Cross-Border Cooperation (CBC) Strategies for Sustainable Development

Rui Alexandre Castanho
University of Dąbrowa Górnicza, Portugal

A volume in the Practice, Progress, and Proficiency in Sustainability (PPPS) Book Series

IGI Global
DISSEMINATOR OF KNOWLEDGE

Published in the United States of America by
IGI Global
Engineering Science Reference (an imprint of IGI Global)
701 E. Chocolate Avenue
Hershey PA, USA 17033
Tel: 717-533-8845
Fax: 717-533-8661
E-mail: cust@igi-global.com
Web site: http://www.igi-global.com

Library of Congress Cataloging-in-Publication Data

Names: Castanho, Rui Alexandre, editor.
Title: Cross-border cooperation (CBC) strategies for sustainable development / Rui Alexandre Castanho, editor.
Description: Hershey : Business Science Reference, 2020. | Includes bibliographical references and index. | Summary: “”This book explores new trends in border areas dynamics and management as well as how cross-border cooperation could or not influences the sustainable development”--Provided by publisher”-- Provided by publisher.
Identifiers: LCCN 2019040397 (print) | LCCN 2019040398 (ebook) | ISBN 9781799825135 (hardcover) | ISBN 9781799825142 (paperback) | ISBN 9781799825159 (ebook)
Subjects: LCSH: Borderlands--Economic aspects. | International economic integration. | Commerce. | Sustainable development.
Classification: LCC HC59.3 .C76 2020 (print) | LCC HC59.3 (ebook) | DDC 338.9/27--dc23
LC record available at https://lccn.loc.gov/2019040397
LC ebook record available at https://lccn.loc.gov/2019040398

This book is published in the IGI Global book series Practice, Progress, and Proficiency in Sustainability (PPPS) (ISSN: 2330-3271; eISSN: 2330-328X)

British Cataloguing in Publication Data
A Cataloguing in Publication record for this book is available from the British Library.

Practice, Progress, and Proficiency in Sustainability (PPPS) Book Series

ISSN:2330-3271
EISSN:2330-328X

Editor-in-Chief: Ayman Batisha, International Sustainability Institute, Egypt

MISSION

In a world where traditional business practices are reconsidered and economic activity is performed in a global context, new areas of economic developments are recognized as the key enablers of wealth and income production. This knowledge of information technologies provides infrastructures, systems, and services towards sustainable development.

The **Practices, Progress, and Proficiency in Sustainability (PPPS) Book Series** focuses on the local and global challenges, business opportunities, and societal needs surrounding international collaboration and sustainable development of technology. This series brings together academics, researchers, entrepreneurs, policy makers and government officers aiming to contribute to the progress and proficiency in sustainability.

COVERAGE

- Eco-Innovation
- Outsourcing
- Innovation Networks
- ICT and knowledge for development
- E-Development
- Socio-Economic
- Environmental informatics
- Strategic Management of IT
- Intellectual Capital
- Green Technology

IGI Global is currently accepting manuscripts for publication within this series. To submit a proposal for a volume in this series, please contact our Acquisition Editors at Acquisitions@igi-global.com or visit: http://www.igi-global.com/publish/.

The Practice, Progress, and Proficiency in Sustainability (PPPS) Book Series (ISSN 2330-3271) is published by IGI Global, 701 E. Chocolate Avenue, Hershey, PA 17033-1240, USA, www.igi-global.com. This series is composed of titles available for purchase individually; each title is edited to be contextually exclusive from any other title within the series. For pricing and ordering information please visit http://www.igi-global.com/book-series/practice-progress-proficiency-sustainability/73810. Postmaster: Send all address changes to above address.

Titles in this Series

For a list of additional titles in this series, please visit:
http://www.igi-global.com/book-series/practice-progress-proficiency-sustainability/73810

Smart Materials for Environmental and Industrial Aplications
Khaled Salah Abou-El-Sherbini (National Research Centre, Egypt) Nasrallah Mohamed Deraz (National Research Centre, Egypt) and Alia Hosni Salama (National Research Center, Egypt)
Engineering Science Reference • ©2020 • 300pp • H/C (ISBN: 9781799829317) • US $215.00

Handbook of Research on Health and Environmental Benefits of Caml Products
Omar Amin Alhaj (University of Petra, Jordan) Bernard Faye (Independent Researcher, France) and Rajendra Prasad Agrawal (Independent Researcher, India)
Medical Information Science Reference • ©2020 • 480pp • H/C (ISBN: 9781799816041) • US $285.00

Interdisciplinary Approaches to Public Policy and Sustainability
Rituparna Das (Adamas University, India) and Nivedita Mandal (Adamas University, India)
Information Science Reference • ©2020 • 320pp • H/C (ISBN: 9781799803157) • US $195.00

African Perspectives on Reshaping Rural Development
Mavhungu Abel Mafukata (Department of Development Studies, University of South Africa, South Africa) and Khathutshelo Alfred Tshikolomo (Limpopo Department of Agriculture and Rural Development, South Africa)
Information Science Reference • ©2020 • 300pp • H/C (ISBN: 9781799823063) • US $195.00

For an entire list of titles in this series, please visit:
http://www.igi-global.com/book-series/practice-progress-proficiency-sustainability/73810

IGI Global
DISSEMINATOR OF KNOWLEDGE

701 East Chocolate Avenue, Hershey, PA 17033, USA
Tel: 717-533-8845 x100 • Fax: 717-533-8661
E-Mail: cust@igi-global.com • www.igi-global.com

Table of Contents

Detailed Table of Contents

OTALEX C is a cross border project elaborated by several entities of the administrations, agencies, and Portuguese and Spanish enterprises. The aim is to develop joint cartography, in addition to the union of territorial and environmental data and their interexchange. SDI-OTALEX C has defined a method capable of assigning the degree of sustainability through the integration of environmental, social, and economic indicators. Thus, a link has been established with consumption and productivity, which promotes the appropriate use of resources and, consequently, the sustainable development of the territory. The benefits for local population of this territory fall within the very term of sustainable development since its objective is to define viable projects and reconcile economic aspects, social and environmental impacts of human activities. To reconcile all these aspects, the SDI makes it possible to contribute to sustainability and to try to envision projects that help to keep the population of these largely depopulated territories.

The promotion of the entrepreneurship has been a challenge in recent years because it is recognised that entrepreneurial activity enhances economic growth. Border regions, because of the possibility of increasing cooperation between economic agents, gained a special status. Still, some of those cross-border regions continue to grow slower than other regions. Authors analyse business dynamics and entrepreneurial activities at a regional basis for the EU. Considering data availability, authors analyse 13 different countries. Indicators under analysis are birth rates, death rates, business churn, and survival rate. This chapter identifies and analyses the existence of significant differences between regions located alongside border areas, and analyses if there exist differences depending on the countries of those regions. To compare business demographic indicators, parametric tests will be used. The results are analysed considering the potential differences between cross-border and non-cross-border regions.

The chapter concerns the implementation assessment of cross-border projects supported by the INTERREG VA Poland - Slovakia 2014-2020 Program. The authors diagnosed the state of implementation of the Program (2018), and analyzed the conditions for managing cross-border projects on the Polish-Slovak borderland. The chapter outlines the role of a cross-border project in management of borderland development, and presents the life cycle of a cross-border project. The authors drew special attention to the results of projects and the administrative burden related to their implementation. The authors carried out quantitative and qualitative research with the participation of Polish and Slovak beneficiaries of the Program to achieve the objectives of the work. The research was supplemented by the desk research analysis covering the selected documents and statistical data (2014 – 2018). The conclusions and recommendations can be useful in the process of programming rules for implementing cross-border projects on the Polish-Slovak borderland and other borderlands after 2020.

Considering the actual panorama of a multi-level governance on EU, the macro-regional strategies - specifying the EU strategy for Danube region (EUSDR) fosters coordination across three dimensions: sector policies; different levels of governance from EU to regional or local, and across administrative boundaries. This chapter analyzes and assesses the ability, challenges, and obstacles of Cross-Border Cooperation (CBC) strategies, projects, and programs to improve integration and cohesion peripheral territories as is the case of the border region of Romania – Serbia, enabling articulating border areas and creating synergies among them. In this regard, it will be considered the latest findings on new insights towards spatial integration in border and transnational contexts. The chapter presents some hypothesis for a good-planned, long-term sustainability for this territory and lesson learned regarding the coordination and management of policies in the EU's system of multi-level governance that could have a wider application and scope.

Climate change has palpable cross-scale implications given the severity of the matter epitomized in the prolonged discussions and negotiations between various parties that incur the consequences of the policy applications. Cross-border adjustment, though seemingly plausible, is a controversial method employed to mitigate the adverse potential impact of carbon emissions through placing an extra cost for the goods imported from countries that lag behind the standards set by multiple global agreements. Exercising cross-border adjustment on international trading activities is likely to have positive reverberations on taming the perils posed by climate change as well as triggering unforeseen perturbations in the interaction of actors involved in the global trading system. This chapter intends to shed light on cross-border adjustments via diagnosing the issues emerging out of the inter-scale interactions and question its effectiveness in micro and macro terms.

The crisis that shook the global financial institutions in 2007/08 revealed the weaknesses and irrationalities of a system that led millions of people, without compatible returns, to the category of "owners" of their home. During the previous decade, the absurd growth of supply in parallel with the progressive increase in real estate value, made housing "the hen of the golden eggs" of the regional and national economy: banks earn with a credit and families with the valuation of homes. This chapter examines the economic context in the crack of the real estate bubble and analyzes as a practical case the incidents of this crisis at international level in the border region of Extremadura.

The current problems in the construction, sale, purchase, offer, or search of housing, present questions about the future of the real estate market, questions that will have to be possible solutions in the medium and long term. This document proposes obtaining primary information through "Opinion survey aimed at the population on housing and its influence on the land market," through an applied methodology and variables associated with the survey. This chapter elaborates a methodological proposal to analyze the situation of the houses for rent in the border city of Badajoz to provide a document of support to the professionals and technicians who are dedicated to the territory and urban planning, to solve the problems about the construction, sale, purchase, offer, or search of housing.

Global economics has two versions. One is the economic realities that are based on our lived world view and explained by our experience of it each day. The other is the complex and theoretical economic view presented by mainstream economists. There is no correlation between the two world views. There is little respect left for the 'predictions' offered by mainstream economics through the use of obfuscating mathematics in practical business decision making. The 2008 financial crisis made this position even more profound. China, the United States, and Europe are the three main contributors to the total productivity of the globe.

In the 21st Century, it is possible to observe a pattern of numerous changes in the sphere of functioning of the cultural institutions also in cities divided by a border. These trends include globalization of culture, development of cultural industries and creative industries, rapid technical and technological growth, occurrence of new cultural management concepts and marketing strategies. Therefore, this chapter presents models of marketing strategies that can be applied in cities divided by a border. Based on individual interviews with 40 experts, four model marketing strategies are proposed which can be used by managers of cultural institutions in cities such as Cieszyn-Czech Cieszyn. Proposed strategies are in relation to specified target markets - residents of a city divided by a border. The practical application aspect of this chapter is evident in the indication of the direction future marketing efforts of cultural institutions should take to improve their market position.

Cross-Border Cooperation (CBC) is described as collaboration with neighbouring countries sharing land or sea borders to cooperate to reduce poverty and inequality among people, and improve living standards for sustainable development of the regions. European Union key objective has been CBC model where bordering countries in balanced partnership, have equal say in program decision-making process for sustainable development to meet common goals. The three factors essential for CBC clearly defined goals, promotion of political transparency, and promotion of connectivity and communication are correlated with the four levels of CBC implementation and public-private-partnerships. This chapter examines the challenge and significance of cross border cooperative relationship between India and Pakistan to disarm and have peace, for achieving 17 sustainable development goals in bordering conflict regions between the two countries for socio-economic progress and prosperity of the millions of people living in South Asia.

This chapter argues that tourism activities, emigration, and cooperation projects can spur growth and sustainable development in rural areas, in general, helping to reduce the existing asymmetries of development, phenomenon that reaches Portugal and other Member States of the Community of Portuguese-speaking Member States (CPLP). The results of a study developed in Portugal evidence that the potential return of a segment of Portuguese emigrants, settled around the world, can contribute to growth and sustainable tourism development in rural areas of Portugal. In this scope, the existence of a Portuguese-speaking cultural heritage allied to the CPLP Strategic Tourism Cooperation Plan can also have a critical role in growth and sustainable development in CPLP.

Nowadays, the high environmental sensitivity and economic constraints, as well as future prospects for development, require a strong sustainable energy policy. Such policies should be based on the local resource valorization – which gains more emphasis in ultra-peripheral territories as the case of the Madeira and Canary Archipelagos. In fact, renewable energy sources become more competitive from the

Preface

Border interactions have reached unprecedented levels in recent decades, not only due to their potential for territorial integration but also considering their role in supranational processes, such as infrastructure construction and planning activities on European territory (Batista et al., 2013; Dominguez and Pires, 2014; Castanho et al., 2016; 2018; 2019, Vulevic et al., 2019; Loures et al., 2019). Nevertheless, experiences of CBC have spread not only in Europe but throughout the world, creating a global network of relationships between people, always trying to create the mutually beneficial scenarios (Domínguez, et al., 2015).

Contextually, borderlands territories are very specific and complex areas, and also very fragile. Thus, their common planning through CBC projects should be deeply analyzed and studied in order to move towards the so-desired sustainable development. In fact, those processes are pivotal to achieve the predefined goals - a common sustainable development and growth. Furthermore, and considering its multidisciplinary, it became crucial to understand this issue from all the different perspectives.

In fact, those principles and strategies gains even more relevance once the territorial strategies play a crucial role in the development and sustainability of regions, not only because of their philosophy of greater or lesser focus on sustainability: social, economic, and environmental - but also the value of funds allocated to each strategy, how these funds are invested by decision makers and political actors – i.e. leading to the issues of political commitment and transparency in relation to such projects and strategies (Ravesteijn et al., 2004; Rabé et al., 2013; Gualini, 2017; Castanho et al., 2019).

Thus, the present book will aim to provide relevant theoretical frameworks and the new trends regarding the border areas dynamics and their management as well as how Cross-Border Cooperation could or not influences the Sustainable Development. It was written for professionals, academics, and also for the general public who want to improve their understanding of the dynamics and patterns of the border environments.

THE NEW CHALLENGES AND TRENDS

Bearing in mind the complexity related to borderlands planning, management, and governance there are several obstacles, opportunities, and challenges that should be considered. Therefore, some challenges related to the Cross-Border Cooperation could be identified within the following themes covered by this monograph:

- Biodiversity Policies and Strategies Accessibility
- C2C (City-to-City Cooperation)
- CBC in Insular or ultra-peripheral territories
- Circular and Green Economy
- Connectivity, and Transportation
- Culture Management
- Environmental Rights and Legislation
- Inter-Organizational Cooperation
- Migratory fluxes - Strategies
- Public Management
- Renewables Energies
- Resources Sharing
- Sustainable Planning and Development
- Territorial Governance and their Common Strategies
- Tourism Management

In fact, many studies (for a summary and review see the first chapter of this book, besides Hooghe, and Marks 2004; Sohn, and Giffinger, 2015; Castanho, 2017; Loures et al., 2018) have identified and studied most of the challenges above-mentioned (see: Buis, 2008; Spirkova, and Ivanicka, 2009; Batista et al., 2013; Faludi, 2013; Nicolini and Pinto, 2013; Medeiros, 2015; Vulevic, 2016; Decoville and Durand, 2017; Gualini, 2017; Stverkova et al., 2018; Castanho, 2019; Gamon and Gómez, 2019; Santos, et al., 2019; among many others).

Contextually, research has also shown how border effect could or not influence the flora and fauna (raptors) diversity in Iberian Territories (see: Raposo et al., 2018) – reviling how biodiversity policies and strategies should be considered in CBC environments.

Furthermore, another newly researches on accessibility, connectivity, and transportation shows how the common strategic planning should be articulated and designed to provide an answer to the border populations as well as to achieve the defined Sustainable Development Goals (SDG´s) (see: Nicolini and Pinto, 2013; Knieling and Othengrafen, 2015; Gamon and Gómez, 2019; or Vulevic et al., 2019).

It also should be highlighted the ongoing challenges regarding the social-economic sustainability pursuit and CBC environments management. In fact, in the last few years many valuable studies and researches have been conducted providing valuable and enriching the literature over this socio-economic issues – i.e. circular and green Economy; culture management; inter-Organizational Cooperation; public Management (see: Nauwelaers, et al.,2013; Reitel, 2015; Naranjo Gómez, 2016; Wróblewski, 2017; Kurowska-Pysz et al., 2018; Stverkova, et al., 2018; Suchacek et al., 2018; are just some few examples of the many existing studies). In fact, in this monograph those themes are further explained through the authors contributions.

Besides, border environments used to be peripheral territories. In this regard, there are the studies conducted on the pursuit on sustainability on ultra-peripheral territories (see: Castanho et al., 2018; Lousada et al., 2019). Also, chapter 12 provides an interesting overview on how this cooperation patterns could be managed in this typology of territories.

There is also the challenge of establishing appropriate policies and strategies that could answer the migratory fluxes. Such challenges exist at two levels. First at an internal/national level – usually from rural to urban areas; creating isolated and low-density areas within the territories. Second at an international level – from country to country or from different continents; usually populational exodus flees from conflicts and/or economic crises. The importance for developing the proper policies and strategies where also reflected in this book (see: chapter 11).

Moreover, research has gained an additional *momentum* considering current developments – i.e. the recent tensions between Crimea (Ukraine) and Russia, the Greek–German frictions, the rise of terrorism in European continent leading to an increasingly fractious debate about free movement in Europe as well as the resurgence of nationalist, extremist sentiments among European citizens (see: chapter 15), among several others issues that in a lower or higher risk jeopardizes the relationships and cohesion between European nations and even the Trans-European Cooperation (Castanho, 2017; Huisseling and Mora Aliseda, 2019). These issues lead us to finding strategies and new approaches, through which it can be possible to achieve a greater territorial cohesion and sustainable development in transboundary territories.

In sum, all those identified challenges and trends will converge to the developing of new strategies and methods for the strategic management and common planning of borderlands. Contextually, the present book covers, not only many of the CBC above mentioned challenges and trends, but also counts with the contribution of some of the most relevant authors and academicians in these specific fields.

ORGANIZATION OF THE BOOK

The book is organized into fifteen chapters. A brief description of each of the chapters follows:

Chapter 1 provides an overall view regarding the Cross-Border Cooperation projects and how can they benefit the regions inserted within the project. The chapter goes even further, exploring a specific CBC project in the Southwest European territories. Bearing in mind the wide scope of this chapter, it fits as a perfect kick-off for starting the studying and discussion over CBC dynamics in the present monograph.

Chapter 2 recognizes the role of entrepreneurial activity in European territories. The authors of this chapter contend that by investing how this theme works or can be influenced in border regions - establishing opportunities and obstacles.

Chapter 3 focuses on Central European Territories and how the implementation of CBC projects supported by the INTERREG should be managed to achieve successful management. Exploring the case of the Polish-Slovakian borderland, therefore, the authors provide directions and guidelines.

Chapter 4 analyzes the Multi-Level Governance System in Southeastern Europe Territories. Contextually, the authors analyze and assess the ability, challenges, and obstacles of Cross-Border Cooperation (CBC) strategies, projects, and programs to improve integration and cohesion in the border region of Romania – Serbia.

Chapter 5 addresses the hot topic of climate change and carbon emissions. Moreover, this chapter aims to provide insights on cross-border adjustments via diagnosing the most relevant issues emerging out of the inter-scale interactions as well as focusing on its effectiveness in micro and macro term.

Chapter 6 presents a view on the crisis that shook the global financial institutions back in 2008. Contextually, the authors analyze the economic context in the crack of the real estate bubble throughout a practical case in a European border region located in the Iberian Peninsula.

Chapter 7 follows the same line of the previous contribution, however, in this case, the authors address the issue of renting in the border cities. Thus, the authors provide some guidelines for the professionals and technicians related to urban planning – aiming to solve the problems regarding the construction processes, sale, purchase, and housing speculation.

Chapter 8 examines the overall impact of the US-China trade conflict on the EU-28 economy. The study explores examine the impact of China's economic strategy on the decline in Chinese Foreign Direct Investment (FDI) in the EU. In fact, this chapter enables to understand the complex patterns of cooperation from different scales and perspectives.

Chapter 9 presents models of marketing strategies that are possible to be applied in cities divided by a border throughout common planning methods of City-to-City

Cooperation. Furthermore, this chapter provides directions for future marketing efforts of cultural institutions.

Chapter 10 analyzes the challenge and significance of border cooperation between India and Pakistan. Also, the work explores relevant issues the possibility those nations to disarm against each other, and have peace, as well as to achieve the Sustainable Development Goals (SDG´s), in the region - through CBC strategies.

Chapter 11 concludes that tourism activities, emigration and cooperation projects can impact positively on growth and sustainable development in rural areas. In this regard, the study explores the asymmetries of development phenomenon that reaches Portugal and the other Member States of the Community of Portuguese-speaking Member States.

Chapter 12 enables a view through the cooperation in insular territories and the strategies used to achieve sustainability – focusing on diverse forms of energy production through natural resources. Thus, the chapter presents a comparison study between *Porto Santo* Island (Madeira, Portugal) and *El Hierro* Island (Canary, Spain).

Chapter 13 analyses the territorial policies for the implementation of the Mercosur Waterway. Therefore, the study concluded that the strategic meaning of the Waterway still needs to be reinforced in an integration context since efforts have not yet been sufficient so that it could be prioritized in the strategic agenda of the countries.

Chapter 14 provides an interesting overview of how the Environmental laws are pivotal to understand and discuss for proper management of transboundary resources. In this regard, the authors bring the case study of the Guaraní Aquifer System located on the territories of Argentina, Brazil, Paraguay, and Uruguay.

Chapter 15 addresses the hot topic of nationalistic independent movements in European territories. In this work, the author analyzes the creation and demarcation of nations during the past, the territorial identity that was formed and the need of the EU to create a European Identity to overcome the threat of independent movements. In this regard, and considering the relevance of the issue nowadays, this chapter was selected to close this monography – to foster the discussion and also to be used as the basis for further studies and researches.

Rui Alexandre Castanho
University of Da̧browa Górnicza, Portugal

REFERENCES

Batista, T., Caballero, C., Ceballos, F., Carriço, C., Mateus, J., & Lopes, H. (2013). IDE-OTALEXC. The first crossborder SDI between Portugal and Spain: Background and development. *Journal of Earth Science and Engineering.*, *3*(6), 393. doi:10.1553/giscience2013s6

Buis H. (2008). The role of local government associations in increasing the effectiveness of city-to-city cooperation. *Habitat International, 2009, 33*(2):190-194. DOI: . habitatint.2008.10.017 doi:10.1016/j

Castanho, R. (2017). Sustainable Urban Planning in transboundary areas: analysis of critical factors for territorial success. (Doctoral Thesis), University of Extremadura (UEx), Spain.

Castanho, R., Cabezas, J., Fernández-Pozo, L., Vulevic, A., Naranjo Gómez, J., Martín Gallardo, J., & Loures, L. (2018). Common Regional Development Strategies on Iberian Territory. Envisioning New Horizons: Post 2020. Chapter in the Book: Enfoques en la Planificación Territorial y Urbanística. Mora Aliseda, J. (ed.), Thomson Reuteurs Aranzadi. pp. 293-303.

Castanho, R., Loures, L., Fernández, J., & Pozo, L. (2016). (in press). Identifying critical factors for success in cross border cooperation (CBC) development projects. *Habitat International, 2016*. doi:10.1016/j.habitatint.2016.10.004

Castanho, R. A. (2019). Identifying Processes of Smart Planning, Governance and Management in European Border Cities. Learning from City-to-City Cooperation (C2C). *Sustainability*, *11*(19), 5476. doi:10.3390u11195476

Castanho, R. A., Lousada, S., Naranjo Gómez, J. M., Escórcio, P., Cabezas, J., Fernández-Pozo, L., & Loures, L. (2018). Dynamics of the Land Use Changes and the Associated Barriers and Opportunities for Sustainable Development on Peripheral and Insular Territories: The Madeira Island (Portugal) [WorkingTitle], IntechOpen, DOI: . Available at https://www.intechopen.com/online-first/dynamics-of-the-land-use-changes-and-the-associated-barriers-and-opportunities-for-sustainable-devel doi:10.5772/intechopen.80827

Castanho, R. A., Vulevic, A., Naranjo Gómez, J., Cabezas, J., Fernández-Pozo, L., Loures, L., & Kurowska-Pysz, J. (2019). Political Commitment and Transparency as a Critical Factor to Achieve Territorial Cohesion and Sustainable Growth. European Cross-Border Projects and Strategies. Regional Science Policy and Practice.

Decoville, A., & Durand, F. (2017). Challenges and Obstacles in the Production of Cross-Border Territorial Strategies: The Example of the Greater Region. *Transactions of the Associations of the European Schools of Planning Journal, 1*(1), pp. 65-78, doi:10.24306/TrAESOP

Domínguez, J. A., Noronha Vaz, T., & Vaz, E. (2015). Sustainability in the trans-border regions? The case of Adalusia e Algarve. *International Journal of Global Environmental Issues, 14*(1¤2), 151-163.

Dominguez, L., & Pires, I. (2014). Cross-border cooperation structures in Europe. Learning from the past, looking to the future. Brussels. *P.I.E. Peter Lang, ISBN-13.*

Faludi, A. (2013). Territorial Cohesion and Subsidiarity under the European Union Treaties: A Critique of the «Territorialism» Underlying. *Regional Studies, 47*(9), 1594–1606. doi:10.1080/00343404.2012.657170

Gamon, W., & Gómez, J. (2019). Main Problems of Railway Cross-Border Transport Between Poland, Germany and Czech Republic. *Sustainability, 11*(18), 4900. doi:10.3390u11184900

Gualini, E. (2017). Political economy of scale in European spatial policy. In *Rethinking European Spatial Policy as a Hologram: Actions, Institutions, Discourses*. London, UK: Routledge.

Hooghe, L., & Marks, G. (2004). Contrasting Visions of Multi-Level Governance. In I. Bache, & M. Flinders (eds.), Multi-Level Governance, Oxford, UK: Oxford University Press, pp. 15-30.

Huisseling, D., & Mora Aliseda, J. (2019). Los Movimientos Soberanistas Como Amenaza a la Integridad Territorial de los Estados y de la UE. Revista Extremeña de Sociología Almenaranº 11, (Online): 2172 – 7538. pp. 59-72.

Knieling, J., & Othengrafen, F. (2015). Planning culture—A concept to explain the evolution of planning policies and processes in Europe? *European Planning Studies, 23*(11), 2133–2147. doi:10.1080/09654313.2015.1018404

Kurowska-Pysz, J., Castanho, R. A., & Loures, L. (2018). Sustainable Planning of Cross-Border Cooperation: A Strategy for Alliances in Border Cities. *Sustainability, 10*(5), 1416. doi:10.3390u10051416

Loures, L., Castanho, R., Naranjo, J., Cabezas, J., & Fernández-Pozo, L. (2019). The influence of cross-border cooperation (CBC) in the fostering of entrepreneurship and regional development – a step closer to achieve major structural changes and sustainable cities within European Territory. Series: Entrepreneurship and Structural Change in Dynamic Territories. In New Paths of Entrepreneurship Development; Carvalho, L., Rego, C., Lucas, M., Hérnandez, I., Viana, A., Eds.; Ed. Springer: Canada, 2019; pp. 371-385

Loures, L., Castanho, R. A., Vulevic, A., Naranjo Gómez, J., Cabezas, J., & Fernández-Pozo, L. (2018). The Multi-variated Effect of City Cooperation in Land Use Planning and Decision-making Processes - a European Analysis. Chapter in the Book: Urban Agglomerations. Ed. InTech. pp. 87-106.

Lousada, S., Silva, P., Castanho, R. A., & Naranjo Gómez, J. (2019). Modelação de sistemas de abastecimento de água. O caso de Ilha da MadeIra. Modelling water system supplies. The case of Madeira island. *Bitacora Urbano Territorial*, *29*(2), 89–98. doi:10.15446/bitacora.v29n2.69381

Medeiros, E. (2015). Territorial impact assessment and cross-border cooperation. Regional Studies. *Regional Science.*, *2*(1), 97–115. doi:10.1080/21681376.2014.999108

Naranjo Gómez, J. M. (2016). Impacts on the Social Cohesion of Mainland Spain's Future Motorway and High-Speed Rail Networks. *Sustainability*, *8*(7), 624. doi:10.3390u8070624

Nauwelaers, C., Maguire, K., & Ajmone Marsan, G. (2013). "The Case of Helsinki-Tallinn (Finland-Estonia) – Regions and Innovation: Collaborating Across Borders", OECD Regional Development Working Papers, 2013/19, OECD Publishing. doi:10.1787/5k3xv0lrt1r6-en

Nicolini, E., & Pinto, M. (2013). Strategic vision of a Euro-Mediterranean port city: A case study of Palermo. *Sustainability Journal, 2013*(5), 3941-3959.

Rabé, P., Toto, R., & Dhima, S. (2013). Analyzing the Likely Impact of European Union Policies on Territorial Planning in Albania. Rotterdam, The Netherlands: Netherlands government (MATRA).

Ravesteijn, N., Evers, D. V. H., & Middleton, D. (2004). Unseen Europe: A Survey of EU Politics and its Impact on Spatial Development in the Netherlands. Rotterdam, The Netherlands: NAI Publishers.

Reitel, B. (2015). Are Cross-Border Urban Spaces European Integration Patterns at Local Level? Analysis of the Management of Urban Areas astride the «French Border». Borders of the European Union: Strategies of Crossing and Resistance.

Santos, R., Castanho, R., & Lousada, S. (2019). Return Migration and Tourism Sustainability in Portugal: Extracting Opportunities for Sustainable Common Planning in Southern Europe. *Sustainability*, *11*(22), 5476. doi:10.3390u11226468

Sohn, C., & Giffinger, R. (2015). A Policy Network Approach to Cross-Border Metropolitan Governance: The Cases of Vienna and Bratislava. *Eur. Plan. Stud. J.*, *23*(6), 1187–1208. doi:10.1080/09654313.2014.994089

Spirkova, D., & Ivanicka, K. (2009). *Dynamics of Bratislava urban and housing development. New models for innovative management and urban dynamics*. Faro, Portugal: University of Algarve.

Stverkova, H., Pohludka, M., Kurowska-Pysz, J., & Szczepanska-Woszczyna, K. (2018). Cross-Border Enterpreneurship in Euroregion Beskydy. *Polish Journal of Management Studies*, *18*(2), 324–337. doi:10.17512/pjms.2018.18.2.26

Suchacek, J., Stverkova, H., & Kasik, J. (2018). Czech Machinery Cluster and Its Role in Sustainable Development of Moravian-Silesian Enterprises during the Post-Transformation Era. *Sustainability*, *10*(2), 239. doi:10.3390u10020239

Vulevic, A. (2016). Accessibility Concepts and Indicators in Transportation Strategic Planning Issues: Theoretical Framework and Literature Review, 2016, Logistics & Sustainable. *Transport*, *7*(1), 58–67.

Vulevic, A., Djordjevic, D., Castanho, R. A., & Cabezas-Fernandez, J. (2019). *Social Marketing and Their Related Challenges for the Limited Access for People Living with a Disability: A Serbian Case Study. Chapter in Book: Case Studies on Social Marketing*. Springer; doi:10.1007/978-3-030-04843_19

Wróblewski, Ł. (2017). Application of marketing in cultural organizations: The case of the Polish Cultural and Educational Union in the Czech Republic. *Cult. Manag. Sci. Educ.*, *1*(1), 79–92. doi:10.30819/cmse.1-1.08

Chapter 1
Benefits of a Spatial Data Infrastructure on the Sustainability of a Southwestern European Territory

Teresa Batista
ICAAM, Universidade de Evora, Portugal

Fernando Ceballos-Zúñiga Rodríguez
Junta de Extremadura, Spain

Cristina Carriço
CIMAC, Portugal

Carlos Pinto-Gomes
Universidade de Evora, Portugal

Luís Fernández-Pozo
Universidad de Extremadura, Spain

José Manuel Naranjo Gómez
University of Extremadura, Spain

José Martín Gallardo
Universidad de Extremadura, Spain

Luís Loures
Research Centre for Endogenous Resource Valorization, Instituto Politécnico de Portalegre, Portugal

José Cabezas
https://orcid.org/0000-0002-7209-3731
Universidad de Extremadura, Spain

ABSTRACT

OTALEX C is a cross border project elaborated by several entities of the administrations, agencies, and Portuguese and Spanish enterprises. The aim is to develop joint cartography, in addition to the union of territorial and environmental data and their interexchange. SDI-OTALEX C has defined a method capable of assigning the degree of sustainability through the integration of environmental, social,

DOI: 10.4018/978-1-7998-2513-5.ch001

and economic indicators. Thus, a link has been established with consumption and productivity, which promotes the appropriate use of resources and, consequently, the sustainable development of the territory. The benefits for local population of this territory fall within the very term of sustainable development since its objective is to define viable projects and reconcile economic aspects, social and environmental impacts of human activities. To reconcile all these aspects, the SDI makes it possible to contribute to sustainability and to try to envision projects that help to keep the population of these largely depopulated territories.

INTRODUCTION

The number of countries in the world, since the middle of last century, has increased almost three times, increasing the number of border areas greatly. Borders are a very complex social phenomenon associated with the confluence of many layers which are related to the territorial organisation of the society, as well as with human psychology, having produced an evolution in the form of interpreting the borders along with changing social investigations. Over the years the borderland studies passed from the field of geography and history, the pioneer disciplines, to the field of interdisciplinary knowledge on rapid expansion, developed in parallel by political scientists, geographers, sociologists, anthropologists, psychologists, ethnologists, lawyers, economists and even experts in technical sciences (Kolosov, 2015; Laine, 2015).

Borders, Boundaries, Frontiers, and Borderland Regions

The border areas, established by the international agreements that delimited them, gave rise to a series of territories of strong dynamics despite being far from the centres of power with a dominant interest in national control, located in the capitals of the new states that they established over time. Although for some authors the borders are always in motion, including concepts such as border construction and reconstruction, search for balances, transboundary flows, undecided borders and the most drastic through the exercise of power, finally by mechanisms of alteration and reconciliation occurs the stability of these peripheral territories (Kornrad, 2015).

Currently, border relations contribute to maintaining the prosperity of the territories of the two countries near the borders, ensuring continuity and promoting links in the globalization environment that has been developing in recent times (Konrad & Nicol, 2011). The border areas contribute to the fact that the population settled in these territories achieves improvements in their economy and social services of all kinds, so that the residents themselves are aware of this situation with respect to other territories of their own countries farther from the border (Allen, 2013; Kurowska-Pysz, Castanho & Naranjo, 2018). These citizens interact and give rise to new approaches to the dynamic frontier concept as Allen indicates (2013),

While the lens of space is useful for understanding processes and activities in a critical sense, I argue that using a dynamic theorization of 'place' augments conventional social and economic analyses of borders by strengthening the links among location, activities, and meanings. Specifically, these links are vital for understanding how different meanings of 'being at' borders are created, modified, and sustained.

From a geographical point of view, national cultures have been understood as a unified entity of areas with nearby cultures in space, with diverse histories and origins, that did not necessarily form a unified and coherent structure (Eriksen & Nielsen, 2001). One of the important points to understand borders and border areas is the local culture that develops on both sides, guided in many cases by the municipal policy that marks the mode of action of their organizations (parties, associations and related movements), which indicate the way forward for the activism of their militants and these in turn influence, by the media or day to day, on all citizens of the border territory (Buis, 2009; Brunet-Jailly & Dupeyron, 2017). Even some authors suggest that there are two key variables to explain how borders and border territories, culture and power originate, are maintained and evolved (Konrad & Nicol, 2011).

However, cross border relations do not always develop harmoniously, in certain areas the needs of the local managers of these administrations, tend to establish links and agreements on both sides of the borders which are only symbolic and for publicity, motivated by the monitoring of the national policies of the two countries or by other supranational agreements marked by supranational organisations or administrations, such as the European Union (Baltà, 2015; Castanho, Loures, Cabezas & Fernández-Pozo, 2017).

The reality, when analysing the relationships among local residents on both sides of the border, it is the presence of a mixture of feelings among which appear negative, resentments and prejudices, with others that tend to the eagerness to achieve a standard of living better and more hopeful in the near future, which leads to misunderstandings and even conflicts with the aspirations of both local governments and their official policy initiatives (Matthiesen & Bürkner, 2002; Baltà, 2015; Markuszewska, Tanskanen & Vila, 2016). Thus the political or economic interests can generate an idea of border situation completely contrary to the reality perceived and observed by the residents, as it could be a false idea of the open and permeable border when in reality it is completely airtight freedom of movement (Kukri, 2014).

Emmanuel Brunet-Jailly and Dupeyron (2017) established that there are two general groups of cases in the behaviour of cross-border communities, on the one hand, that cooperate and develop links that allow them to prosper, and that show strains to carry them to ignore each other surviving in the best possible way.

This last situation is enhanced by what is stated above, the processes of globalization, through ease of access and empowerment of the broadcasting allow individuals confront, assess and decide if government policies to convince them or they simply ignore them or even fight in a determined manner as it is currently happening in Venezuela and Hong Kong (Brunet-Jailly, 2011; Allen, 2013; Ma & Cheng, 2019; Puyosa, 2019; Stromer - Galley, 2019). In this sense Kukri (2014) indicates *Focusing on micro-level and individual cases is a means to critically study institutionalized and dominating ideas of borders, and the colonizing gazes which often result in marginalizing and homogenizing conceptualizations of borderland cultures and identities*.

Emmanuel Brunet-Jailly and Bruno Dupeyron (2017) suggest a general model or framework, derived from the one previously proposed by Brunet-Jailly (2005), to understand borders, which gives rise to a theory of borders that contemplates four analytical objectives equally important: (1) market forces and trade flows, (2) political activities of various administrations of different levels, (3) influence of local cross-border policy, and (4) local cross-border culture. However, the idea remains that a general theory on the frontiers, which synthesizes existing knowledge overcoming barriers between disciplines, would be impossible, although new approaches that overflow the walls between disciplines should not be ruled out (Baltà, 2015; Kolosov, 2015).

And more recently, proposals such as Kireev and Yachin (2019) arise that consider that border studies face internal contradictions that have paved the way for a new polycentric paradigm to arise considering a meta cultural approach, which could even solve one of the great European Union problems, the depletion of integration capabilities.

The digital era underlined the need for interoperability between organizations, and mature solutions are evident in domains such as telecommunications and banking. Initially, the focus was on ensuring interoperability within a single commercial area, mainly at a technical level. It soon became clear that interoperability between companies was also essential and had to include semantic, organizational and legal aspects and acquire a dimension between countries. The private sector has partially met this challenge. However, the public sector faces unique obstacles, such as the non-profit incentive, the organizational complexity of separation of powers, multi-faceted data protection and legal restrictions.

Cross-border Cooperation (CBC)

Cross-border relations reached a global development starting in the seventies of the last century, matching with the increase in political and economic relations worldwide which caused a resurgence of cross-border cooperation (CBC) along with the international border system. With the multiplication of ties between nations at all levels, it was considered that the system created would serve to prevent global conflicts, so it was more interesting to move from the investigation of conflicts to that of political and commercial cooperation, in which they participate from governments to the population of the border areas, through the regional-local political class together with the economic elite of those territories (Zyikov & Sevastianov, 2015).

This reactivation has caused a spectacular increase, in the last half-century, of human interactions caused by several reasons: (1) multiplication of the exchange of relations between governments facilitated by a climate of trust; (2) new supranational cohesion systems between different countries, giving rise to new international communities; (3) national and international non-governmental organizations; (4) involvement of private initiative, from small businesses to large transnational corporations, some with more resources and influence than many states; (5) facilitation of exchanges from transport to access to information through trade, globalization; (6) and finally the aforementioned appearance of a huge number of new states, with their new borders and border territories, which by joining them to the previous five points leads to exponentially multiplying the possible interactions that are occurring in these places, not always positive and trouble-free, sometimes even with very serious conflicts.

CBC projects and strategies are seen as fundamental for territorial cohesion, not only in Europe, but also throughout the world, developing experiences of this kind throughout the planet generating a process, through which integrated spaces emerge that transcend the borders of bordering nations, facilitating that the policies of national states progressively overlap with those of neighbouring nations and organizations (Bonner & Rozental, 2009; Lee & Na, 2010; Castanho et al., 2017). For these experiences to be a success it is essential that they have their own institutional policy that allows them to acquire a joint vision of the project necessary to apply to their border area (Peyrony & Denert, 2012).

Cross-border cooperation despite the benefits it presents can sometimes be hindered by local policy interests that may even attempt to alter national strategies, to the point of being so obvious that they are perceived by border citizens and consequently express their criticisms towards their own administrations (Allen, 2013; Castanho, Loures, Cabezas, & Fernández-Pozo, 2018). And what is more serious cooperation, such as the European Project with the recent events of Brexit in the United Kingdom and others that are occurring within the continent, highlights the gaps that still persist in these processes (McCall, 2015; Dale, 2016; Holmes, 2016; Castanho et al., 2017).

However, many other CBC projects, between EU borders, also demonstrate an example of the success of cross-border cooperation, from the smallest territories such as the EURODE Euroregion, formed by the cities of Kerkrade-Herzogenrath on the Netherlands border- Germany, even the largest, the Country of Lakes Euroregion (Batista et al., 2013; LISER, 2015; Durà, Camonita, Berzi, & Noferini, 2018).

Studies have been carried out on CBC projects in Europe that show a variation in the predominant factors and objectives, depending on whether the economy is better or worse, so they will opt more for access to European funds or, in the second case, the strengthening of their economies and the elaboration of coordinated municipal general plans (Master's Plans). But what they all agree in general is in the connectivity and accessibility between territories, since they perceive it as a means that influences the success of their integration projects (Van Hamme & Pion 2012; ESPON, 2013; Naranjo, 2016; Castanho et al., 2017; Loures et al., 2018).

Cross-border Cooperation and Spatial Data Infrastructures (SDI)

We are currently surrounded by geoinformation, digital cartography dominates our daily activity to be available at all times, to travel in any means of transport, public or private, or to locate and interpret the huge amount of digital images we handle, among many others uses we make of geolocation systems. All that chaotic geoinformation could be structured and subsequently distributed since for some given purpose it could have benefit. To carry out this purpose, what is used is service-oriented maps, whose role is to catalogue, structure and facilitate access to large amounts of georeferenced data of all kinds (Nabeeh, El-Ghareeb & Riad, 2015; Evangelidis, Agrianidis, Perakis, Papadopoulos & Papatheodorou, 2018). CBC initiatives are characterized precisely by their ability to generate this type of information in large quantities, so the application of services-oriented maps on them is considered an obligation.

This obligation is also marked by the INSPIRE Directive (EU, 2007), issued by the European Commission (EC), whose objective is to create a Spatial Data Infrastructure (SDI, in Spanish and Portuguese IDE) that allows the exchange of environmental spatial information, or measures and activities that may affect the environment, among public administrations, also facilitating free access to all this information across all European borders. With this initiative, Europe promotes statistical monitoring, the generation of specific documents and reports, the analysis and comparison between territories in all social, economic and environmental dimensions that facilitate a more sustainable Europe (Cetl, Tomas, Kotsev, de Lima, Smith & Jobst, 2019).

Following the path marked by INSPIRE, the CBC initiatives that resort to the use of SDIs extend throughout the geography of the continent, addressing various themes and covering more or less extensive territories according to the objectives set, and which generally use geoportals that improve governance, economic development of its citizens and cooperation between territories of the continent. Some of these are X-Border-GDI (cross-border geodata infrastructure) developed between Germany and the Netherlands (Craglia & Campagna, 2009), a collaborative program to develop and implement an infrastructure for the supply of cross-border geographic information; Centrope MAP that encompasses regions of the Czech Republic, Slovakia, Hungary and Austria and whose objective is to harmonize cross-border geoinformation essential for political and economic decision making (Schrenk & Pozarek, 2019); and not only on land areas, marine management also finds its application in these applications (Coleman, Rajabifard, & Crompvoets, 2016; Hansen, Reiter & Schrøder, 2017). Outside Europe these technologies are being applied, in America, Africa, Asia and Oceania where the implementation of information management with these technologies is taking place, with special emphasis on sustainable development in the most depressed areas (Craglia & Campagna, 2009; Coleman, Rajabifard, & Crompvoets, 2016).

Within the European area is OTALEX C, the Territorial and Environmental Observatory of Alentejo, Centro and Extremadura, three regions located the first two in Portugal and the last in Spain, and that has the peculiarity of being the first SDI realized on the border between Spain and Portugal (Batista et al. 2013).

Cross-border Cooperation and Sustainable Development

Since it was established in 1987 as a new global paradigm in the Brundtland report, sustainable development has been applied to a multitude of activities, which have stimulated intense discussion and research in all three dimensions, social, economic and environmental issues (UNCED, 1992). Border regions, analysed from a global point of view, are special areas with specific requirements for sustainable development and therefore require greater attention.

Another peculiarity that may affect, from the point of view of sustainability, some border regions is to have different characteristics or geographical conditions with respect to the rest of the territory of neighbouring nations, which can lead to a number of special problems, such as exposure to transboundary pollution, security episodes and underdevelopment in some areas.

CBC projects should be innovative by implementing integrated sustainable development strategies that respond to the needs of the functional territory they cover, the different territories of the EU and neighbouring countries, they must also incorporate these aspects as important tools in the core of their policies in the long term, thus achieving territorial cohesion (Peyrony. & Denert, 2012).

Research on various studies carried out in disparate environments shows that despite the efforts that have been made in recent years to strengthen the CBC in several countries of the world, there is still a long way to go to achieve a sustainable methodology based on objective principles that could contribute to supporting the creation of multiple sustainability benefits (Lee, & Na, 2010; Veemaa, 2012; Boehnke, Rippl, & Fuss, 2015; Castanho, Loures, Cabezas & Fernández-Pozo, 2018).

In the European area any CBC application incorporating distributed map systems should be guided by the INSPIRE directive and is already incorporated among its standards whatever the purpose of the geoportal, it must support sustainable development.

OTALEX C, AN IMPLEMENTATION OF CBC IN SOUTHWESTERN EUROPE.

With the acronym OTALEX C is defined the Territorial and environmental Observatory of cross-border regions of Alentejo, Extremadura and Center, a cross-border collaborative project co-funded by the operational programme cross-border cooperation Spain-Portugal (POCTEP) 2007-2015 for priority cooperation and management joint accessibility and regional planning, in the area of cooperation Centre-Extremadura – Alentejo and priority projects for urban and rural regeneration.

The objective of the Observatory is harmonization of the territorial data in the cross-border space with the aim of developing a joint mapping, as well as the union of territorial and environmental data and the exchange of data, to contribute to the objective of the European Territorial, harmonization of territorial practices strategy. It is intended thereby monitoring the territorial analysis, the study of alterations and pressures on both sides of the border, as well as the consolidation of this cross-border cooperation between different institutions and provide continuity beyond this project.

Given its particular characteristics, OTALEX C has become a distinctive project. It has established a permanent channel of cross-border cooperation between the different levels of administration, from the local (inter-municipal communities and councils, representing the municipalities), to the regional (Junta da Extremadura and CCDRA - Comissão de Coordenação e Desenvolvimento Regional do Alentejo), national (Spanish National Institute of Geography and Portuguese Geographic Institute), institutions of higher education (University of Évora, University of Extremadura and Instituto Politécnico de Castelo Branco) and public companies EDIA (company de Desenvolvimento da Infraestrutura de Alqueva) from two different countries:

Spain and Portugal. This collaboration began with previous projects with a close relationship in the areas of management of the territory and geographical information systems, spread over eigthteen years of continuous cooperation, yet remain and it is stronger and more useful for users.

The initial work was carried out in the territory of the region of Alentejo, in Portugal, and Extremadura, in Spain, so it is initially was the studied area. With the creation of the Euroregion EUROACE in 2009, it became necessary to extend the territorial scope of the Territorial Observatory and environmental Alentejo-Extremadura (OTALEX) to include the region Centro, in Portugal (Figure 1). This is why it established the Territorial Observatory and environmental Alentejo-Extremadura - Centro (OTALEX Ç), which allowed the integration of more information produced by different institutions that developed their skills in these three regions giving in this way, a high level in the quality of the data and the methodology developed, being also the first Observatory with such distinctive features throughout Europe.

The Observatory was chasing, in line with the objectives of the Territorial European strategy (ETE), monitoring and analysis of variations resulting from natural phenomena and, essentially, of human activity on the territory. As important principle give special relevance to environmental values and reconcile with a desirable economic and social development. All this with the aim of improving the quality of life of the inhabitants of these Iberian southwestern areas. Among its objectives also highlighted the integrated development of methodologies of territorial and environmental management with a view to balanced management of these spaces and the introduction of a system of analysis and monitoring of the territorial reality on both sides of the border area. In short, capture all those works in the creation of a Territorial Observatory Alentejo-Extremadura. Through OTALEX C remained a fertile line of collaboration interagency and cross-border, through the exchange of experiences, geographical information and methodologies between both sides of the border and between the different levels of the Administration and other partners.

The lines of work developed over the several common cooperation projects were adapting to innovations coming from European directives and technological advances. In this regard, note that, although when it drafted the initial project is not envisaged, the final result was implanting a spatial data infrastructure (SDI), where disclosure is made through a Web, the name IDE OTALEX (www.ideotalex.eu).

The Observatory is a development that has reached its present configuration from previous projects that have as common objective the cooperation among territories on both sides of the border of the Spanish and Portuguese, encouraging collaboration and exchange of data to one side and the other (Table 1). Over these years have cooperated agencies, incorporated at different times, and others do not currently participate either changed name or skills (Figure 2).

Figure 1. a) Location of OTALEX C territory in the context of the map of Europe. b) Arrangement of the three regions included in the study area: Alentejo (emerald), Extremadura (yellow) and Centro (light green). Source: Mayoral, de la Cruz, Osuna, Rodríguez & Mora, 2015.

JE – Junta da Extremadura; CIMAC - Comunidade ntermunicipal do Alentejo Central; GA - Gobierno de Aragón; MMA – Ministerio de Madio Ambiente; Midi-Pérenné Region (France); CIMAA - Comunidade Intermunicipal do Alto Central (old AMNA), DGT - Direcção Geral do Território (old IGP), DGCE – Dirección General de Catastro de Extremadura; EDIA - Empresa de Desenvolvimento de Infrestruturas do Alqueva, S.A.; UEvora - Universidade de Évora, IPCB - Instituto Politécnico de Castelo Branco, CNIG-IGN - Centro Nacional de Información Geográfica – Instituto Geográfico Nacional, Dip.Badajoz - Diputación de Badajoz – O. A. Área de Igualdad y Desarrollo Local, Dip.Caceres - Diputación de Cáceres – O. A. para el Desarrollo Local; UExt - Universidad de Extremadura

The last projects of CBC, called OTALEX C, proposed the following objectives in his candidacy to POCTEP:

The proposed objectives for the development of OTALEX C are as follows:

- Contribute to the infrastructure of spatial data of Alentejo-Extremadura - Centre to the consolidation of the euro-region Alentejo, Centre, Extremadura (EUROACE), in such a way that the infrastructure constitutes a platform for the exchange of information and institutional collaboration between

Table 1. Background common cooperation projects between Alentejo, Centro and Extremadura Regions (updated of Batista et al., 2013).

Project	Program	Aims	Project Partners	Results
CoordSIG (1997-2001)	INTERREG II C	Coordination of Geographic Information Systems (GIS) and Instruments of Earth Observation.	JE, AMDE (CIMAC), GA, MMA, Midi-Périnée	Standardization of information between Portugal and Spain. Continuous mapping test. Creating the background for cooperation
PlanExAL (2003-2005)	INTERREG III-A	Addressing joint planning strategies on both sides of the Spanish-Portuguese border.	JE, AMDE	Mapping for both sides of the border, orthophotomaps; Study of Widespread Build [1] and Territorial Plan for Alqueva [2].
GeoALEX (2004-2006)	INTERREG III-A	Development of territorial and environmental management model for Alentejo-Extremadura. Creation of common cartography	AMDE (CIMAC), JE, IGP, CNIG-IGN, CCDRA, AMNA (CIMMA), Dip.Badajoz e DGCE	Geographic data and crossborder indicators harmonization. Publication of two books GESTA Model [3] and Common Cartography Object Catalogue scale 1:10000 [4].
OTALEX (2006-2009)	INTERREG III-A	Creation of the Territorial Observatory of Alentejo and Extremadura - OTALEX.	JE, AMDE (CIMAC), IGP, CNIG-IGN, CCDRA, AMNA (CIMMA), Dip.Badajoz e DGCE	Creation of the Territorial Observatory of Alentejo and Extremadura – OTALEX; First crossborder non-pilot SDI – www.ideotalex.eu in 2007; Data harmonization according to international standards – INSPIRE Directive. Publication of OTALEX Results [5] and Corine Land Cover Level 5 [6] books.
OTALEX II (2008-2011)	POCTEP – Cross Border Cooperation Program Spain-Portugal 2007-2013	User services development thought IDE-OTALEX; Management and monitoring environmental system.	AMDE (CIMAC), JE, IGP, CNIG-IGN, CCDRA, AMNA (CIMMA), Dip.Badajoz, UÉvora e UExtremadura	Creation of a physical space for OTALEX in *La Cocosa* (Badajoz, Extremadura, Spain). Improvements on IDE-OTALEX. Eenvironmental Indicators; creation of OTALEX indicator System; Publication of the first Alentejo-Extremadura Atlas [7], OTALEX II Final Results book [8], Land cover/ Land use Map of Évora District, at scale 1:150000 [9], and Alentejo and Extremadura Map, at scale 1:600000 [10].
OTALEX C (2010-2016)	POCTEP – Cross Border Cooperation Program Spain-Portugal 2007-2013	Integration of Centro Portugal region; Development of sustainability indicators; parametric maps of soil; footprint. SDI new services improvement – WPS and WCS New I&D working group; Linked data and SOS	JE, CIMAC, JE, DGT (IGP), CNIG-IGN, CCDRA, Dip.Badajoz, Dip Cáceres, IPCB e EDIA, UÉvora e UExt.	Improvement of IDEOTALEX geoPortal: map viewer, geoprocessing tools (WPS), backoffice, SIO, SOS and linked data.

the national, regional and local administrations with the incidence in this territory.

- Extension of the territorial scope of the territorial Observatory Alentejo-Extremadura, including the central region of Portugal, in such a way that it turns in the Alentejo-Extremadura Territorial Observatory and Center.
- Consolidating the infrastructure of spatial data OTALEX C, expanding its territorial scope and introducing new functions in such a way that it involves the local administration.
- Complete mapping of urban centres.
- Outreach activities and training courses in the physical space OTALEX C.

Figure 2. Chronological distribution of the different projects developed up to OTALEX C and list of partners participating in each of them. Source: http://www.ideotalex.eu/OtalexC/.

COORDSIG	PLANEXAL	GEOALEX	OTALEX	OTALEX II	OTALEX C
1997-2000	2002-04	2004-06	2006-08	2009-11	2011-15
IPCC	AMDE	IGP	IGP	IGP	DGT
AMDE	JE	AMDE	AMDE	CIMAC	CIMAC
JE		JE	JE	JE	JE
MMA		IGN	IGN	IGN	IGN
GA		CCDRA	CCDRA	CCDRA	CCDRA
		AMNA	AMNA	CIMAA	CIMAA
		DB	DB	DB	DB
		GRCE	GRCE	*GRCE*	UEX
			UEX	UEX	Uévora
			UÉvora	UÉvora	EDIA
			EDIA	EDIA	Dip Cáceres
					IPCB

CIMAC=AMDE
CIMAA=AMNA
DGT=IGP=IPCC

- Obtaining data and environmental, socio-economic indicators and sustainability of the central region in order to expand existing ones.
- Progress in obtaining indicators of sustainability in the line of the European sustainable development strategy.

All collected information is published in the geoportal OTALEX C, created in 2007 as the first IDE-border between Portugal and Spain, and the first non-pilot cross-border multilingual Europe. It has a trilingual interface in Spanish, Portuguese and English, and can be accessed through the use of a simple Internet browser, in the address: http://www.ideotalex.eu (Figure 3). This portal includes a standard Viewer with: maps, Web services, a gazetteer, a metadata catalogue, publications, system of indicators and a search engine and semantic display, obtaining in this way to a powerful IDE for cross-border application. This IDE includes in its structure a set of data, services, methodologies, standards and agreements, with which it is possible to view, overlay, consult and analyse geographic information of a territory that is published on the Web, according to a series of well-defined standards, by a group of producers of data and geographical services.

Various aspects following their chronology throughout the various projects discussed can be drawn from the listing of works that appear in the geoportal (Figure 3):

Originally, in CoordSIG, it was worked on standardization processes of the information available on both sides of the border, coordinating, developing and

Figure 3. Home screen of the IDE-OTALEXC geoportal. Source: http://www.ideotalex.eu/OtalexC/.

implementing methodologies with the objective of minimizing the number of gaps in the field of comparable geo-referenced data and quantifiable, using available technologies to achieve better coordination and integration of available GIS. For this, several areas of information were created: Cartography Subsystem, Planning Subsystem, Territorial Subsystem and Communications and finally GIS Coordination. All this allowed the development of a series of methodologies for the compatibility of geographic information that laid the foundations for the integration between the different Portuguese and Spanish cartographies (Figure 4), and which would provide the foundations on which to initiate the projects of subsequent years.

- With PlanExAl, common management strategies were addressed, generating a continuous map on both sides of the border and generating the study and territorial plan of the area of influence of the Alqueva Reservoir, GIS tools continued to prevail.

Figure 4. Controls in the adjustment of the mapping compatibility process for the design of a continuous transboundary map, Ajuda bridge. Source: OTALEX C, 2015.

- GeoALEX was a significant qualitative and especially quantitative leap, due to the number of partners involved in the work. The main objective was to develop a territorial and environmental management model applicable to this border area, harmonizing as much as possible the territorial, socio-economic and environmental indicators available in the two regions (GeoALEX a, 2006; GeoALEX b, 2006). Traditional GIS methodologies were still used and the ArcGIS Geodatabase spatial data model was used (Nuno et al., 2006), which was fed with the series of indicators that were beginning to be collected, mainly with those of an environmental type in the pilot area of the Gévora River (Cabezas et al., 2006).
- In OTALEX, the creation of a cross-border Territorial Observatory of Alentejo and Extremadura was proposed, which meant moving towards methodologies related to spatial data infrastructures (IDE), also resorting to the use of free software technologies. The methodology set by INSPIRE (2007) was followed in the data harmonization process according to international agreements.

- The extension of the project to OTALEX II meant consolidating the cross-border territorial observatory as its main objective while consolidating the work team of OTALEX employees. Especially improvements were made in the design methodologies of the indicator batteries to generate the OTALEX Indicator System that would constitute the IDE power layers. This underwent improvements in the development of its computer systems by adopting new methodologies and potential for publishing geographic information on the WEB.
- Finally, OTALEX C was another important revulsion in the works, but not in the methodologies that had already been consolidated over the years and of the work teams. The reason for this change was caused by the extension of the study territory by incorporating the Central Portugal region to the observatory, which meant covering the entire territory of the EUROACE Euroregion. The most important improvements affected the geoportal (map viewer, web processing of layers) of the IDE-OTALEX C. In the indicator systems the GIS methodologies previously used in the other two were applied to the Central region, adapting the parameters to some peculiarities that incorporated the new territories, such as altitudes, higher population density or new coastal ecosystems.

Summarizing the consequence more palpable in the GIS methodologies used has been the evolution of a system of compatibilization of mapping tools GIS, proprietary software into an IDE for WEB publishing with a greater using free distribution software. It has been used also in the systems of indicators using remote sensing techniques and other tools of smaller broadcasting as it has been to advance methodologies that allow the mapping extension of uses of the territory, through the analysis of images of satellite with algorithms based on the identification of objects (OBIA), or the use, by the Working Group of r & d, a Semantic Web and data from sensors for SOS server.

System of Indicators

The IDE OTALEX C should have a unified data model that allowed save border spaces inherent asymmetries and addressing a joint vision through the monitoring of territorial, environmental and socio-economic variables of the three regions, laying the groundwork for a joint cross-border territorial monitoring system. Some keys to this model are the following:

- Creation of a range of indicators from the inventory of basic data which had limitations on the availability of comparable to one information and across the border. To these constraints is added the need to match the definition, so it was essential the establishment of common criteria necessary to make comparative generalizations. In the case of having varying definitions in terms of the indicators of the two countries, it was decided to harmonize criteria that do not compromise the methodologies and standards accepted in each country.

- The range of indicators was established taking into account the accessibility and consistency of data, factors that ensured the periodic renewal of the same, and the ability to track their evolution in time.
- One of the limitations essential for their treatment both the availability of information was the Cartographic base referred to which, which reflected marked contrast between the different territorial and administrative realities. In the case of Extremadura, the municipalities were chosen and, for Alentejo and Centro, in a first approximation the parishes were chosen by their higher level of detail, but do not have data on some of the indicators available in this level of detail it was decided to also use the division of municipalities to Portugal.

Initially, there were just some territorial and socio-economic indicators that were not also systematized. With the introduction of the environment is thought about creating a structure that would allow sort existing but also add new ones with the progress of the work. Different variables were established around the characteristics of the three border regions and they were structuring constituting the system of indicators (SIO OTALEX). This organization, which was constituted, was based on a hierarchical structure, through 4 categories: *vector, theme, indicator* and, if it was necessary, *subindicator*. The first category distinguished vectors Territorial, environmental, social and economic (Figure 5). Each of these vectors is divided into different topics, that dashing indicators for the same subject matter, and some of these indicators, in turn, were divided into sub-indicators (Figure 6).

Different indicators were defined according to the possibility of describing complex phenomena in a simpler way to explain the reality of the territory, the trends and developments over time. To facilitate the classification and identification of each entity was established a coding system hierarchically structured, open and flexible enough to add more indicators in this system at any time. In this way, an 8-digit sequential code allowed unequivocal identification of each indicator and, at the same time, was a key link between them.

At the same time, it was attributed to each indicator a classification based on the case models proposed by the OECD (1993) of P-E-R (pressure-state-response). This model considers that human activities exert pressures (P) on the environment by altering the quality and quantity of existing natural resources, and as a result,

Figure 5. OTALEX C Indicator System Vectors: Social (purple), Environmental (green), Economic (orange) and Territorial (yellow). Source: OTALEX C, 2015.

Figure 6. Codification of the OTALEX C Indicator System in: vector (green), theme (light green), indicator (orange) and subindicator (brown). Source: OTALEX C, 2015.

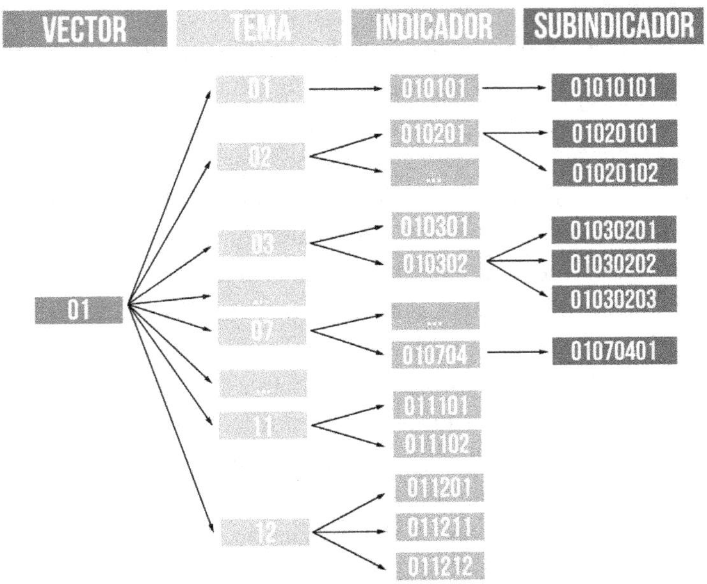

its State (E). On the other hand, society responds (R) to these changes through environmental, economic and sectoral policies. Between the huge number and diversity of existing indicators, choose which is better suited to the objectives was one of the most important works of this CBC, and therefore considered criteria that determinants were:

- Importance and representativeness in the study area.
- Reliability of sources of information.
- Availability and easy to obtain.
- Update capacity
- Ease of interpretation

Through the application of these criteria were structured information in 4-vector and 19 issues, in order to treat different areas for analysis as complete as possible of these border territories (Table 2). More than 60 indicators grouped according to their subject area were treated statistically and demographically. Some of the proposed indicators had to be disposed of either by not having data in both countries, well because they could not be treated in a uniform way, either because the temporal space of reference did not coincide, these being the main problems encountered when working with cross-border information.

Once defined the range of indicators, common to the two countries, data were collected from different official sources Spanish and Portuguese and, later, analysed and treated. After this phase, it was the harmonization of the same and they were incorporated into a geographic database that allowed establishing different relationships between them. This type of organization allowed to store and manage the whole set of data elements and obtained, neatly simplifying analysis models. These models allowed update and integrate new data and information at any time, and its systematic architecture enabled a huge set of structuring, geoprocessing and analysis operations. Once collected, homogenized and analysed all the data, they spent part of the infrastructure of spatial data OTALEX C, which has as main objective to offer to the public around a repository of information common to these regions to allow verify the sustainability of human activities and that serve as a tool in planning and management decision support. All indicators were supplemented by their respective metadata, according to European standards on Standardization of information, registered in the INSPIRE directive (EC, 2007).

With all this territorial information channelled through the IDE OTALEX is suited indicators common to the two countries, comparable and homogenized, serving at the same time with the aim of publicizing them through successive publications, and contributing to the dissemination and consolidation of the cross-border territorial information within the framework of different projects. This could be reached at the

Table 2. System of Indicators of OTALEX C in: four vectors (territorial, environmental, social, economic) and twenty themes. Source: OTALEX C, 2015.

VECTOR	THEME
01. Territorial	01. Weather
	02. Geology And Geomorphology
	03. Hydrography
	04. Soils
	05. Admnistractive Structure
02. Environmental	01. Air
	02. Water
	03. Wastes
	04. Contaminations Sources
	05. Land Use
	06. Environmental Performance Of Urban Areas
	07. Urban Spaces
	08. Noise
	09. Energy
	10. Nature Conservation
	11. Landscape
03. Social	01. Population Dependency
	02. Education Facilities
	03. Health Care
04. Economic	01. Unemployement index
	02. Economic Activities

same time one of the challenges for the consolidation of the data infrastructure: the adaptation of a set of indicators that would allow, in a simple and almost immediate way know the territorial dynamics and make monitoring of this territory, which would treat this space as a continuum.

Work with definitions, criteria, scales, and different sources of information between the two countries have not been an easy task. Nevertheless, the work has reached positive results with the purpose of contributing to the assessment of the sustainability of the territory at all levels: territorial, environmental, social and economic. It has been had tried to improve the work performed, not only with the maintenance of the information and data of the system of indicators but also methodologies and their harmonization at all levels. A clear example was the attribution of the code of administrative units that make up the totality of the project area consists of the country code (PT or is), region (Alentejo, Centre or Extremadura), followed by the NUT and the codes of the municipalities, and the official codification of the National Institute of Statistics (INE) was used. This action contributes to all existing elements are identified uniquely and allows you to perform operations with greater ease and accuracy.

The representation of these indicators appear in the OTALEX C Atlas (OTALEX C, 2013), which displays information comparable and harmonised, summarizes the efforts made by the various entities of the project. Its preparation involved graphic imaging of a wide range of content was developed from previous projects.

One of the latest challenges was the definition and analysis of a sustainability report in order to clarify the status of these regions. When we talk about sustainable development, we intend to define the method through which is intended to ensure the resources of the future without jeopardizing those of the present. To achieve this goal, it has been necessary to add new indicators to the existing battery and what thus constitute in the SIO, a new vector of sustainability. These new indicators are based on the statistical processing of the vectors that already exist (territorial, environmental, social and economic) through the combination and use of one or several of these (Table 3).

Through the creation of the system of indicators OTALEX (SIO) for the web, integrated into the IDE - OTALEX, it got to give added value to the project by providing the necessary tools for more efficient management and operation of the data. This system allowed to offer a set of graphical statistics and thematic maps that presented on maps, they complement the capabilities of the existing platform. Published indicators and updates which are subjected, are reported through the IDE-OTALEX, which constitutes a continuous work and offers to the public not only the possibility of joint information about the cross-border area but also see the evolution of these regions.

RESULTS AND BENEFITS, AND DISCUSSION ON THE CROSS-BORDER COOPERATION OTALEX C

OTALEX C over the years of working in common has provided, as a major milestone for cross-border cooperation, the creation and consolidation of a shared spatial data infrastructure: IDE OTALEX C. The creation of this IDE was the medium on which integrated territorial and environmental information of cross-border regions involved. Among the main achievements of the project was to integrate environmental information and make it available to social, to what was necessary to create a large number of indicators environmental, in its four vectors, that have been mapped and compiled, and with that has made the first Atlas available in this

Table 3. List of sustainability indicators. Source: OTALEX C, 2015.

SUSTAINABILITY	INDICATORS
01. Territorial Matrix	01. Urban Surface
	02. No Urban Surface
	03. Urban Growth Rate
	04. Average Area of Municipal Terms
02. Environmental Quality	01. Protected Area
	02. Burning Area
	03. Burned Area in Protected Areas
	04. Forest Area
	05. Cultivated Area
	06. Water Surface
	07. Biologically Productive Surface
	08. Water Use (Water Footprint)
	09. Aquatic Surface
03. Municipal Metabolism	01. Water Consumption Intensity (Water Efficiency)
	02. Energy Consumption Intensity
	03. Electric Power Balance
	04. Recycling Rate
	05. Density of Green Areas
04. Socioeconomic Dinamics	01. Interannual Population Growth Rate
	02. Municipal Budget
	03. Participation in Municipal Elections
05. Sustainable Mobility	01. Motorization Index
	02. Modal Distribution of Transport
	03. Equipment Distance

area. The geoportal allows any citizen to motorizations of variables and changes in the territorial dynamics.

In this line, there are other experiments carried out in Europe, although subsequent OTALEX c, such as ERGO Masterplan or Redvert or with a more specific theme for renewable energies such as Solar Tirol (Dura, Camonita, Berzi & Noferini, 2018).

As for GRISI project (Craglia & Campagna, 2009) had as objective principal to share experiences in the creation of GIS applications and geoportals, develop capabilities and technical expertise with a view to the adoption of the INSPIRE directive. In some respects very similar to OTALEX C, but remained very low with respect to this in the aspirations of the information collected and the depth of its indicators, being rather an activity of exchange of experience between technicians instead of a useful tool.

Somewhat fuller was X-Border-GDI (Craglia & Campagna, 2009), also serving the lines of INSPIRE, and had a structure of partners like OTALEX C, in which were involved local, regional and national administrations and a series of private organizations. As this reliance on the use of collaborative tools for the transfer and exchange of knowledge and experiences between the partners, also arriving as one of the achievements with OTALEX C that communication and cooperation were two key factors to integrate cross-border SDI.

Centrope MAP that stretches over parts of four countries (Schrenk & Pozarek, 2019), also uses an SDI to collect harmonised cross-border geoinformation, representing on a common system of spatial data through web (WMS) map services compatible with OGC originating in different organizations and institutions throughout the region. Comparing with OTALEX C it is very similar in the technological tools used and on the functionality of its geoportal, counting also with a good amount of socio-economic environmental indicators and not only.

Among other benefits, the CBC has allowed doing an x-ray of the territory as a whole and analyse in-depth the problems and implement solutions. Thus the distribution of the population, has been seen since all these data show that population loss has a great significance in territorial development, so to put in place development is necessary to attract population, mainly young and Entrepreneur betting on the quality of life of rural environments, guidelines referred to in the operational programmes of CBC. The analysis of infrastructures, facilities and services focused from the point of view of its distribution and accessibility, the indicators show in General breakthroughs and an encouraging picture, with quotas of welfare relatively important, that in addition to indirectly has led to the transfer of services to rural environments, although the current crisis is affecting them.

Another benefit that has managed to get this project, observed throughout the many years of collaboration, in addition with virtually with a large number of technicians who have not changed during that time, is to note that you one of the problems most important to advance sustainable development stumbles with the rigidity of the administrations which depends. It depends too much on regional institutions and there is no autonomy to take decisions solely affecting the border area, and these also there is an imbalance between the Spanish and the Portuguese, the latter more dependent of the Central administration. These shortcomings have even been observed by authors outside the project are Tabara et to the. (2018) that carried out a State in the Iberian Peninsula. These imbalances are also in the border area to analyse a particular topic as it is traded, which is weaker in areas close to the border of the Portuguese part (Castanho, Loures, Cabezas & Fernandez-Pozo,

2017)., which you should try to balance as can pose long-term problems (Herrero, A.G.; Xu, J. W. (2017).

Despite the obvious benefits that CBC initiatives provide, as in the Portuguese-Spanish area, avoid risks and barriers that may arise throughout your application, so it is necessary to develop a good coordination mechanism between territories carefully planning initiatives, to mitigate the potential conflicts that may arise between the different systems-politics that Governments develop each of their sides of the border (Miao, 2015). Also detected that one of the big problems is lack of communication (Castanho, Loures, Cabezas, & Fernandez-Pozo, 2017), lack of infrastructures of public transportation passing through the border, which does not provide the permeability and connectivity of these areas border, key aspect together with the commercial exchange and cooperation mechanisms for the success of the sustainable development (Xiao, Cheng, & Wang; 2018).

In order to strengthen cross-border cooperation between non-governmental and non-profit: to make progress in the sustainable development of the countries along the "B & R", there are many aspects, such as installations, Exchange connectivity commercial and cooperation mechanisms, that must be coordinated and resolved by many countries. This requires cross-border cooperation of non-governmental organizations and non-profit. For example, efforts can be made to carry out jointly the study of the master plan and fully consider the balance of interests of all the parties; running joint schools to expand the size of international students; strengthen scientific and technological cooperation, co-build laboratories, extensively carry out exchanges and cooperation among countries along the "B&R"; " celebrate each other the week of tourism promotion, the month of awareness and other activities to jointly create excellent cross-border tourist itineraries with the characteristics of the "B&R"; " and coordinate research on design of routes and technical standards for connectivity facilities.

Analysing, in general, you can see that the territory OTALEX C is quite diverse, with areas from high mountains to coastal areas, with an unbeatable position in environmental values. This is an opportunity in better training and professional qualification of its inhabitants in taking advantage of the natural environment, improving cooperation on shared activities and allowing a better national and international positioning, promoting the dissemination of the products of this type of nature-oriented products.

OTALEX was recognized as a case of good practices of the Programme INTERREG III-A of the Spain-Portugal border cooperation 2000-2006. In 2009, it was invited to the SDI Best Practice Award of the project eSDI-Net + (www.esdinetplus.eu) and received an honourable mention. In 2011, it received an honourable mention from the und (Association of European border regions), in the context of the award und's 2011 (und, 2013). OTALEX C is a member of the infrastructure of spatial data of Spain from March 29, 2011, and is one of three environmental geoportals. It is also a member of the Steering Council of the infrastructure of spatial data of Spain and of the Observatory of sustainability in Spain. It collaborates with several different entities responsible for the management of the territory, like EUROACE, and it belongs to the Portuguese national programme to combat desertification, developed in the framework of the UNCCD (United Nations Convention to Combat the Desertification).

ACKNOWLEDGMENT

The dissemination of this present chapter has been possible thanks to the financial support from the ´European Fund of Regional Development´ (ERDF) and the Government of Extremadura to the research group ARAM through the subsidies with reference GR18054 and to the research group DESOSTE through the subsidies with reference GR18052.

The authors would like to thanks to the great team of OTALEX C and to the POCTEP (Cross-border Cooperation Program for Spain-Portugal) of the ERDF for the co-finance support of the project.

REFERENCES

AEBR - Association of European Border Regions. (2013). Retrieved from http://www.aebr.eu/en/news/news_detail.php?news_id=4 1 (accessed Mar. 24, 2013).

Allen, W. (2013). "I am From Busia!": Everyday Trading and Health Service Provision at the Kenya–Uganda Border as Place-Making Activities. *Journal of Borderland Studies*, *28*(3), 291–306. doi:10.1080/08865655.2013.862756

Baltà, P. J. (2015). *Cross-Border Cooperation and Cultural Communities in Europe*. Brussels, Belgium: Centre Maurits Coppieters.

Batista, T., Caballero, C., Ceballos, F., Carriço, C., Mateus, J., Lopes, H., ... Pinto-Gomes, C. (2013). IDE-OTALEX C. The First Crossborder SDI between Portugal and Spain: Background and Development. *Journal of Earth Science an Engineering*, *6*(3), 393–400.

Boehnke, K., Rippl, S., & Fuss, D. (2015). Sustainable civil-society engagement: Potencials of a transnational civil society in French-German, Polish-German, and Czech-German border regions. *Sustainability*, *7*(4), 4078–4099. doi:10.3390u7044078

Bonner, R. C., & Rozental, A. T. (2009). *Managing the united states-Mexico border: Cooperative solutions to common challenges. Full report of the binational Task Force on the United States-Mexico border*. Washington, DC: Woodrow Wilson Internat.

Brunet-Jailly, E. (2004). Comparing Local Cross-border Relations under EU and NAFTA. *Canadian American Public Policy, 58*, 1–59.

Brunet-Jailly, E. (2011). Special Section: Borders, Borderlands and Theory: An Introduction. *Geopolitics, 16*(1), 1–6. doi:10.1080/14650045.2010.493765

Brunet-Jailly, E., & Dupeyron, B. (2017). Introduction: Borders, Borderlands, and Porosity. In *Borderlands. Comparing Border Security in North America and Europe* (pp. 1–17). Ottawa, Canada: Les Presses de l'Université d'Ottawa, University of Ottawa Press.

Buis, H. (2009). The role of local government associations in increasing the effectiveness of city-to-city cooperation. *Habitat International, 33*(2), 190–194. doi:10.1016/j.habitatint.2008.10.017

Castanho, R. A., Loures, L., Cabezas, J., & Fernández-Pozo, L. (2017). Cross-Border Cooperation (CBC) in Southern Europe—An Iberian Case Study. The Eurocity Elvas-Badajoz. *Sustainability, 9*(3), 360. doi:10.3390u9030360

Castanho, R. A., Loures, L., Cabezas, J., & Fernández-Pozo, L. (2018). Identifying critical factors for success in Cross Border Cooperation (CBC) development projects. *Habitat International, 72*, 92–99. doi:10.1016/j.habitatint.2016.10.004

Castanho, R. A., Vulevic, A., Cabezas, J., Fernández-Pozo, L., Goméz-Naranjo, J., & Loures, L. (2017). Accessibility and connectivity – Movement between cities, as a critical factor to achieve success on cross-border cooperation (CBC) projects. A European analysis. *Sustainable Cities and Society, 32*, 181–190. doi:10.1016/j.scs.2017.03.026

Cetl, V., Tomas, R., Kotsev, A., de Lima, V. N., Smith, R. S., & Jobst, M. (2019). Establishing Common Ground Through INSPIRE: The Legally-Driven European Spatial Data Infrastructure. In *Service-Oriented Mapping. Lecture Notes in Geoinformation and Cartography*. Cham, Switzerland: Springer. doi:10.1007/978-3-319-72434-8_3

Coleman, D., Rajabifard, A., & Crompvoets, J. (2016). *Spatial Enablement in a Smart World. Gilbertville*. GSDI Association Press.

Craglia, M., & Campagna, M. (2009). *Advanced Regional Spatial Data Infrastructures in Europe*. Luxembourg: Office for Official Publications of the European Communities.

Dale, G. (2016). *Karl polanyi: A life on the left*. New York: Columbia University Press.

Durà, A., Camonita, F., Berzi, M., & Noferini, A. (2018). *Euroregions, Excellence and Innovation across EU borders. A Catalogue of Good Practices*. Barcelona, Spain: Universidad Autónoma de Barcelona.

EC - European Commission. (2007). Directive 2007/2/EC of the European Parliament and of the Council of 14 March 2007 establishing an Infrastructure for Spatial Information in the European Community (INSPIRE). *Official Journal of the European Union*, *50*, 1–14.

Eriksen, T. H., & Nielsen, F. S. (2001). A History of Anthropology. London, UK: Pluto Press.

ESPON European Spatial Planning Observation Network. (2013). In *TRACC. Transport Accessibility at Regional/Local Scale and Patterns in Europe*. Brussels, Belgium: European Union. Retrieved from https://www.espon.eu/tracc

Evangelidis, K., Agrianidis, A., Perakis, K., Papadopoulos, T., & Papatheodorou, K. (2018). Web-GIS Development of Geospatial Data Dissemination in EU Operational Programmes. *European Journal of Geography*, *9*(2), 21–36.

Hansen, H. S., Reiter, I. M., & Schrøder, L. (2017). Lecture Notes in Computer Science: Vol. 10441. *A System Architecture for a Transnational Data Infrastructure Supporting Maritime Spatial Planning. Electronic Government and the Information Systems Perspective. EGOVIS 2017* (pp. 158–172). Cham, Switzerland: Springer.

Herrero, A. G., & Xu, J. W. (2017). China's Belt and Road Initiative: Can Europe expect trade gains? *China & World Economy*, *25*(6), 84–99. doi:10.1111/cwe.12222

Holmes, R. (2016). Fascism 2. *Anthropology Today*, *32*(2), 1–3. doi:10.1111/1467-8322.12235

Kireev, A. A., & Yachin, S. E. (2019). Paradigms of Border Studies and the Metacultural Approach. *Journal of Borderland Studies*, *34*(3), 395–412. doi:10.1080/08865655.2017.1344563

Kolosov, V. A. (2015). Theoretical Approaches in the Study of Borders. Introduction to Border Studies (33-59). Vladivostok, Russia: Far Eastern Federal University.

Konrad, V. (2015). Toward a Theory of Borders in Motion. *Journal of Borderland Studies*, *30*(1), 1–17. doi:10.1080/08865655.2015.1008387

Konrad, V., & Nicol, H. T. (2011). Border Culture, the Boundary Between Canada and the United States of America, and the Advancement of Borderlands Theory. *Geopolitics*, *16*(1), 70–90. doi:10.1080/14650045.2010.493773

Kurki, T. (2014). Borders from the Cultural Point of View: An Introduction to Writing at Borders. *Culture Unbound*, *6*(6), 1055–1070. doi:10.3384/cu.2000.1525.1461055

Kurowska-Pysz, J., Castanho, R. A., & Naranjo, J. (2018). Cross-Border Cooperation – The Barriers Analysis and The Recommendations. *Polish Journal of Management Studies*, *17*(2), 134–147. doi:10.17512/pjms.2018.17.2.12

Laine, J. P. (2015). A Historical View on the Study of Borders. In Introduction to Border Studies (14-32). Vladivostok, Russia: Far Eastern Federal University.

Lee, S., & Na, S. (2010). E-waste recycling systems and sound circulative economies in east asia: A comparative analysis of systems in Japan, South Korea, China and Taiwan. *Sustainability Journal*, *2*(6), 1632–1644. doi:10.3390u2061632

LISER. (2015). Opportunities of cross-border cooperation between small and medium cities in Europe. Report written in the scope of the Observatory of Territorial Development, in partnership with the Department of Spatial Planning and Development – Ministry of Sustainable Development and Infrastructure, Luxembourg Institute of Socio – Economic Research. Luxembourg.

Loures, L., Castanho, R. A., Vulevic, A., Naranjo Gómez, J., Cabezas, J., & Fernández-Pozo, L. (2018). *The Multivariated Effect of City Cooperation in Land Use Planning and Decision-making Processes - a European Analysis. Urban Agglomerations* (pp. 87–106). London, UK: InTech.

Ma, N., & Cheng, E. W. (2019). *The Umbrella Movement: Civil Resistance and Contentious Space in Hong Kong*. Amsterdam, The Netherlands: Amsterdam University Press B. V. doi:10.1515/9789048535248

Markuszewska, I., Tanskanen, M., & Vila, J. (2016). Boundaries From Borders: Cross-Border Relationships in the Context of the Mental Perception of a Borderline – Experiences from Spanish-French and Polish-German Border Twin Towns. *Quaestiones Geographicae*, *35*(1), 105–119. doi:10.1515/quageo-2016-0010

Matthiesen, U., & Bürkner, H. (2002). Antagonistic structures in border areas: Local milieux and local politics in the polish – German twin city Gubin/Guben. *GeoJournal*, *54*(1), 43–50. doi:10.1023/A:1021136614586

Mayoral, M., de la Cruz, L., Osuna, J. A., Rodríguez, L., & Mora, P. (2015). *Estudio de Accesibilidad Viaria en el Área OTALEX-C / Estudo de Acessibilidade Rodoviária da Área OTALEX-C*. Retrieved from http://dl.dip-caceres.es/proyectos/otalex2/actividades.html

McCall, C. (2015). State Borders in Europe. In Introduction to Border Studies (180-197). Vladivostok, Russia: Far Eastern Federal University.

Miao, J. (2015). Expectations and Realities: Managing the risks of the "Belt and Road" Initiative. *China Quarterly of International Strategic Studies*, *1*(03), 497–522. doi:10.1142/S2377740015500244

Nabeeh, N. A., El-Ghareeb, H. A., & Riad, A. M. (2015). Integrating software agents and web services in service oriented architecture based cloud services discovery framework. *Journal of Convergence Information Technology*, *10*(1), 2015.

Naranjo, J. M. (2016). Impacts on the social cohesion of mainland Spain's future motorway and high-speed rail networks. *Sustainability*, *8*(7), 624–646. doi:10.3390u8070624

OECD. (1993). *OECD core set of indicators for environmental performance reviews. A synthesis report by the Group on the State of the Environment. OECD Environment Monographs 83*. Paris, France: OECD.

OTALEX C. (2013). *Atlas OTALEX C*. Mérida: Dirección General de Transportes, Ordenación del Territorio y Urbanismo. Consejería de Fomento, Vivienda, Ordenación del territorio y Turismo.

OTALEX C. (2015). *OTALEX C. Historia de un Proyecto Transfronterizo / História de um Projecto Transfronteiriço, 1997 - 2015*. Retrieved from http://www.ideotalex.eu/OtalexC/paginas/Publicacion.jsp

Peyrony, J., & Denert, O. (2012). Planning for Cross-Border Territories: The Role Played by Spatial Information. *Raumforschung und Raumordnung*, *70*(3), 229–240. doi:10.100713147-012-0156-0

Puyosa, I. (2019). Venezuelan Struggle Towards Democratization: The 2017 Civil Resistance Campaign. In *Civil Resistance and Violent Conflict in Latin America. Studies of the Americas* (pp. 85–110). Cham, Switzerland: Palgrave Macmillan. doi:10.1007/978-3-030-05033-7_5

Schrenk, M., & Pozarek, W. (2007). *Centrope MAP: Combining X-Border Information from Multiple Sources for Planning Purposes. Information Fusion and Geographic Information Systems. Lecture Notes in Geoinformation and Cartography* (pp. 96–110). Berlin, Germany: Springer.

Stromer-Galley, J. (2019). *Presidential Campaigning in the Internet Age*. New York: Oxford University Press. doi:10.1093/oso/9780190694043.001.0001

Tàbara, J. D., Cots, F., Pedde, S., Hölscher, K., Kok, K., Lovanova, A., & ... Frantzeskaki, NEtherington, J. (2018). Exploring Institutional Transformations to Address High-End Climate Change in Iberia. *Sustainability*, *10*(2), 161. doi:10.3390u10010161

UNCED. (1992). Programa 21. Documentos oficiales de la Cumbre de la Tierra. Río de Janeiro, Brazil: UN. Retrieved from https://sustainabledevelopment.un.org/milestones/unced

Van Hamme, G., & Pion, G. (2012). The relevance of the world-system approach in the era of globalization of economic flows and networks. *Geografiska Annaler. Series B, Human Geography*, *94*(1), 65–82. doi:10.1111/j.1468-0467.2012.00396.x

Veemaa, J. (2012). Internationalizing the spatial identity of cross-border cooperation. *European Planning Studies Journal*, *20*(10), 1647–1666. doi:10.1080/09654313.2012.713335

Xiao, H., Cheng, J., & Wang, X. (2018). Does the Belt and Road Initiative Promote Sustainable Development? Evidence from Countries along the Belt and Road. *Sustainability*, *10*(12), 4370. doi:10.3390u10124370

Zyikov, A. A., & Sevastianov, S. V. (2015). Transborder Relations. In Introduction to Border Studies (118-138). Vladivostok, Russia: Far Eastern Federal University.

Chapter 2
The Impact of Being a Border Region in Business Demography:
An Analysis in the European Union

Paulo Ferreira
Polytechnic Institute of Portalegre, Portugal & VALORIZA - Research Center for Endogenous Resource Valorization, Portalegre, Portugal & Instituto Politécnico de Portalegre, Portalegre, Portugal

Luis Loures
Research Centre for Endogenous Resource Valorization, Instituto Politécnico de Portalegre, Portugal & VALORIZA - Research Center for Endogenous Resource Valorization, Portalegre, Portugal & Instituto Politécnico de Portalegre, Portalegre, Portugal

Miguel Serafim
Instituto Politécnico de Portalegre, Portalegre, Portugal

ABSTRACT

The promotion of the entrepreneurship has been a challenge in recent years because it is recognised that entrepreneurial activity enhances economic growth. Border regions, because of the possibility of increasing cooperation between economic agents, gained a special status. Still, some of those cross-border regions continue to grow slower than other regions. Authors analyse business dynamics and entrepreneurial activities at a regional basis for the EU. Considering data availability, authors analyse 13 different countries. Indicators under analysis are birth rates, death rates, business churn, and survival rate. This chapter identifies and analyses the existence of significant differences between regions located alongside border areas, and analyses if there exist differences depending on the countries of those regions.
DOI: 10.4018/978-1-7998-2513-5.ch002

To compare business demographic indicators, parametric tests will be used. The results are analysed considering the potential differences between cross-border and non-cross-border regions.

INTRODUCTION

The promotion of the entrepreneurship has been a challenge in the last years all over the world, once it is considered as a source of economic growth, employment creation, and also productivity growth (OECD, 2017). This is a concern all over the world and also in the European Union. Although, the levels of entrepreneurship, which could be evaluated using Eurostat business demographic indicators, are not equal between the different countries and even inside the countries, they are different between regions. Border regions, because of the possibility of increasing cooperation between economic agents, gained a special status, but despite of their dynamism some of those cross-border regions remain growing slower than other regions. So, it is important to evaluate the levels of dynamism of regions and understand if exist any different pattern of business dynamics in cross-border and non-cross-border regions.

Considering this, we propose to analyse business dynamics and entrepreneurial activities at a regional basis, for the European Union. Considering data availability, we will analyse 14 different countries, namely Bulgaria, the Czech Republic, Estonia, Spain, France, Croatia, Italy, Lithuania, Hungary, Austria, Portugal, Romania, Slovakia and Finland. The indicators under analysis are birth rates (the percentage of new firms in a given year), death rates (the percentage of closed firms), business churn (the sum of both previous rates, which could be understood as total dynamics in firms), and survival rate (percentage of firms born 3 years before that continue to be opened).

The objective is to identify and analyze the existence of significant differences between regions located alongside border areas, analysing also if there exist differences depending on the countries of those regions. To make the comparison between the business demographic indicators, and considering the existence of a high number of observations, it will be used parametric tests. The results are analyzed considering the potential differences between cross-border and non-cross-border regions but also depending on the type of border (if those borders are only with EU regions, if share border with EU but also with other countries, if the frontiers are just with other countries or if regions have no frontier).

Our main results show that death rates are not significantly different depending on the regions (meaning probably that some causes for the death of rates are not different in the regions). Business churn shows some difference across regions although not possible to identify clearly in which regions are those differences. Birth rates and survival rates have clearer results, identifying that regions with frontier with other EU regions show higher results, demonstrating the dynamism of entrepreneurship in EU cross-border territories, which is a very interesting finding for regional and local governments to design joint policies for promoting economic growth, using entrepreneurship.

BACKGROUND

Entrepreneurship is often used in several different contexts: newspapers, social media or even politicians' speeches are just some examples. The linkages between entrepreneurship and economic growth, and the capability of being an enhancer of economic development are usually referred in the literature, since entrepreneurship could make countries to prosper economically, increasing citizens' well-being (Acs, Audretsch, Braunerhjelm, & Carlsson, 2012; Galindo & Méndez, 2014, among many others). The effects of entrepreneurship in economic growth are increased in the cases when it is based on knowledge (Audretsch, 2007; Audretsch & Keilbach, 2004a, 2004b, 2007, 2008, among others).

Despite the usual identification of entrepreneurship with the creation of new firms, it is considered that birth rates could be just a part of the whole set of entrepreneurships. In fact, there is not a unique definition for entrepreneurship, but many studies refer to Schumpeter (1934) and its creative destructive paradigm as being in the origin of the concept, when he identified economic dynamics caused by the appearance of more efficient companies, leading to the destruction of other less efficient ones. By this motive, it is used in this study not only information of birth rates but also other demographic statistics indicators to analyse the phenomenon of entrepreneurship, namely death rates, business churn and survival rates.

In the literature is possible to find plenty of studies searching for determinants of firm births, since the possibility of creating a firm as a last resource to earn money, to the identification of a business opportunity (Urbano & Aparício, 2016),

The existing conditions of countries could also be important as influencers of entrepreneurship (Castaño, Méndez, & Galindo, 2015). While in less developed countries entrepreneurship could be seen as the only way of living (Poschke, 2013), in the opposite way the existence of better economic conditions in more developed countries could imply higher firm dynamics (Wong, Ho & Autio, 2005; Angulo-Guerrero, Pérez-Moreno & Abad-Guerrero, 2017). Other countries' characteristics like social conditions (Davidsson & Honig, 2003), the existence of better physical and infrastructural conditions (Woolley, 2013; Audretsch, Heger, & Veith 2015), high levels of R&D (Caves, 1974; Javorcik, 2004; Ayyagari & Kosová, 2010) are also important drivers of entrepreneurship.

The generality of those studies have in common the use of country information in their analysis. Although, recently border areas gained a special interest, once they present singular characteristics, namely the cooperation between economic agents in those territories (Kurowska-Pysz, 2016; Sohn & Giffinger, 2015; Spirkova & Ivanicka, 2009). The difference of development between cross-border regions, when compared with the remaining (Lima, 2012; Pires, 2008; Medeiros, 2005) rely the importance of continue to study these particular regions. But despite the recognized importance of cross-border territories, caused by the proximity and economic interactions, there are few studies analyzing the differences in cross-border's business demography (Capello, Caragliu & Fratesi, 2018).

The cross-border cooperation started to call the attention even in the academic world. The high share of population living in this type of territory, in some cases the lack of common policy-making and the necessity of filling these gaps make important to study this type of regions (see, for example, Castanho, Loures, Fernandez & Pozo, 2018).

The existence of scarce information on business demography studied in a subnational level and the fact that the study in cross-border territories is even smaller, makes significant the approach used in this study, which distinguish between cross-border and non-cross border regions regarding to birth rate, death rate, business churn, and survival rate. Moreover, it is also distinguished the behaviour considering the type of frontier, once some regions just share borders with other EU regions, while others share borders with EU regions but also non-EU countries or share borders just with non-EU countries. Finally, it is also possible to find regions with no frontier at all.

DIFFERENCES IN BUSINESS DEMOGRAPHY IN EU CROSS-BORDER REGIONS

Material and Methods

It is made an assessment about the existence or not of differences in business demography indicators for the European Union NUTS3 regions. Due to date availability, just regions of 14 countries are analysed, namely Bulgaria, the Czech Republic, Estonia, Spain, France, Croatia, Italy, Lithuania, Hungary, Austria, Portugal, Romania, Slovakia and Finland. In total the analysis assesses 497 regions. The indicators under analysis are birth rates (the percentage of new firms in a given year), death rates (the percentage of closed firms), business churn (the sum of both previous rates, which could be understood as total dynamics in firms), and survival rate (percentage of firms born 3 years before that continue to be opened).

Table 1. Data under analysis

	Number of regions	Observations
Bulgaria	28	2015 for death rates and business churn
Czech Republic	14	2015 for death rates and business churn
Estonia	5	No data for survival rates
Spain	59	2013 for death rates and business churn
France	101	No data for survival rates
Croatia	21	2015 for death rates and business churn
Italy	110	2015 for death rates and business churn
Lithuania	10	No data for survival rates
Hungary	20	2015 for death rates and business churn
Austria	35	2015 for death rates and business churn
Portugal	25	2015 for death rates and business churn
Romania	42	2015 for death rates and business churn
Slovakia	8	2015 for death rates and business churn
Finland	19	The data is all for 2016

It is always used the last year with available information, which is, in general, 2016. The exceptions are referred in Table 1. Some of the regions do not have information for survival rates, so in that particular index just the remaining are used (see also Table 1 for obtain that information).

Two different analysis are made. Firstly, it is compared directly the business demographic indicators between cross-border and non-cross-border regions. Considering the existence of a high number of observations, it was used the t-test to detect those differences between independent samples, with the following hypotheses:

H0: Means are equal for cross-border and non-cross-border regions
H1: Means are different for cross-border and non-cross-border regions

In order to control the equality of variances in the different samples, it was applied the Levene's Test for Equality of Variances, with the hypotheses:

H0: Variances are equal for the different samples
H1: Variances are not equal for the different samples

Because the pattern of borders is different all over the European Union, regions were divided in four different groups: i) those which doesn't have any frontier; ii)

*Table 2. Results for the equality of means for the different indicators. * and ** identify rejection of the null hypothesis with significance levels of, respectively, 5% and 1%*

	Birth rate	Death rate	Business churn	Survival rate
Cross-border average	9.7996	8.1197	17.9059	58.3841
Non-cross-border average	9.1010	7.7728	16.6022	55.2850
Levene's test	8.905**	0.089	7.019**	12.376**
T-Test	2.661**	0.142	3.123**	4.515**

those which have only frontier with other EU regions; iii) those which have frontier with EU regions but also with other countries; iv) those which just have frontier with non-EU countries. Having several factors, the chosen methodology to test the difference between regions was the one-way ANOVA, with the hypotheses:

H0: All means are equal, for the different groups
H1: At least one mean is different from the remaining groups

To confirm the homogeneity of groups, it was used the Tukey HSD test.

RESULTS

The analysis started with the calculation of the difference of the indicators between regions with and without frontier, with the results present in Table 2. There, it is possible to identify that cross-border regions show higher values in the indicators than non-cross-border ones. And excepting the case of death rates, the remaining

*Table 3. Results for the one-way ANOVA for the different indicators. * and ** identify rejection of the null hypothesis with significance levels of, respectively, 5% and 1%*

	Birth rate	Death rate	Business churn	Survival rate
Frontier with EU regions	10.891	7.7728	17.9363	60.2100
Frontier with EU regions and other countries	9.6483	7.6854	18.6023	58.5407
Frontier just with other countries	9.5345	7.8334	17.3326	56.7058
No frontier	9.1010	8.3029	16.6022	55.2850
ANOVA F test	4.544**	1.347	3.869**	9.136**

*Table 4. Results for Tukey-HSD test, for multiple comparisons. * and ** identify rejection of the null hypothesis with significance levels of, respectively, 5% and 1%*

		Birth rate	Death rate	Business churn	Survival rate
Frontier with EU regions	Frontier with EU regions and other countries	-2.2003	1.1249	-0.7036	-1.1061
	Frontier just with other countries	0.2342	0.9941	0.7412	1.4482
	No frontier	1.9555	1.9491	2.8444	4.4194**
Frontier with EU regions and other countries	Frontier with EU regions	2.2003	-1.1249	0.7036	1.1061
	Frontier just with other countries	2.0398	-0.2290	1.1391	1.9847
	No frontier	3.3560**	-0.1686	2.2374*	3.4358**
Frontier just with other countries	Frontier with EU regions	-0.2342	-0.9941	-0.7412	-1.4482
	Frontier with EU regions and other countries	-2.0398	0.2290	-1.1391	-1.9847
	No frontier	0.9654	0.1390	0.9707	1.2084
No frontier	Frontier with EU regions	-1.9555	-1.9491	-2.8444*	-4.4194**
	Frontier with EU regions and other countries	-3.3560**	0.1686	-2.2374	-3.4358**
	Frontier just with other countries	-0.9654	-0.1390	-0.9707	-1.2084

differences are statistically significant. So, it seems that cross-border regions show higher entrepreneur levels.

When splitting the existence of frontier in the categories explained in the previous section, and when the ANOVA tests are applied, the results are the ones of Table 3. The death rate is the unique indicator that does not have significant evidence of difference among the groups under analysis. In the remaining cases, there exist differences or at least one group of regions.

Table 5. Homogeneous subsets resulting from the Tukey-HSD test, with a maximum significance subset of 0.05

	Birth rate		Death rate	Business churn	Survival rate	
Frontier with EU regions	X		X	X	X	
Frontier with EU regions and other countries	X		X	X	X	
Frontier just with other countries	X	X	X	X	X	X
No frontier		X	X	X		X
Significance	0.706	0.072	0.598	0.091	0.078	0.606

Based on the results of the Tukey HSD tests for multiple comparisons between groups (results in Table 4), it is possible to separate the groups in homogeneous subgroups (Table 5).

As expected, for death rate just one group is formed, because means are not different. Although, for business churn it is also just possible to identify one subgroup, according to the Tukey-HSD procedure. Despite the rejection of the one-way ANOVA test, this is a possible result because both tests (ANOVA and Tukey) have different testing power.

DISCUSSION, SOLUTIONS AND RECOMMENDATIONS

Looking at Table 4, it is possible to find some differences between the “No frontier” group and the one of “Frontier with EU regions and other countries”, meaning that regions without any frontier behave someway differently from the others. But the most interesting results is that, both for birth rate and survival rate, it is possible to separate one group composed by regions with “No frontier” and with “Frontier just with other countries” (despite in this case, these regions have some linkage with the subgroup composed by regions with frontier with EU). So, besides the fact that having a frontier has some impact on the entrepreneurial activity, the fact that the impact is higher when sharing frontier with other EU countries identify the relevance of belonging to the EU.

The results of this study show the existence of some differences in specific business demography indicators in the EU, at the regional level. In particular, entrepreneurial dynamic seems to be higher in the cross-border regions of the EU which share frontier with other EU regions, result of utmost importance considering the policy orientations it might be defined regarding business and company creation and development.

FUTURE RESEARCH DIRECTIONS

Despite the interest of this work and its results, it is necessary to highlight the existence of some possible limitations, namely the fact that the work just accounts for the difference in business indicators but do not analyse any possible determinants of those differences. The difficulty on obtaining relevant data for those possible determinants is on the basis of this limitation and is clearly a starting point for future research. Moreover, the extension of this analysis to other disaggregated regional levels, like municipalities, would be also relevant, once again depending on data availability. Finally, considering the obtained results it would be interesting to assess in a near future the impacts of the Brexit in the business dynamics between Ireland and the UK.

CONCLUSION

After the development of the present research, the obtained data enabled us to put forward noteworthy conclusion regarding the impact of border proximity in business demography. Moreover, the obtained results confirm the efficiency of the envisioned methodology to ascertain the impact of location on business demography, thought out the use of parametric tests.

Additionally, a relevant conclusion obtained from the assessed data is that there is a significant difference among border regions based on the integration, or not, of the neighbour country belongs to the EU. This strengthens not only the theory according to which economic integration fosters trading markets among neighbour countries, but also the fact that border regions might benefit from their proximity to countries with which they have no trade barriers.

ACKNOWLEDGMENT

This research was supported by Fundação para a Ciência e a Tecnologia [grant UID/ECO/04007/2019]

REFERENCES

Acs, Z., Audretsch, D., Braunerhjelm, P., & Carlsson, B. (2012). Growth and Entrepreneurship. *Small Business Economics*, *39*(2), 289–300. doi:10.100711187-010-9307-2

Angulo-Guerrero, M., Pérez-Moreno, S., & Abad-Guerrero, I. (2017). How economic freedom affects opportunity and necessity entrepreneurship in the OECD countries. *Journal of Business Research*, *73*, 30–37. doi:10.1016/j.jbusres.2016.11.017

Audretsch, D. (2007). Entrepreneurship capital and economic growth. *Oxford Review of Economic Policy*, *23*(1), 63–78. doi:10.1093/oxrep/grm001

Audretsch, D., Heger, D., & Veith, T. (2015). Infrastructure and entrepreneurship. *Small Business Economics*, *44*(2), 219–230. doi:10.100711187-014-9600-6

Audretsch, D., & Keilbach, M. (2004a). Does entrepreneurship capital matter? *Entrepreneurship Theory and Practice*, *28*(5), 419–429. doi:10.1111/j.1540-6520.2004.00055.x

Audretsch, D., & Keilbach, M. (2004b). Entrepreneurship capital and economic performance. *Regional Studies*, *38*(8), 949–959. doi:10.1080/0034340042000280956

Audretsch, D., & Keilbach, M. (2007). The localisation of entrepreneurship capital: Evidence from Germany. *Papers in Regional Science*, *86*(3), 351–365. doi:10.1111/j.1435-5957.2007.00131.x

Audretsch, D., & Keilbach, M. (2008). Resolving the knowledge paradox: Knowledge-spillover entrepreneurship and economic growth. *Research Policy*, *37*(10), 1697–1705. doi:10.1016/j.respol.2008.08.008

Ayyagari, M., & Kosová, R. (2010). Does FDI facilitate domestic entrepreneurship? Evidence from the Czech Republic. *Review of International Economics*, *18*(1), 14–29. doi:10.1111/j.1467-9396.2009.00854.x

Capello, R., Caragliu, A., & Fratesi, U. (2018). Measuring border effects in European cross-border regions. *Regional Studies*, *52*(7), 986–996. doi:10.1080/00343404.2017.1364843

Castanho, R., Loures, L., Fernandez, J., & Pozo, L. (2018). Identifying critical factors for success in Cross Border Cooperation (CBC) development projects. *Habitat International*, *72*, 92–99. doi:10.1016/j.habitatint.2016.10.004

Castaño, M., Méndez, M., & Galindo, M. (2015). The effect of social, cultural, and economic factors on entrepreneurship. *Journal of Business Research, 68*(7), 1496–1500. doi:10.1016/j.jbusres.2015.01.040

Caves, R. (1974). Multinational Firms, Competition and Productivity in Host Country Markets. *Economica, 41*(162), 176–193. doi:10.2307/2553765

Davidsson, P., & Honig, B. (2003). The Role of Social and Human Capital among Nascent Entrepreneurs. *Journal of Business Venturing, 18*(3), 301–331. doi:10.1016/S0883-9026(02)00097-6

Galindo, M., & Méndez, M. (2014). Entrepreneurship, economic growth, and innovation: Are feedback effects at work? *Journal of Business Research, 67*(5), 825–829. doi:10.1016/j.jbusres.2013.11.052

Javorcik, B. (2004). Does foreign direct investment increase the productivity of domestic firms? In search of spillovers through backward linkages. *The American Economic Review, 94*(3), 605–627. doi:10.1257/0002828041464605

Kurowska-Pysz, J. (2016). Opportunities for cross-border entrepreneurship development in a cluster model exemplified by the Polish-Czech border region. *Sustainability, 8*(3), 230. doi:10.3390u8030230

Lima, F. (2012) *As dinâmicas territoriais no espaço de fronteira na fachada atlântica peninsular: a eurocidade Valença/Tuy*. Retrieved from http://ler.letras.up.pt/uploads/ficheiros/9963.pdf (accessed on 21 February 2017).

Medeiros, E. A. C. (2005). *Coesão territorial nas NUTS III de fronteira de Portugal Continental. A iniciativa Interreg III-A e o desenvolvimento regional. O caso da NUT III do Alentejo Central* (Unpublished master's thesis). Universidade de Lisboa, Portugal.

OECD. (2017). *The geography of firm dynamics: measuring business demography for regional development.* Paris, France: OECD. Retrieved from http://dx.dol.org/10.1787/9789264286764-en

Pires, I. (2008). *A integração dos mercados ibéricos: um processo dependente e territorialmente diferenciado?* Lisboa, Portugal: Centro de Estudos Geográficos, Universidade de Lisboa.

Poschke, M. (2013). 'Entrepreneurs out of necessity': A snapshot. *Applied Economics Letters, 20*(7), 7. doi:10.1080/13504851.2012.727968

Schumpeter, J. (1934). *The theory of economic development*. Harvard University Press.

Sohn, C., & Giffinger, R. (2015). A policy network approach to cross-border metropolitan governance: The cases of Vienna and Bratislava. *European Planning Studies, 23*(6), 1187–1208. doi:10.1080/09654313.2014.994089

Spirkova, D., & Ivanicka, K. (2009). Dynamics of Bratislava urban and housing development. In T. Panagoupolos (Ed.), *New models for innovative management and urban dynamics* (pp. 37–52). Faro, Portugal: University of Algarve.

Urbano, D., & Aparicio, S. (2016). Entrepreneurship capital types and economic growth: International evidence. *Technological Forecasting and Social Change, 102*, 34–44. doi:10.1016/j.techfore.2015.02.018

Wong, P., Ho, Y., & Autio, E. (2002). Entrepreneurship, innovation and economic growth: Evidence from GEM data. *Small Business Economics, 24*(3), 335–350. doi:10.100711187-005-2000-1

Woolley, J. (2013). The creation and configuration of infrastructure for entrepreneurship in emerging domains of activity. *Entrepreneurship Theory and Practice, 38*(4), 1042–2587.

ADDITIONAL READING

Cavaco, C. (1997). Servicios y nuevas oportunidades en los territorios rayanos. In L. Trigal, L. González, & F. Guichard (Eds.), *La articulación territorial de la Raya Hispano-Portuguesa* (pp. 191–198). Lisboa, Portugal: Centro de Estudos Geográficos.

Cumming, D., Johan, S., & Zhang, M. (2014). The Economic Impact of Entrepreneurship: Comparing International Datasets. *Global Perspectives on Entrepreneurship, 22*(2), 162–178.

Ferreira, P., & Dionísio, A. (2016). Entrepreneurship rates the fuzzy-set approach. *Eastern European Business and Economics Journal, 2*, 111–128.

Guiso, L., & Schivardi, F. (2011). What determines entrepreneurial clusters? *Journal of the European Economic Association, 9*(1), 61–86. doi:10.1111/j.1542-4774.2010.01006.x

Hessels, J., van Gelderen, M., & Thurik, R. (2008). Entrepreneurial aspirations, motivations, and their drivers. *Small Business Economics, 31*(3), 323–339. doi:10.100711187-008-9134-x

López Trigal, L. (1997). Las redes urbanas de la raya hispano-portuguesa. In L. Trigal, L. González, & F. Guichard (Eds.), *La articulación territorial de la Raya Hispano-Portuguesa* (pp. 199–205). Lisboa, Portugal: Centro de Estudos Geográficos.

Navarro-García, A., Schmidt, A., & Rey-Moreno, M. (2015). Antecedents and consequences of export entrepreneurship. *Journal of Business Research, 68*(7), 1532–1538. doi:10.1016/j.jbusres.2015.01.047

Shane, S. (2009). Why encouraging more people to become entrepreneurs is bad public policy. *Small Business Economics, 33*(2), 141–149. doi:10.100711187-009-9215-5

KEY TERMS AND DEFINITIONS

ANOVA test: Test used to analyse the existence of not of differences in means among different groups.

Birth Rate: The percentage of firms created in a given year, based on the existing firms. It is one possible measure of entrepreneurship.

Business Churn: The sum of birth and death rates, which could be considered as firms' dynamics, according to Schumpeter.

Business Demography: The whole set of indicators that could explain business dynamics.

Death Rate: The percentage of firms that close in a given year, being a possible indicator of firms' dynamics.

NUTS III: Territorial units corresponding to sub-regional level.

Survival Rate: The percentage of firms which continue to work, after a given time span.

Tukey HSD test: Test used to identify differences in means between pairs of groups.

Chapter 3
The Assessment of the INTERREG VA Program:
Support for the Polish-Slovak Cross-Border Projects

Joanna Kurowska-Pysz
University of Dąbrowa Górnicza, Poland

Antonio Paulo Cargnin
https://orcid.org/0000-0002-1212-0793
State Government of Rio Grande do Sul, Federal University of Rio Grande do Sul, Brazil

Bruno de Oliveira Lemos
State Government of Rio Grande do Sul, Brazil

Aldomar Arnaldo Rückert
Federal University of Rio Grande do Sul, Brazil

ABSTRACT

The chapter concerns the implementation assessment of cross-border projects supported by the INTERREG VA Poland - Slovakia 2014-2020 Program. The authors diagnosed the state of implementation of the Program (2018), and analyzed the conditions for managing cross-border projects on the Polish-Slovak borderland. The chapter outlines the role of a cross-border project in management of borderland development, and presents the life cycle of a cross-border project. The authors drew special attention to the results of projects and the administrative burden related to their implementation. The authors carried out quantitative and qualitative research with the participation of Polish and Slovak beneficiaries of the Program to achieve the objectives of the work. The research was supplemented by the desk research

DOI: 10.4018/978-1-7998-2513-5.ch003

analysis covering the selected documents and statistical data (2014 – 2018). The conclusions and recommendations can be useful in the process of programming rules for implementing cross-border projects on the Polish-Slovak borderland and other borderlands after 2020.

INTRODUCTION

Cross-border projects support the implementation of structural policy of the European Union (EU). The structural policy has a significant impact on both pace and directions of development of border regions and their cohesion. The term: cross-border region denotes a system of border areas connected by the same social and cultural affinities and/or social and economic co-dependence (BUFON, 2013). At cross-border areas there is a need for cross-border co-operation at a certain level among local actors (e.g. cross-border management of catchment areas, cross-border labour force-migration). The nature and type of cross-border areas is changing both spatially and temporally. During recent decades, dynamic changes in the capacity of borders to separate have been typical, especially in Central Europe (JASCHITZ, 2013).

Cross-border cooperation develops on the borderland and consists in creating a network of connections that help develop socio-economic cooperation and give way to cultural and social barriers in local communities (PERKOWSKI, 2010, KUROWSKA-PYSZ, 2015). Cross-border cooperation creates wide opportunities for establishing new neighbourhood relations and expanding the existing contacts between local communities on the border, through a series of activities aimed at achieving common goals, e.g. promotion of the region, attracting investors, development of tourism, etc.

The functioning of various types of connections in the cross-border region contributes, among others to: eliminating negative aspects of peripheral location of border areas, using development opportunities resulting from the proximity of a neighbouring country, developing European integration and international cooperation, penetrating socio-cultural influences, spreading innovation (PROBST, BÜCHEL, 1997)

The essence of cross-border cooperation is an establishment of new social and economic relations, as well as expansion of previous contacts between borderland communities, through a series of actions that allow for achieving common goals, for example through the promotion of the region, attracting investors, the development of tourism, but also the creation of clusters. The partners themselves define the scope and objectives of the cooperation, according to their needs and in line with their expectations. Bilateral cooperation and networking, in various forms, can be carried on, among others, by the following entities at cross-border market (SZROMNIK,

2010): governments at all levels; public utility companies, government entities; companies and holding companies; NGOs: associations, clubs, foundations, etc.; clusters.

The experience of recent years proves that cross-border cooperation usually contributes to visible, beneficial infrastructural changes on the borderlands, especially in terms of infrastructure. It should be mentioned that at the same time it stimulates integration and deepens mutual trust of local communities (KLATT, WASSENBERG, 2017). Therefore, the social capital of the borderland is strengthened, development is dynamized and many secondary effects are achieved, e.g. support for the development of tourism also stimulates development of local entrepreneurship in tourism-related services. Cross-border projects are effective but complex projects, often implemented with the use of special EU funds obtained from the INTERREG Program (INTERREG: The European Territorial Co-operation, 2018). As a rule, the EU support covers only the selected thematic areas and is available to entities within the agreed financial framework. A process of applying for a grant supporting the cross-border projects, then the implementation of this type of projects as well as maintaining their results should be realized on specific conditions. Although the methodology of cross-border projects management is rather difficult, interest in making the use of EU funds for such kind of cooperation is much greater than their availability. A possibility of obtaining EU grants e.g. from the INTERREG Program, is a decisive condition for undertaking or developing cross-border cooperation for many entities. It should be pointed that in many cases the entities which initiate the partnership and prepare together the application form for UE funds, cut the cooperation in the situation when their application is rejected. That is why one can't find many cross-border projects which are not supported by EU funds. Generally, they are rather project implemented by companies in the field of cross-border entrepreneurship but unfortunately it is very difficult to find any official data regarding this. This kind of project are not registered. However, the conclusions from much research show that the companies are the group of entities not strongly involved in cross-border cooperation (KUROWSKA-PYSZ, CASTANHO, LOURES, 2018). More often the companies develop the cross-border business alliances on capital market.

The specificity of cross-border projects, which constitutes a significant research issue for the development of cooperation on borderlands, has become an inspiration for the authors of the chapter. The use of the INTERREG Program for the implementation of projects focused on cross-border cooperation plays an important role in management of organization functioning in the area of borderland and influences the process of implementation of the EU cohesion policy areas after 2020. The conclusions and recommendations from the presented article can be useful in the process of programming rules for implementing cross-border projects on borderlands after 2020.

EUROPEAN UNION FUNDS AS AN INSTRUMENT SUPPORTING DEVELOPMENT OF CROSS-BORDER COOPERATION

Most countries and regions of the EU are struggling with development disparities, occurring, among others, as a result of specific location. Borderland areas, e.g. border areas of neighboring countries, constitute a good example of the areas particularly vulnerable to developmental disparities (DOŁBZASZ, RACZYK, 2010, p. 16). Development processes within the borderland areas are less dynamic when compared to agglomerations and it is caused by historical, geopolitical and infrastructural conditions and urban processes. Endogenous potential of most of the border regions is too weak to effectively stimulate development processes, therefore they are supported by the European Union funds (EUROPEAN COMMISSION, 2007). The EU cohesion policy constitutes a platform of cooperation for government, local, central, regional and local units. It should be added that it performs the same function for the benefit of international organizations as it aims at adjusting economic and social conditions in all regions of the European Union. The cohesion policy constitutes the main investment policy of the EU - it supports employment, business competitiveness, economic growth and sustainable development. It is oriented towards improving quality of life of citizens. The cohesion policy enables to achieve the objectives of economic growth described in the "Europe 2020" strategy.

One of the biggest problems for defenders of cohesion policy is the difficulty in providing a credible economic case for the policy, based on conclusive evidence of effective results. After more than thirty years of intervention, the contribution of Cohesion policy to economic development and growth remains contested and uncertain (BACHLER, GORZELAK, 2007). A wide range of results are reported in a vast literature on the subject, ranging, at best, from positive correlations between Structural Funds intervention and growth to, at worst, negative impact (MANZELLA, MENDEZ, 2009).

About EUR 351.8 billion (approx. 1/3 of the EU budget) was allocated to the cohesion policy for 2014-2020 to support the necessary projects, but also to stimulate further public and private financial investments. It is estimated that in this field for 2014-2020 will be investments of around EUR 450 billion. European territorial cooperation represents one of the thematic areas of the cohesion policy. It is an instrument serving to motivate regions and cities from different EU member countries to cooperate and learn from each other within the joint programs, projects and networks. Cross-border, international and interregional programs obtain awarded funding from the European Regional Development Fund (REGULATION (EC) NO 1080/2006 OF THE EUROPEAN PARLIAMENT AND OF THE COUNCIL OF 5 JULY 2006 ON THE EUROPEAN REGIONAL DEVELOPMENT FUND, 2006). In accordance with the EU guidelines, financial assistance from this fund is directed, among others, to "naturally disadvantaged" areas characterized by specific territorial features resulting, e.g., from mountain landscape or sparsely populated areas. These areas are treated with special consideration and they can benefit from the so called "special support" aiming at compensation for their "disadvantageous position" (EUROPEAN REGIONAL DEVELOPMENT FUND, 2014). This fund finances all of the EU programs which are oriented towards provision of the support described above, as it can be exemplified by the INTERREG Program.

The INTERREG Program implemented in 1990 is the Community initiative, which initially covered only cross-border cooperation between neighboring borderland regions (EUROPEAN COMMISSION, DG REGIO, 2000). Later, the INTERREG Program has expanded to encompass transnational and interregional cooperation (PERKMAN, 2003, pp. 153-171). The program is subject of the Commission's Directorate-General for Regional and Urban Policy and it co-finances, among others, development of many activities aiming at dynamization of cooperation between organizations having a diverse formal status and cooperating within the internal borderland regions of the Community. It also promotes creation and development of cooperation networks along the internal borders of the Union (EUROPEAN COMMISSION, 2000). A crucial goal of this cooperation is to strengthen partnership between organizations operating on the borderlands and to eliminate barriers in the process of communication. Last, but not least, it should be added that cooperation helps to create conditions conducive to transfer of knowledge and experience. Finally, it enables to make use of possibilities available for organizations from cooperating regions (MEDEIROS, 2018, pp. 69-93).

Territorial planning and territorial cooperation play significant roles in borderlands development (CARGNIN, RUCKERT, LEMOS, 2018). European territorial cooperation and investment in employment and growth are defined as two objectives of the cohesion policy for 2014-2020. During this period, the program operates under the auspices of the INTERREG VA Program agenda and is based on 11 investment priorities (PRIORITIES FOR 2014-2020, 2014). The investment priorities are considered the thematic pillars of implementing the "Europe 2020" strategy for the benefit of smart, sustainable economic growth facilitating also social inclusion. In practice, at least 80% of the budget for each cooperation program must focus, at the maximum, on four thematic pillars among eleven priority areas of the European Union (INTERREG, WWW), co-financed by the European Regional Development Fund and the European Social Fund (INTERREG, WWW). These objectives concern the support for research, technological development and innovation; development of information and communication technologies, increasing the competitiveness of small and medium-sized enterprises, supporting low-carbon economy and adaptation to climate changes, risk prevention and management; environmental protection; promoting sustainable transport, promoting employment and supporting labor mobility; promoting social inclusion and fighting poverty; investing in education, skills and lifelong learning, and improving efficiency of public administration. The INTERREG VA Program has a budget of EUR 10.1 billion, which supports, among others, 60 INTERREG VA cross-border cooperation programs, along 38 internal borders of the Union. The Community allocates EUR 6.6 billion. The Cross-border Cooperation Poland-Slovakia 2014-2020 Program belongs to one of the programs mentioned above.

CONDITIONS OF DEVELOPMENT OF CROSS-BORDER COOPERATION IN INTERREG VA POLAND - SLOVAKIA 2014-2020 PROGRAM

The INTERREG VA Poland-Slovakia 2014-2020 Program was approved by the European Commission (EC) on 12 February 2015 According to the Partnership Agreement signed with the EC, activities performed under the program implemented in the period 2014-2020 take into account the territorial dimension of the Polish-Slovak borderland, as well as the socio-economic parameters.

The goal of the Program is to promote international cooperation and to strengthen integration of the Polish-Slovak borderland, with consideration of the local perspective (Micro-Project Fund). Program priorities might be perceived as the activities complementing the European Union Strategy for the Baltic Sea Region and the European Union Strategy for the Danube Region. The main objective of the Program (CROSS-BORDER COOPERATION PROGRAM INTERREG V-A POLAND-SLOVAKIA 2014-2020, 2014) is to overcome common problems which characterize the Polish-Slovak borderland, and to face and perform three important challenges:

1. Protection, strengthening and development of the main potential of the area, e.g. natural and cultural heritage.
2. Improvement of transport infrastructure.
3. Development of education, including non-compulsory education, increasing lifelong learning opportunities, better adaptation to the job market.

In Table 1 there are presented four Priority Axes (PA) included the Program:

- PA1. Protection and development of the natural and cultural heritage of the border area
- PA2. Sustainable cross-border transport
- PA3. Development of cross-border education and lifelong learning

Table 1. Thematic objectives and investment priorities in the Program

Thematic objective	Investment Priority
PA1 Preservation and protection of natural environment and support efficient resources management	Preservation, protection, promotion and development of the natural and cultural heritage (6c)
PA2 Promoting sustainable transport and removing bandwidth shortages in operation of the most important network infrastructure	Increasing regional mobility by connecting secondary and tertiary nodes to the TEN-T infrastructure, including multimodal nodes (7b)
	Developing and improving environmentally – friendly and low carbon transport systems, in order to promote sustainable local mobility (7c)
PA3 Investing in education, trainings and vocational training aiming at acquisition of skills and lifelong learning	Investing in education, training and vocational training for skills and lifelong learning by developing and implementing joint education, vocational training and training schemes (10 *European Territorial Cooperation – crossborder cooperation)*
PA4 Technical support	Ensuring high quality management and effective implementation of the Program. Achievement of this objective will affect a process of achieving objectives defined for other priority axes, as well as efficient use of ERDF resources (European Regional Development Fund).

Source: The INTERREG VA Poland-Slovakia 2014-2020 Program
Elaboration: authors

- PA4. Technical Support

Thematic objectives and investment priorities, i.e. areas of eligible activities, have been defined for projects under each priority axis.

Standard projects (project partners jointly implement activities and incur costs on both sides of the borderland) can be implemented in all priority axes of the Program, while microprojects only in PA1 and PA3. Microprojects are local projects (simplified funding procedure, smaller budget in comparison with standard projects). They can be implemented as:

- joint microprojects (partners jointly apply for funds, implement activities and bear costs on both sides of the borderland)
- individual microprojects (one project partner applies for funding, partners jointly implement activities on both sides of the borderland, but these activities are financed only by the partner applying for funds).

The role of the Managing Authority in the Program is performed by the Polish Ministry of Investment and Development, while the role of the Slovak national institution is performed by the Ministry of Agriculture and Rural Development of

Figure 1. Eligible geographical area of the INTERREG VA Poland-Slovakia 2014-2020 Program
Source: The INTERREG VA Poland-Slovakia 2014-2020 Program
Elaboration: https://pl.plsk.eu/o-programie (access: 19.02.2019)

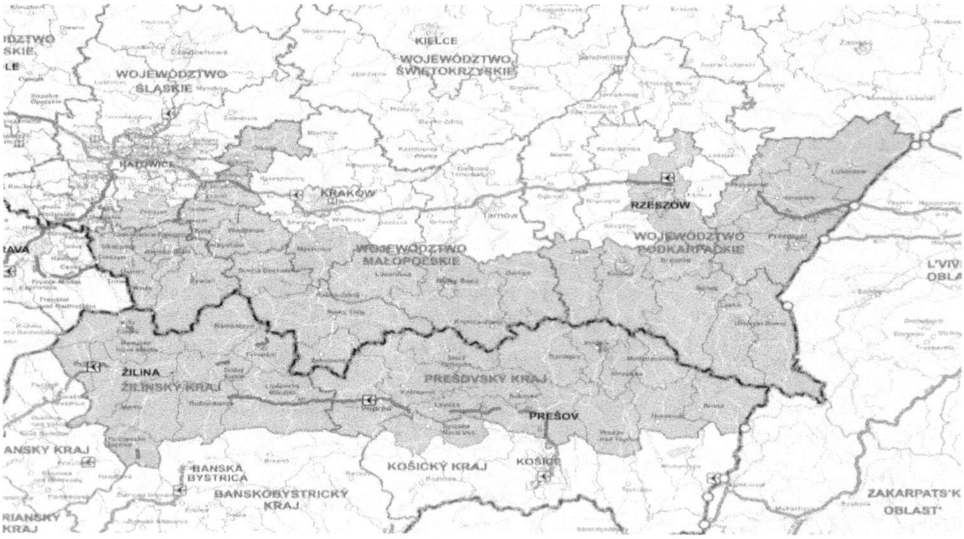

the Slovak Republic. The function of the national controller is performed both in Poland and Slovakia. A person performing this position is responsible for the process of assessing the eligibility of activities and costs in the Polish-Slovak projects. The Joint Technical Secretariat of the Program located in Cracow is responsible for the process of applying for standard projects, process of implementation of these projects, their settlement and monitoring, as well as for supervising the sustainability of their results.

Similar activities regarding microprojects are carried out by the following Euroregions: Beskidy, Tatra Mountains, Carpathians which are represented by the Polish associations and Slovak territorial units of higher level. The Euroregions are also responsible for the cross-border cooperation management on local level (BÖHM, 2014). In literature Euroregions are also discussed as a separate cross-border functional areas or cross-border tourism destinations (STUDZIENIECKI, 2005, pp.26-32).

The Program support covers the Polish-Slovak borderland area defined as NUTS III-level. The borderland area which is eligible for support under the Program is presented in the Figure 1. Thematic objectives and investment priorities, i.e. areas of eligible activities, have been defined for projects under each Priority Axe.

Different entities can apply for support from the Program, including:

Table 2. Data on the number of partners and standard projects contracted under the Program till the end of 2018

	In total	*PA1*	*PA2*	*PA3*	*PA4*
Number of partners in projects - Poland	97	61	14	5	17
Number of partners in projects - Slovakia	92	68	12	7	5
Total number of partners in projects	**189**	**129**	**26**	**12**	**22**
Total number of standard projects	**73**	**34**	**12**	**5**	**22**

Source: The Ministry of Investment and Economic Development in Warsaw
Elaboration: authors

- local governments, central administration, public institutions and other units of the public finance sector,
- scientific units, universities, schools and kindergartens,
- cultural institutions,
- non-governmental (non-profit) organizations, e.g. chambers of commerce, associations of entrepreneurs, tourist organizations, organizations supporting regional development,
- technology transfer centers, business incubators, technology incubators,
- Euroregions and European Groupings of Territorial Cooperation.

Local government units, public institutions as well as central administration (it is determined, among others, by the scope of activities which can be financed and the required budget of the project) submit the biggest number of applications for co-financing standard projects in the Program. In turn, in the case of microprojects, local government units and non-governmental organizations constitute the largest group of beneficiaries. These groups of entities are also the key stakeholders of cross-border cooperation activities. As it was mentioned in the text, companies are generally less visible in such kind of partnership because they are excluded of using EU funds such as INTERREG VA Program. This discourage them to establish the partnership but at the same time they have also different interest. They are focused on profits, not social impact of their cooperation, what is a domain of EU cohesion policy.

The highest level of the use of allocated funds from the European Regional Development Fund is observed in PA2 (99.23%), while the lowest level - in PA3, i.e. 22.38% of the allocation.

Activities aimed at protection of the cultural and natural heritage enjoy the biggest interest, i.e. PA1 (the largest number of partners and the largest number of projects), although this axis is dominated by projects with smaller budgets n (only

Figure 2. The degree of the use of allocation of funds for standard projects from the European Regional Development Fund till the end of 2018
Source: The Ministry of Investment and Economic Development in Warsaw
Elaboration: authors

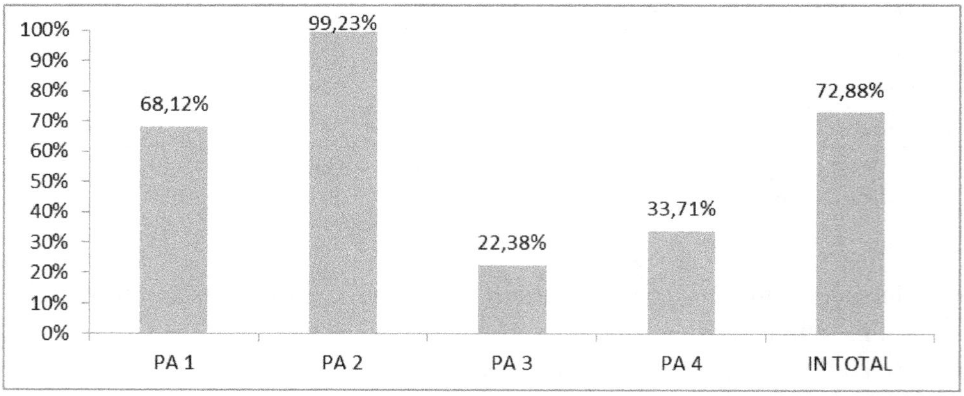

68% of allocation is used). In projects oriented towards improvement of the road infrastructure (PA2), all available allocation (approx. 99%) has been already used, although the number of partners and projects is much smaller than in the case of PA1 (it results from the nature of road investments characterized in most cases by high budgets – hence a limited number of projects is possible). PA3, concerning the development of education is much less popular. Only 5 projects were contracted for 12 partners, while the use of allocation is estimated around 22%.

It is caused, among others, by a relatively small number of entities authorized to apply and higher attractiveness of other sources of financing educational activities. PA4 is addressed only to entities which are involved in the process of implementing the Program. Indicators for program implementation illustrate the impact of the Program on development of cross-border cooperation on the borderland. Values of the selected indicators for Program implementation at the end of 2018 are presented below.

In PA1, a large number of projects and partnerships is translated into a high level of indicators for program implementation, and indirectly into the directions of development of cross-border cooperation. In the case of PA2, it turns out that the average cost of 1 km of road is lower than it was assumed in the Program, hence due to the use of 99.23% of the allocation, it was possible to achieve over 500% of indicator value regarding the length of reconstructed or modernized roads. The standard projects in the Program are supplemented by the Microprojects Fund. It should be also mentioned that in the financial European Union perspective 2014-2020, 12% of the Program budget (i.e. EUR 18 598 646.75) was spent on the micro-

Table 3. Selected indicators for program implementation (2018)

Priority Axis (PA)	Indicator name	Level of indicator for Program implementation (December 2018) in relation to the direct objective of the Program for this year
PA1	Length of new, modernized or improved cross-border recreational trails	**560,68%**
PA1	Number of new cross-border tourist products	105,92%
PA1	Number of modernized elements of cultural heritage objects	**57,14%**
PA2	Length of reconstructed or modernized roads	503,65%
PA3	Number of joint local initiatives for employment	38,18%
PA3	Number of participants in joint local employment initiatives	**244,00%**

Source: The Ministry of Investment and Economic Development in Warsaw
Elaboration: authors

projects (90% of this amount was spent on the micro-projects in PA1 and 10% of this amount was spent on the micro-projects in PA3). The number of micro-projects implemented in Euroregions at the end of 2018 is presented in the Figure 3.

Having analyzed the Microprojects Fund, we can state that many more projects are implemented in PA1. Only 22 out of 221 micro-projects are implemented in PA3 . It is a result of the available allocation and thematic areas of the projects (much broader scope of eligible activities can be implemented in PA1 than in PA3). Microprojects implemented under PA1 are characterized by a larger scale of influence

Figure 3. Number of micro-projects divided by priority axes (PA)
Source: The Ministry of Investment and Economic Development in Warsaw
Elaboration: authors

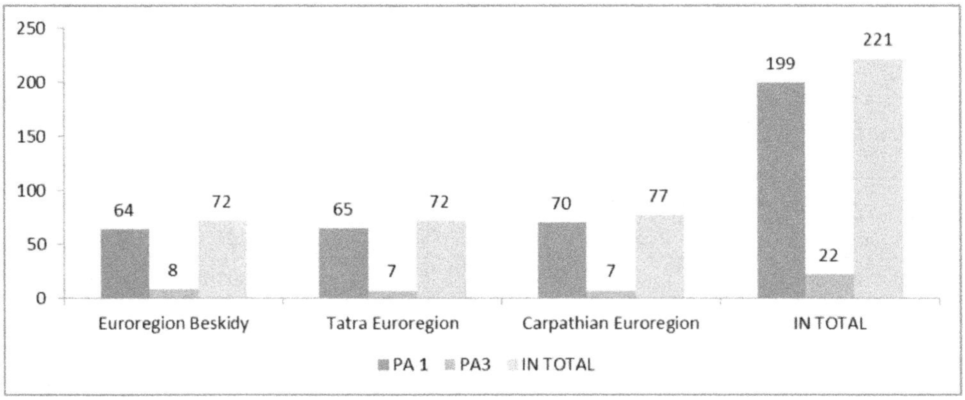

Figure 4. Number of micro-projects implemented in individual Euroregions
Source: The Ministry of Investment and Economic Development in Warsaw
Elaboration: authors

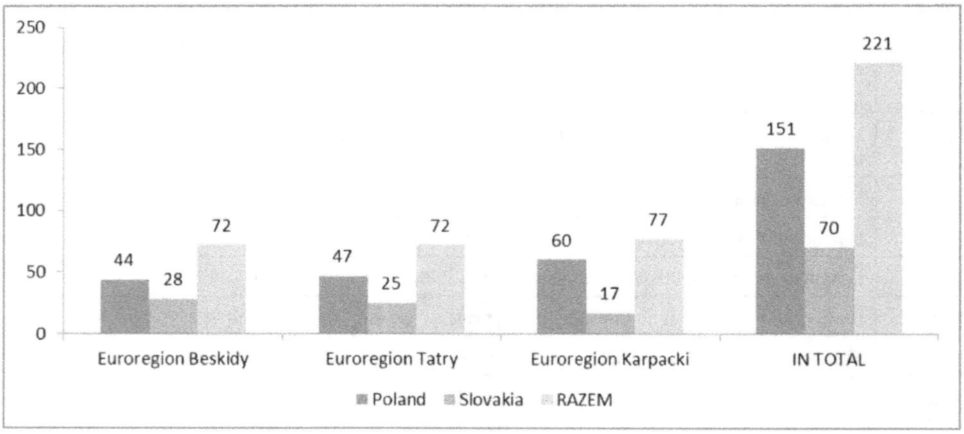

on achievement of the objectives and results of the Program results when compared to the microprojects implemented under PA3. A comparable number of projects is implemented in individual Euroregions. It is presented in Figure 4.

In the Microprojects Fund, the number of applications submitted by the lead partner on the Polish side (about 150) is over two time higher than in the case of the Slovak side (about 70). The level of contracting funds from the Microproject Fund by the end of 2018 indicates that the greatest progress was achieved in PA1 (Table 4).

The analysis presented above indicates that the Program creates good opportunities for the development of cross-border cooperation on the Polish-Slovak border, however, it supports only the selected directions of joint activities and selected groups of beneficiaries. It is in line with the "Europe 2020" strategy outlining general directions of the development of the European Union by 2020. As it turns

Table 4. Level of contracting funds for implementation of micro-projects in Euroregion (divided by PA), 2018

Partner within umbrella project	PA1	PA 3	Together
Euroregion Beskidy	54,93%	54,20%	54,86%
Tatra Euroregion	69,50%	40,80%	66,63%
Carpathian Euroregion	79,85%	65,00%	78,37%

Source: The Ministry of Investment and Economic Development in Warsaw
Elaboration: authors

out from other European documents - one of the key principles of cohesion policy concerns thematic concentration.

In practice, it turns out that the Program for the Polish-Slovak borderland should focus on four key issues maximally. As a result of the SWOT (Strength, Weakness, Opportunity, and Threat) analysis carried out for the Polish-Slovak border area, only the thematic areas of cross-border cooperation falling under PA1, PA2 and PA3 were chosen for support. With the aim of ensuring the lowest administrative burden, the elements presented below were provided for the Program beneficiaries in the years 2014-2020 (APPENDIX NO. 1 TO THE HANDBOOK FOR BENEFICIARIES OF THE INTERREG V-A POLAND-SLOVAKIA PROGRAM), namely:

- simplifying project documentation and procedures for making changes to projects
- maintaining a communicative website of the Program with current information
- strengthening and extension of the consultation network for applicants and beneficiaries
- simplified methods of settlement of certain expenses
- improving the functioning of electronic tools supporting the process of applying for funds and project management.

CROSS-BORDER PROJECT MANAGEMENT - SELECTED ISSUES

A cross-border project is one-off undertaking or is part of long-term cross-border cooperation between two or more organizations. The cross-border project is characterized by (LEWIS, 2001, p. 5; JURAN, 2003, p. 24; PROJECT MANAGEMENT INSTITUTE, 2000, p. 10):

- novelty and distinguishing from routine activities
- specificity (defined time limits for project implementation and budget)
- uniqueness (unique products and results occurring on both sides of the border)
- defined objectives, tasks and expected results.

Projects are accompanied by different types of risk, which, among others, can be the result of complexity of the cross-border environment (BINDER, 2016).

Their implementation requires project partners to involve human, material and financial resourced along with specialized knowledge (BUDNIKEVICH, 2017). Additionally, the cross-border project meets the following requirements (KUROWSKA-PYSZ, 2019):

- it is implemented jointly by at least two partners from neighboring borderland regions of at least two countries
- it embraces tasks carried out on both sides of the border
- it involves representatives of all cooperating organizations, who cooperate together in a cross-border project team
- project results bring positive results for both project partners and target groups on both sides of the border
- it generates the so-called cross-border effect, i.e. in the form of favorable changes in specific development areas of the entire borderland, e.g. culture, education, economy, etc., understood as sustainable impact of its results on project partners, on both parts of the borderland and on implementation of the objectives of the cross-border cooperation program (MINISTRY OF REGIONAL DEVELOPMENT, 2007, www).

As key critical factors which influence the cross-border project can be recognized some elements coming out from cross-border project environment (e.g. government support; law and administrative rules) as well as some elements directly connected with the partners (e.g. motivation for cooperation; knowledge, competences and skill for cross-border cooperation development; funds and human resources) as well as some macro factors (e.g. GDP in border regions, unemployment level).

Key partnership principles in cross-border projects concern, among others, equal rights and obligations of project partners, transparency in mutual relations and equal benefits from cooperation (SIMO, 2017). When planning a cross-border project, it is required to take into account a number of assumptions, which concern, among others, a process of elimination of barriers to the development of cross-border cooperation (KUROWSKA-PYSZ, CASTANHO, NARANJO GÓMEZ, 2018, pp. 134-147) and ensuring project compliance with:

- border development strategies
- needs of partners and other stakeholders on both sides of the border
- potentials and resources of cooperation partners.

The project should result from the true willingness to start cross-border cooperation and should enable each partner to achieve the expected results.

Very important is also the project team which should include the both partners staff. Generally their duties are: cross-border project management, promotion and communication activities but according to the specific project field there are also included other persons responsible for the specific project activities. The quality of project team work depends on their motivation, competences as well as the communication effectiveness (KUROWSKA-PYSZ, 2019).

The project should be implemented in a manner which is conducive to strengthening trust between partners and removing barriers to communication and cross-border cooperation. It ought to be carried out in such a way that after its completion partners are still interested in continuing joint cooperation and involve other organizations in cross-border cooperation activities. A cross-border project can be financed from own resources of partners and/or external resources (returnable and non-returnable, public and commercial), among others, it can be financed from the INTERREG VA Program (INTERREG, www). In the process of applying for funds from the INTERREG VA Program, partners are frequently required to fill in extensive project documentation. After the award of the EU support, a given project is implemented in accordance with the content of the application form and in accordance with the EU guidelines regarding the financing of cross-border cooperation.

Organizations jointly implementing cross-border projects co-financed by the INTERREG VA program are required to jointly meet at least three out of four criteria. The criteria are presented below (EUROPEAN PARLIAMENT, www):

a) joint preparation of the project
b) joint implementation of the project by partners participating in all tasks serving the purpose of implementation of the project objectives
c) joint personnel, e.g. cross-border team representing all partners
d) joint financing of the project from a common budget, which includes expenses incurred by all project partners on both sides of the border.

The INTERREG VA Program applies the lead partner principle, which means that one of projects partners takes full responsibility for the entire project and its financial settlement, as well as for the sustainability of its results (minimum 5 years on INTERREG VA Poland-Slovakia Program 2014-2020). Other partners in the cross-border project fulfill their tasks in accordance with the project and the partnership agreement and liable in the event of irregularities in the scope of expenditure declared by them. In the context of the implementation of a cross-border project, one can mention a specific life cycle performed in accordance with the model adopted by the European Commission. It is a sequence of stages a given project has to go through on both sides of the border – from its beginning to its completion. The subsequent stages are defined by milestones, indicating progress in achieving the planned effects of the project (EUROPEAN COMMISSION, 2007, p. 32). It is characterized by the phases shown in Figure 5.

The next stages of implementing cross-border projects supported by funding from INTERREG VA Program are presented in the table below.

After completion of the first project life cycle, further development of cross-border cooperation in the next projects and their life cycles is desirable. It also gives

Figure 5. The life cycle of a cross-border project
Source: Project management. Handbook, Project Management Poland Association, Warsaw 2009, p. 54
Elaboration: authors

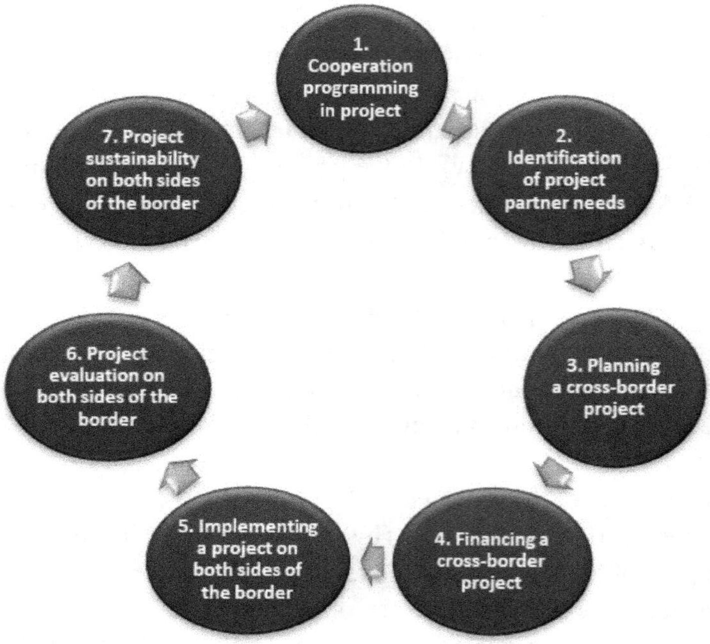

the possibility of the cross-border use of the synergy effect and complementarity of tasks to be performed. It can be exemplified by joint implementation of several further projects by the same project partners, e.g. the project on protection of cultural and natural heritage (WRÓBLEWSKI, KASPEREK, 2019).

Dynamic changes taking place in organizations, occurring as a result of learning process and inter-organizational cooperation, cause that competent managers become involved in the process of implementation of cross-border projects. It should be added that the managers undertaking project implementation are well prepared to manage such structures. They should be responsible for development of organizational culture in the cooperating entities. Organizational culture itself is a component of intangible resources of the organization, which are becoming more and more important in achieving its competitive advantage and ensuring sustainable development.

Organizations implementing cross-border projects using funds obtained from the INTERREG VA Program should also ensure proper implementation of the control function, including:

Table 5. Life cycle of a cross-border project co-financed from INTERREG VA Program (all EU borders)

Project stages	Requirements resulting from funding obtained from the INTERREG VA Program (all EU borders)
1. Cooperation programming 2. in cross-border project	Ensuring eligibility, among others, of: partners, types of activities, types of costs, period and place of project implementation, etc.
3. Identification of project partners needs on both sides of border	Determination of the detailed scope of the project, required expenditure(including financial one) and the expected results of cross-border cooperation in the project.
4. Planning 5. a cross-border project	Conclusion of a partnership agreement in the project. Preparation of the application for co-financing of a cross-border project from the INTERREG VA Program.
6. Financing of cross-border project	Conclusion of a contract for co-financing a given project. The contract provides funds from the INTERREG VA Program for implementation of the project on both sides of the border. The partners' own contribution to the project.
7. Implementing 8. a project on both sides of the border	Project implementation in accordance with the content of the application form and the EU guidelines. Fulfillment of the requirements of information and promotion of the EU funds. Communicating with project stakeholders on both sides of the border. Keeping project documentation in accordance with the requirements. Achievement of planned results. Development of the project report.
9. Project evaluation on both sides of the border	Project assessment by the Managing Authority in terms of: – the degree of implementation of the planned objectives and results – disbursement of funds in accordance with the schedule and budget in efficient, purposeful and economical manner – achieving the planned cross-border effect.
10. Keeping the project durability on both sides of the border	Control of the project performed by institutions and bodies appointed for this purpose. The control verifies: maintaining project sustainability, cooperation of partners and the cross-border effect of the implemented project for a period of 5 years from the moment of its completion.

Elaboration: authors

1. Implementation of the project in a way which ensures that each partner achieves the assumed objectives and effects of cooperation, which must be consistent with the objectives of the INTERREG VA program and with the content of the approved application.
2. Ensuring that the project has a proper and acceptable relation between input and output (in relation to all resources used in the project, including non-financial ones).
3. Compliance with all requirements regarding the issue of partnership and implementation of cross-border projects (eligibility, budget, implementation time, scope of the project) resulting from the guidelines concerning the

Figure 6. Overlapping of life cycles of subsequent cross-border projects characterized by the similar thematic areas
Elaboration: authors

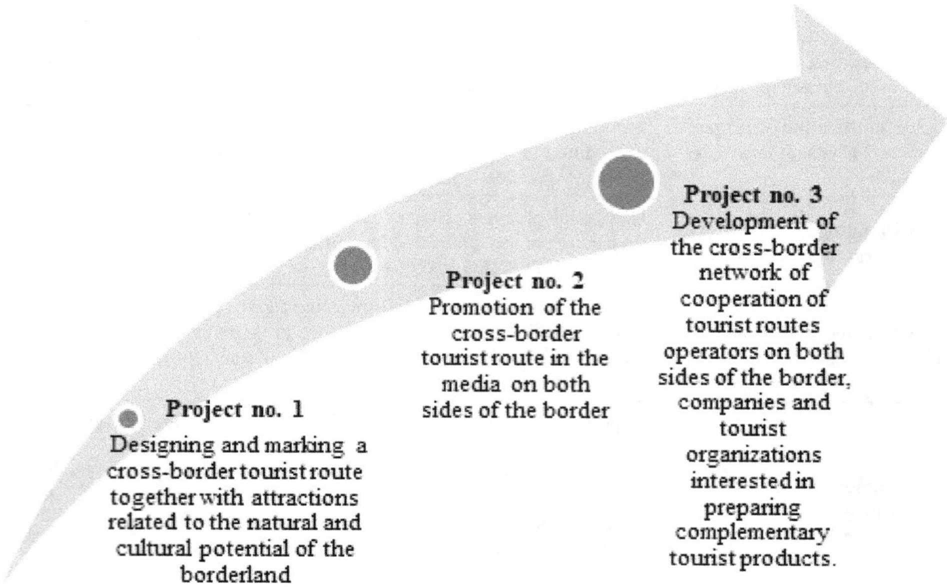

disbursement of the European Union, under pain of losing all or part of the EU funding.

4. Ensuring that project partners are able to communicate and cooperate well with each other, which facilitates proper project management, continuation of cooperation after its completion (e.g. developing a strategy for further cooperation), and minimilization of cooperation barriers.
5. Agreeing on the process of ensuring project sustainability, considering the fact that project partners provide all required resources (e.g. human, financial, material, etc.) guaranteeing the maintenance or further development of cross-border cooperation and maintaining project objectives

RESEARCH METHODOLOGY, DISCUSSION OF RESEARCH RESULTS

The aim of the work was to assess conditions for implementation of cross-border projects as exemplified by the INTERREG VA Poland-Slovakia 2014-2020 Program. The authors diagnosed the state of implementation of the Program at the end of 2018 and analyzed the conditions for implementing cross-border projects on the Polish-Slovak borderland. Additionally, the role of cross-border projects in management of the borderland development was also outlined. The authors drew special attention to the results of projects and administrative burdens related to their implementation. The quantitative research (CATI - computer-assisted telephone interviewing, CAWI - computer-assisted web interview) with the participation of the Polish and Slovak beneficiaries of the Cross-Border Cooperation Program Republic of Poland - Slovak Republic 2014-2020 (48 Polish respondents and 22 Slovak respondents who represented partners of standard projects and micro-projects implemented until the end of 2018) was performed to achieve the aim of the work. This part of the research required to answer the following questions:

1. Were the objectives of the Program comprehensible at the stage of applying for funds?
2. Which thematic areas are can be excluded from the Program?
3. Was the implementation method of the Program friendly to applicants and beneficiaries?

In turn, a total number of 30 respondents, i.e. the Polish and Slovak beneficiaries of the INTERREG VA Poland - Slovakia 2014-2020 Program, participated in the qualitative research (6 focused group interviews). This part of the study concerned answers to the following research questions:

1. Which success factors decided about the success of the project?
2. What results were obtained as a result of implementation of cross-border projects and were they sustainable?
3. What kind of positive changes are generated by the Program?

This research was supplemented by the desk research analysis of program documents, application forms and project implementation reports. The research was carried out in 2018-2019.

In Figure 7 it is shown that the vast majority of respondents confirm that at the time of starting preparation for the projects, objectives of the Program were understandable to them (nearly 100% of respondents stated this fact).

Detailed research shows that in PA1 the scope of eligible activities overlapped to a large extent with the needs of project partners. In the case of PA2 and PA3, most of the respondents stated that they do not have an opinion in this matter, as they have not yet prepared such projects. PA3 was identified as an unnecessary thematic area. This thematic area evokes the least interest, which is also confirmed by the desk research analysis regarding the state of implementation of the Program, indicating

Figure 7. The level of understanding the the objectives of the Program at the stage of applying for funds; Question: Did you understand the objectives of the Program at the stage of applying for funds?
Source: authors study based on the survey
Elaboration: authors

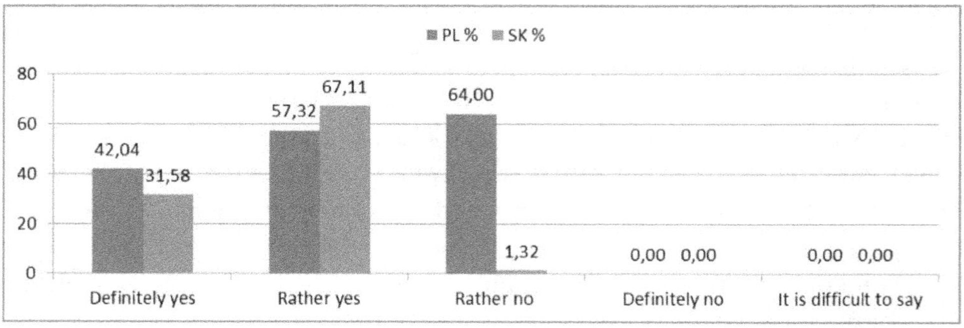

Figure 8. Assessment of the usefulness of thematic areas in the Program; Question: Which thematic areas are can be excluded from the Program?
Source: authors study based on the survey
Elaboration: authors

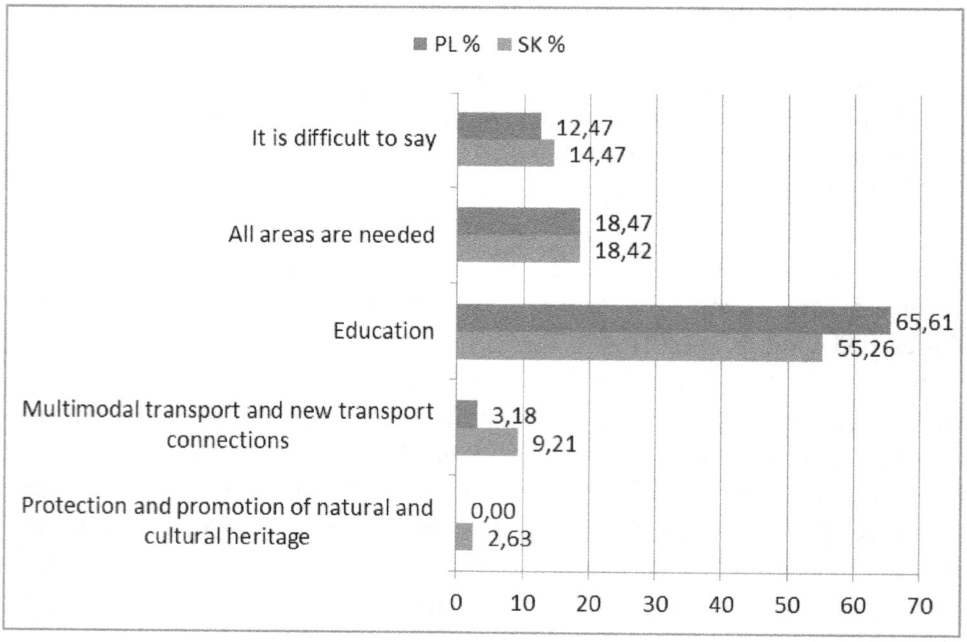

objective limitations in the use of the INTERREG Program for development of cross-border cooperation in the field of education and vocational training (Figure 8).

Respondents of the survey also assessed conditions created for the needs of projects in the Program at the stage of applying for funds, project implementation and its settlement. Detailed assessment is presented in table 6.

Respondents positively assessed both schedules of calls for proposals and a method of preparing the EU application form with appendings. Evaluation of the quality of support provided for applicants applying for standard and micro-project projects was more diverse. In this respect, Euroregions obtained better results, while the support of the Joint Technical Secretariat was assessed as sufficient by a smaller number of beneficiaries of standard projects. Over 20% of Polish respondents and nearly 20% of Slovak respondents did not have an opinion on this matter. The analysis of respondent responses regarding the project evaluation criteria indicates that in the case of micro-projects these criteria were more understandable than in the case of standard projects. The vast majority of respondents positively assessed the principles of contract award and availability of information on the principles of the Program implementation. Diversified evaluations, regarding support of the institution in the Program at the project preparation stage, were also confirmed in the question about the effectiveness of cooperation with the Joint Secretariat and Euroregions. Euroregions which cooperate with beneficiaries of micro-projects were assessed definitely better. In turn, cooperation with a project partner was assessed very well – it has to be added that most of the respondents considered partnership cooperation to be positive.

The conclusions from the research conducted by means of the focus group interview method are presented below.

Firstly, the issues specified below have been identified as the key success factors in cross-border projects:

- well-chosen partnership
- competences and skills of cross-border projects managers
- adjusting the scope of the project to the needs of its recipients

Secondly, the noticeable results of implementing cross-border projects include:

- development of cross-border cooperation between partners,
    - protection of cultural and natural heritage,
    - integration of Polish and Slovak local communities,
    - providing new services and new products available on both sides of the border,
    - increased tourist recognition of the borderland.

Table 6. Evaluation of the implementation method of cross-border projects co-financed from the Program

	Standard projects Poland %	Standard projects Slovakia %	Microprojects Poland %	Microprojects Slovakia %
Call for proposal schedule				
Correct	85,11	72,73	87,27	94,44
Incorrect	6,38	0,00	0,00	3,70
It is difficult to say	8,51	27,27	12,73	1,85
Competition documentation				
Comprehensible	80,85	81,82	87,27	81,48
Incomprehensible	8,51	4,55	2,73	3,70
It is difficult to say	10,64	13,64	10,00	14,81
Support from the Program institutions at the application stage				
Sufficient	68,09	72,73	83,64	90,74
Insufficient	8,51	9,09	0,91	1,85
It is difficult to say	23,40	18,18	15,45	7,41
Criteria of application evaluation				
Adjustment to conditions of project preparation	70,21	72,73	85,45	85,19
Non-adjustment to conditions of project preparation	8,51	13,64	2,73	0,00
It is difficult to say	21,28	13,64	11,82	14,81
Contract award principles				
Clear	82,98	95,45	91,82	96,30
Unclear	4,26	0,00	0,00	1,85
It is difficult to say	12,77	1,55	8,18	1,85
Availability of information about the Program				
Sufficient	91,49	86,36	95,45	94,44
Insufficient	6,38	4,55	0,91	1,84
It is difficult to say	2,13	9,09	3,64	3,70
Cooperation with the Joint Secretariat/Euroregions				
Effective	55,32	68,18	82,73	92,59
Ineffective	25,53	9,09	0,00	0,00
It is difficult to say	19,15	22,73	17,27	7,41
Cooperation with a Project Partner				
Effective	95,74	100,00	93,64	92,59
Ineffective	0,00	0,00	0,91	1,85
It is difficult to say	1,26	0,00	5,45	5,56

Elaboration: authors

The results of the project related to the cross-border cooperation of project partners and to the scope of cross-border projects are considered the most lasting.

Thirdly, the key positive changes generated by the Program included:

- strengthening contacts between the Polish and Slovak community on the borderland,
- broadening knowledge about the neighboring country,
- greater appreciation of the cultural and natural values of the borderland,
- better use of the borderland for tourist purposes, whilst ensuring protection of the area,
- increasing cultural awareness,
- change in the way of spending free time by borderland residents,
- improving the quality of cross-border transport infrastructure.

CONCLUSION

Cross-border projects (both standard projects and microprojects) implemented with the support of INTERREG VA Poland - Slovakia 2014-2020 Program are implemented in conditions allowing to achieve their expected results. It is, among others, evidenced by positive opinions of beneficiaries, regarding the support of the Program institutions: Joint Technical Secretariat and Euroregions at the stage of preparation and implementation of projects. It is also confirmed thanks to the Program indicators, which in the period of its implementation (i.e. 2014-2018) have been exceeded in many cases. Program beneficiaries are familiar with the the possibilities of using it for their own, specific needs, hence the supply of projects exceeds available allocations (in PA1 and PA2).

A process of preparing the application documentation requires extreme care in planning a cross-border project in terms of its budget, project activities and their results. Demonstrating the impact of the project on durability of the cooperation between projects partners and achievement of the cross-border effect constitute very significant elements. The cross-border effect maintenance is verified five years after the end of the project. One of the key criteria for assessing cross-border projects is also their impact on implementation of the European Union cohesion policy [regional policy] in the area of borderland support. Achievement of the objectives of cohesion policy regarding territorial cooperation is performed by means of over 60 cross-border cooperation programs. As a result of the synergy effect which has been achieved, cross-border cooperation will be significantly strengthened in the European Union in the years 2014-2020. From this perspective, cross border cooperation is considered an important instrument supporting borderland areas.

The life cycle of a cross-border project, co-financed from the INTERREG VA Program, includes seven phases of its implementation which are clearly distinguished. Each phase of the project life cycle has a significant impact on further development of cross-border cooperation between partners. The most mature level of cross-border cooperation occurs at the last phase, e.g. the phase number seven (Figure 5). After its completion, it is possible to move on to the next life cycle of the project, characterized by higher level of cross-border cooperation, encompassing, e.g. more advanced activities or tasks which are complementary to those which have been implemented previously. Under the 2014-2020 perspective, it is required to concentrate funds from the European Regional Development Fund on maximally four priority areas. It means that the INTERREG VA Program does not support in a sustainable manner all possible directions of cross-border cooperation, but only the selected ones (KUROWSKA-PYSZ, SZCZEPAŃSKA-WOSZCZYNA, 2017). In the INTERREG VA Poland - Slovakia 2014-2020 Program, three thematic objectives, regarded as the most significant priority areas for the borderland, were supported. In practice, it turned out that only two priority areas were selected accurately (protection of cultural and natural heritage and road projects). On the other hand, projects related to education and vocational training did not attract much interest. It indicates that the thematic objectives to be supported by the Program were chosen wrongly. As a result, thematic objectives which will be supported by the Program should be more carefully assessed under the next EU perspective. It will allow to avoid spending the EU funds on projects that do not significantly affect the borderland.

It is worth observing that the thematic objectives of the Program are equally carried out by standard projects and microprojects implemented in Euroregions. Microprojects affect borderland communities more locally. The level of interest in implementation of micro-projects is similar in the whole borderland area. Euroregions, responsible for supervising their implementation, are evaluated very well. In the case of standard and microprojects, calls for proposals for projects related to the protection of cultural heritage were much more popular in comparison to their educational counterparts (WRÓBLEWSKI, DZIADZIA, DACKO-PIKIEWICZ, 2018).

Regardless of the thematic objective of implemented cross-border projects, all respondents evaluated highly cooperation with a project partner, regarded as one of the aspects of managing joint ventures. The factor concerning successful project partnership has been also considered one of the key determinants of the project success. In turn, the development of cross-border cooperation was defined as one of the most important and long-lasting project results. Therefore, the research outcome confirmed that as a result of the implementation of cross-border projects, in accordance with the conditions specified by the INTERREG VA Poland - Slovakia

2014-2020 Program, it is possible to implement these projects on the basis of the life cycle presented in Figure 5. Obtaining synergies and complementary results of cross-border cooperation, through joint transition of partners to the subsequent life cycles of jointly implemented projects, is also achievable.

REFERENCES

APPENDIX NO. 1 TO THE HANDBOOK FOR BENEFICIARIES OF THE INTERREG V-A POLAND-SLOVAKIA PROGRAM (State as of 31.12.2018), Retrieved from https://pl.plsk.eu/zapoznaj-sie-z-dokumentami. May 24, 2019.

Bachtler, J., & Gorzelak, G. (2007). Reforming EU Cohesion Policy. *Policy Studies*, *28*(4), 309–326. doi:10.1080/01442870701640682

Binder, J. (2016). *Global project management: communication, collaboration, and management across borders*. Routledge. doi:10.4324/9781315584997

Budnikevich, I. M. (2017) Implementation Of Partnership Marketing Concept In Corss-Border Cooprration Programs Of Bukovyna Cross-Border Area. *Ecoforum Journal*, 6(2).

Böhm, H. (2014). A comparison of governance forms for cross-border co-operation within the EU. *Journal of Cross-border Studies*, *2014*, 9.

Bufon, M. (2013). Researching Elements of Cross-Border Social Cohesion: The Case of Slovene Border Areas. *European Countryside*, *5*(2), 89–101. doi:10.2478/euco-2013-0006

Cargnin, A. P., Ruckert, A. A., & Lemos, B. (2018) Territorial planning and La Plata Basin borders. 2018.

Cross-Border Cooperation Program Interreg V-A Poland-Slovakia 2014-2020, Available at https://pl.plsk.eu/zapoznaj-sie-z-dokumentami. June 16, 2019.

Dołbzasz, S., & Raczyk, A. (2010). *Cross-border cooperation in Poland after EU accession* (p. 16). Warsaw, Poland.

EUROPEAN REGIONAL DEVELOPMENT FUND. Available at https://ec.europa.eu/regional_policy/en/. August, 1, 2014.

EUROPEAN COMMISSION. (2000). Fundusze Strukturalne 2000-2006, Ewaluacja ex-ante oraz wskaźniki dla programu Interreg, Dokument roboczy nr 7, Brussels, Belgium.

EUROPEAN COMMISSION. (2007). *Aid Delivery Methods* (p. 32). Guidelines on the Programming, Design, and Management of General Budget Support.

INTERREG: The European Territorial Co-operation. Available Oct. 1, 2018.

Jaschitz, M. (2013). Key factors for successful territorial cohesion: Cross-border cooperation–how can some EU instruments create a new geography. *European Journal of Geography*, *4*(4), 8–19.

Juran, J. M. (2003). *Juran on Leadership for Quality* (p. 24). Simon and Schuster.

Klatt, M., & Wassenberg, B. (2017). Secondary foreign policy: Can local and regional cross-border cooperation function as a tool for peace-building and reconciliation? *Regional & Federal Studies*, *27*(3), 205–218. doi:10.1080/13597566.2017.1350652

Kurowska-Pysz, J., & Szczepańska-Woszczyna, K. (2017). The analysis of the determinants of sustainable cross-border cooperation and recommendations on its harmonization. *Sustainability*, *9*(12), 2226. doi:10.3390u9122226

Kurowska-Pysz, J. (2019). *Zarządzanie partnerstwami transgranicznymi organizacji uczących się*. Warsaw, Poland: PWN.

Kurowska-Pysz, J., Castanho, R. A., & Naranjo Gómez, J. M. (2018) Cross-border cooperation: the barriers analysis and the recommendations. *Polish Journal of Management Studies*, pp. 134-147.

Kurowska-Pysz, J. (2019) Zarządzanie partnerstwami transgranicznymi organizacji uczących się, PWN, 2019.

Kurowska-Pysz, J., Castanho, R., & Loures, L. (2018). Sustainable Planning of Cross-Border Cooperation: A Strategy for Alliances in Border Cities. *Sustainability*, *10*(5), 1416. doi:10.3390u10051416

Kurowska-Pysz, J. (2015) The Circumstances of Knowledge Transfer within the Scope of the Cross-Border Czech-Polish Projects 2014-2020, Forum Scientiae Oeconomia, 3(3).

Lewis, P. J. (2001). *Project planning, scheduling and control* (3rd ed.). The McGraw Hill Companies.

Manzella, G. P., & Mendez, C. (2009). The turning points of EU cohesion policy, Working Paper Report to BARCA Report.

Medeiros, E. (2018). The role of European Territorial Cooperation (ETC) in EU cohesion policy. In *European Territorial Cooperation* (pp. 69–93). Springer. doi:10.1007/978-3-319-74887-0_5

MINISTRY OF REGIONAL DEVELOPMENT. Effects of cross-border cooperation of Polish regions in 2004 -2006. Available at https://www.ewt.2007-2013.gov.pl/Wiadomosci/Documents/broszura_INTERREG_IIIA.pdf

Perkman, M. (2003). Cross-border regions in Europe. Significance and drivers of regional cross-border co-operation. *European Urban and Regional Studies*, *10*(2), 153–171. doi:10.1177/0969776403010002004

Perkowski, M. (2010). *Współpraca transgraniczna. Aspekty prawno-ekonomiczne*. Białystok: Fundacja Prawo i Partnerstwo.

Priorities for 2014-2020. Available at http://ec.europa.eu/regional_policy/pl/policy/how/priorities. June, 16, 2018.

Probst, G., & Büchel, B. S. (1997). *Organizational learning: The competitive advantage of the future*. Prentice Hall.

Project Management Institute. (2000). *A Guide to the Project Management Body of Knowledge* (p. 10).

REGULATION. (EC) NO 1080/2006 OF THE EUROPEAN PARLIAMENT AND OF THE COUNCIL OF 5 JULY 2006 ON THE EUROPEAN REGIONAL DEVELOPMENT FUND, EUROPEAN TERRITORIAL COOPERATION. Available at http://ewt.slaskie.pl/article/1279787593. August, 1, 2019.

Simo, B. (2017) The Analysis Of Absorption Capacity Of Project Beneficiaries Contributing To Cross-Border Programmes Based On The Most Fundamental Criteria. *APSTRACT: Applied Studies in Agribusiness and Commerce, 10*(1033-2017-145), pp. 100-93.

Studzieniecki, T. (2005). Euroregions - new potential destinations. *Tourism Review*, *60*(4), 26–32. doi:10.1108/eb058463

Szromnik, A. (2010). Marketing terytorialny. Oficyna Wydawnicza Wolters. Warsaw, Poland: Kluwer.

Wróblewski, Ł., Dziadzia, B., & Dacko-Pikiewicz, Z. (2018). Sustainable Management of the Offer of Cultural Institutions in the Cross-Border Market for Cultural Services - Barriers and Conditions. *Sustainability*, *10*(9), 3253. doi:10.3390u10093253

Wróblewski, Ł., & Kasperek, A. (2019). Euroregion as an Entity Stimulating the Sustainable Development of the Cross-Border Market for Cultural Services in a City Divided by a Border. *Sustainability*, *11*(8), 2232. doi:10.3390u11082232

Chapter 4
Cross-Border Cooperation (CBC) in a Multi-Level Governance System in Southeastern Europe Territories:
How to Manage Territorial Governance Processes in Serbia-Romania Border Space

Ana Vulevic
https://orcid.org/0000-0001-5150-4477
Institute of Transportation-CIP, Belgrade, Serbia

Vidomir Obradovic
https://orcid.org/0000-0002-3462-8002
Faculty of Natural Science and Mathematics, University of Banja Luka, Bosnia and Herzegovina

Rui Alexandre Castanho
Faculty of Applied Sciences, WSB University, Poland & Environmental Resources Analysis Research Group (ARAM), University of Extremadura, Spain

Dragan Djordjevic
MC Transport Design and Simulation, Belgrade, Serbia

ABSTRACT

Considering the actual panorama of a multi-level governance on EU, the macro-regional strategies - specifying the EU strategy for Danube region (EUSDR)

DOI: 10.4018/978-1-7998-2513-5.ch004

fosters coordination across three dimensions: sector policies; different levels of governance from EU to regional or local, and across administrative boundaries. This chapter analyzes and assesses the ability, challenges, and obstacles of Cross-Border Cooperation (CBC) strategies, projects, and programs to improve integration and cohesion peripheral territories as is the case of the border region of Romania – Serbia, enabling articulating border areas and creating synergies among them. In this regard, it will be considered the latest findings on new insights towards spatial integration in border and transnational contexts. The chapter presents some hypothesis for a good-planned, long-term sustainability for this territory and lesson learned regarding the coordination and management of policies in the EU's system of multi-level governance that could have a wider application and scope.

INTRODUCTION

In last decades, European integration policy has helped to reduce the fragmentation of the European territory (Dominguez, & Pires, 2014). In this context, the spatial policy is an instrument serving the Union's internal and external policies and contributes directly to achieving the goals of the Europe 2020 Strategy, smart, sustainable and inclusive growth. Borders are the sovereign 'interface' between countries (Henrikson, 2010), and their degree of openness, which can change over time, depending on the situation with regard to the process of Europeanisation (Decoville, & Durand, 2017). "In strategic planning, planners need to think increasingly in terms of open, porous borders despite the fact that in concrete planning activities, politics, and governance, the region continues to exist largely in the form of bounded and territorial political units" (Paasi, & Zimmerbauer, 2015).

Although the INTERREG programs were intended to support cooperation across national boundaries, they were often criticized for creating additional boundaries through the definition of the program's areas of cooperation. In recent years, EU macro-regional strategies promote a specific approach to addressing the functional interlinkages between territories (Dühr, 2011). EU macro-regional strategies introduce a new layer of governance to the existing 'many vehicles for multilateral cross-border cooperation already at work in the EU and broader European space' (Dangerfield, 2009). There are four EU macro-regional strategies covering the Baltic Sea Region, Danube Region, Adriatic and Ionian Region and the Alpine Region. EUSDR (EU strategy for Danube region) was adopted in 2011 and nine EU member states are involved in the Strategy: Austria, Bulgaria, Croatia, Czech Republic, Germany, Hungary, Romania, Slovakia and Slovenia, as well as five non-EU member states, Bosnia Herzegovina, Moldova, Montenegro, Serbia, and Ukraine. However, the challenge now lies in the implementation of the EU macro-regional strategies and their performance over a longer period of time and in the new instruments need to realize their added-value. Danube - the macro-region has been composed of 14 states of very different sizes and administrative structures, and different principles of the administrative systems, different level of governance performance which reflecting the different development paths. “Good governance” is the basis and ultimate objective for the institutional capacity building.

The countries display various institutional capacities most of them lacking the strategic and operational capacity to respond to new challenges, the involvement of civil society and other stakeholders in the decision-making processes is still limited (INTERREG, 2014, INTERACT, 2012; 2017). The approach of addressing problems in an integrated manner on a transnational level was already recognized as an efficient tool by the countries situated within the Danube river basin. Based on the experience accumulated, there are some elements of the implementation which need to be further strengthened or developed in order to enhance the operation and effectiveness of EUSDR’s governance system.

The present research aims to analyze the ability, challenges, and obstacles of strategies in coordination and governance dimension to concretely improve border integration, create synergies among them and to examine how the Europe 2020 objectives of promoting sustainable, inclusive and smart economic development can be promoted by macro-regional authorities in Serbia-Romania border space. In this regard, the present research adopts a twofold perspective, addressing both the European level and the macro-regional level coordination and governance. In this context, it will be highlighted the Romania Serbia border space because it is in the scope of the EUSDR strategy, it is the financial-economic depressed region with declining population and has complex governance arrangements. This study try to answer on some of the policy questions: How to promote sustainable and inclusive regional development strategies, taking into account the changing role of coordination and governance regional authorities and the proliferation of stakeholders in functional territories? Which are key differences between EU macro-regional strategies and transnational cooperation programs? Which are challenge and obstacles in coordination and governance dimension in Serbia-Romania border space contributing to the Union strategy for smart, sustainable and inclusive growth?

Recent research and experiences show that Danube macro-regional cooperation is time-consuming and complex, and it will likely succeed if a strong political commitment regarding the macro-regional level is carried out (Dühr, 2011). There are some elements of the implementation which need to be further developed in order to enhance the effectiveness of EUSDR’s governance system.

BACKGROUND

Territorial Governance is an objective, vision, dimension, or priority of several European strategic and flagship documents, such as Europe 2020, Territorial Agenda 2020, and Europe Territorial Vision 2050. However, these documents do not address the Western Balkan region (TG-WeB, 2018, p.11).

The Europe 2020 strategy, according to the European Commission (EC) (2017) «puts forward three main priorities to make the EU a smarter, more sustainable and more inclusive economy and growth»:

- Smart growth: developing an economy based on knowledge and innovation.
- Sustainable growth: more competitive economy, resource efficient, greener and
- Inclusive growth: developing a high-employment economy in order for social and territorial cohesion.

Regarding with role of the Cross-Border Cooperation in the European strategy, The European Territorial Agenda 2020 defining the importance of CBC claiming and territorial integration as a "key factor in global competition facilitating better utilization of development potentials and the protection of natural environment" (INTERACT, 2012; 2017) fostering at integrating the territorial dimension within different policies at all levels of governance. Key challenges and potentials for territorial development have been defined with European Territorial Agenda 2020. Today, although there are many attempts to explain CBC programs of strategies and projects and indicate their significance, many of them are very broad and do not solve challenges beyond national boundaries and do not have common planning, common strategies, and management (INTERACT, 2012; 2017). Regarding multilevel governance, Europe 2020 Strategy „has improved coherence in the European multi-level governance system(s). However, boosting Europe's global competitiveness and the transition to a sustainable knowledge-based economy requires more efforts than those set-in motion by the Europe 2020 Strategy" (Böhme, et. al, 2014).

Common Regional Development Strategies/ Macro Regional Strategies

In spatial planning literature, there is a lack of theoretical references on how the projects and strategies affect the real spaces of the border. This lack of conceptual tools makes it difficult to produce cross-border territorial strategies that can effectively articulate border territories and create synergies between them in a way that involves institutional aspects, functional reality, ideational representations, and elements related to differences in territorial contexts (Faludi, A. 2010; Kuzmin, & Kravchenko, 2014; Kurowska-Pysz, 2015; Reitel, B., 2015; RESSI, 2017, Castanho, et. al, 2017). Cross-border integration has been covering different aspects. One of them is institutionalization between local and regional actors across borders (Scott, 1999, Sohn, et.al., 2009, Dörry, & Walther, 2015).

Macro-regional strategies for functional macro-regions are new strategies for new territorial forms of integration. These strategies and their programs have encouraged full Integration into a Macro regions area framework and achieved coverage of a big territory with a high diversity of regions and sometimes with conflicting interests. The EU macro-regional strategy level is lifted by transnational cooperation into the sphere of EU multi-level governance with a stronger role for supranational institutions. Especially, the European Commission as coordinator of the macro-regional strategies can provide some stability that intergovernmental cooperation often misses.

Macro-Regional Strategies in INTERREG Programs

Macro regional strategies and a transnational cooperation program operating in the same cooperation area. Both working on common issues for the territory, supporting cooperation and have some key differences: the core idea, themes addressed, funding aspect and how it's implemented and managed (INTERACT, 2012; 2017). They are based on different policy and/or legal frameworks, internal governance structures and administrative procedures, different sets of rules or thematic priorities (ICPDR, 2014).

The main role of transnational programs is to use their resources for funding transnational projects with the strategic dimension, providing the ground for projects to test their experimental ideas and pilot new or alternative approaches and solutions in the thematic field of respective programs. However, Macro-Regional strategies (MRS) go far beyond projects and programs thematic focus and define a political-strategic framework for cooperation on the macro-regional level. From the perspective of a program, which supports MRS, to the financing of the governance structure of MRS reduce program capacity in achieving its targets and brings administrative burdens (Dühr, 2011; INTERACT, 2012; 2017).

BORDER INTEGRATION AND THE NEW CBC GOVERNANCE SYSTEM/COMPLEX GOVERNANCE ARRANGEMENTS

Regarding of the working definition of multilevel governance (MLG) in the 'White Paper on MLG' overall principles of MLG deriving from the White Paper are participation, representation, partnership, subsidiarity, proportionality, proximity, solidarity and mutual loyalty. This principle is dependent on different corresponding qualities of governance, because of multi-level governance lead to coordinated action by the European Union, the Members and local and regional authorities, based on partnership and aimed at drawing up and implementing EU policies.

Territorial Governance is place-based and addresses territorial diversities, be those natural, social, cultural, historical, or ethnic. The region is rich in its diversity, which is a unique asset to its development, but often also creates a basis for disputes. Any reform should address these diversities and should not be implemented uniformly (TG-WeB, 2018, p.11).

Macro-regional strategies introduce a new layer of governance to the existing 'many vehicles for multilateral cross-border cooperation already at work in the EU and broader European space' (Dangerfield, M. 2009). Complex governance arrangements and the need to ensure long-term political commitment present further challenges for EU macro-regional strategies. EU macro-regional strategies seek to achieve coordination across three dimensions: horizontally (across sector policies), vertically (across different levels of governance from EU to regional or local), and geographically (across administrative boundaries) (Dühr, 2011).

Territorial Governance is based on decentralised approaches, which strengthen democracy, bring about efficiency, and enhance the principle of partnership. The governments of the Western Balkans, on the other hand, have recently shown a strong tendency towards governance centralization (instead of developing decentralisation mechanisms) (TG-WeB, 2018, p. 11).

CHALLENGES AND OBSTACLES IN THE CREATING OF MACRO REGIONAL BORDER TERRITORIAL STRATEGIES

The experience with the transnational INTERREG programs has shown that broad frameworks with largely generic funding priorities rarely result in projects of real significance for the macro-region (Géphyres & Radboud, 2010). It is therefore important that policy priorities and actions are specific to the macro-region, and not merely replicate EU policy objectives. It can be issues that are currently not dealt with appropriately within a country and by nation-states acting alone, and issues that may in future not be dealt with satisfactorily by nation-states acting alone as a consequence of changing framework conditions (political, economic, environmental, social, or else) (Dühr, 2011).

Healey (2007) argues that only if the strategy is sufficiently focused and convincing will it be able to generate 'mobilizing force' that ensures the long-lasting support of actors. The strategy must have the potential for 'transformative force', for the institutionalization of approaches and of cooperation structures, and the new 'communities of practice' at macro-regional scale (Dühr, 2011).

National, regional and local capacity has to be strengthened to ensure that all the bodies are able to work with their cross-border counterparties, as well as to coordinate the different policies. Countries are likely to proceed at a different speed in the alignment with EU legislation and in the access to financial instruments, by hindering the implementation of the macro-regional approach. A weak political perception which is not able to understand the outcomes and challenge that the area integration is essential both for the economic strengthening of countries and the whole European integration process. Existing experience related macro-regional strategies shows that the quality and stability of governance mechanisms are essential for an effective implementation (EC, 2014).

CASE SERBIA - ROMANIA BORDER SPACE

Study Area

The study area includes a relevant part of the territory of this two countries (9 NUTS 3 units are included in the area, 6 districts in Serbia and 3 counties in Romania) (http://ec.europa.eu/regional_policy/what/future/experts_documents_en.cfm#2). The study area is in the core of the Danube basin and of the European Danube macro region and the geography of the area is heterogeneous and complex. Regarding the population number it is balanced on the two sides of the border. The plains are located in the north (the Banat), and in the south east, and mountains are the Southern Carpathians range, Western end of the Southern Carpathians, the Veliki Krš, Mali Krš and Stol mountains, dominated by karst formations. In Romania the Mehedinţi Mountains.

The Danube produces many opportunities/needs for cooperation and cross-border interaction. Other smaller rivers crossing area have relevant impact: Tisa, Timiş, Cerna, Caraş Nera. The eligible area for the programming period 2014-2020 under the IPA CBC programme Serbia Romania will include three counties of Romania, and the six districts of the Republic of Serbia.The eligible area includes a relevant part of the territory of the two countries.

The study area is at the centre of the European Danube Macro Region. The two partner countries include a large share of the river basin, their total surface

Figure 1. Study area
Source: Romania-Serbia IPA CBC Programme 2014–2020, Territorial Analysis SECOND DRAFT 2014

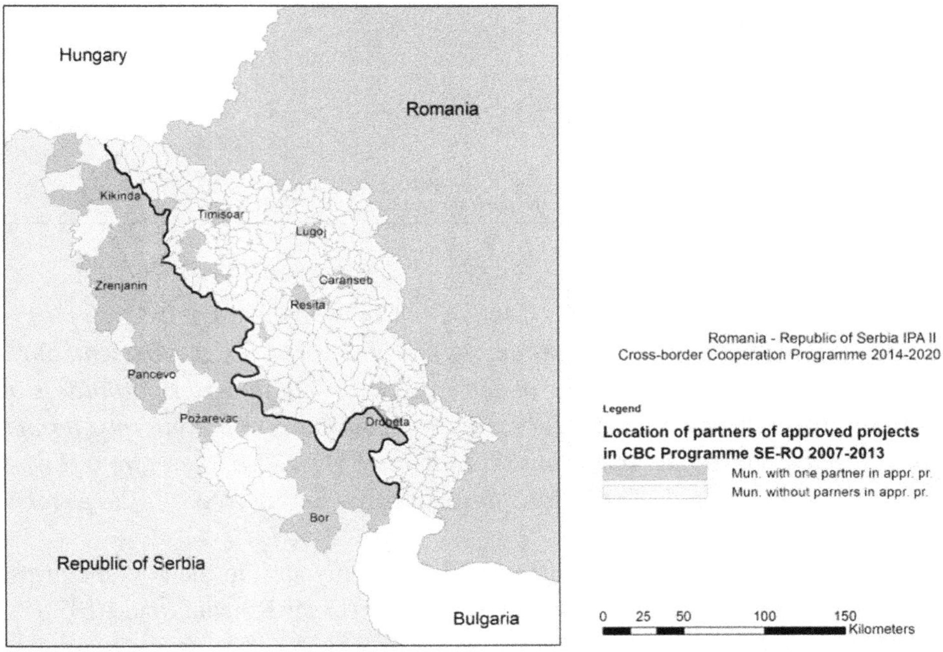

representing 10% of the basin in Serbia and 29% in Romania (http://www.icpdr.org/main/danube-basin/countries-danube-river-basin).

The total area is 40.596 sq.km (53,1% in Romania/ 46,9% in Serbia), including the Romanian counties Timiş, Caraş-Severin and Mehedinţi, and the Serbian districts (Severno Banatski, Srednje Banatski, Južno Banatski, Braničevski, Borski, Podunavski).

As we can see at Figure 1 the two NUTS2 regions belong in Romania, and two NUTS2 regions in Serbia. The three Banat districts (NUTS3) belong to the Vojvodina, an administrative entity classified as NUTS2 statistical region according to the law 46/2010. The Braničevski, Borski and Podunavski districts belong to the NUTS2 statistical region of Southern and Eastern Serbia. In Romania, Mehedinti County belongs to the Development Region South West. The two counties of Caraş-Severin and Timiş belong to the development Region West (Romania-Serbia IPA CBC Programme 2014 – 2020).

The eligible territory in Republic of Serbia represents 20,8% of the total, a larger share than in Romania, were the three eligible counties represent just 9% of the national territory. The length of the border in the eligible territories between

Table 1. General policy framework

General policy frameworks in Serbia- Romania border space
INTERREG program/IPA CBC PROGRAM The Europe 2020 strategy The EU Strategy for Danube Region (EUSDR) The South-East Europe 2020 Strategy (SEE 2020) Territorial Agenda of the European Union 2020 National plan of the Republic of Serbia Regional Development Strategy Republic of Serbia CBC and Interregional Programs accessible in the program area (e.g. CBC HU-RS)

Romania and Republic of Serbia is 546 km, out of which 290 km (53,1%) on the Danube river. The length of the border in the programme area represents 26% of the external borders of Republic of Serbia, and 17% of the external borders of Romania. Along this common border there are 5 constantly operating road border crossings and 2 constantly operating railroad crossings. Also, there are 6 fluvial ports in Serbia, and 3 on the Romanian shore (Romania-Serbia IPA CBC Programme 2014 – 2020, p. 8)

The population in the eligible area is almost evenly split in the two countries, according to the demographic data in 2011, 1.244.509 live in Romania and 1.137.179 live in Republic of Serbia. Thus, within the border area, 52,2% of the population is living in Romania, and 47,7% is living in Republic of Serbia. The population has been decreasing from 2,584 million in 2002, with a steep decline in the last years due to both negative migratory and demographic balance.

General Policy Framework

The Romanian Partnership Agreement highlights the central role of the CBC programs in case Romania, for the contribution to the Europe 2020 Strategy with highlight the importance of promoting the EUSDR, as macroeconomic strategies offer a new, more substantial and consistent cooperation platform. The planned interventions related to the EUSDR include five different areas, namely transport (e.g.: development of bridges and port infrastructure), network of settlements (e.g.: connecting Bucharest and the Danube river), environment (e.g.: protection of the Danube Delta), society (e.g.: improvement of social infrastructure) and economy (e.g.: exploiting the agricultural, energy and tourism potential of the Danube area) (INTERREG, 2014).

The Republic of Serbia according to the National plan, have affirming one of the priorities of its foreign policy – an improvement of regional cooperation to develop relations with immediate neighbors and countries in the region of South-East Europe.

Table 2. Main outcomes based on the territorial analysis (TA) in Romania-Serbia border space

Main outcomes	Based on the Territorial analysis (TA) in Romania-Serbia border space
Socio – cultural	• EU support for social inclusive growth • Growing social and cultural ties between RO and RS • Integration in the macro regional framework of EUSDR. • Declining population, especially of young active people • Unemployment rates are still high in the territory • Indicators shows potential the region has as a tourist-magnet • Marketing and advertisement strategies are not coordinated among these countries
Financial – Economic	• The region is financial-economic depressed • GDP/per capita values are considerable low • Strategies for investor´s magnet should be considered
Resources Sustainability	• Several infrastructures are duplicated in nearby areas/territories • Poor quality of local and intraregional transport infrastructures for moving within the eligible area • Severe limitations to accessibility in rural and mountainous areas • European strategies for environmental protection in macro regions, offering additional support to local strategies (Danube region)
Political - Strategic	• Lack of political commitment towards EU 2020 goals and EU standard´s • Transparency and political commitment should be increased • Common Master-Plans and long-term objectives should be considered • Lack of political commitment towards EU 2020 goals and EU standard´s • Transparency and political commitment should be increased • Common Master-Plans and long-term objectives should be considered

In the strategy of Serbia, regional cooperation represents a central contribution to the strengthening of bilateral relations with the neighbors and the states from the South - East Europe region. The Republic of Serbia is actively contributing especially to the EUSDR, thus assigning a special role to the CBC Program with Romania, for the contribution to the wider strategy, and the creation of an integrated framework for the achievement of the Strategy objectives (Romania-Serbia IPA CBC PROGRAM, 2014).

Below are summarized the main policy frameworks in Serbia- Romania border space.

Based on the territorial analysis (TA) in Romania-Serbia border space Table 2 present main outcomes in socio – cultural, financial – economic, resources sustainability and political – strategic fields.

When we analyze regional governance regimes in Europe which take into account both the specific governance characteristics of the various countries as well as the way they each chose to manage and implement EU cohesion policy, in Romania case which entered the EU in 2007, there is continuity with a centrally managed cohesion policy. Through ESPON 2020 they have not yet successes develop

Table 3. Challenge and obstacles in coordination and governance dimension in fourfold manner in Serbia-Romania border space contributing to the Union strategy for smart, sustainable and inclusive growth.

MAIN OUTCOMES	BASED ON THE TERRITORIAL ANALYSIS (TA) IN ROMANIA SERBIA BORDER SPACE
Socio – cultural	• EU support for social inclusive growth • Growing social and cultural ties between RO and RS • Integration in the macro regional framework of EUSDR • Declining population, especially of young active people • Unemployment rates are still high in the territory • Indicators shows potential the region has as a tourist-magnet • Marketing and advertisement strategies are not coordinated among this countries
Financial – Economic	• The region is financial-economic depressed • GDP/per capita values are considerable low • Strategies for investor´s magnet should be considered
Resources Sustainability	• Several infrastructures are duplicated in nearby areas/territories • Poor quality of local and intraregional transport infrastructures for moving within the eligible area • Severe limitations to accessibility in rural and mountainous areas • European strategies for environmental protection in macro regions, offering additional support to local strategies (Danube region)
Political - Strategic	Lack of political commitment towards EU 2020 goals and EU standard´s Transparency and political commitment should be increased Common Master-Plans and long-term objectives should be considered Lack of political commitment towards EU 2020 goals and EU standard´s Transparency and political commitment should be increased Common Master-Plans and long-term objectives should be considered

autonomous meso-level institutions, have a strong mono-centric character, with a capital that dominates in terms of population and economic development, in all issues that contribute to influencing the development trajectories of other regions (RESSI, 2017, INTERREG, 2014).

Policymaking in Serbia requires reform of the public administration, professional monitoring and evaluation, proper planning at strategic and policy level, effective execution management with a focus on performance, and coordination of activities within the government itself as well as in cooperation with other state authorities and civil society.

The governance dimension, as well as coordination (transnational, political and cross-sectoral) of macro-regional strategies, are the key to their success according to recent studies carried out by Chilla, & Sielker; 2016, Sielker, 2016; Gänzle & Kern, 2008; Durh, 2011. and INTERACT, 2017. Regarding with review the relevant policy documents in Serbia and Romania, the reports from the European Commission (EC), 2013; 2014; INTERACT Program, 2012; 2017, that different coordination aspects in fourfold manner are identified and adapt in Table 3. as outcomes, challenge and obstacles in Serbia-Romania border space contributing to the Union strategy for smart, sustainable and inclusive growth and to the achievement of economic, social and territorial cohesion.

CONCLUSION

The present Paper allows understanding the EU macro-regional strategies introducing a new, complex layer of governance dimension and to examine how the Europe 2020 objectives of promoting sustainable, inclusive and smart economic development can be promoted by macro-regional authorities in Serbia-Romania border space. Focusing on the Romania Serbia CBA it is possible to understand the distance that exists between the EU 2020 strategy goals. Nevertheless, and analyzing Table 2, it is possible to identify the several opportunities for sustainable, inclusive and smart growth that these regions have. At the same time, it is necessary for the Serbia as one of Western Balkan country recognize that integration is not equal to accession. In this sense, intra-regional integration should become a priority for the Serbia next to current processes of EU integration and accession.

Moreover, by analyzing the cross-border area it is noticed that the multi-level challenge of cross-border cooperation needs soft, flexible forms of territorial governance. Contextually, recent experiences show that macro-regional cooperation is complex and time-consuming, and it will likely succeed if a strong political commitment regarding the macro-regional level is carried out. Multilevel governance system has to be improved in Romania and Serbia border spaces.

In line with the argument presented above, the improvement of territorial governance constitutes an important aspect within a wide range of different policy fields. Regarding that the relations between the study area and the Danube Region through Romania-Serbia IPA CBC Programme 2014 – 2020 was analyze in the following main fields: regional development, mobility, energy, environment, risks, and socioeconomic development. In the same time that are the most urgent topic areas in which territorial governance needs to be improved to ensure progress towards more efficient policy making and European integration are all listed below.

Regarding regional development and cohesion Serbia as Western Balkan country should become part of EU programs that support evidence-based policy making, such as ESPON.

In some areas a strong interdependency between the eligible area and the larger Danube region can be identified. These areas are dominated by international and interregional factors, with impacts that largely overcome the regional dimension.

Some examples: reduction and prevention of pollution of land, water and air by industrial and urban sources, control and mitigation of environmental risks, development of the integration of the European Transport Networks. In these areas the action of the CBC programme partners should be focused on the integration of the local with the global strategies at the level of Danube region. (Romania-Serbia IPA CBC Programme 2014 – 2020, p. 8).

Unemployment and low rate of activities are another common and serious challenge in the study area which suffer of a demographic decline, with aging of the population particularly severe in the marginal areas. The long history of cross border interaction, and the recent experience of cooperation under the current program, created a relevant potential for common actions in this field as well as in the field of social services in marginal areas, or social and cultural inclusion.

A sustainable use of natural resources, in particular water, by developing and managing environmental infrastructures, by protecting natural resources can be addressed as "protecting the environment, promoting climate change adaptation and mitigation, risk prevention and management" The actions in the field of environmental protection and sustainable development are also those where the strongest synergies with the Danube regions strategy can be pursued. (Romania-Serbia IPA CBC Programme 2014 – 2020).

The study area has good accessibility to national and European transport networks, but suffers of a poor quality and inefficiency of local networks, for both transport infrastructure and public services. The severity of this challenge is worsened by the risks of marginalization of the remote rural areas, in particular those close to the borders, and those in the mountains.

Promoting sustainable transport and improving public infrastructures - in particular common action for soft innovations in the provision and management of public services, for the establishment of innovative systems for public transport, for the provision of basic utilities to remote areas, could benefit of joint actions and sharing of experiences across the border (Romania-Serbia IPA CBC Programme 2014 – 2020, p. 112).

REFERENCES

Böhme, K., Finka, M., Gustedt, E., Schön, P., Sielker, F., & Zillmer, S. (2014). *Response to the European Consultation on the Future of the Europe 2020 Strategy*. Academy for Spatial Research and Planning.

Castanho, R., Cabezas, J., Fernández-Pozo, L., Vulevic, A., Gómez, N., Gallardo, J. M., & Loures, L. (2018). Common Regional Development Strategies on Iberian Territory. Envisioning New Horizons: Post 2020. – Enfoques En La Planificación Territorial Y Urbanística. 1ª Ed., Enero 2018, Thompson Reuters, pp. 293 – 304.

Chilla, T., & Sielker, F. (2016). Measuring the Added-Value of the EUSDR – Challenges and Opportunities. Discussion Paper. University Of Erlangen-Nuremberg.

Decoville, A., & Durand, F. (2017). Challenges and Obstacles in the Production of Cross-Border Territorial Strategies: The Example of the Greater Region. *Transactions of the Associations of the European Schools of Planning Journal, 1*(1), pp. 65-78, Doi: doi:10.24306/Traesop.2017.01.005

Dominguez, L., & Pires, I. (2014). *Cross-Border Cooperation Structures in Europe. Learning from the Past, Looking To the Future.* Brussels, Belgium: P. I. E. Peter Lang. doi:10.3726/978-3-0352-6452-4

Dörry, S., & Walther, O. (2015). Contested 'Relational Policy Spaces' In Two European Border Regions. *Environment & Planning A, 47*(2), 338–355. doi:10.1068/a130315p

Dühr, S. (2011). *Baltic Sea, Danube and Macro-Regional Strategies: A Model for Transnational Cooperation in the Eu?* Notre Europe.

ESPON RESSI- Regional Strategies for Sustainable and Inclusive Territorial Development 2017: Regional Interplay and EU Dialogue Targeted Analysis Annex 2. Governance Regimes, Opportunities and Challenges for European Cities and Regions Version 30/11/2017.

Faludi, A. (2010). *Cohesion, Coherence, Cooperation: European Spatial Planning Coming of Age?* Abingdon: Routledge. doi:10.4324/9780203842324

Gänzle, S., & Kern, K. (2008). A 'Macro-Regional' Europe in the Making? Theoretical Approaches and Empirical Evidence (pp. 99–120). London, UK: Palgrave Macmillan. Added Value of the Regional Development Fund (ERDF) (No. 2008. Ce.16.0.at.016). Final Report. Zoetermeer.

Géphyres, E., & Radboud, P. (2010). *Ex-Post Evaluation of INTERREG 2000-2006 Initiative financed by the Regional Development Fund (Erdf). Panteia, Eure Consult S.A., Policy Research and Consultancy. – University Nijmegen no. 2008. ce.16.0.at.016). Final Report.* Zoetermeer: Panteia.

Healey, P. (2007). *Urban Complexity and Spatial Strategies - Towards a Relational Planning For Our Times. (RTPI Library Series).* London, UK: Routledge.

Henrikson, A. K. (2010). Border Regions as Neighborhoods. In D. Wastl-Walter (Ed.), *The Ashgate Research Companion to Border Studies* (pp. 85–102). Farnham: Ashgate.

ICPDR – EUSDR PA4 & PA5 COORDINATIO. (2014). Joint Paper on Cooperation and Synergy for the EUSDR Implementation.

INTERACT. (2017). Added Value of Macro-Regional Strategies Project and Programme Perspective. Final Report of the Study. EU.

INTERACT Programme. (2012). INTERACT Handbook. – Practical Handbook for Ongoing Evaluation of Territorial Cooperation Programs. Updated Version. Retrieved from http://Wiki.Interact-Eu.Net/Display/Pc/Practical+Handbook+For+Ongoing+Evaluation

Kurowska-Pysz, J. (2015). Assessment of Trends for the Development of Cross-Border Cultural Clusters at an Example of Euroregion Cieszyn Silesia. *Forum Scientiae Oeconomia.*, *3*(1).

Kuzmin, O., & Kravchenko, I. (2014). Cross-Border Cooperation of Enterprises: Essence and Significance.

Paasi, A., & Zimmerbauer, K. (2016). Penumbral Borders and Planning Paradoxes: Relational Thinking and the Question of Borders in Spatial Planning. *Environment & Planning A*, *48*(1), 75–93. doi:10.1177/0308518X15594805

Regio, D. G. (n.d.). Draft implementing acts. List of ETC programmes. Retrieved from http://ec.europa.eu/regional_policy/what/ future/experts_documents_en.cfm#2

Reitel, B. (2007). Are Cross-Border Urban Spaces European Integration Patterns At Local Level? Analysis of the Management of Urban Areas astride the "French Border". – Borders of the European Union: Strategies of Crossing and Resistance.

Report from the Commission to the European Parliament, the Council, the European Economic and Social Committee and the Committee of the Regions Concerning the Governance of Macro-Regional Strategies. Brussels. 20.5.2014 Com (2014) 284 Final

Romania-Serbia, I. P. A. (2014). *CBC Programme 2014 – 2020.* Territorial Analysis SECOND DRAFT.

Scott, J. (1999). European and North American Contexts for Cross-Border Regionalism. *Regional Studies*, *33*(7), 605–617. doi:10.1080/00343409950078657

Sielker, F. (2016). A Stakeholder-Based Eu Territorial Cooperation: The Example of European Macro-Regions. European Planning Studies. Doi: Http://Dx.Doi.Org/10.1080/09654313.2016.1221383

Sohn, C., Reitel, B., & Walther, O. (2009). Cross-Border Metropolitan Integration in Europe: The Case of Luxembourg, Basel and Geneva. *Environment and Planning. C, Government & Policy*, *27*(5), 922–939. doi:10.1068/c0893r

TG-WeB. (2018). *Position paper on territorial governance in the Western Balkans*. The Western Balkans Network on Territorial Governance.

Chapter 5
Scale Matters:
Cross-Scale Dynamics of Cross-Border Carbon Adjustments

Asli Tasbasi
Işık University, Turkey

Pınar Yeşim Sarıca
Işık University, Turkey

Ahmet Hakan Yüksel
https://orcid.org/0000-0001-9195-9265
Işık University, Turkey

ABSTRACT

Climate change has palpable cross-scale implications given the severity of the matter epitomized in the prolonged discussions and negotiations between various parties that incur the consequences of the policy applications. Cross-border adjustment, though seemingly plausible, is a controversial method employed to mitigate the adverse potential impact of carbon emissions through placing an extra cost for the goods imported from countries that lag behind the standards set by multiple global agreements. Exercising cross-border adjustment on international trading activities is likely to have positive reverberations on taming the perils posed by climate change as well as triggering unforeseen perturbations in the interaction of actors involved in the global trading system. This chapter intends to shed light on cross-border adjustments via diagnosing the issues emerging out of the inter-scale interactions and question its effectiveness in micro and macro terms.

DOI: 10.4018/978-1-7998-2513-5.ch005

INTRODUCTION

The proposal that we have entered a new geological epoch called *Anthropocene* is consistent with the enormous impact of human activity on earth, particularly since the Industrial Revolution. Indeed, not only the magnitude, but the pace of anthropogenic threats over the ecosystem through unsustainable production and consumption patterns is extremely worrying. Stunning rates of ice melting have been detected, the number of mammals, birds, fish and reptiles has declined and the species in wetlands, lakes and rivers have decreased dramatically. To cap it all, rapid increases in temperature indicate that in the next century, our planet is going to be warming at a minimum rate of 20 times than the historical average.

One of the most important causes of the destruction on earth and the ecosystem is climate change, while the dominant cause of climate change is human economy, of which global trade is a central part. Therefore, trade and how to internalize the environmental externalities associated with it has become an inherent and perennial issue for those inquiring the nexus between economic activity and environmental burden. Emissions of carbon dioxide as the leading contributor to climate change on the other hand is a global externality as supported by evidence, and is coupled by increased trade and economic growth.

As the most undoubted truth, effective mitigation of climate change depends heavily on the reduction of carbon emissions. However, absence of explicit international cooperation on a common climate regime and correspondingly binding regulations is widely accepted to be the obstacle in front of an absolute global commitment to a carbon-free world. The two most contentious issues regarding national endeavors aiming to curtail emissions are the resultant cost disadvantage for domestic firms and carbon leakage, which implies an increase of carbon emissions in countries without climate precautions due to emission reducing actions taken in other countries. Several policy measures have been initiated to alleviate these concerns; yet, feasibility in theory does not always hold true for functioning in practice.

This chapter broadly questions whether cross-border adjustments may be operative as carbon equalization measures, and be economically efficient, environmentally responsible, legally approvable and politically practical. Kernel of the work is to deal with the inter-scale interactions associated with import and export carbon reduction adjustments at the border, around which the necessity to refrain from discriminative or restrictive trade implementations is discussed.

The chapter proceeds as follows. Section two presents related literature to set the background and extract the motivation of the work. Section three discusses that adaptation to climate change begs for an appropriate context given the emergent dynamics of the interaction between scales. Section four presents the concluding remarks.

BACKGROUND

Though theoretical roots of border tax adjustments (BTAs) go back to David Ricardo in the eighteenth century, it is the 1968 OECD Report that defined BTAs as fiscal equalization measures based on the destination principle (OECD, 1968: 39). In 1970, WTO Working Party took over this definition in principle, but stated that the adjustments should not necessarily be made at the border; instead, they could be applied on internationally traded goods in general. The main idea was that the domestic taxes would be levied on domestic products no matter what the tax system was in countries of export or import.

Border adjustments related to environment on the other hand, are induced to other countries in order to level the field, *i.e.* to prevent competitive disadvantage. They are fiscal mechanisms developed nationally, to disburden domestic producers, particularly in energy-intensive sectors, who have to face foreign competitors from countries that lack appropriate environmental commitments.

Border adjustments target carbon reduction, that is why they can also be named as border carbon adjustments. Be they in the form of a quota restriction or a border tax, these adjustments have been widely discussed in the literature, providing arguments both against and for.

Among the vast array of literature on climate adjustments at the border, some elucidatory studies include but are not limited to the following. World Bank (2016) report gives an outline of existing and rising global carbon pricing instruments, including national and subnational endeavors. The report also concentrates on the significance of adjusting and integrating carbon pricing strategies to more extensive policy inputs. The report gives new modelling analysis to show the pivotal advantages that an international carbon market built up under Article 6 of the Paris Agreement could give in decreasing the costs to countries of accomplishing their emission targets. Condon and Ignaciuk (2013) provide a broad literature review which can be referred as a comprehensive source on BCAs and alternatives where they compare the existing studies in terms of competitiveness and leakage.

Most studies which discuss the applicability of border adjustment mechanisms tend to evaluate the elements of a possible border adjustment mechanism to be adopted in the EU alongside the Emissions Trading System (ETS) (Monjon and Quirion, 2010; Asselt and Brewer, 2010), since it is the most efficient carbon pricing system that has ever put into life, leaving aside the fact that it covers only the 40% of EU emissions.) Asselt and Brewer further discuss the issue for US. The authors propose concrete design options, such as the preference of allowances to import taxes, their amounts and the necessity to apply adjustments to basic materials instead of consumer products (Asselt and Brewer, 2010).

Fischer and Fox (2012) evaluate in their study four policies that can be combined with unilateral emission pricing and look for the conditions that are mostly effective in reducing greenhouse gas emissions. Among border charge on imports, border rebate for exports, full border adjustment, and domestic output-based rebating, none is found to be as effective as it is supposed to be in reducing global emissions. In addition, each policy is considered to have economic and legal drawbacks.

Shiell (2014) derives an optimum set of BTA for a coalition of countries working cooperatively to abate greenhouse gas emissions, under an exogenous emissions reduction target. Comparing the domestic and global target strategies, Shiell suggests that using constant domestic target to test the effectiveness of carbon based BTA's is wrong. Instead, "under a global target, the optimal BTA consists of the terms of trade component and an induced foreign emissions component".

Branger and Quirion (2013) claim that BCAs can reduce carbon leakage by 10 percentage but they are approached cautiously since they shift partially the abatement costs from abating countries to non-abating countries. In a detailed report Cosbey et. al (2012) provide guidance on the implementation of BCAs, from what is meant by leakage and competitiveness to identification of countries and domestic sectors that should be covered by a BCA. The report carefully defines the appropriate level of adjustment and the allocation of revenues. The report concludes by describing how a fair practice in the application and elaboration of BCA regimes should be governed. Cosbey (2012) draws attention to the difficulties involved in designing and practicing a BCA regime, particularly in terms of the objectives, effectiveness and compliance with trade law.

Kortum and Weisbach (2016) investigate border adjustments in terms of which goods they should apply to, which emissions from the production of those goods should be taxed, and from and to which countries they should apply. The authors find that the economic cost of border adjustments is so high that it requires good justification put forth in terms of the acquisition of social welfare.

Compliance of border adjustments with the prevalent international trade law is another side of the issue that is dissected in the literature. Weber (2015) questions the BCAs within the WTO's legal framework and emphasizes that border adjustments should legally be justified within the WTO law.

Holzer and Shariff (2012) draw attention to possible advantages of including BCAs in PTAs, underlying that this would refrain from trade retaliation against unilateral imposition of BCAs, and that is more feasible in legal terms. Horn and Mavroidis (2011) find in their study that the WTO regime cannot be considered as a major barrier to adopt BTAs, yet, the authors note that the allocation of the burden of proof could be an issue.

In a recent study, Bueb et al. (2016) present the most thorough analysis of border adjustment mechanisms hitherto, anatomizing the issue in terms of instruments to employ, carbon content appraisal, targeted sectors/products, countries to be affected and coverage of carbon flows. The authors point at the economic, political and legal difficulties in implementation, yet, conclude that these difficulties are not insuperable as long as nations are committed to “profound and voluntary transformation of the society” for a carbon free energy transition.

Empirical studies are less in number, signaling to a gap in the field. Winchester et al (2010) conduct a model which concludes that the implementation of BCAs brings along two contrasting effects. Whereas they decrease the carbon leakage by two-thirds, they “significantly reduce welfare” and their contribution to global emissions is quite low.

Alexeeva-Talebi et al (2008) compare border tax adjustments (BTA) and integrated emission trading (IET) policies in a stylized two-country model and find that the two function better in different areas. According to the findings of the study, while BTA is a better tool in domestic competitiveness, IET is more efficient in emissions reduction.

A study by Böhringer et al (2012) provides quantitative evidence that while BCAs can effectively mitigate leakage and help easing the adverse impacts on energy intensive industries which implement carbon reducing measures, the “global cost saving” is negligible.

The model developed by Wetzel and Peterson (2012) shows that BCA can only provide “moderate” efficiency and reduce leakages on a limited scale. leakage. The authors note that better implementation brings about higher costs and that in some cases BCAs could be exploited as a backdoor trade policy instrument in order to achieve terms of trade gains.

It is not an easy task to contribute to the literature whose main research topics, methods and main findings are addressed above. The main motivation of this study is to compile the existing literature on cross border adjustments, which have been on the agenda in recent years in order to control and eliminate the negative effects of climate change which is a matter of all people, regardless of socio-cultural or economic background, living in the world. In an attempt to determine in which aspect of the topic there may be a deficiency or a gap, cross-scale interaction can be identified to play a decisive role in the design of cross-border strategies.

Dealing with climate change related policy actions from a cross-scale perspective is a knotty endeavor. Not only it is challenging to take a stance on such a contentious issue, but also the innate complexities embedded in the dynamic nature of cross-scale interactions increases the number subtleties of the matter. On one side of the argument there are proponents of the existence of scales who conceptualize the matter as the vertical differentiation in which social relations are embedded within (Brenner, 2005), platforms of absolute space in a wider sea of relational space (Smith, 2000), different levels of space that refers to the geographic level of social activity

(Spicer, 2006) as well as the detractors who ontologically refute the existence of the very matter itself (Thrift, 1995; Smith, 2003; Marston, *et.al.*, 2005). Nevertheless, there is a substantial body of literature inclined toward analyzing the repercussions of climate change related policy actions in cross-scale context.

One of the potential reasons for the entrenched lethargy in the global actors is likely stem from the fact that success of any attempt to mitigate and adapt to climate change has spatial and temporal implications, which are rather neglected, driven by the divergent interests of decision makers (Adger, *et.al.*, 2005). As a matter of fact, adaptation to climate change begs for an appropriate context given the emergent dynamics of the interaction between scales given the difficulty of making inferences about upscale results from micro scales and downscale results of macro models to micro sites (Peterson, 2000). Another reason is the inadequacy of micro scale actors to interpret the signals that are in fact portent of the things to come due to climate change as it is usually hard for companies to comprehend climate impacts on business as climatic stimuli is perceived to be among many other drivers for change that the organization is supposed to confront (Berkhout, *et.al.*2006). Uncertainties associated with the type, the occurrence, the scale and the location of upcoming climate-related events makes the situation even more intriguing. Ergo, the cross-border adjustment as an adaptive implementation appears to be a multi-dimensional issue that requires to take an inter-scale stance on climate change adaptation endeavors.

MAIN FOCUS OF THE CHAPTER

Taking a Cross-Scale Stance on Climate Change Adaptation

Adaptation-oriented decisions taken to cope with anticipated adversaries associated with anthropogenic climate change cultivate the 'meaning' as such serves as the reason for further development of remedial methods that aim to augment the level of adaptiveness to this severe threat posed by the global community. Occasional congestion of climate change negotiations and efficiency of the adaptive implementations going awry, seemingly stem from cost-oriented concerns of decision makers. Taking a *ceteris paribus* stance, although literally plausible, on explaining the nature of the obstacles on the way to deal with climate change adaptation is nevertheless misleading. Relative weight placed on priorities, aspirations and expectations leads to diverse range of meanings harvested from the espoused values emphasized by different actors at different scales, which fill the space that serves as the essential framework of all modes of intellectual endeavor. Ergo, when it comes to align (especially country) priorities and processes, scale matters (Haddad, 2005). Space, in conjunction with time, provides a fundamental ordering system interlacing every

Table 1. Philosophical views of space

Absolute space	*Relative space*
Space can exist independent of any matter.	Space exists only with reference to things and processes
Space as a 'container'	Space is defined by things and processes
Associated primarily with inventory and mapping	Associated primarily with studies of forms, patterns, functions, rates, diffusion
Euclidean space	May involve non-Euclidean (transformed) space

Source: Meentemeyer, 1989

face of thought (Sack, 1980). Meentemeyer (1989) provides definitions of absolute and relative space drawing on the philosophical views of the very concept (Table 1).

Space frequently alters its meaning as spatial relations among things are generally described and perceived differently in different situations, such as distances, patterns and shapes literally take on dissimilar appearances and can be described differently from different viewpoints (Sack, 1980). The point of view presented by absolute space enables us to create images of sub-containers within a container and to excogitate felicitous classification schemes, whereas the relativistic point of view defines space by the spatial elements and processes (Meentemeyer, 1989).

Given the fact that success of climate change adaptation depends of the spatial and temporal scale (Adger, et.al. 2005), time is always related to space. What takes place in time is having a spatial implication (existence in real world or in the mind-sets of humans). What exists in space is also affecting and relating to time and temporal processes. (Hedaa and Törnroos, 2002). Slawinski and Bansal (2012) examine how an organization's time perspective is related to its response to climate change and reveal two patterns of responses. They label those two patterns as 'focused' and 'integrated' with an attempt to state the nature of two patterns they have found in firms' responses to climate change. Their research reveals that focused firms accentuate linear time, which is evident in a lower tolerance for uncertainty and a tendency to dismiss the past and the long-term future in their climate change decisions. On the other hand, integrated firms have higher tolerance for uncertainty, draw on previous experience and have the tendency to see time as cyclical and connected events over time.

Scale, extending from its roots in cartography, "refers to the physical dimensions of observed phenomenon, or the content or extent of scale, such as a segment of a territory" (Nightingale, 2015). Like cartographic projections and controlled distortions, scales allow us to portray disparate views of spatial relations and, given the systematical interrelations, coordinate these views and perspectives with a standard yet flexible description of space, which delivers a "frame of reference abstracted from the material world and with regard to which the material objects and their relationships can be identified and described" (Sack, 1980). Scale has been conceptualized by many researchers though there is a vast array of scholarly positions on the matter. One set of scholar approaches conceptualize scale as a "vertical differentiation in which social relations are embedded within a hierarchical scaffolding of nested territorial units" (Brenner, 2005), "the spatial level, local, national or global, at which presumed effect of location is operative (Agnew, 1993) and "platforms of absolute space in a wider sea of relational space" (Smith, 2000). However, detractors postulate that "global, national and local scales do not exist as such" (Smith, 2003) and "we may be best served by approaching scale not as an ontological structure which 'exists', but as an epistemological one – a way of knowing or apprehending" (Jones, 1998). It would be timely, at this point, to draw the line between level and scale. Nightingale (2015) casts light on this subtlety as follows:

Scale, however, is not equivalent with level. "Rather, level refers to locations upon a scale, or the way that scale is organized. The national scale—i.e. territory or population—are not the same as the national level which refers to various institutions and actions—i.e. national government—that apply to the entire nation. Scale and level are often conflated, but when a more careful conceptualization of scale is used, it becomes possible to understand that for example, the scale of knowledge, is not the same as the level at which that knowledge is mobilized or the level of the actors who use it. In this view, 'local knowledge' is not scaled to the local, but rather refers to the level of the actors who hold that knowledge." The scale of 'local knowledge' is most often global given that local level actors incorporate understandings from a wide range of worldwide sources to form their own perceptions and conceptions of the world. "So, while it may be called 'local knowledge', 'local' signals the level of the actors rather than the extent or content of the knowledge itself."

Analyzing scales requires exploiting hierarchy theory to be able to extract meaning from the cross-scale interactions. Hierarchy theory has been derived from systems theory does not assume that a system is hierarchically constructed, rather, separates the world into hierarchical levels with an attempt to simplify the analysis of cross-scale interactions (Simon, 1974; Peterson, 2000). Peterson (2000) mentions the difficulty of upscaling results from small scales to large scales as well as down-scaling the results of global models to local sites and emphasizes four scaling problems, which are non-linearity and heterogeneity, different processes dominate at different scales, cross-scale connections and emergent properties. These problems become salient during analysis of cross-scale dynamics for implementing climate-change adaptation actions. The dynamic nature of connections between levels of governance entails elaboration on the way scales are constructed. "Relationships between macro and micro scales and the interactions between macro-structure and micro-agency significantly shape the way our world works" (Wilbanks and Kates,

1999). As a consequence of increased complexity, emergence of qualitatively distinct new phenomena should be dealt with appropriately in order to be able to achieve successful adaptation measures that qualify equitable, effective, efficient and legitimate outcomes (Adger, et.al., 2005). Any attempt to stave off the paucities in climate-change related adaptation research and unfold adaptation processes entails to grasp the insights of the interrelationships between organizations (micro scale) and various other actors (scales located at other hierarchical levels).

Organizations at the micro-scale confront couple of problems on the way to adjust their strategic orientations towards climate-change related changes in the environment. Busch (2011) postulates three of those problems. One of them is the lack of organizational capability to anticipate ecosystem dynamics as the disruptions in natural environment are far from pursuing predictable courses. Second, it is extremely difficult to develop specific knowledge of the environment-related uncertainties, due to the problem of chaos and complexity. *In situ* complexity on inter-scale governance system might limit penetration rate of expected decision makers (for instance, local governments) in relation to planning and risk management issues (Preston *et.al.*, 2008).

Organizations have the tendency "to draw upon the repertoire of responses already open to them instead of investing in research and development to identify new options" (Berkhout, et.al., 2006). At this point, significance of context emerges as the heart of the matter for those who would like "to understand why a given challenge has arisen in the adaptation process by considering the cross-scale context of the governance system" (Mukheibir *et.al.*, 2013). Such context is exacerbated by the inter-dependent nature of decision making between agents on scale (Adger *et.al.,* 2008) as well as "mediating processes such as power, values and structures" (Bosomworth and Handmer, 2008). Third, environmental disruptions are usually rapid and massive, which exceeds resilience levels of organizations. Berkhout, et.al. (2006) also stress the importance of organizations as interpretation systems and highlight their failure to recognize and interpret evidence from experience as significant, which might be construed as an impediment for developing polycentric institutions that are capable of converging inter-scale priorities. "Proactive adaptation is a collective process and is contingent on the interaction" of entire participants, namely organizations, (Mukheibir *et.al.*, 2013) thus, increasing intensity of complexity via enhancing "interaction resonance, which signifies richness of information flow that is generated and maintained through interactions over time" (Goldstein *et.al.*, 2010). Adaptive multi-level governance put special emphasis on comprehending the priorities of an inter-connected social-ecological system, the stressors and drivers of change that are actually influential on the very process of adaptation of a social-ecological system encompassing interactions and feedback loops of divergent scales (Bunce *et.al.*, 2010).

CONCLUSION

Climate change has been a standout amongst the most serious issues confronting the planet in recent years that need to be addressed, as its outcomes are unfurling right in front of us. From an international economics perspective, a conceivable method for eliminating the market failure stemming from climate change is to internalize the negative externality through types of border adjustments that go towards helping those influenced and supporting endeavors of constraining the negative outcomes.

This chapter attempts to emphasize border climate adjustments in terms of inadequacy of micro scale actors to interpret the signals that are in fact portent of the things to come due to climate change. The chapter points out the complexity of making inferences from upscale results from micro scales and downscale results of macro models to micro sites. It is specified that uncertainties associated with the type, the occurrence, the scale and the location of upcoming climate-related events makes the situation even more intriguing. It is not intended in the chapter to provide policy recommendations or action plans, but rather underline the urgency of recognizing the essence of cross-scale integration to cut the pace of climate change and ultimately eliminate all the factors that lead to it given the current vulnerability of the planet.

Highlighting the importance of a micro -firm level- approach, it is obvious that the content of the chapter calls for further research on the awareness, acceptance and coming into action at different scales of global labor market and industrial relations. Transition to low carbon economy for an ecologically sustainable future is expected to affect industrial relations, workers and working conditions through the implementation of cross border adjustments (Martinez-Fernandez et al, 2010). That is why one of the next steps of future research may be analyzing possible effects of cross border adjustments on labor markets.

Possible adverse consequences on labor markets should be scrutinized as well as the net employment growth of the move towards a low-carbon economy. In depth work is needed to make by policy makers in countries about climate change regulatory measures planned to be implemented or currently being implemented on their potential impact they have on labor markets. In sectors with relatively large amounts of CO_2 emissions, workers will be highly vulnerable to the direct effects of wide array of regulatory measures on climate change due to increasing production costs. Poschen (2015) explains that the common belief in the beginning that regulations for climate change might lead to unemployment due to increasing costs for the firms has falsified.

In today's globalized world, social inequalities are still colossal and economic up and downs seem to keep on having a huge effect on social conditions and thus on the labor markets. Challenges of climate change will be just as dramatical, particularly due to structural changes of climate change adaptation and mitigation measures directly. But a switch to a low carbon economy would mean shifting from old jobs to new green ones if global green employment policies are adopted. This is a future promising topic to anatomize.

All in all, this study leads to future derivative studies that require an in-depth examination of all the components that live within the organic structures of institutions operating at different scales. Given the lack of empirical evidence due to insufficient number of empirical studies the use of simulations to predict the effects of cross-border adjustment on social welfare in future studies may serve to achieve global consensus on designing cross border strategies, paving the way to both improve social conditions and increase total surplus in the economy.

REFERENCES

Adger, W. N., Arnell, N. W., & Tompkins, E. L. (2005). Successful adaptation to climate change across scales. *Global Environmental Change*, *15*(2), 77–86. doi:10.1016/j.gloenvcha.2004.12.005

Agnew, J. (1993). Representing space: Space, scale & culture in social science. In J. Duncan, & S. Ley (Eds.), *Place / cultural representation* (pp. 251–271). London, UK: Routledge.

Alexeeva-Talebi, V., Löschel, A., & Mennel, T. (2008). Climate Policy and the Problem of Competitiveness: Border Tax Adjustments or Integrated Emission Trading? ZEW *Discussion Papers*, No. 08-061.

Asselt, H., & von. (2010). Addressing competitiveness and leakage concerns in climate policy: An analysis of border adjustment measures in the US and the EU. *Energy Policy*, *38*(1), 42–51. doi:10.1016/j.enpol.2009.08.061

Berkhout, F., Hertin, J., & Gann, D. M. (2006). Learning to Adapt: Organizational Adaptation to Climate Change Impacts. *Climatic Change*, *78*(1), 135–156. doi:10.100710584-006-9089-3

Böhringer, C., Balistreri, E. J., & Rutherford, T. F. (2012). The role of border carbon adjustment in unilateral climate policy: Overview of an Energy Modeling Forum study (EMF 29. *Energy Policy*, (34): 97–110.

Branger, F., & Quirion, P. (2013). Climate policy and the 'carbon haven' effect. *Wiley Interdisciplinary Reviews: Climate Change*, *5*(1), 53–71.

Brenner, N. (2005). *New state spaces: urban governance and the rescaling of statehood*. New York: Oxford University Press.

Bueb, J., Hanania, L. R., & Le Clezio, A. (2016). Border adjustment mechanisms Elements for economic, legal, and political analysis. WIDER Working Paper (20).

Busch, T. (2011). Organizational adaptation to disruptions in the natural environment: The case of climate change. *Scandinavian Journal of Management*, *27*(4), 389–404. doi:10.1016/j.scaman.2010.12.010

Condon, M., & Ignaciuk, A. (2013). Border Carbon Adjustment and International Trade: A Literature Review. *OECD Trade and Environment Working Papers*. OECD Publishing.

Cosbey, A. (2012). *It ain't easy: The complexities of creating a regime for border carbon adjustment* (pp. 1–8). Entwined. Issue Brief.

Cosbey, A.; Susanne Droege, S.; Fischer, C., Reinaud, J.; Stephenson, J.; Weischer, L., & Wooders, P. (2012). A Guide for the Concerned: Guidance on the elaboration and implementation of border carbon adjustment. Entwined, *Policy Report.*

ETUC. (2006). Climate Change and Employment: Impact on Employment in the European Union-25 of Climate Change and CO2 Emission Reduction Measures by 2030. Available at www.tradeunionpress.eu/Web/EN/Activities/Environment/Studyclimatechange/rapport.pdf, accessed 5 November 2018.

Fischer, C., & Fox, A. K. (2012). *Journal of Environmental Economics and Management*, 64(2), September 2012, pp. 199-216

Hedaa, L., & Törnroos, J. A. (2002). Towards a theory of timing. In R. Whipp, B. Adam, & I. Sabelis (Eds.), *Making Time Time & Management in Modern Organization* (pp. 31–45). New York: Oxford University Press.

Holzer, K., & Shariff, N. (2012). *The Inclusion of Border Carbon Adjustments in Preferential Trade Agreements: Policy Implications* (pp. 1–27). Milan, Rome: Trade and Climate Change.

Horn, H., & Mavroidis, P. C. (2011). To B(TA) or Not to B(TA)? On the Legality and Desirability of Border Tax Adjustments from a Trade Perspective. *World Economy*, *34*(11), 1911–1937. doi:10.1111/j.1467-9701.2011.01423.x

Jones, K. (1998). Scale as epistemology. *Political Geography*, *17*(1), 25–28. doi:10.1016/S0962-6298(97)00049-8

Kortum, S., & Weisbach, D. (2016). *Border Adjustments for Carbon Emissions: Basic Concepts and Design. Resources for the Future* (pp. 1–43). Discussion Papers.

Marston, S. A., Jones, J. P. III, & Woodward, K. (2005). Human geography without scale. *Transactions of the Institute of British Geographers*, *4*(30), 416–432. doi:10.1111/j.1475-5661.2005.00180.x

Martinez-Fernandez, C., Hinojosa, C., & Miranda, G. (2010). Green jobs and skills: the local labour market implications of addressing climate change. OECD/LEED Local Employment and Economic Development Program.

Meentemeyer, V. (1989). Geographical perspectives of space, time, and scale. *Landscape Ecology*, *3*(3-4), 163–173. doi:10.1007/BF00131535

Monjon, S., & Quirion, P. (2010). How to design a border adjustment for the European Union Emissions Trading System? *Energy Policy*, *38*(9), 5199–5207. doi:10.1016/j.enpol.2010.05.005

Mukheibir, P., Kuruppu, N., Gero, A., & Herriman, J. (2013). Overcoming cross-scale challenges to climate change adaptation for local government: A focus on Australia. *Climatic Change*, *121*(2), 271–283. doi:10.100710584-013-0880-7

Nightingale, A. J. (2015). Challenging the romance with resilience: communities, scale and climate change. In W. Harcourt, & I. L. Nelson (Eds.), Practicing Feminist Political Ecologies. Moving Beyond Green Economy. Zed Books. Chicago Distribution Center.

OECD. (1968). Border tax adjustments law. Report of the Working Party adopted on December 2, 1970.

Peterson, G. D. (2000). Scaling Ecological Dynamics: Self-Organization, Hierarchical Structure, and Ecological Resistance. *Climatic Change*, *44*(3), 291–309. doi:10.1023/A:1005502718799

Poschen, P. (2015). *Decent Work, Green Jobs, and the Sustainable Economy*. Sheffield, UK: Greenleaf.

Preston, B., Brooke, C., Measham, T., Smith, T., & Gorddard, R. (2008). Igniting change in local government: Lessons learned from a bushfire vulnerability assessment. *Mitigation and Adaptation Strategies for Global Change*, *14*(3), 251–283. doi:10.100711027-008-9163-4

Sack, R. D. (1980). *Conceptions of Space in Social Thought: A Geographic Perspective*. London, UK: Macmillan. doi:10.1007/978-1-349-16433-2

Shiell, T. (2014, April). Who Cares about Carbon Leakage? The Economics of Border Tax Adjustments under Incomplete Climate Treaties. Department of Economics Faculty of Social Sciences University of Ottawa. Working Paper, #1403. pp. 1-22.

Slawinski, N., & Bansal, T. (2012). A matter of time: The temporal perspectives of organizational responses to climate change. *Organization Studies*, *33*(11), 1537–1563. doi:10.1177/0170840612463319

Smith, N. (2000). Scale. In R. J. Johnston, D. Gregory, G. Pratts, & M. Watts (Eds.), *The Dictionary in Human Geography* (pp. 724–727). Oxford, UK: Blackwell.

Smith, R. G. (2003). World city topologies. *Progress in Human Geography*, *27*(5), 561–582. doi:10.1191/0309132503ph447oa

Spicer, A. (2006). Beyond the convergence-divergence debate: The role of spatial scales in transforming organizational logic. Organization Studies, (27), 10, 1,467-1,483.

Thrift, N. (1995). A hyperactive world. In R. J. Johnston, P. Taylor, & M. Watts (Eds.), *Geographies of global change: remapping the world in the late twentieth century* (pp. 18–35). Oxford, UK: Blackwell.

Weber, R. H. (2015). Border tax adjustment – legal perspective. Springer. *Climatic Change*, *133*(3), 407–417. doi:10.100710584-015-1414-2

Weitzel, M., & Peterson, S. (2012). Border Carbon Adjustments: Not a Very Promising Climate Policy Instrument. Kiel Policy Brief. no 55.

Wilbanks, T., & Kate, R. W. (1999). Global change in local places: How scale matters. *Climatic Change*, *43*(3), 601–628. doi:10.1023/A:1005418924748

Winchester, N., Paltsev, S., & Reilly, J. (2010). Will border carbon adjustments work? MIT Joint Program on the Science and Policy of Global Change. Report no. 184, 1-22.

World Bank. Ecofys & Vivid Economics. (2016). State and trends of carbon pricing. Washington, DC: International Bank for Reconstruction and Development/The World Bank.

KEY TERMS AND DEFINITIONS

Border Climate Adjustments: Border climate adjustments refer to import fees levied by carbon-taxing countries on goods manufactured in non-carbon-taxing countries. The rationale that sets the grounds for border adjustments is to ensure a level playing field in international trade while internalizing the costs of climate change into prices of goods and services.

Climate Change: Climate fluctuations, by definition, exist in the usual weather. This could be measured through the amount of rain a place gets in a year. Or it could be observed as a temperature change of a usual temperature pertaining to a place. However, melting of ice and snow caused oceans to rise due to the warming of earth's climate. This, inevitably, triggers a series of consequences leading to emergent global problems.

Environmental Politics: Environmental politics could briefly be explained as the examination of the way environmental issues are dealt with given the prevailing political systems which looks at how governments are supposed to balance environmental issues with their other priorities such as education, economy, etc.

International Trade: International trade consists of economic transactions that are made between countries through exporting and importing of multifarious goods. The first type of trade occurs when a certain range of goods are beyond the productive capability of a country or when the current production falls short. The second type of trade, which happens to be more complicated than the first type mentioned above, occur even when a country possesses the capability of producing the goods or supplying the services, though, still imports them.

Chapter 6
Economic Context of the Real Estate Bubble Crack:
Case of a Border Region - Extremadura

Julián Mora Aliseda
Universidad de Extremadura, Spain

Jacinto Garrido Velarde
Universidad de Extremadura, Spain

Consuelo Mora
Fundicotex, Spain

ABSTRACT

The crisis that shook the global financial institutions in 2007/08 revealed the weaknesses and irrationalities of a system that led millions of people, without compatible returns, to the category of "owners" of their home. During the previous decade, the absurd growth of supply in parallel with the progressive increase in real estate value, made housing "the hen of the golden eggs" of the regional and national economy: banks earn with a credit and families with the valuation of homes. This chapter examines the economic context in the crack of the real estate bubble and analyzes as a practical case the incidents of this crisis at international level in the border region of Extremadura.

ANALYSIS OF THE INTERNATIONAL ECONOMY 2007-2008

During 2007 the economy of the planet enjoyed a remarkable development, around 5%. Although, in the last quarter of the year, global economic growth began a

DOI: 10.4018/978-1-7998-2513-5.ch006

moderation phase as a result of permanent financial turbulence. The uneasiness of the financial markets comes from the sector of high-risk or subprime mortgages in the United States, and as a result of the deficit balances in the banks' balance sheets intensified and began to influence the stock markets of the entire planet.

In this new context, at the beginning of this year, the IMF reduced the global growth forecasts for the entire year of 2008 to 4.5%. Production in the United States slowed considerably in the last months of 2007 and this trend has continued throughout 2008, with the slowdown in domestic consumption, the stagnation of corporate profits and the worsening dollar price. Likewise, the economy of the European Union lost the inertia of recent years and most macroeconomic indicators began to fall, as well as the more domestic ones that expressed a lack of confidence on the part of businessmen and consumers.

Japan slowly recovers from the housing sector crisis of the 1990s and increases the confidence of its economy because its banks are in a stronger situation than the Americans or Europeans, even so their economy has not just seen the light at the end of the tunnel. Meanwhile, emerging countries, despite their reduction in the pace of their exports, continue to grow above 4%, especially in the cases of China, India and Brazil, while Russia will grow to 3%. These economies have benefited from strong domestic demand and the high price of the raw materials they export (food and energy), although the financial chaos situation is reaching them and this will force them to reduce their economic projections.

Global inflation increased throughout 2008 in both advanced and emerging market economies due to the rising prices of raw materials and energy. The rise in food prices, in particular corn, soybeans and wheat, has been produced due to the pressures generated by the increase in the use of corn and other food products for the production of biofuels, the rise in demand of emerging market countries, not forgetting the inability of supplies due to adverse weather conditions in some countries such as Australia where drought reduced wheat production by 60%.

For its part, the relevant growth in demand has kept the prices of oil and other products such as metals at high levels. Until now, the world economy has been able to absorb the sustained escalation of oil prices during the last five years without suffering a significant impact. The supply in the world oil markets remains low. Despite OPEC's capacity has expanded, the reaction of the global supply has been slow in the face of a demand for oil products that has continued to grow, especially in the fast-growing emerging market countries, joining with all this shortage of capacity of refining. However, as of the month of June where the historical maximum was reached on the price of oil (147 dollars per barrel), it experienced a brutal fall, until being in the present month of December 2008, at 35 dollars per neighbourhood, the lowest price since 2004.

The main challenge facing global monetary policy is to balance the arising risks from the increase in inflation and the atony of economic activity. In addition, risks persist due to the continuity of global imbalances in a context of greater financial volatility. Therefore, it is necessary to address a greater regulation that allows to ensure appropriate transparency regarding risks, such as exposures which are not included in the balance sheets, in order to ensure that markets can adequately assess the price of risk in a world in which financial instruments have become extremely complex. Credit conditions have tightened throughout 2008 due to growing concern over the impact of problems in the high-risk mortgage market in the United States. Uncertainty regarding the distribution of losses generated a significant decrease in liquidity in some segments of the financial markets. The central banks of the main world economies, which before the turbulence were generally tightening monetary policy to contain the incipient inflationary pressures, since mid-2007 and several times throughout 2008, have been forced to inject liquidity into financial markets to stabilize short-term interest rates, given the existing disturbances in them.

The main currencies have maintained the trends observed in previous periods. The US dollar has continued to weaken. The euro has appreciated, although less than the yen. The Chinese currency, the Renminbi, has continued its gradual appreciation against the US dollar, despite the current account surplus of China has increased even more, favouring the growth of the international reserves of this country.

An analysis by the large blocks of the world economy must begin with the United States where the impact of turbulence on financial markets was most noted. The fall in investment spending, particularly in the residential sector, has been one of the main causes of the slowdown in the US economy that grew in 2007 by 2.6%. The unemployment rate reached 5% of the active population and the price level increased by 4.1%.

Japan grew by around 2%, but domestic demand remains the pending issue. The emerging countries of Asia continued to experience intense growth during 2007 and somewhat slow down during the first half of 2008. The expansion was channelled by China, where the real GDP grew by 11.4% thanks to the acceleration of exports and investment. Chinese growth has a bias towards heavy industry, a large difference between countryside and city and a preference towards investment and exports to the detriment of private consumption. Another pressing problem of the Chinese economy is the rising inflation and the need to maintain monetary stability. Also in India, the intensification of domestic demand, particularly investment, supported a growth of 8.7%. Volatility in global financial markets has had a limited impact on this geoFigureical block (International Monetary Fund, 2008).

Central African continues experienced a notable growth of 6.1% in 2007 and 5.3% in the first half of 2008. This progress is largely based on the entry into service of new production plants in exporting countries of oil like Angola and Nigeria. Although the fastest growth is recorded by oil exporting countries, most other economies are expanding rapidly, overcoming their secular backwardness.

The long period of high growth in the Middle East continues to be backed by high oil prices and robust domestic demand, registering in 2007 an increase of 5.9% and 5.7% in the first half of 2008. The increase in GDP in the oil-exporting countries were also supported by the expansion in the non-oil sectors, driven by the increase in public spending financed by oil revenues, foreign capital inflows and the rapid growth of domestic private credit.

In Latin America, the pace of expansion has moderated to 4.6% in the first half of 2008, as a result of the slowdown in activity in the United States that has influenced Mexico and Central America, especially through trade links and, in addition, to the somewhat slower growth of remittances sent by migrant workers (International Monetary Fund, 2008).

In economies of recent incorporation into the EU, growth is still noticeable. Expenditure on production platforms and housing led to investment while the improvement of labour markets and easy access to credit continued to underpin invest and consumer spending, especially in the Baltic countries and in southern and south-eastern Europe. The region's growth was 5.7% in 2007 and of the same order in the first half of 2008, based on the important transfers of the EU structural funds and the incentives that continue to stimulate outsourcing from Western Europe (Eurostat, 2008).

The economic development of the euro zone was reflected in 2.6% in 2007. The engine of this growth was the general acceleration of investment spending, especially in Germany, the rebound in construction and the robust expansion of exports. Private consumption remains weak. The harmonized consumer price index was 3.1% year-on-year. In this context, the ECB decided to maintain intervention interest rates at 4% during the final months of the year, reiterating the presence of upward risks to medium-term price stability.

ANALYSIS OF THE SPANISH ECONOMY 2007-2008

The recent evolution of the Spanish economy, according to the National Accounting figures and their forecasts (Bank of Spain, Economic Bulletin, September 2008), is undergoing substantial changes in its behaviour in the current year, where the contraction has been made very palpable.

Spain currently has, with the updated municipal register, a population of 46,063,500 inhabitants (+ 1.9%, compared to 2007), of which 5,220,600 inhabitants are foreigners, which represents 15.5 per 100 of the total population. Without the

Figure 1. Growth of the Spanish economy
Source: INE and National Accounting.

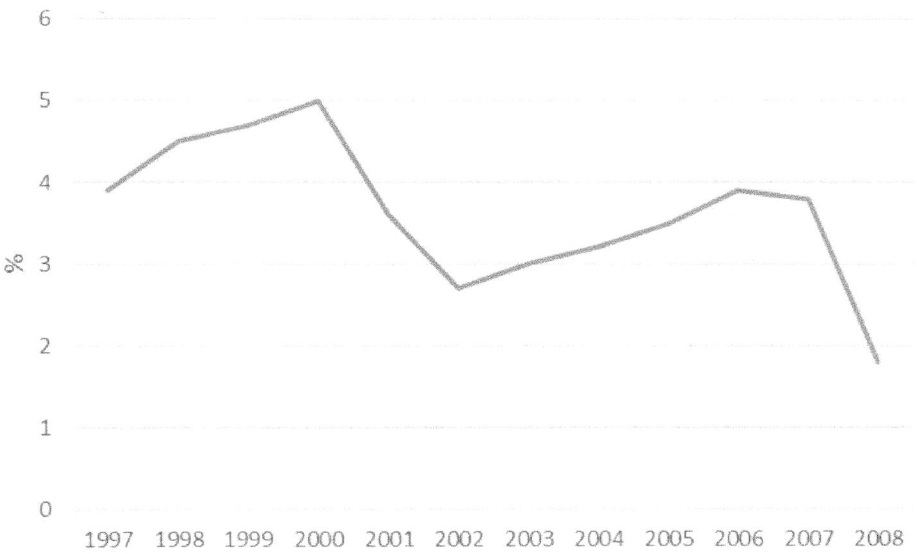

presence of foreigners, our country would have negative population growth and would not have experienced the spectacular economic development of the last decade.

The GDP of Spain in 2007 showed a profile of slight deceleration, closing the year with an average increase of 3.8%, one tenth less than in 2006. Even so, the growth of the Spanish economy was higher than that of the Euro Zone and that of the EU as a whole, whose rates were 2.7% and 2.9%, respectively. According to Eurostat 2006 data, Spain with 22,152 euros exceeded Italy in GDP per capita in parity of power of purchase, that is to say, 105% of the GDP per capita of the average of the Europe of the 27, but it is still five percentage points below the countries of the Eurozone.

The Spanish Gross Domestic Product at market prices amounts to 1,049,848 million euros. Of these, 27,342 correspond to the agricultural and fishing branches (2.60%), 27.807 to the energy branches (2.65%), 141.838 to the industrial branches (13.51%), construction amounts to 115.181 million euros (14.40%) and services with 628.627 million euros reach 59.88%. Finally, net taxes on products account for the remaining 6.96%.

If at the beginning of 2007 the growth rate of the national product reached a maximum of 4.1%, during the following quarters and, especially, in the last months of the year a lower intensity of the growth rate was observed (3.5% in the fourth quarter of 2007) that had its main origin in the slowdown in national demand.

Figure 2. GDP growth at basic prices by Autonomy in 2007
Source: FUNCAS. Cuadernos de Información Económica nº 203

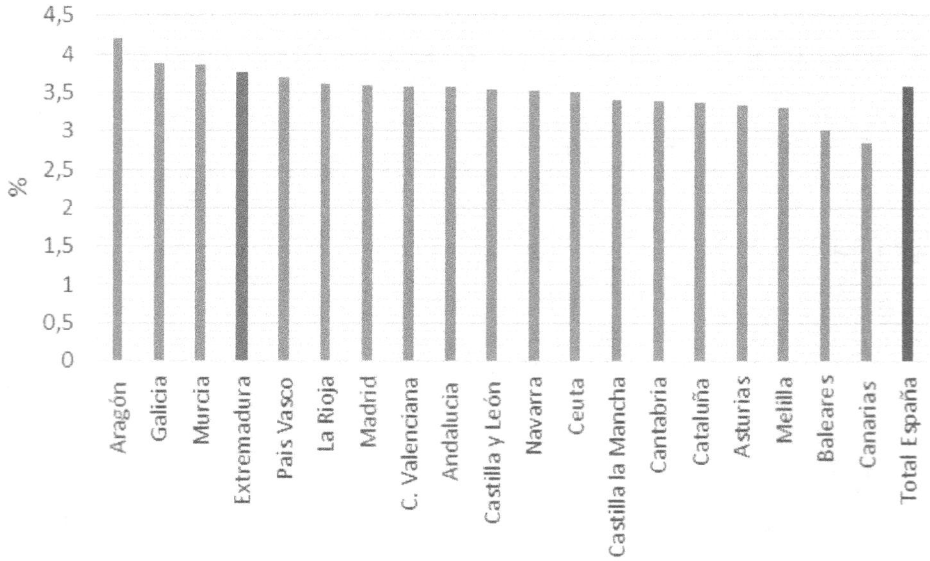

During the first semester of 2008, the GDP has been reduced to a growth of 1.8% (Figures 1 and 2). This intensification in the pace of GDP slowdown has been the result of the lower strength of national demand, whose annual growth rate decreased by 1.3 percentage points (pp), to 1.4%, which was partially offset for the improvement of the foreign sector, whose contribution to the growth of the economy became positive for the first time in seven years. All components of internal spending slowed except public consumption and investment in other constructions. Thus, the expansion rate of private consumption decreased by 1 percentage point, up to 1.2%, while the growth rate of investment in capital goods slowed down by almost 3 pp, to 2.3%. However, the component that underwent the most rigorous adjustment was the investment in housing, whose rate of variation was cut by more than 5 percentage points, to -6.3%.

Regarding foreign trade, it should be noted that both exports and, above all, imports of goods and services slowed down, growing at rates of 4.1% and 2.3%, respectively, well below the previous quarter (4.3% and 4.1%). From the supply perspective, the moderation of the activity affected all branches, with the exception of non-market services and, especially, energy, and employment advanced at a rate of 0.4% (1pp less than in the first quarter of 2008). The loss of dynamism of this variable was more pronounced than that of the product, which meant that the growth rate of apparent labour productivity continued to increase moderately (by two tenths, up to 1.4%).

The activity rate in the second quarter of 2008 was 59.76, which means an annual growth of 0.90%, while the unemployment rate reached 10.44% of the active population, with growth 2.4% year-on-year. (INE, 2008). Unemployment has increased in all sectors, largely motivated by the completion of a large part of the residential work, which has induced effects on other sectors and subsectors of activity (Figure 3).

This fact, and the end of the summer season, causes the service sector to lead the increase in unemployment: 56,897 (3.8%). The largest percentage increase is registered in the group without previous employment: 15,160 people (6.4%), many of them young people who have finished their studies in this month.

The variations in the rest of the sectors are the following: under construction, 14,241 (3.3%), industry, 7,002 (2.1%) and agriculture 2,067 (2.4%). By sex, male unemployment stands at 1,218,732, rising 56,541 (4.8%) and female unemployment in 1,406,636, increasing by 38,826 (2.8%).

In relation to the previous year, male unemployment rises by 431,381 (54.7%) and female unemployment is 176,624 (14.3%). Among young people under 25, unemployment rises in September by 30,111 people (10.4%) compared to the previous month, and among those over 25 it rises by 65,256.

The number of contracts registered during the month of September has been 1,501,595, which represents a decrease of 94,326 (-5.9%) over the same month last year. The accumulated contracting reaches 12,736,235, which means 1,121,147 contracts less (-8%) than in the same period of the previous year.

In September 173,481 contracts of indefinite nature, have been registered, the third best figure of the month of September, after those of the last two years, in full force of the labour reform. Indefinite hiring represents 11.6% of the total contracts signed and represents a reduction of 18,808 (-9.7%) over the same month of the previous year.

In cumulative quantities, 1,490,192 contracts have been made until September 2008, with a year-on-year reduction of 172,582 (-10.3%).

Analysis of the Economy of Extremadura in 2007-2008

Extremadura is a region with an extension that amounts to 41,633 km^2 (the fifth in size, assuming 8.2% of the national area), and a population that totals 1,089,900 inhabitants (representing 2.4%, of the set of demoFigureic staff in Spain), resulting in a really low density (26.18 inhabitants / km^2).

According to the National Institute of Statistics of Extremadura, it grew 3.9% in 2007, two tenths above the same macromagnitude for the whole of Spain, which

Figure 3. Unemployment rate in Spain from 2004 to 2008
Source: INE and Ministry of Labour and Social Affairs

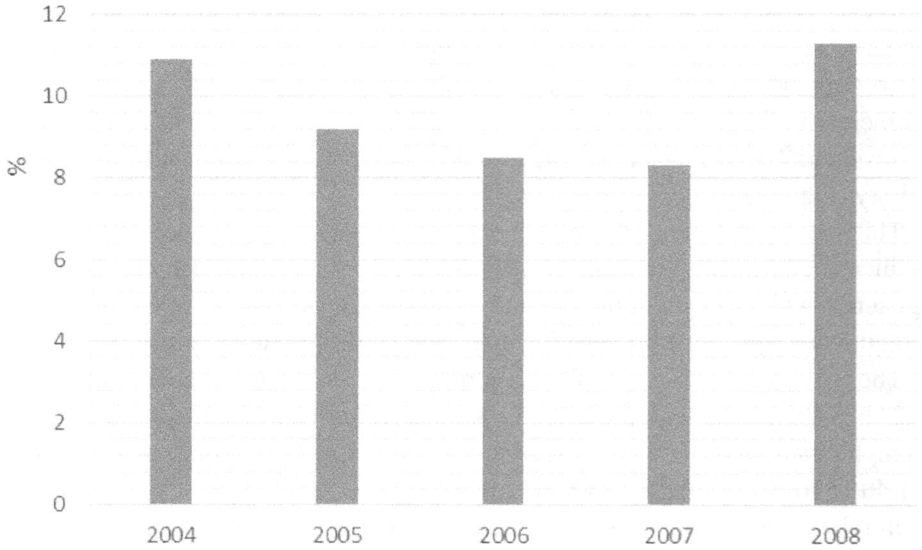

stood at 3.7%. By sectors, the agriculture in Extremadura increased by 3.9% and in Spain by 3.3%; the industry 3% and 4%, respectively; construction 4.3% and 4%, and the GVA of services increased in Extremadura by 3.4% and 3.8 in Spain. For the year 2008 the results are less optimistic, even so Extremadura is resisting the crisis better than other Spanish regions (Figure 4).

According to these data, another year it was the construction sector that contributed most to the growth of GVA in our region, while the industry was the one that had the least favourable behaviour.

The estimations of the Regional Accounting of Spain of the INE are in line with the previous ones, although they show some sectoral variations. The regional GVA grew 4%, and in terms of GDP pm 3.9%, very slightly above the same growth rates of both macromagnitudes for the national group, which were 3.9% and 3.8%, respectively.

For the INE, the sector whose GVA grew the most was energy, with 7.1%; the services followed, 4.2%; Next, agriculture, livestock and fishing stood at 3.8%; then the construction, 3.4%, and finally the industry, 2.6%.

From these data it is agreed that construction has become the sector that has helped most of Extremadura's growth in recent years, but that for the first time in 2007 increases to a lesser extent than the growth rate of the Extremadura economy as a whole.

Figure 4. Comparison of productive sectors between Extremadura and Spain.
Source: Hispalink, February 2008

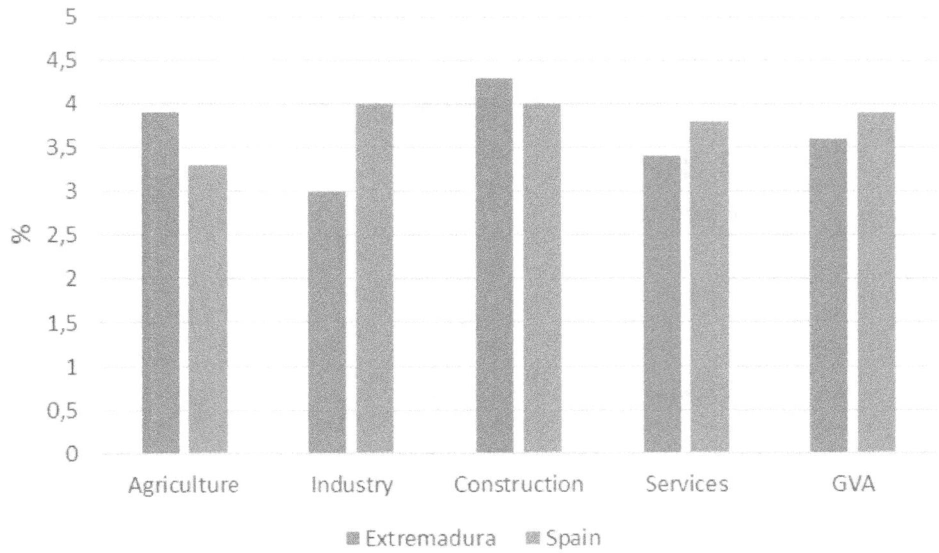

The Savings Banks Foundation gives Extremadura a slightly lower growth, as

Table 1. Data by economic sector for 2006/2007 comparative between Spain and Extremadura

	2006				2007				Real Growth 07/06	
	Extremadura		Spain		Extremadura		Spain			
	€ Million	% of total	€ Million	% of total	€ Million	% of total	€ Million	% of total	Extremadura	Spain
Agriculture	1857,3	11,88	34505,2	3,87	1980,9	11,82	38083,9	3,57.	2,70	1,58
Marine Fishing	0,0	0,0	1742,9	0,19	0,0	0,0	1820,1	0,18	0,0	1,04
Energy and Water	678,4	4,32	26779,0	2,85	734,8	4,29	28,882,2	2,84	3,20	2,81
Processing Industry	1088,4	8,82	151683,0	18,15	1133,5	8,72	160288,0	15,88	3,10	2,61
Construction	2339,5	14,93	106628,9	11,35	2599,8	15,17	117040,0	11,59	3,80	3,69
Private Services	6635,1	42,35	507223,3	58,99	7190,5	42,81	546913,2	54,18	4,30	4,07
Public Services	3089,9	19,72	110846,2	11,80	3308,8	19,90	118741,5	11,78	3,80	3,60
Total	15666,6	100	990408,5	100	16875,9	100	1009566,9	100	3,76	3,58

Source: INE

Figure 5. Contribution of each Sector at basic prices. Extremadura vs Spain 2007
Source: FUNCAS. Cuadernos de Información Económica nº 203

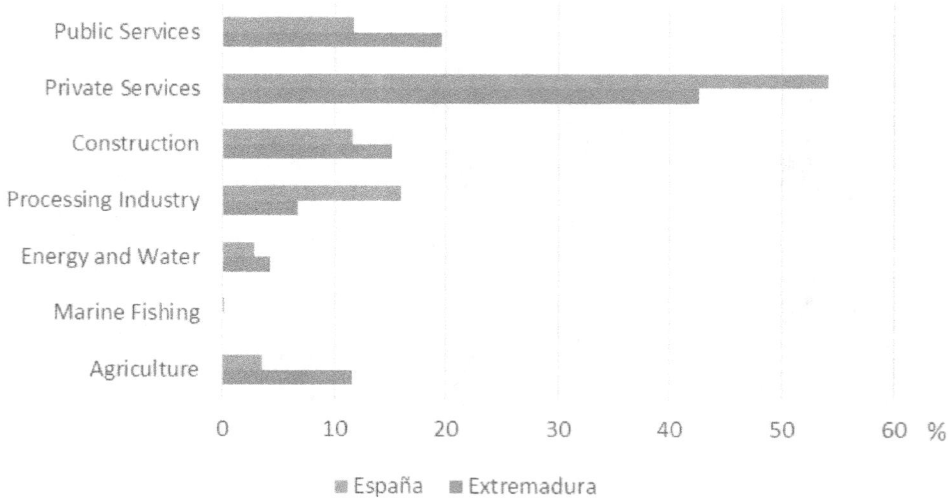

it points out that the Gross Domestic Product at basic prices increased by 3.76% in 2007, above the increase experienced by the Spanish economy, which it did at a rate 3.58%, almost two tenths less. By sectors, private services contributed the most to regional growth, 4.3%, while in Spain they increased 4.07%; construction continued, 3.8% in our region and 3.69% in the whole country; public services were then placed, 3.6% in both cases; energy and water, 3.2% and 2.81%, respectively; the processing industry, 3.1% and 2.61%, and finally agriculture, 2.7% in Extremadura and 1.58% in the whole of Spain.

The Table 1 gives an account of employment and productivity data. The latter is obtained by dividing GDP between jobs, and decreased by 0.04% in Extremadura, while in Spain it increased by 0.66%. In 2006, these two percentages, respectively, were 3.25% and 2.08%

CONCLUSION

The previous Figures elaborated from the data offered by FUNCAS, show a very unique aspect when it comes to the economic analysis: the productive structure of Extremadura and Spain. Comparing both, interesting conclusions are drawn in the case of our Autonomous Community. It indicates that it has a way to getting closer to the national average in terms of this structure and, therefore, in terms of production.

In Extremadura agriculture still has a great weight. In 2007, regional GDP contributed 11.62%, slightly below the 11.86% of the previous year. In the Spanish case, these percentages were, respectively, 3.57% and 3.67%.

The opposite of the above is the processing industry. The percentage that this sector represented in 2007 on regional GDP was 6.72%, and 6.82% a year before. In Spain these percentages were, respectively, 15.88% and 16.15%. Several conclusions can also be drawn from this reality. The first is that, both in Extremadura and in Spain, the contribution of the industrial sector decreased. Secondly, and in the case of our region, that 6.72% implied that the GDP of this sector over the regional total accounts for an economy with low levels of industrialization.

Regarding the energy and water sector, its contribution to regional GDP was 4.29%, and 4.32% in 2006. In the national group, these percentages were 2.84% in 2007 and 2.85% the previous year. Therefore, a distortion can also be seen here, which would be very much in favour of Extremadura if it were not because the production of electricity, which is a lot in terms of GDP, does not represent so much in terms of income, since a part of the added values that are generated go outside the region (Figure 5).

Construction is of great importance in Extremadura. The weight of this sector is much higher in our region, compared to what it means nationally. In 2007, construction GDP represented 15.17% of regional GDP, and 14.93% in 2006. National contributions, respectively, were 11.59% and 11.35% (Figure 5)

The set of services contributed 62.2% to Extremadura's GDP in 2007, and 62.07% a year earlier. In Spain as a whole, these two percentages were, respectively, 65.93% and 65.79%. Therefore the services have a lower weight in our region, but where the difference is greater when it distinguishes between private services and public services, with a great weight, as we will see, of the latter in the Extremadura economy.

In 2007, private services accounted for 42.61% in Extremadura, and 42.35% the previous year. In Spain they were, respectively, 54.17% and 53.99%. In turn, public services accounted for 19.59% and 19.72% in 2006 in our region, while in our country they were 11.76% and 11.8%, respectively.

As a synthesis, of the comparison between Extremadura and Spain of the weight of the different productive sectors in their respective GDP, clear imbalances are observed in the Extremadura case: the still notorious weight of agriculture and livestock in regional production; a relatively small importance of the processing industry; an oversized energy and water sector, compared to the same sector at the national level, which also contributes little in terms of income; a construction sector that has a high incidence in regional production; a much smaller subsector of private services in our region, while public services, which are financed with public resources, are decisive for our GDP. Correcting this situation and all these structural imbalances, is the main commitment to the future of Extremadura in the economic plane.

REFERENCES AND ADDITIONAL READING

Andrés, J., & Ferri, J. (2017). *Precio de la vivienda, empleo y PIB en España. Estudios sobre la Economía Española (09)*. FEDEA.

Arellano, M., & Bentolilla, S. (Eds). (2009). La burbuja inmobiliaria: causas y responsables. En Los orígenes inmobiliarios de la crisis actual, capítulo 7 en Antonio Cabrales et al. (Eds). Banco de España. Retrieved from http://www.bde.es

Ayuso, J., & Restoy, F. (2006). Precios de la vivienda y de los alquileres: Un enfoque de valoración de activos de equilibrio. *Journal of Empirical Finance*, *0609*, 371–388. doi:10.1016/j.jempfin.2005.10.004

Banco Mundial. Retrieved from http://www.bancomundial.org

Barlevy, G. (2007). Economic theory and asset bubbles. *Economic Perspectives*, *31*(3), 44–59.

Gómez Bujía, D. (2016). La crisis inmobiliaria española, motivaciones y perspectivas. Trabajo de fin de grado. Universidad da Coruña.

Case, K. E., & Shiller, R. J. (2003). Is there a bubble in the housing market? Cowles Foundation Paper(1089), 299-362.

de Molina, M., & Luis, J. (2010). *La economía española en la crisis mundial*. Banco de España.

Doménech, R. (2011). *El impacto económico de la construcción y de la actividad inmobiliaria*. BBVA Research.

Domínguez, B. G. (2009). Creación y destrucción de la burbuja inmobiliaria de España. En La primera crisis global: procesos, consecuencias, medidas. Revista ICE Nº: 850.

Eurostat. (2008). Retrieved from http://www.ec.europa.eu/eurostat

Fondo Monetario Internacional. (2008).

Fuentes Castro, D. (2009). Una nota sobre el exceso de oferta de viviendas y la duración del ajuste del sector. Boletín Económico del ICE (2958), 15-24.

Funcas. (2007). Cuadernos de Información Económica nº 203.

García Montalvo, J. (2003). La vivienda en España: desgravaciones, burbujas y otras historias. Perspectivas del sistema financiero (78), 1-43.

Hornero, A. (2008). La crisis de las hipotecas subprime y el riesgo de credit crunch. *Revista de Economía Mundial*, (18): 195–204.

Instituto Nacional de Estadística. (2008).

Instituto Nacional de Estadística. Retrieved from http://www.ine.es

Leal Maldonado, J., & Martínez del Olmo, A. (2017). Tendencias recientes de la política de vivienda en España. *Cuadernos de las relaciones laborales, 35*(1), 15-41.

López, T. J. (2009). Crisis in mobiliaria, crisis crediticia y recesión económica en España. En Papeles de Europa. Vol. 19-2009, (pp. 82-107).

López García, M. Á. (2011). *Precios de la vivienda, booms inmobiliarios y política impositiva: ¿podría España haber sido diferente?* Huelva: XIV Encuentro de Economía Aplicada.

Fernández Luna, M. (2016). Análisis económico de la crisis del sector inmobiliario en España (2007-2013). (Doctoral thesis). Universidad de Sevilla.

Torrero Mañas, A. (2010). La crisis financiera y sus efectos sobre la economía española. Universidad de Alcalá de Henares.

Ministerio de Economía y Hacienda. Gobierno de España. Retrieved from http://www.mineco.gob.es

Ministerio de Fomento. Gobierno de España. Retrieved from http://www.fomento.gob.es)

Naredo, J. M. (2009). La cara oculta de la crisis. El fin del boom inmobiliario y sus consecuencias. En Revista de economía crítica, 7 (pp. 118-133).

Rodríguez López, J. (2006). *Financiación de la vivienda en un contexto de tipos de interés crecientes*. Lleida: IX Semana de Estudios Urbanos.

Rodríguez López, J. (2008). La situación del mercado de vivienda en España. Boletín Económico del ICE (2951), 11-23.

Romero, A. (2004). "Migraciones". En Tendencias Demográficas durante el siglo XX en España. Instituto Nacional de Estadística, 207-253.

Rubio de Juan, M. A. (2006). *Flujos de inversión de no residentes en inmuebles residenciales. Flujos de inversión de residentes en inmuebles residenciales fuera de España*. Estudios y Publicaciones del Ministerio de la Vivienda en España.

Sánchez Vera, P., & Riella, A. (2010). Globalización y perspectivas de la integración regional. Murcia: edit.um.

Scanlon, K., Lunde, J., & Whitehead, C. (2008). En respuesta a las viviendas y crisis financieras: Préstamos hipotecarios, productos de hipotecas y las políticas del gobierno. *Revista Internacional de Política de Vivienda*, *11*(1), 23–49.

Servicio Público de Empleo Estatal. Retrieved from http://www.sepe.es

Suárez, J. L. (2016). Proyección de las necesidades de vivienda en España. IESE Business School.

Chapter 7
Analysis of Housing for Rent in Borderlands:
A Case Study Approach From the Iberian Peninsula

Jacinto Garrido Velarde
Universidad de Extremadura, Spain

Betina Cavaco de São Pedro
Universidad de Extremadura, Spain

Consuelo Mora
Fundicotex, Spain

ABSTRACT

The current problems in the construction, sale, purchase, offer, or search of housing, present questions about the future of the real estate market, questions that will have to be possible solutions in the medium and long term. This document proposes obtaining primary information through "Opinion survey aimed at the population on housing and its influence on the land market," through an applied methodology and variables associated with the survey. This chapter elaborates a methodological proposal to analyze the situation of the houses for rent in the border city of Badajoz to provide a document of support to the professionals and technicians who are dedicated to the territory and urban planning, to solve the problems about the construction, sale, purchase, offer, or search of housing.

DOI: 10.4018/978-1-7998-2513-5.ch007

INTRODUCTION

The right to housing is a commodity of the first necessity that is recognized in the Universal Declaration of Human Rights[1]. The European Union, despite not having direct competence in housing policy, which is understood as a domain of the national responsibility of each Member State, adhered to the new commitments agreed at the II Conference on Hungarian Settlements - Habitat II[2].

The Habitat Agenda puts the issue of housing at a higher level of social commitment, or the creation of conditions, so that citizens have "adequate housing for all", which, in general terms, means: provide security in the purchase of housing, promote the right to decent housing, provide equal opportunities in access to land ownership, promote equal opportunities in access to credit. For the Habitat Agenda «living in a suitable home, it is not simply having a roof over your head; A suitable home must also be sufficiently large, bright, heated and ventilated, offer a certain privacy, be physically accessible, must allow you to live safely and allow you to enjoy the safety of your occupation, present a stable and durable structure, be equipped with infrastructure, basic, to be adequate from an ecological and sanitary point of view ... in short, to be located at a reasonable distance from workplaces and basic services, all for an acceptable price».

Reviewing the different European legislations, the common objective of the policies in all countries, it could be summed up in the same premise: the right of all citizens to access decent housing. In Spain, for example, the right to housing is recognized in article 47 of the Constitution as follows: «All Spaniards have the right to decent and adequate housing. The public authorities shall promote the necessary conditions and establish the pertinent norms to enforce this right, regulating the use of the land in accordance with the general interest to prevent speculation. The Community will participate in the capital gains generated by the urban action of public entities».

Note that, if the right to adequate housing is included among the fundamental rights of man, the existence of this right does not necessarily imply public production or property ownership by individuals. That right refers only to use.

Although several countries, particularly the Mediterranean ones, tried to achieve the social objectives of housing through measures to increase the supply in the market, property titling is not the only means of ensuring accessibility and quality of housing for family aggregates of weaker yields. In fact, as regards the satisfaction of this social good, most of the interventions are aimed at financial support, both directly, through the delivery of subsidies or indirect, such as the reduction of fiscal expenses.

As Alonso Rodríguez (2002) argues, in many European countries other dimensions begin to appear in the objectives of housing policy that try to go a little further in regard to the ability to choose in reference, both to the diversity of the property regime and to social cohesion and the variety of social classes, ages and circumstances of the housing enclaves; or the right not only to housing, but also to a healthy, safe and ecologically sustainable environment, the right to the city and the right to quality of life; or even the right to a home with a reasonable price. In this sense, housing ceases to be a right to guarantee itself and begins to be understood as an active and fundamental part of the city's policy from a sustainable and environmental point of view, where care for the environment and the city prevails existing against excessive growth.

MATERIALS AND METHODS

The sample is composed of 200 individuals, where 71.6% are registered and 28.4% are floating population.

Of the 200 people surveyed, 55% belong to the female sex; and, 45%, male.

98% of the population surveyed are of Spanish nationality; the rest of the population, 2%, corresponds to people of different nationality from the Spanish; Among them, the majority are Brazilian, Portuguese and Cuban nationals.

Civil Status

In Figure 1 below on the marital status of the Badajoz respondents, 47.6% of the surveyed population is single; 42.9% are married (or are in fact partners); 5.4% belong to the group of divorced or separated; and 4.1% are widowers.

Figure 1. Marital status of respondents from Badajoz.

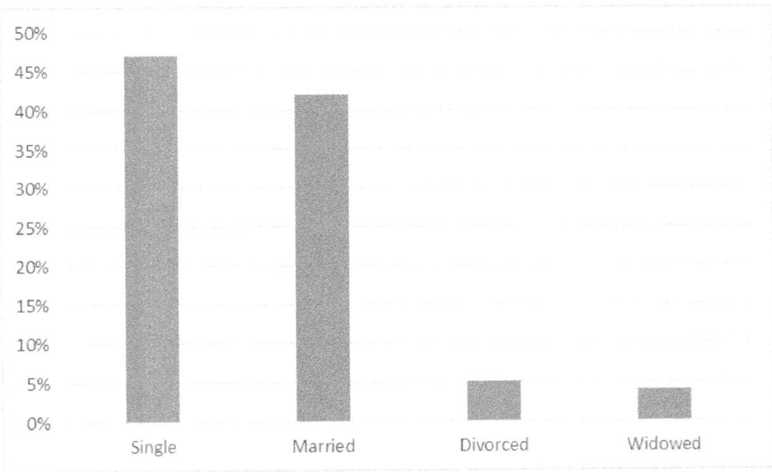

Figure 2. Level of studies of the Badajoz respondents.

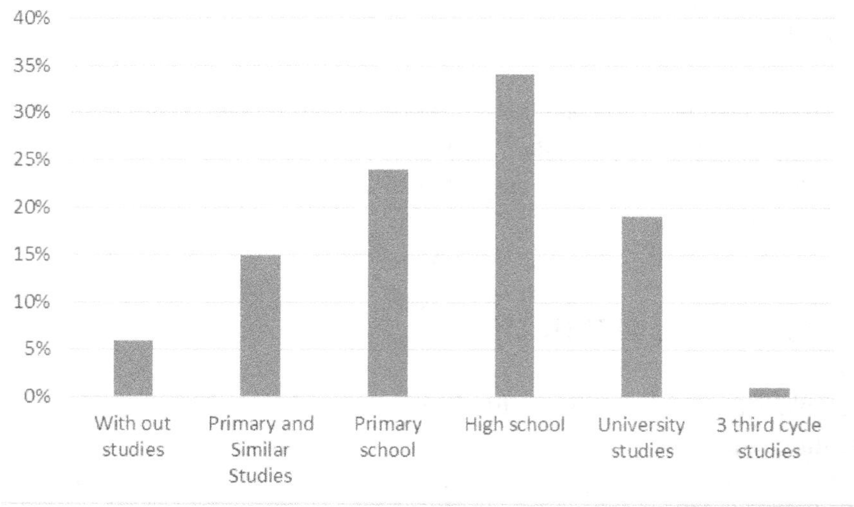

Education Level

Employment Situation

Figure 3. Employment situation of Badajoz respondents

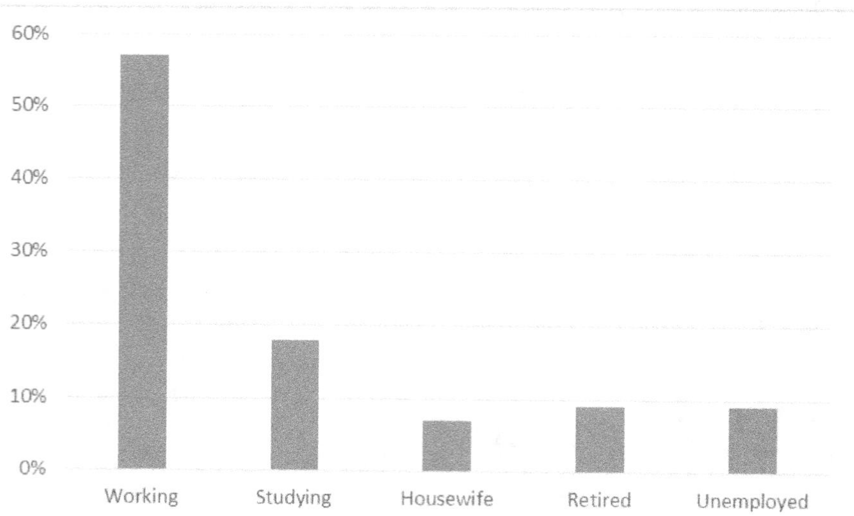

Figure 4. Figure on the Social Security contribution scheme of those who work

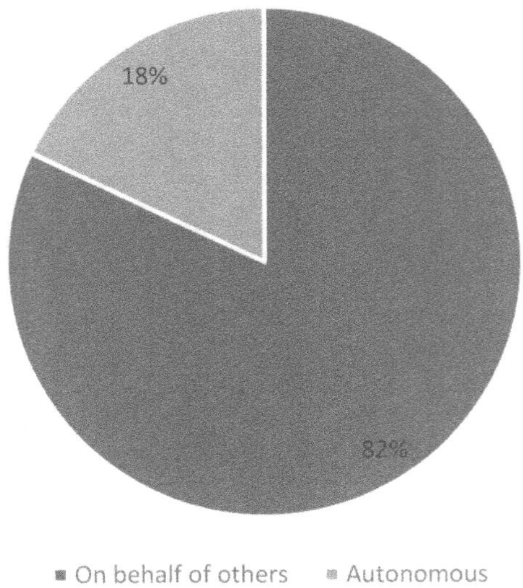

Social Security Quotation Regime

Type of Contract

Figure 5. Type of contract for workers who are employed by others.

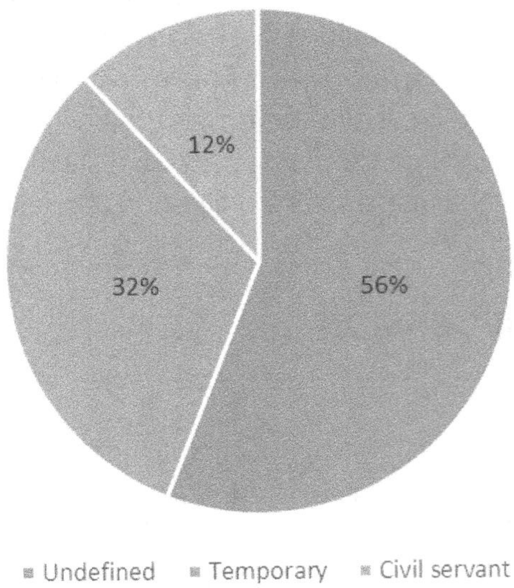

Figure 6. Monthly income

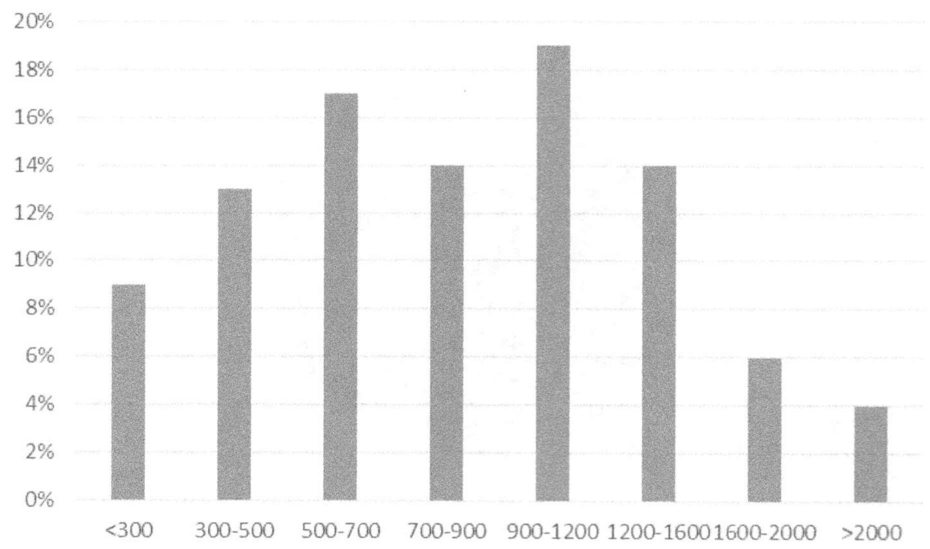

Salary

As for the monthly income we can note that the highest percentage (18.7%) belongs to monthly income of between 900 and 1,200 €; It also highlights the range of 500 to 700 €, which has a weight of 16.5% over the total population. In Figure 6, the ranges of values represent the monthly income with their respective percentages.

53.3% of the surveyed population have no monthly income of over 900 €.

And there is 22.4% of the population that has monthly income of less than 500 €.

As an indicative note, those that reach monthly yields between 2,000 € and 2,400 € correspond to 1.8% of the population surveyed; while 1.1% earn from 2,400 to 2,800 €; and 1.2% had revenues exceeding 2,800 €. It should be noted that 3.3% of the population surveyed did not answer the question of monthly income.

RESULTS AND DISCUSSION

Type of Tenure

Of the population surveyed in Badajoz there is a percentage of 72.1% that lives on the property and 27.9% of the population is rented (as shown in Figure 7). As an indicative note, there is 0.7% of the total population that are in a mixed regime,

Figure 7. Figure on the type of tenure

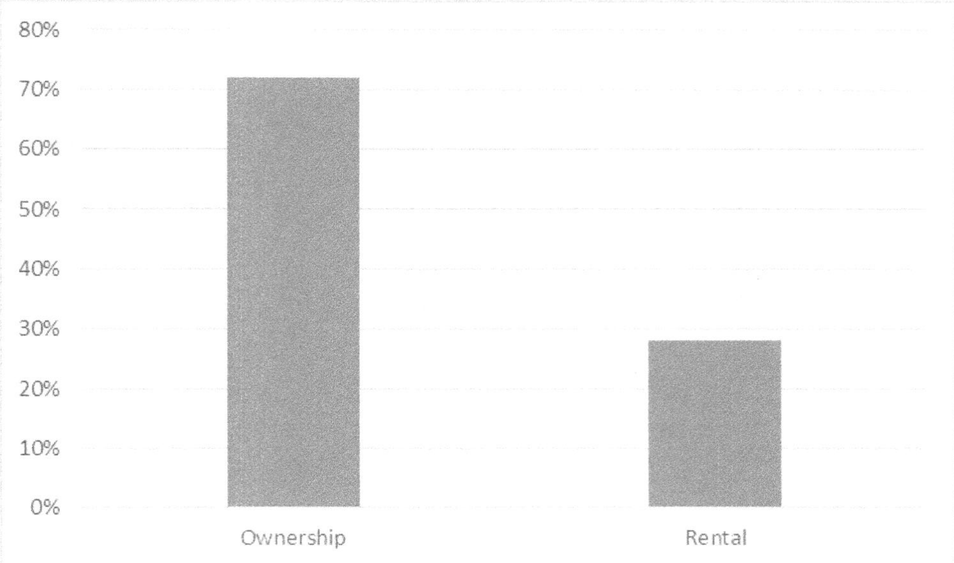

whose value is included in the rental scheme. The mixed regime indicates that the individual is in the municipality where he is surveyed on a rental basis, although he has a property in another place, therefore having his fixed residence in another municipality.

Type of Residence

As can be seen in Figure 8, of the total population surveyed (200 people), almost 38.8% reside in a block house of their own; 29.9% own a single-family home; 3.0% live in apartments; and 0.4% live in a study of their property.

Of the total surveyed population, it can also be said that, in relation to rent, 22.9% reside in rental in block dwellings; 2.2% have rented a single-family home; 1.4% live on rent in an apartment; and, 0.6%, in one study.

Of the mixed regime, the percentages do not exceed 0.5% in the four typologies (single-family, block, apartment and studio).

Residence for Rent

The analysis carried out below focuses only on the individuals that are renting. Of the total surveyed population, 27.9% are on a rental basis. Of that 27.9%, their experience and their perspective on rent are analysed.

Figure 8. Figure on the type of residence of those who are in property and rent

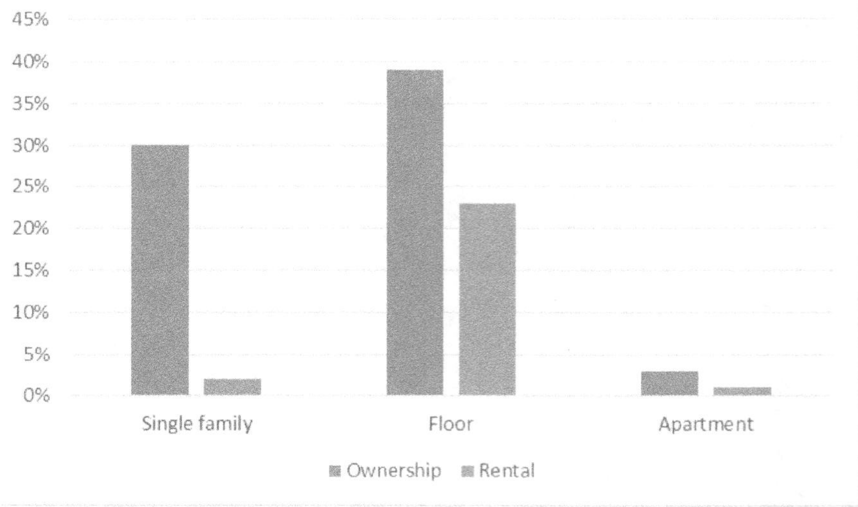

Rental Time

About the time they have been renting, and as presented in Figure 9, 55.8% have been living on rent for 1 to 5 years; 29.4% live on rent for more than 5 years; and 15.3% were in this situation less than 1 year ago.

Figure 9. Figure about the time they have been renting.

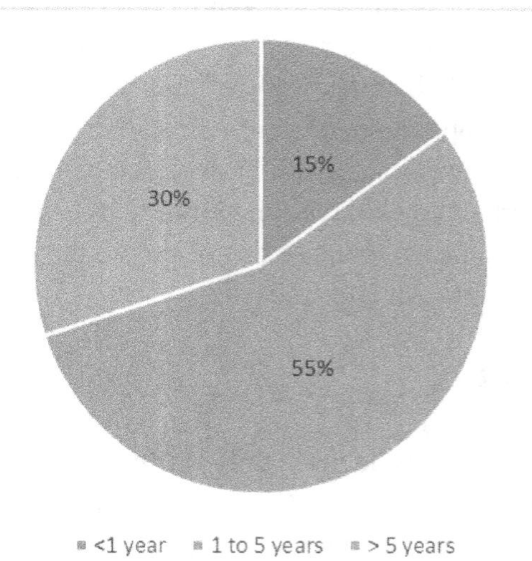

Figure 10. Figure on the main reason for living in rent.

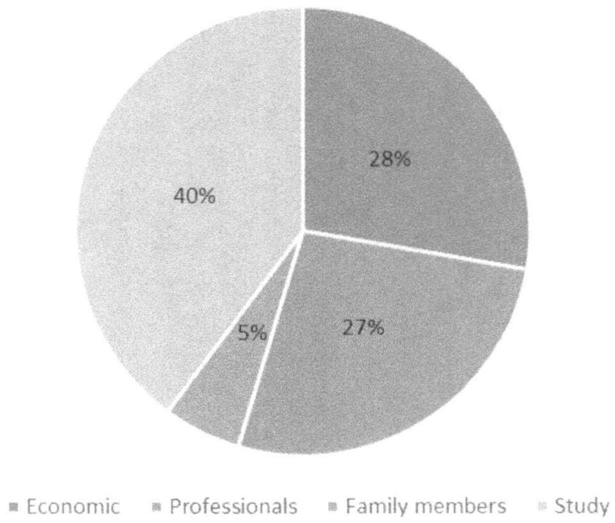

Reason for Living for Rent

Of the almost 28% of the population that is renting, 42.8% indicated that the main reason for being in this situation were the studies; 30.0% rent for economic reasons; 20.8% consider professional reasons the main reason to rent; and 5.8% indicated family reasons. Figure 10 shows the commented percentages. As an indicative note there was only 0.6% of responses that indicated "other" as the main reason for renting.

Temporary or Permanent Rental

When asked about whether they considered renting as something transitory or definitive in their lives, 88.2% said they considered rent something transitory; while 11.8% of the surveyed population that is for renting responded that they considered it final. It is shown in Figure 11.

Preferred Location

When asked in which area they preferred to live those who are renting, 75.1% opted for the Badajoz Centre area; 7.0% indicated the southern zone; 6.7% prefer the North zone; 2.6% considered the Northwest area; and 2.2% like the East to live. 0.3% of respondents replied that they preferred the Northeast (Figure 12).

Figure 11. Figure on considering rent as transitory or definitive.

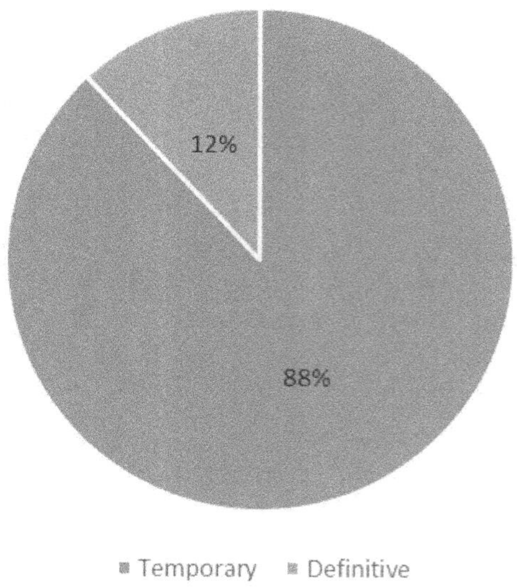

It is still mentioned that the West, Southeast and Southwest zones had the same percentage weight in the total preferences of the respondents who are for rent, that is, 1.6%. 1.3% did not answer this question.

Figure 12. Figure on the preferred location to live.

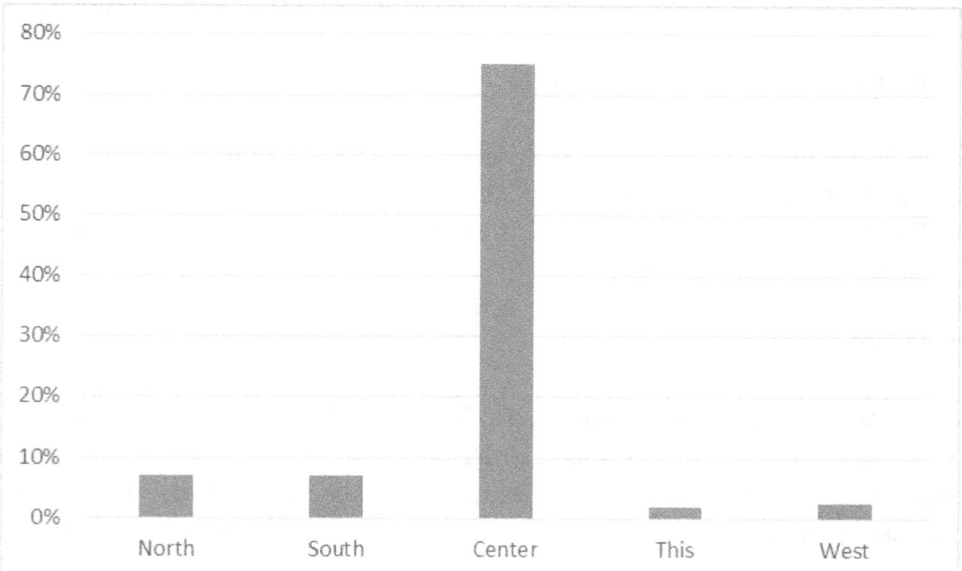

Figure 13. Figure on the preference when renting.

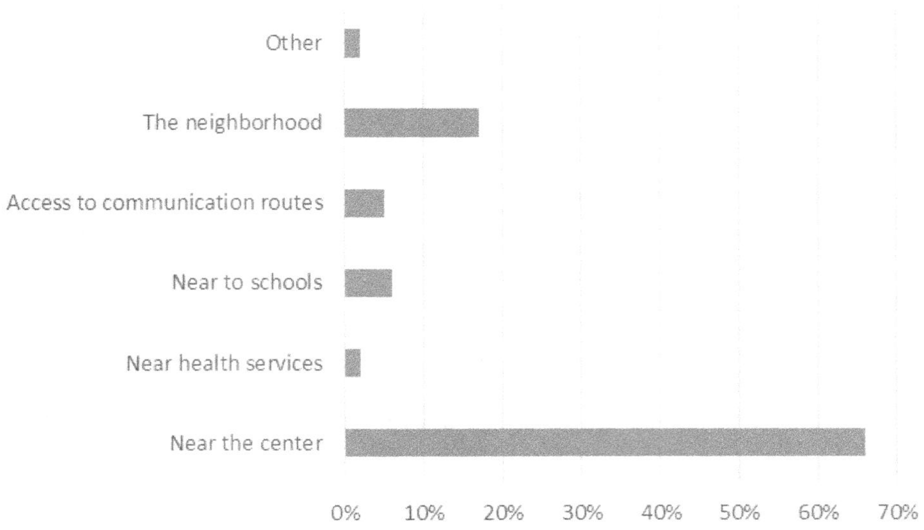

Preference When Renting

When asked about what is the first thing they would consider when renting, as can be seen in figure 13, of those who are renting, 65.5% answered the proximity to the centre; while 16.9% take into account the neighbourhood / neighbourhood before; 6.4% prefer to live near educational services / schools; For 5.4% of respondents who are for rent, access to communication channels is the first thing they would consider when renting a home; 2.2% seek proximity to health services and, the same percentage, considered "another" reason. As an indicative note, 1.3% did not answer.

Rented Housing With or Without Furniture

On the preference of renting a home with or without furniture, of which they are for rent (remember that they represent 27.9% of the total), 77.0% prefer a furnished home, while 23.0% prefer one that is unfurnished (Figure 14).

Rental Price Of Housing

Of the population of Badajoz that is renting, 50.5% pay from 300 to 400 € per month; 24.3% spend between 400 and 500 € for their home; 22.0% pay between

Figure 14. Figure on the preference of having a rented house with furniture or without furniture.

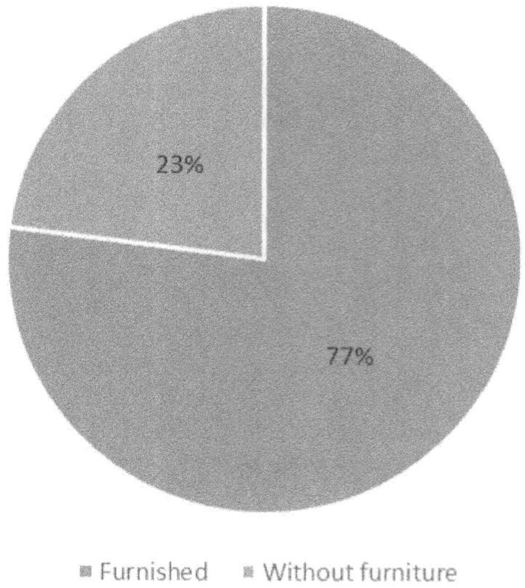

200 and 300 € per month; 2.9% pay from € 500 to € 600; and 0.3% spend on rent more than 600 € (Figure 15).

Figure 15. Figure on the payment of rent (whole house).

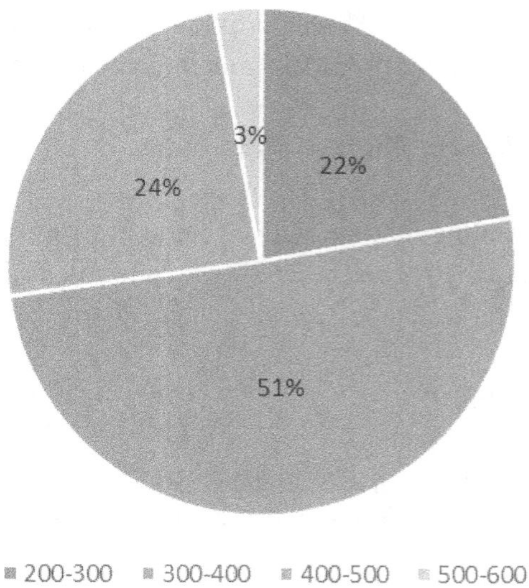

Figure 16. Figure on the percentage of rent (whole house).

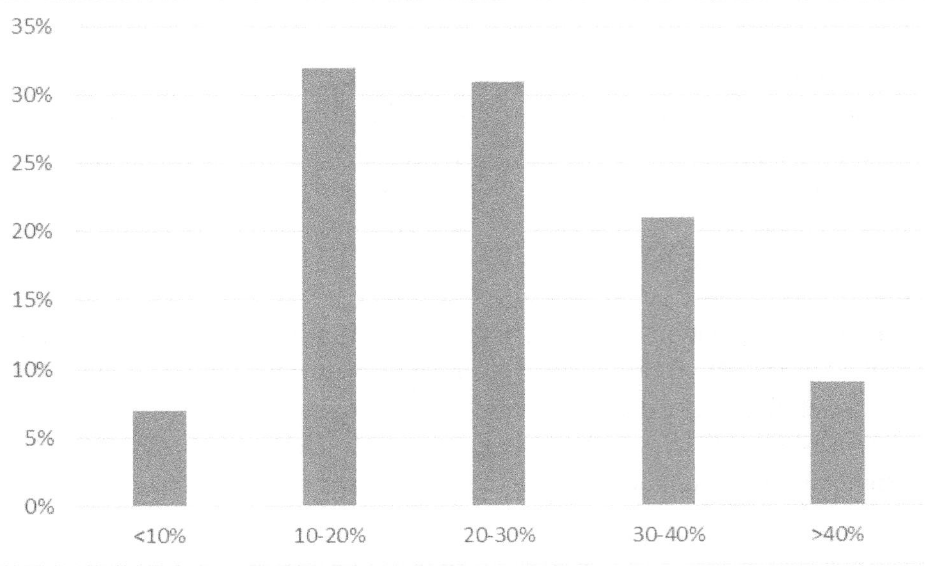

Figure 17. Figure on the main rental problem

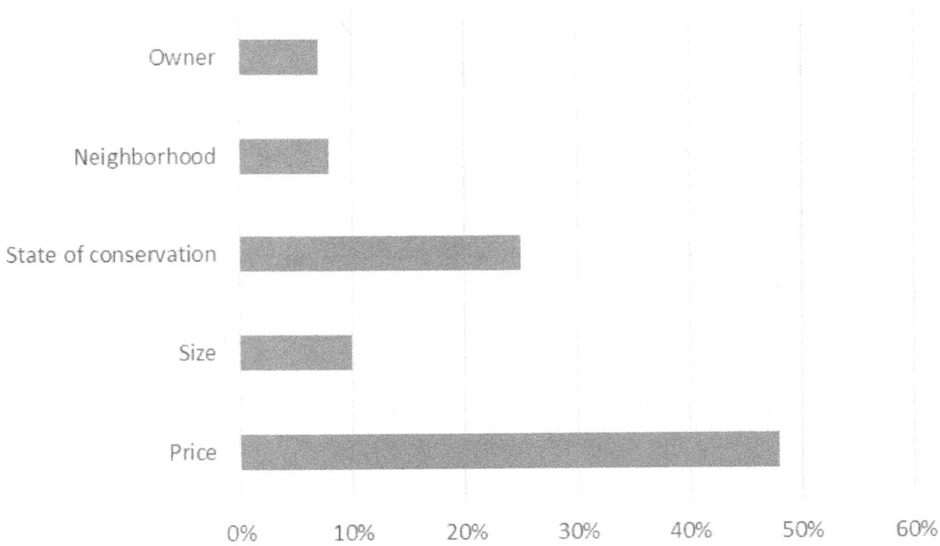

Percentage of Income to Pay the Rent

On the percentage of monthly income that goes to the rental of a house, and as can be seen in Figure 16, 32.3% spend between 10% and 20% to pay the rent; 30.7% have a monthly rental expense of 20% to 30% of their income; 20.8% spend between 30 and 40% of their monthly income; 8.6% of rental respondents pay more than 40% of their income in a home; 7.3% allocate less than 10%. 0.3% did not answer.

Main Rental Problem

The surveyed population living on rent (which represents 27.9% of the total respondents) replied that the price was the main problem with the rental (with 47.9% of the answers); almost a quarter (24.9%) responded that the state of conservation of the houses was; 10.2% said the main problem was size; 8.3% considered it to be the neighbourhood / community; and for 7.0% the owners were the main problem. 1.3% answered "other" and 0.3% did not answer the question (Figure 17).

CONCLUSION

The following conclusions are drawn from this study:

1. Of the 200 respondents, more than 80% have been living for rent for more than 1 year, of which 55% have been living in this type of residence for 1 to 5 years.
2. Note that in the city of Badajoz, because it is a university city, 42% live on rent for study reasons and 30% for economic reasons
3. From the answers of the respondents, it is extracted that almost 90% of those who live on rent do so temporarily until their economy allows them to have a home on the property, something very characteristic of Spanish society.
4. In relation to the characteristics of living more than 50% prefer to rent a home in the centre of the city and furnished.
5. Highlight that respondents allocate between 10% and 30% of their rent salary and consider that the main problem of this type of housing is the price, so in the long run they find it more profitable to mortgage and pay a mortgage monthly of smaller amount than the monthly rent of a house for rent.

REFERENCES AND ADDITIONAL READING

Andrés, J., & Ferri, J. (2017). *Precio de la vivienda, empleo y PIB en España. Estudios sobre la Economía Española (09)*. FEDEA.

Arellano, M., & Bentolilla, S. (Eds). (2009). La burbuja inmobiliaria: causas y responsables. En Los orígenes inmobiliarios de la crisis actual, capítulo 7 en Antonio Cabrales et al. (Eds). Banco de España. Retrieved from http://www.bde.es

Ayuso, J., & Restoy, F. (2006). Precios de la vivienda y de los alquileres: Un enfoque de valoración de activos de equilibrio. *Journal of Empirical Finance*, *0609*, 371–388. doi:10.1016/j.jempfin.2005.10.004

Barlevy, G. (2007). Economic theory and asset bubbles. *Economic Perspectives*, *31*(3), 44–59.

Gómez Bujía, D. (2016). La crisis inmobiliaria española, motivaciones y perspectivas. Trabajo de fin de grado. Universidad da Coruña.

Case, K. E., & Shiller, R. J. (2003). Is there a bubble in the housing market? Cowles Foundation Paper(1089), 299-362.

de Molina, M., & Luis, J. (2010). *La economía española en la crisis mundial*. Banco de España.

Doménech, R. (2011). *El impacto económico de la construcción y de la actividad inmobiliaria*. BBVA Research.

Domínguez, B. G. (2009). Creación y destrucción de la burbuja inmobiliaria de España. En La primera crisis global: procesos, consecuencias, medidas. Revista ICE 850.

Fuentes Castro, D. (2009). Una nota sobre el exceso de oferta de viviendas y la duración del ajuste del sector. Boletín Económico del ICE (2958), 15-24.

García Montalvo, J. (2003). La vivienda en España: desgravaciones, burbujas y otras historias. Perspectivas del sistema financiero (78), 1-43.

Hornero, A. (2008). La crisis de las hipotecas subprime y el riesgo de credit crunch. *Revista de Economía Mundial*, (18): 195–204.

Leal Maldonado, J., & Martínez del Olmo, A. (2017). Tendencias recientes de la política de vivienda en España. *Cuadernos de las relaciones laborales, 35*(1), 15-41.

López, T. J. (2009). Crisis inmobiliaria, crisis crediticia y recesión económica en España. En Papeles de Europa. Vol. 19-2009, (pp. 82-107).

López García, M. Á. (2011). *Precios de la vivienda, booms inmobiliarios y política impositiva: ¿podría España haber sido diferente?* Huelva: XIV Encuentro de Economía Aplicada.

Fernández Luna, M. (2016). Análisis económico de la crisis del sector inmobiliario en España (2007-2013). (Doctoral thesis). Universidad de Sevilla.

Torrero Mañas, A. (2010). La crisis financiera y sus efectos sobre la economía española. Universidad de Alcalá de Henares.

Naredo, J. M. (2009). La cara oculta de la crisis. El fin del boom inmobiliario y sus consecuencias. En Revista de economía crítica, 7 (pp. 118-133).

Rodríguez, A. R. (2002). Análisis Comparado de las políticas de suelo y vivienda aplicadas en países europeos con fines sociales y ambientales. En el Congreso "La política de vivienda en España desde la perspectiva de otros modelos europeos", Ibiza (España), 30 de Noviembre de 2002. Instituto Juan de Herrera de la Escuela Técnica Superior de Arquitectura de Madrid y La Agencia de Ecología Urbana de Barcelona, que fue dirigido por José Manuel Naredo y Fernando Roch.

Rodríguez López, J. (2006). *Financiación de la vivienda en un contexto de tipos de interés crecientes*. Lleida: IX Semana de Estudios Urbanos.

Rodríguez López, J. (2008). La situación del mercado de vivienda en España. Boletín Económico del ICE (2951), 11-23.

Romero, A. (2004). "Migraciones". En Tendencias Demográficas durante el siglo XX en España. Instituto Nacional de Estadística, 207-253.

Rubio de Juan, M. A. (2006). *Flujos de inversión de no residentes en inmuebles residenciales. Flujos de inversión de residentes en inmuebles residenciales fuera de España*. Estudios y Publicaciones del Ministerio de la Vivienda en España.

Sánchez Vera, P., & Riella, A. (2010). Globalización y perspectivas de la integración regional. Murcia: edit.um.

Scanlon, K., Lunde, J., & Whitehead, C. (2008). En respuesta a las viviendas y crisis financieras: Préstamos hipotecarios, productos de hipotecas y las políticas del gobierno. *Revista Internacional de Política de Vivienda, 11*(1), 23–49.

ENDNOTES

1 Adopted and proclaimed by the General Assembly in its resolution 217 A (III), of December 10, 1948.

2 Held from June 3 to 14, 1996 in Istanbul

Chapter 8
United States-China Trade War 2019:
Its Impacts on European Economies

Hassan Syed
https://orcid.org/0000-0003-2114-2473
BPP Law School, UK

Sema Yilmaz Genç
https://orcid.org/0000-0002-3138-1622
Kocaeli University, Turkey

ABSTRACT

Global economics has two versions. One is the economic realities that are based on our lived world view and explained by our experience of it each day. The other is the complex and theoretical economic view presented by mainstream economists. There is no correlation between the two world views. There is little respect left for the 'predictions' offered by mainstream economics through the use of obfuscating mathematics in practical business decision making. The 2008 financial crisis made this position even more profound. China, the United States, and Europe are the three main contributors to the total productivity of the globe.

INTRODUCTION

Global economics has two versions. One is the economic realities that are based on our lived world view and explained by our experience of it each day. The other is the complex and theoretical economic view presented by mainstream economists.

DOI: 10.4018/978-1-7998-2513-5.ch008

There is no correlation between the two world views. There is little respect left for the 'predictions' offered by mainstream economics through the use of obfuscating mathematics in practical business decision making. The 2008 financial crisis made this position even more profound. China, the United States, and Europe are the three main contributors to the total productivity of the globe. The global GDP stands at USD 80 trillion (World Bank, 2019).

The US and EU contributed 50% to the global GDP in 1980. In 2019 the US and EU combined share went down to 31%. Asian economies contribute 63% to the global GDP as of 2019. China takes the lion's share of 33%. Africa only adds 2% to the global GDP. The United Kingdom contributes 1% to the global GDP (Desjardins, 2019).

The reality of global economics is not the result of the forces of free markets or any of the economic equilibrium theories. The global economic situation is the outcome of intense global politics. The global economic policies also have strong influences from the world's largest military force, the United States. The United States has over 700 military bases around the world. These military bases allow the United States to leverage economic and political advantages from other nations (Davis, 2011). The US economic policies are firmly linked to its foreign policy. The foreign policy is guided by the US geopolitical and geo-economic interests combined.

It is still an enigma of how the US objectives for military dominance and economic hegemony are decided and translated into policy. The recent rise of the far-right movement in the United States is still not fully understood by the political scientists. Some attribute this far-right movement to the mass exodus of Central and South American populations escaping poverty and civil unrest in their countries and lining-up at the borders of the United States. Other's see it as a consequence of deteriorating racial relations in America due to the economic marginalisation of non-whites and fuelling of racial politics by politicians like Donald Trump. Regardless of the reasons, it is evident that the United States' internal politics and its foreign policy objectives for economic and political hegemony are distinct (Inwood, 2019). Since the 1980s, China has emerged as a global production powerhouse. The 1980's famous 'Four Modernisation' policies of Deng Xiaoping called for reforms in China. Deng Xiaoping set ambitious goals for reforms in China's defence capability, agricultural production, industrial outputs and innovations in science and technology (Zhang & Feng, 2019). The meteoric rise of China from the 1980's to date in all the four realms is a testimony to the discipline and political cohesion of the Chinese nation. There is no parallel in the contemporary world economic history of such massive national transformation. China has achieved the impossible and envious state of economic prosperity regardless of being the most populous country in the world. China's spectacular transformation has transfixed the attention of global power players in the United States and Europe. The current US-China trade war is linked to the perceived threat by the policymakers in the United States of the Chinese growing global economic influence. The US-China trade war, including its influence on Europe, is perhaps also linked with the American urgency to deal with the rising global influence of China in all spheres of global politics. This paper explores the impact of the US-China trade war and its impact on Europe emerging from the discourse in the contemporary political and economic literature. The findings of this paper are the result of the inference drawn by the authors from their literature review.

HISTORICAL CONTEXT

Europe between the first and second world wars was a continent of declining empires and wrangling nation-states that were embroiled in conflicts. The conflicts were the result of European colonial decline globally. The conflicts were also the result of trying to carve out their influence in global economics. The transforming world of the early 20th century was also a fight for economic survival by the declining European empires. The European mercantile society was facing the threat of the free-market economy through political discourse (Paine, 2019).

The European monarchies were desperate to hold on to their colonial legacies. The European societies were facing emancipation and reconciliation of religious dogmas between Christianity and Semitism. The fears of weaning European mercantilism and shifting political alliances resulted in the present-day map of Europe. It is a sad historical fact that the fight between European ideologies resulted in 40 million death in World War I and 70 million death in World War II. The genocide of Jewish people during World War II with 6 million killings was the result of the Christian-Jewish ideological clash. More than 6 million civilians perished in Anatolia and Armenia during the First World War The exact number of casualties from both the wars have never been known (Johnson, 2019).

The Europe that emerged from the ashes of the two great wars seemed to have lost its grip on the global geopolitics. The United States and the Soviet Union led the world as the new global powers between the 1950's until 1989. The bipolar world shifted to a unipolar one because of the disintegration of the Soviet Union in 1989. The United States imposed a new world order as the only superpower. The communism of Lenin and Stalin took its last breaths when the few remaining Eastern European states became members of the European Union. EU-28 became a powerful economic block. The EU also became a symbol of successful regional unity for mutual cooperation and shared prosperity.

The 2016 UK's Brexit referendum shook the foundations of EU-28. It must be mentioned that it was UK's Prime Minister Winston Churchill who floated the idea of a United Europe in his famous address at Zurich University on 19 September

1946. Churchill proposed the idea of a 'United States of Europe'. EU's first steps as an economic community started to emerge in 1950 with the establishment of the European Coal and Steel Community. The six founding members of the 1950 Steel and Coal Community were Belgium, France, Germany, Italy, Luxembourg, and the Netherlands. The Treaty of Rome in 1957 formally established the European Common Market. It was not till the unification of Germany that the idea of a union became a reality with the Maastricht Treaty on European Union in 1993 (Wiesner, 2019).

The establishment of the European Central Bank (ECB) in 1988 and the 1999 adoption of single currency Euro marks the global entrance of Euro-Zone as a formal economic block with its distinct economic policies. In 1989 the idea of the European Economic Area (EEA) was floated and adopted to allow non-EU member states of Switzerland, Iceland, Liechtenstein, and Norway to negotiate trade agreements favourable to EU-28 and European Free Trade Association (EFTA) states. Switzerland which is one of the four members of EFTA did not sign the EEA Agreement and has independent trade arrangements with EU-28.It is still no clear if the economic policies of the Euro Zone are in fact aligned or distinct from the economic agendas of EU-28. EU-28, Euro-Zone, EEA, and EFTA are a melting pot of diverging socio-economic and socio-political interests (Boldeanu & Tache, 2016).

This short albeit historical introduction of the United States and the EU shed light on the complexity of the trade and economic situation globally. This also reflects the complex geopolitics for global influence that is perceived to favour the United States as the only global power. Europe as EU-28 wielded economic influence but it had to remain subservient to the United States for its own survival. The rise of China as a global economic power has shifted the balance in favor of China. The EU-28 did reconcile their position for their economic advantages with China while continuing to support and favour the United States for its geopolitical influence.

The US is in a different situation with China's growing global influence due to its economic prosperity. The United States is having difficulty with allowing China to share the stage as the second global power. It is this complex geopolitical situation that was brewing between the US and China which took the shape of a trade war. EU-28 is engaged in its internal strife due to Brexit however, the EU is firmly attached to any consequences due to the political and economic fall-out of the US-China trade war.

GEOPOLITICS OF US-CHINA TRADE

A simplistic view of the current US-China trade war would assume that the United States under the leadership of President Trump seeks to establish trade parity with China. The balance of trade and the so-called large trade deficit that the US has with China is not a simple mathematical equation. It is quite complex. The US sends components to China which are assembled or manufactured as finished goods by the Chinese. These finished goods are then sent back to the US as cheaper consumer products. The cost-effective production of these US component-based Chinese finished goods fuels consumer spending in the USA (Kraemer, Linden & Dedrick, 2011). The US economy is a 100% consumptions based economy. Chinese finished goods that use the US components are almost 90% of the goods exported to the US (Norton, 2019). All finished Chinese consumer goods that have US components are still considered Chinese exports. This subtle fact is always obscured and hidden from the narratives being presented by the US media in their portrayal of China as depriving the US market of jobs and revenue. The fact is that US components drive most of the finished goods exported back to the United States from China. These cheaply assembled goods then drive consumer spending in the United States. The latest research on the positive impact of Chinese goods imported in the United States refers to lowering the purchase costs for average consumers (Bai & Stumpner, 2019).

The fact is that the so-called US trade deficit with China between 2012 and 2018 only grew by USD 100 billion. US consumer spending for 2018 stood at USD 13.9 trillion. Chinese consumer goods only comprise 3% of the total US consumer spending (Hale, et al. 2019).

As the figure below shows, US automobiles are one of the key US exports to China. In 2018, US automakers sold roughly 28 million automobiles in China in

Figure 1. U.S. Trade Deficit With China
Source: Kimberly Amadeo, June 22, 2019- www.thebalance.com

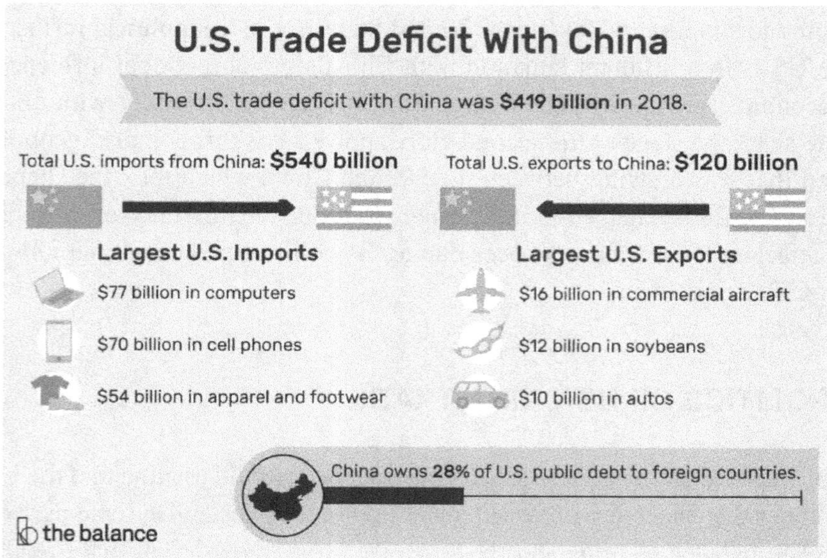

contrast to 17 million in the local U.S markets. China allows the US farming sector to export a major share of its produce. China owns 28% of US debt. China is the largest owner of US debt at USD 1.3 trillion (USCBC, 2018).

Our above analysis provides the following evidential deductions:

- China benefits from producing large volumes of consumer products that have US components. The large volume production results in cheaper pricing. The cheaper production cost benefits are passed on to US consumers.
- The US component-based cheaply produced finished Chinese products fuel consumer spending in the US. Chinese consumer exports of USD 540 billion to the US total only 4% of the total US consumer spending of USD 13.9 trillion in 2018.
- US exports to China in 2018 stood at USD 128 billion. This is an 86% increase since 2008. US exports to the rest of the world increased by only 21% for the same period.
- China is the largest market for US automobiles that is even larger than the US market for the US auto manufacturers.
- China consumers more US agricultural products than any other country in the world.
- US services export to China stood at USD 52 billion in 2016. US services exports to China increased more than 300% between 2007 and 2006. The US services exports to the rest of the world increased by 50%.

The above deductions do not reflect any major anomalies in the trade relations between the US and China. Both countries seem to be benefiting from the economic and trade relationships with each other. The question of the reason for a trade war becomes even more confounding. The conventional wisdom of 'Not fixing something which is not broken' seems to be missing here. What is then the real reason behind the US-China trade war? There is no simple answer to this question. The plausible answer to this question perhaps lies hidden in the historical underpinnings of geopolitical relations between contemporary China, the United States, and Europe that we have just eluded to in the introduction. The plausible answer also lurks in the shadows of US global political interests that are now directly colliding with global Chinese influence. Also in the middle of this complex mix is the US and Europe's complicated relationship which is based on the historical influence of the UK on US politics since the US civil war of the 18th century.

Unfortunately, the contemporary political and economic analysts would try to coerce the simple view that the US-China trade war is about bringing jobs back to the US. Another simple view posits that the US-China trade war is about forcing China to open its markets to the so-called 'Free Market Economy' system of western capitalism. These views miss the cardinal point that China remains the biggest holder of US debt at US$1.123 trillion. The total US debt as of February 2019 stood at US$19.4 trillion. The US also has US$120 trillion in unfunded future liabilities on the US Federal government balance sheet (Siddiqui, 2019).

The present political system in the United States is heavily influenced by families that have deep relations with the elite in the British aristocracy and politics. The famous story of British tea dumped in the Boston harbour in December 1773 regales the US federalists to this day. Such stories promote the illusion of American distinction from the British politic to prevail. The special relations between the British and the American politicians and policymakers have multiple dimensions. President George Bush, President Ronald Regan, Alan Green Span, and other prominent policymakers have been bestowed with the knighthood of the British Crown. These special relations impact US foreign policy and trade commitments. It also allows British policymakers to hedge their risks when confronted with complex geopolitical situations. These relations also have an impact on the current US-China trade war (Yu, 2019).

The discovery of oil in the Middle East has shaped global politics and economic policies since the early 1900's. The US and the UK have always presented a united front when tackling the politics surrounding the Middle East oil since both the countries have controlled the world oil supply since its mass discovery in the early 1900's. The monarchs of Saudi Arabia, UAE, Bahrain, and Kuwait continue to provide the American and British companies with large incentives that are not granted to other nations. US dollar acts as the exchange currency for OPEC oil trade. This makes the US dollar as the globally significant currency. The US and UK installed the present Arab monarchies in Saudi Arabia, UAE, Kuwait, Qatar, etc. These oil-rich Arab states under the US and UK influence ensure that the US dollar remains the dominant US currency for the foreseeable future. Any demise of these Arab monarchies will also mean that Russia, Venezuela, Iran, etc. will get rid of the US dollar-dominant OPEC trades.

China has been trying to forge stronger ties with these Middle Eastern states. The Chinese have also started to mix their currency with the US dollar oil trade. The Chinese efforts have been met with a mixed reaction from the US and UK policymakers. The result is an increase in the US, UK, France, and German arms supply to these oil-rich Arab states. The US and the EU countries have lent their support to the Saudi led invasion of Yemen. These oil-rich Arab states are dependent monarchies which cannot survive without the US and EU's help. These Arab monarchies are also despondent and rule with brutal policies. The US and EU have advised these Arab states to deal with China's at-an-arms distance. None of these non-democratic Arab monarchies would survive without US and EU military support. These Arab rulers exchange their oil wealth with the US and EU governments for their survival.

China is trying to enter the equation for its own economic interests that undermine the US and EU influence with these Arab states.

Iran is the adversary of Saudi radical Islam in the Middle East. Those who are knowledgeable about the ideological differences between the Saudi radical Islam and Iran's Islamic government would prefer Iran over Saudi Arabia any day. The Saudi extremist version of Salafi ideologies has given birth to the Taliban, ISIS, Bokoharam just to name a few. China has suffered extremism at the hands of the Saudi-funded madrassah franchise in its Xingjian region. Foreign fighters from Afghanistan and Pakistan infiltrated the Chinese region to try and plant their extremist ideologies amongst the Chinese Muslims in the Xingjian region (Datta, 2014). The people of Xinjiang affiliate their origins with the Turkish people as the Turkmans. There were no extremist elements in the region before the rise of US-sponsored Mujahideen in Afghanistan during the Afghan-Soviet war of 1979. After the demise of the Soviet Union, the Saudi regime diverted funding of their extreme ideology to poor Islamic countries in Asia and Africa. The madrassah-franchise of the Saudi ideology is the vehicle for Saudi funding to these poor Islamic countries. The US has always looked the other way in terms of Islamic extremism funding by the Saudi regime (Prokop, 2003). China has a strategic interest in trying to curb extremism in its regions bordering Central Asia. Rise in Islamic extremism along China's Belt and Road routes strategically favours the United States. China can be manipulated if there is instability inside China. This is also an important factor to consider in the US-China trade war.

Iran sits on the mouth of the Strait of Hormuz along with Pakistan. China has leased the deep seaport of Gwadar from Pakistan for 100 years. Chinese presence at the very mouth of the Strait of Hormuz and the development of an oil terminal at the Gwadar port would mean that China will not have to carry its oil from the Middle East especially Iran through the Strait of Malacca. The British interests in Singapore and Brunei will be deeply jeopardized if China cannot be controlled in its naval movements or its marine trade routes. China's BRI strategy further exacerbated the policy dilemma for US and UK policymakers who were trying to create some form of international alliance against China in the South China sea. China's BRI strategy simply removed the South China Sea issue from the table and focused its trade routes through Pakistan-Iran-Turkey and Central Asia all the way to Europe (Shariatinia & Azizi, 2017).

China Belt and Road strategy coupled with the geopolitics of oil in the Middle-East has the potential to tilt the balance of power in China's favour. The BRI strategy aims to connect Asia with Europe through a network of roads and railway that will provide crucial trade routes with Central Asia. The Central Asian region with its vast natural resources and trade potential has been sitting landlocked for the past 200 years. The BRI strategy will provide the necessary physical logistics and ensuing economic advantage to the Central Asian countries. The United States becomes a redundant party in this equation. Europe gains access to another large population of Central Asia passing through Iran and Turkey all the way to China. This Euro-Asian trade and social connectivity places China as the center of power. This scenario has been played as a doomsday scenario by China's critics in Washington and Europe (Callahan, 2016).

How does Europe's interest fit into this complex geopolitical picture of oil and gas in the Middle East? Europe is the second-largest consumer of oil and gas in the world after the United States. Only the UK and Norway (Non-EU) are the two oil producers in Europe. Europe has a heavy reliance on natural gas from Russia. Both Norway and the UK have lost almost 50% of their oil production capability in the last decade. The scenario of China BRI strategy influencing or dominating the Middle East-North Africa (MENA) and Central Asian natural resources aligns the European agenda with China. The UK is haranguing to leave EU at all costs, cheered on by Trump and even without a deal under Boris Johnson. Such a situation raised the possibility of the rest of the EU aligning itself with China for their economic interests as a Euro-Asian trade block under BRI. The US is desperate to dislodge this possibility and all possible pressure is being applied to China to negotiate this position with the US. The US would seek some reassurances from China through the US-China trade war negotiations for keeping the US interests as part of the deal.

EU has been benefiting from Chinese investment since the last decade. UK, Germany, and France received 85% of total China's European investments in 2017. This major chunk of Euro 30 billion Chinese investments gave a tremendous boost to the UK, French and German economies post 2008 financial crisis. The rest of Europe had to contend with what was left over from the Chinese investments in Europe. The EU plays a vital role in negotiating the third-country trade agreements with the EU-28. Some of the criticism levelled against Brussels is justified in that the larger economies of EU-28 negotiate trade terms that are beneficial to their economies (Casarini, 2008). The state-dimension of power influence in Brussels is widely acknowledged. The EU institutional powers are relegated as secondary powers once EU-28 policies are being dictated by Germany, France or the UK. The EU-US trade relationship is the result of political powers dictating the terms to the Brussels' institutions (Tallberg, 2008). In this scenario, one can appreciate the US concerns over China's increasing influence on the governments of Germany, France, and the UK as the leading economies and decision-makers of EU-28. The figure below shows the spread of Chinese investments in Europe in 2017. It reaffirms the analysis about the state-dimension of power within the EU-28.

The UK has been making subtle moves to engage with China outside the EU-28 since 2013. The UK Treasury announced in June 2014 that the City of London Renminbi business volume increased by 140% in 2013. The City of London Renminbi

Figure 2. Chinese investment in EU-28, 2017
Source: Rhodium Group

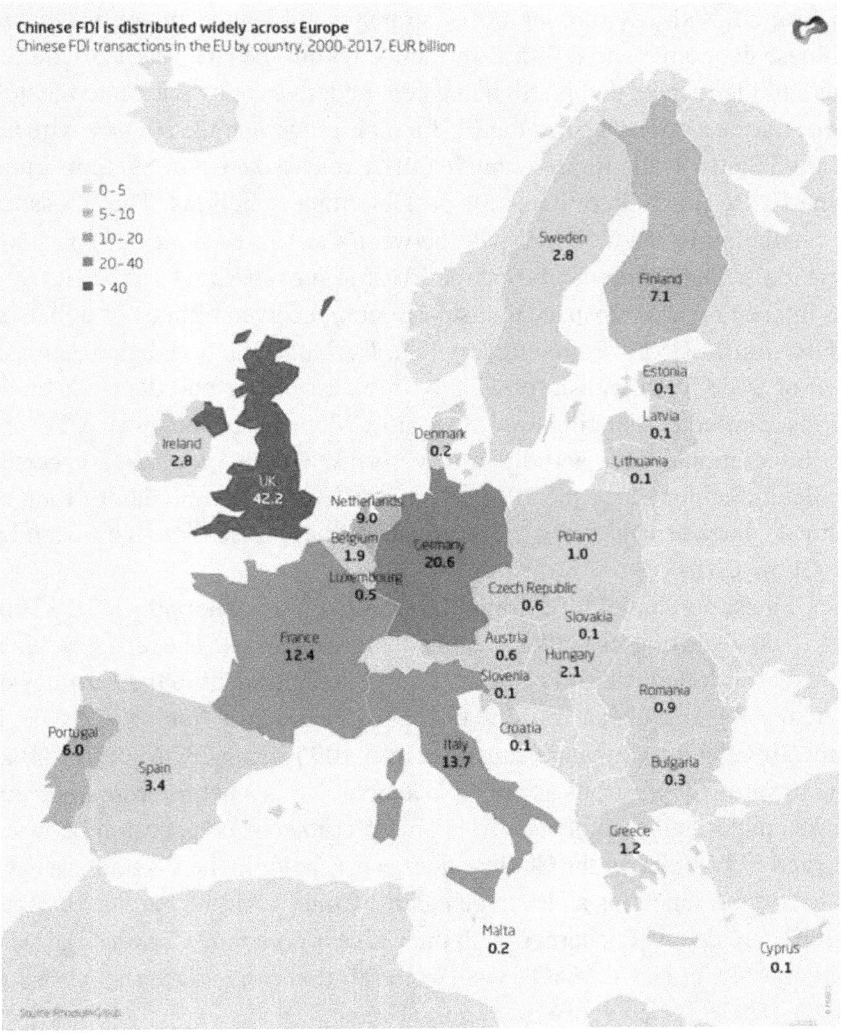

trading amounts to 62% of the total Renminbi trade outside Mainland China and Hong Kong. The EU-28 does not figure anywhere in this scenario. Similarly, the United States is the UK's largest trade partner in both exports and imports. EU-28 has taken sides in the US-China trade war. The first signs of this appeared in 2018. China offered the EU-28 an alliance against the US unilateral imposition of trade sanctions during the June 2018 World Trade Organisation (WTO) Summit in Beijing (Herszenhorn & Von Der Burchard, 2019). This development was never fully discussed or reported in the western media nor fully discussed by economic analysts in the western world. A China-EU alliance against the US at WTO would mean a slow and painful economic death for the US outside of continental United States. The US is slowly running out of strategic and long term options to counter the Chinese economic and political influence within the EU. The US-China trade war has a hidden aspect that is still being kept under wraps by the United States that concerns trade sanctions against the EU for their growing trade alliance with China. The United States Trade Representative Office released a list of 89 items imported from the EU to the United States for possible trade sanctions. The US sanctions are in retaliation to the WTO dispute between the United States and EU aircraft maker Airbus. The US demands that the EU stop subsidizing Airbus as it threatens the US interest in the Aerospace industry. Boeing received billions of dollars in tax subsidies from the US government every year. The United States is being increasingly accused of trade unilateralism especially in its assertions and demands at WTO. The US is accused of dictating terms to almost 200 other countries at WTO forums against international trade and diplomacy norms. The WT has taken exception to this unilateral approach of the US and advised a more reconciliatory tone rather than threats of trade sanctions against countries that refuse the US unilateral trade terms (Chow, 2019).

The Chinese purchased 140 Airbus planes in 2017 for a whopping USD 23 billion. Boeing is slowly losing its market share in China to Airbus. The recent Boeing 737 Max crashes in Indonesia and Ethiopia has put a major dent in the earnings of the US Aerospace giant. China was one of the major users of Boeing 737 Max in its booming air industry. China has cancelled over 100 Boeing 737 Max aircraft and is moving towards EU's Airbus as the replacement. US is a net loser in this scenario. EU makes major gains in this deal. This indirect intense competition between US Boeing and EU Airbus for the Chinese market is a factor in the US trade war against China to use the sanctions as leverage against China's Airbus purchases. Both the US and EU are deeply concerned with the Chinese company Commercial Aircraft Corporation of China, COMAC's C-919 aircraft that can replace the Airbus A320 and Boeing 737 Max category of aircraft (Huang, 2019).

China launched the Asian Infrastructure Investment Bank (AIIB) in 2016. AIIB is based out of Beijing. It has one hundred members worldwide. AIIB is China's response to the US-based World Bank and IMF. AIIB has an impressive list of projects that are a game-changer in Asia and the Middle East. The diminishing role of IMF and the World Bank is running the US agenda in the region that has been amplified by China's majority investment in the AIIB funded projects. Australia, India, Israel, Saudi Arabia, and UAE are staunch US allies in the world. All these countries have joined AIIB. A total of USD 96 billion has been invested by the AIIB across its member states in a short span of almost 3 years. AIIB is a major concern for US policymakers. The present US-China trade war has elements of

AIIB's growing influence globally and the US anxiety over the loss of credibility by the US-appointed IMF and World Bank leadership.

BRICS (Brazil, Russia, India, China, South Africa) is an association of countries with a shared vision on the global geopolitical issues confronting the world. The BRCIS was launched in 2009 in Russia. The BRICS countries launched the BRICS Contingent Reserve Arrangement in July 2014 for a total value of USD 200 billion. China contributed USD 100 billion for the fund. The BRICS have the potential to sway India and Brazil from under the US influence. The BRICS have caused major concerns for the United States. The US cannot control the South American regimes without having effective control over the Venezuelan oil and resource-rich Brazil. The United States CIA has a long history of interfering in the Brazilian elections and tactics of covert regime changes. The 2004 declassified documents of the US State Department revealed the role of CIA in installing the Brazilian military dictator Castelo Branco government in 1964 (Pringle, 2018). The current President of Brazil is a staunch support of Trump politics and has refused to allow any recognition of the rights of the indigenous Amazon people. The Chinese growing influence on the 'third-shore' of the United States raises serious concerns for the US influence in South America and the Caribbean. The accumulated impact of AIIB and BRICKS through China's investment in various projects also underpins the US-China trade work (Cavanna, 2019).

Chinese Belt and Road Initiative (BRI) is a game changer for 70 of the poorest countries in the world. China has emerged as the world leader in addressing poverty, global threats to the environment and promoting trade between countries that have been devastated by the policies of IMF and World Bank. The BRI strategy is the center of severe criticism by mainstream economists in the US, UK, and Europe. There are multi-million grants being given to Universities and Think-Tanks in some of the BRI participating countries to raise false-alarms about China's perceived 'take-over' of the world through its 'soft-power'. The fact is that China BRI strategy is not only misunderstood but most of the pseudo-experts have never visited China nor studied Chinese philosophy to comprehend the Chinese way of life (Xing, 2019).

At the heart of the arguments presented above is the US fear of losing its hegemony globally. The US had built an extensive network of military bases around the world after the Second World War. The United States emerged as the net-sum winner post-second world war. The Marshall Plan and Bretton Woods Conference established the US control over the ruined economies of Europe and Asia. The United States used its huge cash reserves and excess production post-second world war as aid to the battered economies of Europe (Acharya, 2018). The Chinese rise has threatened the US control over Europe and Asia. It is also threatening the US global military bases as countries are exceedingly raising concerns over the presence of the US troops and missile systems on their soil. The US attributes these happenings to Chinese influence that is offering the world with another choice for alignment with a world power. The United States is now entering a century of another global power taking away its global dominance due to the sheer size of their economy and their ability to yield soft power without having to build and maintain hundreds of military bases around the world.

EU-CHINA & EU-US RELATIONS

EU had its moment of truth during the early 2009 Greek sovereign debt crisis. Germany stands suspect of financial imperialism during the entire episode of the Greek debt crisis. Angela Merkel, the German Chancellor set aside ethics when she failed to informed the German Bundestag about the real motive behind Germany's efforts during the Greek crisis (Zafiropoulou, Theodosiou & Papakonstantinou, 2015). Germany wanted the Greek bailout on its dictated terms. The clear and factual reason was the German government's implicit involvement with the Deutsche Bank bail-out post-2008 financial crisis. The bail-out of Deutsche Bank was carried out on the backs of Greek people (Münnich, 2015). The Greek crisis was a moment for the EU-28 to straighten its house and create policies that protected the entire EU and not just the dominant economies of Europe. The EU-28 failed in that and continued with its policies of protectionism towards financially dominant economies within the EU.

The crisis also led to revelations by German news media outlet SPIEGEL exposing the covert work of CIA and German foreign intelligence agency BND (SPIEGEL Staff, 2015). The intelligence agencies were working together to covertly spy on German media as well as politicians who were seen opposing the US interests within the EU. The Greek financial crises exposed the fissures within the EU economic policymaking and their covert alliance with the US geopolitical interest. The details of this dark side of economic policymaking manipulated through the use of covert intelligence resources seriously undermined any claims of legitimacy by the EU policymakers in Brussels. The role of the US intelligence agencies in protecting the US economic interests within the EU also exposes the lack of adherence to the democratic system in US policymaking. While these important factual details have been carefully removed from the public eye, they remain a contentious topic between the US-EU and the China-EU trade talks. China increased its investments in Europe post the crisis and the US has been concerned about the increasing Chinese influence in the EU-28 (Steinbock, 2012).

The Greek Minister of Finance Yanis Varoufakis resigned from his office to protest the harsh terms of the bailout package offered by the EU and the IMF. He later detailed and revealed the entire episode of the German government's negative role in the negotiations to save German banks at the cost of Greek people. The Greek crisis had led to the GREXIT sentiments in the country. In 2013 IMF admitted partially its role in ruining the Greek economy. IMF apologized for the 'miscalculated' hyper-inflated taxes and the disastrous consequences for the most vulnerable sections of the Greek society (Elliott & Smith, 2013). Merkel's efforts to bail out the German banks at the cost of the people of Greece were termed as the economic death spiral (Jones, 2015). Varoufakis, who is an accomplished economist, came out clean about the mess within the EU and its financial institutions. Varoufakis also questioned the legitimacy of the EU's actions that led to the Greek financial crisis (Varoufakis, 2017).

The Greek financial crisis is a great context to understand the future of the EU as a single economic market. The EU's 2017 GDP stood at Euro 14 trillion. Germany has the largest share as the EU member state of 21%. UK (15.2%) and France (14.9%) are the other two leading economies of the EU. The top three economies account for over 51% of the total EU GDP. With the UK potentially preparing to exit in October this year, Italy with an 11% share would climb up to number three. France and Germany would retain the top spots.

Germany acts as the defacto 'Grown-up' in the policy-making domain of the EU. The Greek crisis helps us to understand the German position. Greece was treated as the 'child' in the German 'Grown-up' attitude in talking down to the Greeks during the crisis. The situation is not likely to change with UK's exit from the block. These mirky and shaky economic policymaking practices within the EU allow the US to manipulate the situation and drag the EU further into the US-China trade war.

UK is not leaving the block due to its own devices. UK has been contemplating reverting to its individual position with the Continent of Europe during the cold war. The disintegration of the USSR and the placement of NATO allies encircling Russia by using the EU has proven successful for US policymakers. Countries like Poland have taken a very hard stand against Russia after the demise of the USSR. The Russian economy and its own internal problems prevent it from flexing any muscles internationally. The UK understands the oil-based economy of Russia as its Achilles heel. The UK can leverage better economic bargains by exiting the EU and aligning with the US to assist in isolating Russia internationally. China and Russia are trying to improve their ties. Russia is a member of AIIB as well as BRICS. Russia is also participating in the China BRI strategy. The United States sees value in using the UK separately from the EU against Russia. The UK has been trying to pressure the Russian economy due to Russia annexation of Crimea from Ukraine. The US and UK combined sanctions will help keep Russia out of global markets. EU has not reciprocated to the US-UK pressure on sanctions against Russia. Germany and the rest of Europe are heavily reliant on Russian gas for their industrial production. US-China trade war has an impact on Russia as China is forced to reduce its financial investments to Russia due to a decrease in its revenues. US continues to ride on Russia and is reinforced by the UK in the restricting any Russian rise on the global scene (Bond, Odendahl & Rankin, 2015). The Russian sanctions are also linked with the US-China trade war including their impact on EU-28.

The United States is now fully focused on China. Europe will have to make do with its own worries. Until and unless Brussels is not able to put its house in order, the EU-28 future will be linked to the socio-political and socio-economic demands of its three leading economies. Germany and France continue to dominate and tame any nationalist sentiments rising within the remaining EU members. EU as a block provides moral support to the US in times like the US-Iran crisis. EU is careful to criticize China openly. The UK has taken a separate position to fuel overt and covert support for disturbances and riots in Hong Kong. The UK perceives that its overt and covert involvement with Hong Kong violence will help deal with the rising threat of Chinese influence around the world. This move by the UK is linked with the US-China trade war. These disturbances in Hong Kong fueled with the help of the US and UK administrations, also helps to divert the public attention away from the emerging socio-economic issues in their own countries.

The EU has its European Union Military Committee (EUMC) under the Treaty of Lisbon. The purpose is the have a common defense and deterrence strategy for the block. In November 2018, both Merkel and Macron drew the ire of Trump by stating that the EU could no longer rely on the United States for its defense. Both Merkel and Macron endorsed EU President Jean-Claude Juncker's idea about a European army (Kucera, 2019). Both France and Germany are the world's leading suppliers of conventional weapons and allied war machines. The University of the Bundeswehr in Munich has published papers on integrated Bundeswehr's Rapid Response Forces Divisions comprising military units from various EU countries under command of the Germans. This EU move is perhaps a step by Brussels to draw the attention of the US towards its ability to leverage favours even if the UK leaves the EU. This move perhaps reminds the US that the UK leaving the Eu does not diminish the role of EU in the global geopolitics. The US would have to treat the EU with respect and allow preferential treatment in matters of economics and trade.

The enhanced military preparedness by the United States, UK, and the EU raises many questions even at the economic policy level. US-China trade war is one of the key components of those questions. The recent sudden 'pro-democracy' violent protests in the streets of Hong Kong have left many political scientists bewildered. The UK Prime Minister prorogued the UK Parliament from meeting and discussing anything pertaining to his plans for a so-called 'hard Brexit'. The UK Supreme Court termed the move by the Prime Minister as unlawful. There are talks of Trump impeachment in the US Congress. EU economy is stagnant.

In the midst of all this, China, Africa, and Asia continue to thrive and trade with each other. Afterall, two-third of the world's population is in Asia and Africa. The US continues to twist the arms of its allies in Europe and Australia. It has minor allies in the Middle East who are the Arab despondent monarchies. The United States has to make some hard choices internationally. China is not going to reverse its continuing success just to appease the United States. Countries like Australia sit on the periphery of global politics. They can still decide and chose which way to go when it comes to the interest of their people. Europe is most definitely in the midst of the US-China trade war on many levels. Europe will have to decide and chose a path that is beneficial for the entire Europe and not just the top three economies. The future of the EU depends on these reforms that have nothing to do with the US-China trade war.

CONCLUSION

President Trump has emerged as the most divisive US president in recent history. He loves controversies and thrives under the media spotlight. President Trump has provoked opposition Congress members to 'go back' to their countries of origin. Three of those members of Congress are born Americans. President Trump has chosen the most controversial aspects of American politics to rouse public debate during the last year of his presidency. There is no clear way to predict the winners or losers in Trump's chosen trade-war with China. China has a philosophical history that dates back thousands of years. Those of us who have studied in China and remain, students of China, understand the Chinese way of dealing with confrontations. China is not the land of short-term strategies. China will have a strong and cogent response to the US short-term strategy aims for the US-China trade war.

EU aligns itself with the US when it comes to bashing China for its internal affairs. EU is also first in line when there are any lucrative trade or investment deals on the table from China. China does not miss these choices. The US has made it amply clear that it is going to act unilaterally against China. EU or for that matter any country that does not align itself with the US will face similar trade sanctions. The US will act in this unilateral manner as long as it lives under the illusion of being the dominant global power. China has been hedging its economic success by peacefully engaging in strategic moves to protect its national interests. The AIIB, BRICS, BRI and other such initiatives are all Chinese efforts to ensure that its investments in other countries are safe. The large base of the Chinese economy now includes 800 million Chinese consumers who are now able to absorb the Chinese production surplus locally. This major policy consideration is sometimes ignored by western critics of China.

China has modernised its military but has not engaged in spreading its military might by building military bases around the world. China will protect its sovereignty at all costs. China will not let another 'Opium-war' come to its door-steps. The US is facing its opioid crisis through over-prescription by its doctors. There is no one else to blame for it. The US pharmaceutical industry has made trillions of dollars from this comfortable arrangement between the doctors and US pharmaceuticals at the costs of the American patients. Most recently the US media started a campaign to blame China for its opioid crisis.

Both the US and Canada have liberalised the use of recreational and medicinal marijuana. It has sky-rocketed as a billion-dollar industry. It is a bewildering policy initiative by a country that is already reeling from high suicides from opioid crisis and depression. China is careful to side-step this mess. EU also has to navigate its way through this crisis as it's only a matter of time before such 'liberalisations' would be openly demanded across the EU by the US marijuana industry.

The EU is in the cross-fire of the US-China trade war in the areas of aerospace, military spending and the political fall-out of China's global influence through AIIB, BRICS and BRI. EU is best advised to choose sides only if the EU-28 can collectively decide their future. In the present state of decision making, Germany seems to be bank-rolling the EU policy-making with minor aid from France. EU is not heading in a direction of great unity and economic harmony. The rising tide of anti-immigrant, anti-Islam and anti-China sentiments within the EU will fuel far-right nationalism. EU has to democratise its own policy-making process in Brussels to make cogent and realistic socio-political and socioeconomic choices in this highly polarised world.

REFERENCES

Acharya, A. (2018). *The end of American world order*. John Wiley & Sons.

Bai, L., & Stumpner, S. (2019). Estimating US consumer gains from Chinese imports, *Banque de France Working Paper No. 718.*

Boldeanu, F. T., & Tache, I. (2016). The financial system of the EU and the Capital Markets Union. *European Research Studies*, *19*(1), 59.

Bond, I., Odendahl, C., & Rankin, J. (2015). *Frozen: The politics and economics of sanctions against Russia*. Centre for European Reform.

Callahan, W. A. (2016). China's Belt and Road Initiative and the New Eurasian Order. Norwegian Institute of International Affairs, 22.

Casarini, N. (2008). What Role for the European Union in Asia? An Analysis of the EU's Asia Strategy and the Growing Significance of EU-China Relations. *Current Politics and Economics of Asia*, *17*(1), 59–82.

Cavanna, T. P. (2019). *Unlocking the Gates of Eurasia: China's Belt and Road Initiative and its Implications for US Grand Strategy (May 2019)*. Texas National Security Review.

Chow, D. C. (2019). United States Unilateralism and the World Trade Organization. BU Int'l LJ, 37, 1.

Datta, S. K. (2014). *Inside ISI: The Story and Involvement of the ISI, Afghan Jihad, Taliban, Al-Qaeda, 9/11, Osama Bin Laden, 26/11 and the Future of Al-Qaeda*. Vij Books India Pvt Ltd.

Davis, S. (2011). The US military base network and contemporary colonialism: Power projection, resistance and the quest for operational unilateralism. *Political Geography*, *30*(4), 215–224. doi:10.1016/j.polgeo.2011.04.003

Desjardins, F. (2019). *The Economies Adding the Most to Global Growth in 2019.* Retrieved from https://www.visualcapitalist.com/economies-global-growth-2019/

Elliott, L., & Smith, H. (2013). *IMF 'to admit mistakes' in handling Greek debt crisis and bailout.* Retrieved From https://www.theguardian.com/business/2013/jun/05/imf-admit-mistakes-greek-crisis-austerity

Hale, G., Hobijn, B., Nechio, F., & Wilson, D. (2019). How Much Do We Spend on Imports?. *FRBSF Economic Letter*, 1.

Herszenhorn, D., & Von Der Burchard, H. (2019) *EU scores at China summit with assist from Trump*. Retrieved from https://www.politico.eu/article/eu-china-summit-result-assist-donald-trump/

https://www.spiegel.de/international/germany/the-nsa-and-american-spies-targeted-spiegel-a-1042023.html

Huang, Y. (2019). US–China economic tensions: origins and global implications. *China International Strategy Review*, 1-12.

Inwood, J. (2019). White supremacy, white counter-revolutionary politics, and the rise of Donald Trump. *Environment and Planning C. Politics and Space*, *37*(4), 579–596.

Johnson, C. (2019). *Tin Cans and Greyhounds: The Destroyers that Won Two World Wars*. Simon and Schuster.

Jones, E. (2015). The forgotten financial union. In The future of the euro, 44-69. doi:10.1093/acprof:oso/9780190233235.003.0003

Kraemer, K. L., Linden, G., & Dedrick, J. (2011). Capturing value in Global Networks: Apple's iPad and iPhone. *University of California, Irvine, University of California, Berkeley, y Syracuse University, NY.* http://pcic. merage. uci. edu/papers/2011/value_iPad_iPhone. pdf. Consultado el, 15.

Kucera, T. (2019). What European army? Alliance, security community or postnational federation. *International Politics*, 1–18.

Münnich, S. (2015). Readjusting imagined markets: Morality and institutional resilience in the German and British bank bailout of 2008. *Socio-economic Review, 14*(2), 283–307. doi:10.1093er/mwv014

Norton, M. A. (2019). *Testimony before the US-China Economic Security Review Commission Hearing on "An Emerging China-Russia Axis? Implications for the United States in an Era of Strategic Competition"*. Jeanne L. Wilson Shelby Cullom Davis Professor of Russian Studies.

Paine, J. (2019). Democratic Contradictions in European Settler Colonies. *World Politics*, 1–44.

Pringle, R. W. Jr. (2018). *The Costs of Hidden Involvements. Lindsey A. O'Rourke: Covert Regime Change*. Ithaca, NY: America's Secret Cold War Cornell University Press.

Prokop, M. (2003). Saudi Arabia: The politics of education. *International Affairs, 79*(1), 77–89. doi:10.1111/1468-2346.00296

Reports, U. S. C. B. C. (2018). *US Exports to China*. Retrieved from https://www.uschina.org/reports/us-exports/national

Shariatinia, M., & Azizi, H. (2017). Iran–China Cooperation in the Silk Road Economic Belt: From Strategic Understanding to Operational Understanding. *China & World Economy, 25*(5), 46–61. doi:10.1111/cwe.12213

Siddiqui, K. (2019). The US Dollar and the World Economy: A Critical Review. *Athens Journal of Business & Economics.*

Staff, SPIEGEL. (2015). *SPIEGEL Targeted By US Intelligence.*

Steinbock, D. (2012). The Eurozone debt crisis: Prospects for Europe, China, and the United States. *American Foreign Policy Interests, 34*(1), 34–42. doi:10.1080/10803920.2012.653719

Tallberg, J. (2008). Bargaining power in the European Council. *Journal of Common Market Studies, 46*(3), 685–708. doi:10.1111/j.1468-5965.2008.00798.x

Varoufakis, Y. (2017). *Adults in the room: My battle with Europe's deep establishment*. Random House.

Wiesner, C. (2019). Inventing the EU: But as a Democratic Polity or a Balance of Powers? In *Inventing the EU as a Democratic Polity* (pp. 85–96). Cham, Switzerland: Palgrave Macmillan. doi:10.1007/978-3-319-94415-9_6

World Bank. (2019). *World Bank national accounts data, and OECD National Accounts data files*. Retrieved from https://data.worldbank.org/indicator/NY.GDP.MKTP.KD.ZG

Xing, L. (2019). China's Pursuit of the "One Belt One Road" Initiative: A New World Order with Chinese Characteristics? In *Mapping China's 'One Belt One Road' Initiative* (pp. 1–27). Cham, Switzerland: Palgrave Macmillan. doi:10.1007/978-3-319-92201-0_1

Yu, M. (2019). Introduction to the special issue on understanding the current China-US 'Trade War'. *China Economic Journal, 12*(2), 97–99. doi:10.1080/17538963.2019.1616919

Zafiropoulou, M., Theodosiou, A., & Papakonstantinou, A. (2015). *Discourse analysis report of official and political documents for Greece: Public discourse analysis of the Greek crisis: the case of Greek politicians' perceptions of the Germans and Readers' online comments about Chancellor Merkel's visits to Athens*, FRAGMEX Research Programme Report.

Zhang, Y., & Feng, W. (2019). Deng Xiaoping and China's Reform and Opening-Up. In *Peaceful Development Path in China*. Singapore: Springer. doi:10.1007/978-981-13-1439-1_2

Chapter 9
Marketing Strategies of Cultural Institutions in a City Divided by a Border:
The Case Study for the City of Cieszyn-Czech Cieszyn

Łukasz Wróblewski
WSB University, Poland

Marcin Lis
WSB University, Poland

ABSTRACT

In the 21st Century, it is possible to observe a pattern of numerous changes in the sphere of functioning of the cultural institutions also in cities divided by a border. These trends include globalization of culture, development of cultural industries and creative industries, rapid technical and technological growth, occurrence of new cultural management concepts and marketing strategies. Therefore, this chapter presents models of marketing strategies that can be applied in cities divided by a border. Based on individual interviews with 40 experts, four model marketing strategies are proposed which can be used by managers of cultural institutions in cities such as Cieszyn-Czech Cieszyn. Proposed strategies are in relation to specified target markets - residents of a city divided by a border. The practical application aspect of this chapter is evident in the indication of the direction future marketing efforts of cultural institutions should take to improve their market position.

DOI: 10.4018/978-1-7998-2513-5.ch009

INTRODUCTION

Over the last twenty years, along the borders of member states of the European Union, including the Polish and Czech border, the intensification of various types of activities aimed at supporting cross-border cooperation in the field of culture can be observed. Among other things, these activities serve to blur the borders and divisions between the local communities and to shape their new quality (they should become a place of meetings, and not divisions) (Perkman, 2003; Castanho, Naranjo Gómez, Kurowska-Pysz, 2019; Wróblewski, Kasperek, 2019). On the Polish and Czech border, in particular in a city divided by a border, such as Cieszyn and Czech Cieszyn (Český Těšín), it is expressed in the growing number of cultural events which are being organised, and which are often implemented as part of cross-border cultural projects co-financed from the funds of the European Union (Kurowska-Pysz, 2016; Wróblewski, Dziadzia, Dacko-Pikiewicz, 2018). Nevertheless, this situation poses new challenges for the managers of the cultural institutions of Cieszyn and Czech Cieszyn and requires the implementation of the new marketing strategies. This, however entails taking responsibility for culture, which, on the one hand, requires an even deeper examination of the cultural offer available on both sides of the border (its quality, saturation with artistic content or availability), and on the other hand, is determined by an in-depth analysis of the needs of both Polish and Czech addressees of this offer. Therefore, it seems reasonable to propose model solutions of marketing strategies to cultural institutions, which can become an inherent part of their mission and strategic objectives. An example of such strategies are utility strategies, relating to specific target markets in a city divided by a border such as Cieszyn and Czech Cieszyn. However, to prepare successful marketing strategies in the cultural sector (in cities divided by a border also), there should be a balance between attitudes towards culture, which include the claim that culture has its own inherent value which must be protected at all costs, and the views of people who think that, just like any other form of human activity, culture must pay for itself, and it is therefore essential to take the available audience into account. We must keep in mind that the mission of many cultural institutions (e.g. theaters, operas, museums, and concert halls) is seeking various forms of expression. Therefore, not only concerts and performances which are known to have the support of the broad community are performed (Kolb, 2005; Schroeder, 2005: 1291-1305; Rentschler, Shilbury, 2008: 60-71; Boorsma, Chiaravalloti, 2010: 297-317; Jyrama, Ayvari, 2010: 723-735; Lehman, Wickhman, 2014: 133-141; Dacko-Pikiewicz, Wróblewski, 2017: 17-34). We should also look at the reasons for implementing different marketing strategies in culture with reference to the ongoing lifestyle changes of the consumers of the cultural offer. In addition, an important role is played by the internationalization of the circulation of cultural goods and services, as well as by the problems with introducing products that have been created outside the so-called broadcasting centers (e.g. the Hollywood cluster) into global circulation. At the same time, among the reasons to implement marketing strategies in the cultural sector, the development of information and communication technologies plays an important role, triggering new opportunities for creating and distributing cultural goods and services, and communicating the related values to consumers of culture. Ongoing technological development changes the position of cultural players in the market. Given the fact that marketing is a multi-paradigmatic category, there are specific grounds for the implementation of various marketing strategies by entities in the cross-border cultural sector (Wróblewski, Dacko-Pikiewicz, Cuyler, 2017: 302-314).

BACKGROUND: CITY CIESZYN-CZECH CIESZYN AS A RESEARCH AREA

The area of analysis in this chapter is the city which, due to political decisions that took place at the end of World War I, has been divided into Cieszyn and Czech Cieszyn (Český Těšín) for over 100 years. It is a system of cities which in 2007 entered the so-called Schengen area, and therefore visa-free traffic without border controls. Cieszyn, with approximately 36,000 residents and Czech Cieszyn (approximately 25,000 residents) are the main towns in the Cieszyn Silesia region and the Euroregion Śląsk Cieszyński located on the River Olza. This region lies in the border area of southern Poland and north-eastern Czech Republic, in the close vicinity of Slovakia. Originally, Cieszyn Silesia belonged to the Great Moravian Empire. Before 991, it became a part of the Polish state, and at the turn of 1289 obtained the status of a separate Duchy of Cieszyn which became part of the Czech crown in 1327. After the Piast dynasty ceased to exist in 1653, the Duchy became the property of the Habsburg family. For a century and a half, the entire area belonged to one state, the Austro-Hungarian Empire. This condition lasted until its dissolution in 1918. At that time, there was a conñict over this territory which, on July 28, 1920, by the decision of the Council of Ambassadors of the Great Powers at the conference in SPA, was divided between the newly reborn Poland and the newly formed Czechoslovakia. Artiðcially dividing the historically, ethnographically and socially homogeneous area (including the town of Cieszyn into Cieszyn and Czech Cieszyn) became the cause of mutual Polish-Czech animosities, grievances and conñicts that blocked the creation of the Polish-Czech cross-border market for cultural services for many years (Kowalczyk, Nawrocki, 1999: 196-202, Werpachowski, 2014: 1525, Wróblewski, 2016: 50-52). Cieszyn and Czech Cieszyn are special not only because of their history, unique location and terrain, but they are also famous for numerous cultural entities and many exceptional cultural events, some of which, as shown by research conducted in 2014, are known and appreciated both in Poland and the Czech Republic (Wróblewski, 2014: 68-72). These are primarily the events of the Film Review 'Cinema on the Border' (Filmová přehlídka Kino na hranici) or the Theatre Festival 'Without Borders' (borderfestival.eu).

The cultural offer of both cities are many institutions whose proposals are not limited to recipients on one side of the river, along which the border extends. Despite the small size, the city as a whole has two theatres. On the Polish side, it is the Theatre named after Adam Mickiewicz, on the Czech side it is a theatre with a double, namely Polish and Czech scene. What is particularly interesting is the fact that the Polish scene located in Těšínské Divadle is financed by the Czech marshal's office without subsidies from Polish sources. Two large cultural centres operate in the city as a whole: Cieszyn Culture Centre National House and Kulturní a společenské středisko Střelnice. Important points of culture are the Municipal Library in Cieszyn, the Municipal Library in Český Těšín (Městská knihovna Český Těšín), Reading Room and Literary Café Avion (Čítárna a kavárna Avion), known internationally and dealing in design Cieszyn Castle, Museum of Cieszyn Silesia, or Cieszyn Historical Library (Książnica Cieszyńska) which has had many unique publications from the last five hundred years. Sustainable development for both cities is also the activity of associations. The most visible are: Association for Regional Development and Cooperation 'Olza', Euroregion Cieszyn Silesia, Polish Cultural and Educational Association, Congress of Poles in the Czech Republic, Association 'Culture on the Border', Association Člověk na hranici (Man on the Border), Polish-Czech-Slovak Solidarity, Association Education Talent Culture. More or less significant initiatives and places in private hands also cannot be overlooked . Such places also enrich cultural offer and work for the image of cities, as well as large local government institutions. These include Literary Café Kornel i Przyjaciele, Tea Room Laja, Klub Dziupla, Blady Dawn Bar (Bledý úsvit), or events like a series of charity concerts called Activate Good. A large number of cultural entities actively involved in Cieszyn and Czech Cieszyn directly generate a rich and diverse artistic offer in terms of culture. The analysis of substantive reports of Cieszyn's local government cultural institutions shows that only the self-government cultural institutions of Cieszyn in 2016 organized over 1,600 cultural events of various nature, in which (as estimated by the organizers of these events) over 265,000 people took part. In order to get a more complete idea of the richness of social and cultural capital of Cieszyn and Czech Cieszyn, the cultural offer of private cultural entities and non-governmental organizations operating in the sphere of culture should also be taken into account, as well as the offer of cultural entities located on the other side of the border in Czech Cieszyn.

METHODOLOGY OF THE CONDUCTED RESEARCH

The main purpose of the conducted research was to proposed models of marketing strategies which can be used by managers of cultural institutions in a city divided by a border in relation to specified target markets. In order to obtain reliable results, an inductive method was used, i.e. the method of incomplete numerical induction. It is inductive reasoning, the premises of which do not exhaust the entire universe of objects to which the general principle expressed in the conclusion of the reasoning refers. Here, the premises are specific sentences, while the conclusion is a general sentence, and each premise follows logically from the conclusion. It is a method in which a general principle is derived from a limited number of details (Lisiński, 2016: 14).

Bourdieu (1994:229), indicates not without a reason that "the mysteries of culture have their catechumens, their initiates, their holy men, that 'discrete elite' set apart from ordinary mortals". Although this statement seems to be a mental shortcut, it is beyond doubt that on the territory of a divided city, such as Cieszyn and Czech Cieszyn, it is possible to find experts who, owing to their education and functions performed in the field of broadly understood culture, have a more extensive and detailed knowledge than other residents of the town. Therefore, in order to obtain a more complete picture of the issues analysed in this chapter, primary research was conducted using the interview method in the form of individual in-depth interviews (IDI) with 40 experts – directors of cultural institutions, marketers, creators, animators and organisers of cultural events in Cieszyn (20 persons) and Czech Cieszyn (20 persons) – Appendix 1. The interview questionnaire (in Polish and in Czech) contained 17 questions in total, seven of which were short, based on association and completion, while the remaining 10 questions were open and in-depth. The interviews were carried out between February and June 2018.

In addition, as complementary research, a consultation meeting were carried out. A consultation meeting of experts with the use of brainstorming techniques with key stakeholders in the cross-border market for cultural services in Cieszyn and Czech Cieszyn, e.g.: Mayors of Cieszyn and Czech Cieszyn, representatives of the Cieszyn Silesia Euroregion, local governments, representatives of cultural institutions, third sector cultural organisations,the heads of culture and promotion departments of both cities). The meeting, which took place in the Municipal Ofðce in Czech Cieszyn on 7 November 2018, was attended by a total of 16 experts (9 from the Czech side and 7 from the Polish side).

The research which was carried out was part of two Polish-Czech cross-border projects co-ðnanced by the European Regional Development Fund-Interreg V-A Programme Czech Republic-Poland under the Micro-Projects Fund of the Cieszyn Silesia Euroregion-Těšínské Slezsko and the state budget:

- The “Programme for Cieszyn and ˇCzech Cieszyn Culture” project implemented in 2017–2018;
- The “Czech Cieszyn/Cieszyn InEurope” project implemented in 2018–2019.

RESULTS

Characteristics of Residents as Separated Target Markets of Cultural Institutions in Cieszyn and Czech Cieszyn

Based on material obtained from individual interviews with 40 experts, as well as conclusions from the consultation meeting of experts with the use of brainstorming techniques, it is possible to divide the culture recipients of the Cieszyn and Czech Cieszyn into segments. Taking into account both the artistic and aesthetic competences of the consumers of the cultural offer (those present and potential), and the intensity of marketing activities in cultural institutions in Cieszyn and Czech Cieszyn, experts identified four main customer segments:

- Residents associated with art professionally,
- Residents with a positive attitude towards art,
- Residents indifferent to cultutal offer,
- Residents reluctant towards art.

Residents associated with art professionally are a customer segment which is often included in the so-called art world (artists, critics, employees of cultural institutions, etc.), which evaluates the artistic offer and often determines the success of a given artistic project (which in turn can translate into financial success). In Cieszyn and Czech Cieszyn, they are, for example, artists, academic workers associated with the University of Silesia (Art Department, Art Education Department), or directors of public cultural institutions. This segment has the expertise necessary for the proper reception of art and is knowledgeable about both the market for the creation and dissemination of art. Therefore, in comparison with other segments, it is relatively insusceptible to the marketing activities of cultural institutions. This group primarily looks for information about the artistic offer in traditional media, on the Internet, and in magazines devoted to cultural issues. It makes its market decisions autonomously and when choosing a cultural event to participate in, it is directed primarily by the message of the work and its content, which is much more important than the promotion of the event, or the price of admission. These customers have a high level of requirements and highly diverse expectations, not all of which can be met by cultural institutions. These are people for whom being with art is a way of life, and the main motivation for participating in a particular artistic event is intellectual development and communicating with authors, artists, and other people.

Table 1. Experts participating in the in-depth interviews

Item	Experts participating in the research (IDI – in-depth interviews)	
	Experts on the Polish side (Cieszyn)	Experts on the Czech side (Český Těšín)
1	Director of the Cieszyn Castle	Director of the Youth Centre in Český Těšín
2	Director of the Cieszyn Cultural Centre "Dom Narodowy"	Director of Albrechtova střední škola Český Těšín
3	Director of the Cieszyn Library	Director of the Association "Człowiek na Granicy" (Man on the Border) in Český Těšín
4	Director of the Adam Mickiewicz Theatre in Cieszyn	Deputy Director, coordinator of cultural projects Mateřská škola, základní škola a střední škola Slezské diakonie
5	Director of the Municipal Library in Cieszyn	Vice-President, project manager in the Polish Youth Association in the Czech Republic – club "Dziupla" in Český Těšín
6	Director of the Museum of Cieszyn Silesia	Project coordinator, organisational employee of Otwarte Pracownie/Otevřené Ateliéry
7	Director of the Festival "Viva il Canto", Associate Dean for Promotion and Artistic Activities of the University of Silesia, Faculty of Fine Arts in Cieszyn	Employee of the Literary Cafe "CAFE AVION" in Český Těšín
8	Head of the Cultural Education Department in the Faculty of Ethnology and Educational Science of the University of Silesia, Branch in Cieszyn	Member of the Association EducationTalentCulture based in in Český Těšín
9	President of the Polish Cultural and Educational Union in the Czech Republic	Theatre director, artist of the Theatre in Český Těšín
10	President of the Association "Kultura na Granicy" (Culture on the Border), Director of the Film Festival PL "Kino na Granicy" (Cinema on the Border)	Member of the Cultural Committee of the town of Český Těšín
11	Secretary of the Polish-Czech-Slovak Solidarity, Regional Branch in Cieszyn	Coordinator of the Polish-Czech projects in the Půda Association in Český Těšín
12	Head of the Culture, Sports, Tourism and NGO Department of the Poviat Starosty in Cieszyn	Head of the PR Department, Spokesperson of the Muzeum Těšínska in Český Těšín
13	Director of the "Na Granicy" Political Critique Centre	Coordinator of the Polish-Czech projects in the Municipal Library in Český Těšín
14	Director of the Museum of Printing in Cieszyn	Animator of the Cultural Centre Slezanek, Český Těšín
15	President of the Management Board of the Creative Women's Club in Cieszyn	Animator of the Youth Centre in Český Těšín
16	Manager of Polish-Czech projects in the Polish Cultural and Educational Union in the Czech Republic	Culture referent in the town of Český Těšín
17	Journalist of "Głos" – Polish newspaper in the Czech Republic	Director of the Project "Every Czech Reads to Kids"
18	Member of the Main Board of Macierz Ziemi Cieszyńskiej	Director of the Association "Asociace obecne prospěšných služeb" in Český Těšín
19	Treasurer of the "Rotunda" Association in Cieszyn	Coordinator of cultural projects in the Cultural Centre "Střelnice" in Český Těšín
20	President of the OFKA Social Cooperative in Cieszyn	PR manager in the town of Český Těšín

Source: own work.

Residents with a positive attitude towards art create a segment not professionally involved with art, but participating in the artistic events organized by cultural institutions. In Cieszyn and Czech Cieszyn, they are, for example, members of the Polish Cultural and Educational Association in the Czech Republic or students of the Silesian University (Art Department, Department of Cultural Education). Cultural needs occupy a relatively high position in the hierarchy of values in their life, but compared with the previous segment, their spending on culture is lower. It should be noted that although such forms of activity like going to a museum, gallery, library or theater are considered by this group of people as valuable, they are not implemented frequently. When choosing an artistic event in which they will participate, in addition to the content and message of the work, they often pay attention to comfort. In making their purchasing decisions, a significant role is played by the place where the artistic event will take place. It should also be noted that these customers are sensitive to the promotion of a cultural event and the artistic offer of cultural institutions is more suited to their expectations. Therefore, convincing them to participate in a particular artistic event should not pose a major difficulty to the institutions. This group, compared with people associated with art professionally, is somewhat less prepared for the reception of art, so next to individual development and leisure, the main motivating factor for participation in an artistic event is cultural education.

Those indifferent to cultural offer of Cieszyn and Czech Cieszyn are a segment of customers who occasionally participate in cultural events, especially high culture (theatre, museum, classical music). In comparison with the previous segments of customers, the cultural needs of this group of residents of Cieszyn and Czech Cieszyn occupy a low position in the hierarchies of their life values and are felt with a lower intensity. Their market decisions depend to a greater extent on the price and the places where the cultural event will be held. Expenditures on participation in culture are at a relatively low level. However, among the behavioral patterns of a large part of this group, attention should be paid to the display effect (snobbery), which can be interpreted as a regularity describing the tendency of the customer to be similar to others. This group is particularly vulnerable to the marketing activities of cultural institutions. This group seeks information about the cultural offer above all in the press and in Internet (social media) and the family is also a source of information. It should be emphasized that they do not read magazines devoted to cultural issues.

The residents reluctant towards art is the least educated segment and at the same time the worst prepared for the reception of art. Deficiencies in education, in particular concerning knowledge of culture, often lead to a misunderstanding of art which, in turn, creates an aversion towards it. This is a group of people who are not interested in events in the field of culture, as they often perceive them as boring, designed for social elites or snobs. Therefore, the activities of cultural institutions in Cieszyn and Czech Cieszyn must be aimed at changing this specific group‘s perception of the institution itself and its offer. This task is very laborious, time consuming, and also very expensive. This group, although it is a strategic challenge for many cultural institutions in Cieszyn and Czech Cieszyn, cannot constitute the main segment on which these institutions focus their marketing efforts.

Through separating the market segments presented, as well as determining the direction in which the cultural institution's artistic offer is moving (elitism, popularity), experts participating in the research indicate it is possible to use one of the following four marketing strategies:

- Elitist art strategy,
- Art emphasizing strategy,
- Strategy of increasing sensitivity to art,
- Art popularization strategy.

The elitist art strategy is mainly designed for people associated with art professionally. In relation to residents with a positive attitude towards art, the use of the art emphasizing strategy seems to be the most appropriate. In regard to those indifferent to cultural offer, the strategy for increasing sensitivity to art should be used, and for residents reluctant to art, the art popularizing strategy.

Elitist Art Strategy

The implementation of the elitist art strategy by the cultural institution in Cieszyn and Czech Cieszyn is associated with the development of an artistic offer of the highest quality. The priority of this strategy is to popularize works of art whose level can match that of global cultural heritage and revive and enhance it. This is achieved through patronage extended by the cultural institution to the most valuable works of global cultural heritage, individual creators, and artists with significant achievements, or by promoting new prestigious investments, unique at an international level (e.g. the organization of new museum exhibition or organization an international theatre festival). The marketing is focused on a relatively narrow group (mostly people associated with art professionally), which is looking for an original, exclusive offer of the highest quality, made up of both classic works of art, as well as modern/avant-garde ones. Therefore, the strategy may be used by cultural institutions of Cieszyn and Czech Cieszyn focused on marketing which, when seeking market opportunities, often market a new offer, paying particular attention to its acceptance by the public. Addressees of the elitist art strategy are mostly well off, therefore according to Engel's law, the Katona effect, as well as the Veblen paradox, they are willing to allocate more funds to satisfying their needs in the field of culture. This fact, as well as an original cultural offer of the highest quality, entitles the cultural institution to use a prestigious price strategy, which makes it possible for the organization to achieve a satisfactory income. In the elitist art strategy it also seems to be the most appropriate to use the exclusive distribution strategy, the informing promotion strategy, and the image promotion strategy. However, other combinations are possible. It is very important that marketing activities facilitate the creation of a positive image of the cultural institution, which is both exclusive and prestigious. The most important advantage of using this strategy is the originality and high quality of an ambitious artistic offer. One of the main disadvantages is the high price, which is a barrier to accessing culture for those less privileged. Therefore, cultural institutions in Cieszyn and Czech Cieszyn that want to effectively promote cultural offer into residents should not only use this strategy. It seems necessary to combine it with the art emphasizing strategy, or even with the strategy of increasing sensitivity to art.

Art Emphasizing Strategy

The art emphasizing strategy is addressed to people with a positive attitude towards art, and its main goal is to distinguish the artistic offer of the cultural institution from competing products. Institutions seek to create such a position of their offer in the minds of buyers that it is seen as exceptional or even unique. Essentially, this should not pose major problems since cultural institutions, as one of the few, uphold the highest values through their activity. Theodor Adorno (1991), the author of the most systematic and most critical analysis of popular culture, and also high culture, says that in contrast to popular music - the reception of which is always passive, endlessly repeated, confirming the world as it is - art, for example symphonic music, refers to the pleasure derived from the imagination, proposing participation in a world as it could be (Storey 2003: 89-94). Therefore, this is a strategy in which a very important role is played by the positioning of the artistic offer. The positive perception of art and the positive attitude of the client in relation to the artistic offer results in the customer‘s readiness to a specific behavior, e.g. formulation of the intent to make a purchase or making a purchase. Using this strategy, however, requires the cultural institution of Cieszyn and Czech Cieszyn to move away from the passive transmission of information and replace it with stimulation and developing the ability to have a deeper participation in art, and also an individual understanding of the phenomena, processes, and people who create it. At the same time, this cannot be easily absorbed into the institution‘s specific programs and activities. Employees of cultural institutions of Cieszyn and Czech Cieszyn, in addition to personal predisposition, must have enormous substantive knowledge, abilities, and real skills, e.g. to take innovative, creative actions in addition to those basic ones related to reawakening and stimulating individual needs and interests. Institutions in cities divided by a border wishing to apply this strategy should strive for maximum penetration of the current market through appropriate promotional activities among residents of both side of border (mainly the strategy of building loyalty) and distribution activities (the strategy of selective distribution). It is also possible to achieve through the use of the neutral price strategy, which is based on the prices of competing products. The main advantage of the art emphasizing strategy is that it puts a lot of emphasis on the development of long-term relationships between the cultural institutions and the existing customers of their offer. Unfortunately, acquiring new customers of the artistic offer is a secondary issue here, which is its weakness.

Strategy of Increasing Sensitivity to Art

Hypothetically, it can be assumed that every person is sensitive to art, regardless of the level of culture, profession, environment, etc., but it must be added that this trait is not stable and is easily influenced by all these factors which affect the human psyche. It is formed through contact with art, acquiring experiences, and broadening the scope of reflection on artistic phenomena and, although it manifests itself spontaneously, it cannot occur without the appropriate stimuli. What stimulates it is the specific qualities of objects, e.g. rhythmic or expressive qualities, and particularly complicated structures occurring in art, harmonious or disharmonious, referred to as aesthetic structures (Kolb, 2005). The purpose of the strategy of increasing sensitivity to art is therefore to bring the people who are indifferent to art into contact with the offer of cultural institutions more frequently, and consequently stimulate their sensitivity to art. These activities rely heavily on ensuring the proper distribution of tickets and, more importantly, the services themselves. The cultural institution in a city divided by a border, in order to popularize its offer among the broadest possible group of people indifferent to art and to stimulate their ability to interpret art, should organize artistic events not only in its headquarters, but also in places closer to the target group (schools, parks, or churches). It is also important that the distribution of services (the selective distribution strategy) is supported by appropriate pricing strategies. It seems that the most appropriate strategy is the compensation price strategy, but promotion strategies, in particular the stimulating strategy, can be adopted. An important advantage of this strategy is that the cultural institutions of Cieszyn and Czech Cieszyn has the possibility of obtaining a customer segment which has not participated regularly in cultural events before, while the disadvantage is the relatively high cost of customer acquisition in relation to the low revenues earned from ticket sales.

Art Popularizing Strategy

A person's response to external stimuli regarding art (a cultural institution's offer) can be negative (Kolb, 2005). This reveals itself in perceiving certain negative attributes of a given product; expressing negative feelings towards the product; demonstrating a tendency to avoid the acquisition of the given services (Hill, O'Sullivan, 2003). In such cases, cultural institutions in cities divided by a border should adopt the art popularizing strategy. Its main purpose is to change the image of the organization, resulting in a change in the perception of the institution and its offer in the minds of customers. It must be remembered that in the cultural sector, we come into contact with certain psychological regularities of customer behavior. For example, a regularity consisting in assigning certain characteristics to products according to their appearance and other physical properties is very important. The assessment of a given object is made from the point of view of social judgments, which are considered correct and valid. It is widely recognized, for example, that formal attire is required in the theatre or concert hall which, for a certain group of customers, can be embarrassing. In other words, a cultural institution must attempt to change the beliefs of the customer through its impact on the cognitive element of the customer's attitude or to change the customer's feelings, which affect his emotions (e.g. ambition aspects), or attempt a simultaneous change of beliefs and feelings. To achieve this, modification appears necessary, as well as the adaptation of the cultural institution's of Cieszyn and Czech Cieszyn existing products to existing attitudes. This, however, poses a risk that they will become closer to entertainment than art. At the same time, it is necessary to use intensive distribution, which offers potential customers the possibility to come into contact with the institution's offer in places not yet associated with high culture (stadium, street, town square, etc.).

The appropriate shaping of price is also important. It should not be a barrier in the decision making process on participation in an artistic endeavor and therefore the symbolic (minimum) price strategy seems the most appropriate. Of course, a special role in promoting art is played by appropriate promotion, which should be directed at changing the image of the cultural institution. The main advantage of the popularization strategy is that the perception of the institution and its offer is altered by those people who have a reluctant attitude to art. This, in turn, leads to changing the attitude from reluctant to neutral or even to positive. Its most significant drawback is the commercialization of the cultural institution's offer, due to which it begins to manifest qualities closer to entertainment than art.

CONCLUSION

The beginning of the twenty-first century has brought significant changes in the functioning of cultural institutions in a cities divided by a border, but above all in the mentality of people - artists, creators, and especially the heads of arts organizations. They must confront new market realities, such as globalization, increasing competition within the sector, the wider sphere of entertainment, and the increasingly accelerated deployment of new technologies. The customers are also changing, ceasing to be merely the recipients of art and becoming the creators of the market. Both these circumstances, as well as the high competition in other spheres, the wider sphere of entertainment in general, and leisure activities has meant that a large number of cultural institutions in a cities divided by a border have changed their product orientation and began to operate in accordance with market orientation. This change, however, still raises a lot of controversy and is met with opposition from many representatives of the so-called art world. The adoption of a market oriented approach is for many heads (especially artistic directors) of cultural institutions still synonymous with the creation and dissemination of culture under the dictation of its recipients. Of course, the possibility of applying many model solutions known from source literature, i.e. strategies that are perfect for large corporations, are limited in the activities of cultural institutions. Some of them, however, can be modified and successfully used also in cultural institutions in a cities divided by a border. It should be remembered that the product offered by cultural institutions is very specific, so we must make sure that a balance is maintained between opinions about culture, with its inherent value and the need to protect it at all costs, and also the opinion that - like any other form of human activity - it should be profitable. Appropriate strategic or marketing management in the activities of cultural institutions can significantly contribute to the maintenance of this balance.

In this place it is also worth emphasizing, that Cieszyn and Czech Cieszyn as one of the few cities divided by international border have prepared a cross-border "Program for Culture". The program was developed in cooperation with the author of the chapter in 2018 and contains a diagnosis of the state of culture in Cieszyn and Czech Cieszyn, which became the basis for preparing four proposal of marketing strategies presented in this chapter. The data presented in "Program for Culture" shows that the vast majority of the residents of Cieszyn (69%) had not made use of the offer of the cultural institutions located in their town. The situation was even less optimistic regarding the inhabitants of Czech Cieszyn. In 2017, as many as 84% of inhabitants did not even once use the cultural offer available on the Polish side of the town. The presented data also show that Poles living in Cieszyn very rarely visit cultural institutions that are located on the other side of the border (more then 88% never use of cultural offer in Czech Cieszyn). The more then 51% surveyed residents of Czech Cieszyn declared, that they had not made use of the offer of the cultural institutions in Czech Cieszyn. Therefore, in the opinion of the authors, in the city Cieszyn - Czech Cieszyn seems to be the most appropriate application of "Art popularizing strategy".

Of course, the above considerations do not exhaust the problem, rather, they are only a modest contribution to further research. Cities divided by an international border in Europe constitute a very heterogeneous category, which is internally diverse in many respects. In many cases, the only element connecting them with each other is the fact that there is an international border dividing the city into two parts. Therefore, the research conclusions (proposed strategies) presented in this chapter cannot be adopted to all cities divided by a border. They may, however, be a good starting point for developing a joint cross-border cultural policy in cities that, like Cieszyn and Czech Cieszyn, are located in the European Union and the Schengen Area. The next step is to conduct similar research in cities located on the external border of the European Union. The examination of various case studies and viewpoints should contribute more fully to the explanation of the phenomenon described.

ACKNOWLEDGMENT

The research which was carried out was part of two Polish-Czech cross-border projects co-ðnanced by the European Regional Development Fund-Interreg V-A Programme Czech Republic-Poland under the Micro-Projects Fund of the Cieszyn Silesia Euroregion-Těšínské Slezsko and the state budget:

- The "Programme for Cieszyn and Czech Cieszyn Culture" project implemented in 2017–2018
- The "Czech Cieszyn/Cieszyn InEurope" project implemented in 2018–2019.

REFERENCES

Adorno, T. W. (1991). *The Schema of Mass Culture. The Culture Industry: Selected Essays on Mass Culture*. London, UK: Routledge.

Boorsma, M., & Chiaravalloti, F. (2010). Arts marketing performance: An artistic-mission-led approach to evaluation. *The Journal of Arts Management, Law, and Society*, *40*(4), 297–317. doi:10.1080/10632921.2010.525067

Bourdieu, P. (1994). *Distinction. A social Critique of the Judgement of Taste*. Cambridge, MA: Harvard University Press.

Castanho, R. A., Naranjo Gómez, J. M., & Kurowska-Pysz, J. (2019). How to Reach the Eurocities? A Retrospective Review of the Evolution Dynamics of Urban Planning and Management on the Iberian Peninsula Territories. *Sustainability*, *11*(3), 602. doi:10.3390u11030602

Dacko-Pikiewicz, Z., & Wróblewski, Ł. (2017). Spatial range of the inñuence of the philharmonic institutions in Katowice. *Forum Scientiae Oeconomia*, *5*, 17–34.

Hill, L., O'Sullivan, C., & O'Sullivan, T. (2003). *Creative Arts marketing, Linacre House*. Oxford, UK: Jordan Hill.

Jyrama, A., & Ayvari, A. (2010). Marketing contemporary visual art. *Marketing Intelligence & Planning*, *28*(6), 723–735. doi:10.1108/02634501011078129

Kolb, B. M. (2005). *Marketing for Cultural Organizations: New strategies for attracting audiences to Classical Music, Dance, Museums, Theater and Opera*. London, UK: Thomson Learning.

Kowalczyk, A., & Nawrocki, T. (1999). Współpraca transgraniczna w „miastach podzielonych - na przykładzie miast Słubice-Frankfurt nad Odrą oraz Cieszyn-Czeski Cieszyn. In A. Mync, & R. Szul (Eds.), *Rola granicy i współpracy transgranicznej w rozwoju regionalnym i lokalnym* (pp. 188–202). Warsaw, Poland: Europejski Instytut Rozwoju Regionalnego i Lokalnego Uniwersytetu Warszawskiego.

Kurowska-Pysz, J. (2016). Opportunities for Cross-Border Entrepreneurship Development in a Cluster Model Exempliðed by the Polish–Czech Border Region. *Sustainability*, *8*(3), 230. doi:10.3390u8030230

Lehman, K., & Wickham, M. (2014). Arts-Marketing and Marketing Strategy Development: Modeling The Marketing Activities of Visual Artists across Their Career. *Academy of Taiwan Business Management Review*, *9*(2), 133–141.

Lisiński, M. (2016). Metody naukowe w metodologii nauk o zarządzaniu. *Przegląd Organizacji* 4.

Perkmann, M. (2003). Cross-Border Regions in Europe: Signiðcance and Drivers of Regional Cross-Border Co-Operation. *European Urban and Regional Studies*, *10*(2), 153–17. doi:10.1177/0969776403010002004

Rentschler, R., & Shilbury, D. (2008). Academic assessment of arts management journals: A multidimensional rating survey. *International Journal of Arts Management*, *10*(3), 60–71.

Schroeder, J. E. (2005). The artist and the brand. *European Journal of Marketing*, *39*(11/12), 1291–1305. doi:10.1108/03090560510623262

Storey, J. (2003). *Cultural Studies and the Study of Popular Culture*. Athens, GA: University of Georgia Press.

Werpachowski, L. (2014). Regionalna współpraca transgraniczna na Śląsku Cieszyńskim. Doświadczenia i perspektywy, in Kasperek, A. (Ed.), Euroregion Śląsk Cieszyński – Těšínské Slezsko. Współpraca transgraniczna i międzyregionalna prowadzona w obszarze trójstyku polsko-czesko-słowackiego. Cieszyn-Katowice: Polska Akademia Nauk Oddział w Katowicach-Stowarzyszenie Rozwoju i Współpracy Regionalnej "Olza", pp. 15-25.

Wróblewski, Ł. (2014). Wpływ kultury i przemysłów kultury na wizerunek Euroregionu Śląsk Cieszyński, in Kasperek, A. (Ed.), Euroregion Śląsk Cieszyński – Těšínské Slezsko. Współpraca transgraniczna i międzyregionalna prowadzona w obszarze trójstyku polsko-czesko-słowackiego, Cieszyn-Katowice: Polska Akademia Nauk Oddział w Katowicach-Stowarzyszenie Rozwoju i Współpracy Regionalnej „Olza", pp. 37-82.

Wróblewski, Ł., Dacko-Pikiewicz, Z., & Cuyler, A. (2017). The European Union consumer behaviour in the festivals market in Poland. *Polish Journal of Management Studies*, *16*(2), 302–314. doi:10.17512/pjms.2017.16.2.26

Wróblewski, Ł., Dziadzia, B., & Dacko-Pikiewicz, Z. (2018). Sustainable Management of the Offer of Cultural Institutions in the Cross-Border Market for Cultural Services—Barriers and Conditions. *Sustainability*, *10*(9), 3253. doi:10.3390u10093253

Wróblewski, Ł., & Kasperek, A. (2019). Euroregion as an Entity Stimulating the Sustainable Development of the Cross-Border Market for Cultural Services in a City Divided by a Border. *Sustainability*, *11*(8), 2232. doi:10.3390u11082232

Chapter 10
Cross-Border Cooperation for Bilateral Trade, Travel, and Tourism:
A Challenge for India and Pakistan

Anita Medhekar
https://orcid.org/0000-0002-6791-4056
Central Queensland University, Australia

Farooq Haq
https://orcid.org/0000-0002-1620-9226
Canadian University of Dubai, UAE

ABSTRACT

Cross-Border Cooperation (CBC) is described as collaboration with neighbouring countries sharing land or sea borders to cooperate to reduce poverty and inequality among people, and improve living standards for sustainable development of the regions. European Union key objective has been CBC model where bordering countries in balanced partnership, have equal say in program decision-making process for sustainable development to meet common goals. The three factors essential for CBC clearly defined goals, promotion of political transparency, and promotion of connectivity and communication are correlated with the four levels of CBC implementation and public-private-partnerships. This chapter examines the challenge and significance of cross border cooperative relationship between India and Pakistan to disarm and have peace, for achieving 17 sustainable development goals in bordering conflict regions between the two countries for socio-economic progress and prosperity of the millions of people living in South Asia.

DOI: 10.4018/978-1-7998-2513-5.ch010

INTRODUCTION

Cross-Border Cooperation (CBC) is relatively a new phenomenon of the 21st century. It—CBC is described as collaboration with neighbouring countries sharing land, mountains, rivers or sea borders, in order to cooperate to reduce poverty, inequality and improve living standards in the region (Castanho, Loures, Cabezas, & Fernández-Pozo, 2017; DeSousa, 2012; Timothy, 2009). The three main objectives of CBC are: (i) Promoting economic and social development in border areas. (ii) Addressing common challenges (example-public health, education, poverty, environment, safety and security of population). (iii) Putting in place better conditions for movement of persons, goods and capital between countries (European Commission, 2019). Examples of successful development under CBC for bilateral relationship for partnering, cooperation, trade, travel and tourism exist across countries bordering Germany (Krätke, 2002), US-Canadian border (Timothy, 2009), Adriatic (Bufon, 2002), Sweden-Finland (Prokkola, 2008), European Union (EU) countries (DeSousa, 2012) and Portugal-Spain and Norway-Sweden (Medeiros, 2010).

According to De Sousa (2012) who established that, CBC provided a positive initiative for territorial co-operation and institutional innovation, that provides a platform for dialogue on economic development, growth, peace and prosperity between countries. Gordon (2009) emphasized that CBC also supports neighbouring countries against transnational crime, human trafficking and terrorism. Similarly, Heusala and Koistinen (2018) suggested a strategy to counter international crime and improve infrastructure construction and policy planning by adopting CBC approach for improving bilateral relationships. The CBC for bilateral trade can be best applied if the goals of cooperation between members are focused on political commitment, healthcare, transportation, tourism and border conflicts and obstacles facing any two countries (Castanho et al., 2018; Medeiros, 2018). Whereas, Wróblewski and Kasperek (2019), discussed sustainable development of Polish-Czech local cross-border markets for cultural services in cities divided by international borders. Further, sustainability is the foundation, for today's leading global framework of international cooperation to meet the three pillars of sustainable development such as, economic growth, social equity, and environmental protection 2030 agenda for sustainable development (IISD, 2019; UNSDP, 2019).

Due to rising economic and political crisis in the region, there is an urgent need and call for CBC for bilateral trade and mutual understanding between India and Pakistan and amongst the South Asian Association for Regional Cooperation (SAARC) group of eight (G-8) Afghanistan, Bhutan, Bangladesh, India, Maldives Nepal, Pakistan, and SriLanka, member countries. India and Pakistan share nearly 1.7 billion people with diverse religious spiritual orientations, languages and thousands of year's old rich cultural heritage. This multi-faith diversity provides a competitive edge to be a world leader in the market of spiritual tourism as a vehicle for global peace and set an example of effective functioning of a common market with a common currency in Asia (Haq & Medhekar, 2015, 2017). Therefore, political will for peace dialogue between India and Pakistan is necessary for CBC to bring about (i) peace and disarmament, (ii) socio-economic transformation, and (iii) economic progress and prosperity between the two nations and for the wider SAARC region to function efficiently and effectively to have a positive impact (Medhekar & Haq, 2019). Political will for bilateral peace dialogue to solve border dispute over Kashmir, will help to achieve not only CBC goals for the two nations, but also the three pillars of sustainable development (i) economic growth, (ii) social equity, and (iii) environmental protection including the United Nations 17-sustainable development goals (17-SDGs), introduced in September 2015, and widely adopted by businesses, educational institutions, governments, and non-government organisations (IISD, 2019; UNSDP, 2019).

Cross-Border Cooperation between India and Pakistan for bilateral trade, travel, and tourism can offer many business opportunities for economic development, growth, prosperity and peace between the two nations (Hall & Page, 2012). It can also spread to all eight SAARC countries. Gordon (2009) further proved that SAARC could be used to build confidence and provide a post-hoc platform for cooperation among member nations in general, India and Pakistan specifically. Given the historical and cultural affinity between the two countries, CBC for sustainable peace to achieve common goals and mutual benefit should not be an issue (Medhekar & Haq, 2019; Seung-Hyun, Shenkar, & Li, 2008). Gordon (2009, p. 86) specified the main weakness of bilateral CBC between India and Pakistan as: “although information exchange appears in the exhortatory policy, it does not occur to any significant degree”.

Historically, India, Pakistan, Bangladesh and some parts of Nepal and Afghanistan were one country for centuries. However, since the partition of India or Hindustan in 1947, cross border cooperation and bilateral talks have failed to bring about peace over Kashmir, for sustainable development of the region. Since February 2019 and recent events due to revoking the seven decades of autonomous status to Jammu and Kashmir in August 2019, the bilateral relationship between the two countries have again become hostile and diplomatic ties, trade and two train routes are suspended, and countries again seem to be on the brink of war (Chaudhary & Jacob, 2019). Both the countries have fought three wars over Kashmir and millions of dollars are spent on defense expenditure, which could have been spent for development purposes. Reasons include lack of political commitment to peacefully cooperate since partition, political mistrust, incidence of cross-border terrorism, numerous wars between the two nations over Kashmir in 1965, 1971, 2002 and cross-border skirmishes (Medhekar & Haq, 2019; Sugunakararaju & Akhtar, 2015).

The recent February 2019 air-attack by India on Pakistan, August-2019 Kashmir issue, on again and off again friendship trains and bus service across borders and the blame game, which never seems to see peace-lamp at the end of the tunnel. Moreover, the message of hate, hostility and religious nationalism across nations has been selling well to win votes from large number of extremists on both sides. War, mistrust and lack of political will has had a continuous negative impact to have any permanent peace solution for future generations of the two countries through bilateral dialogues, to promote trade, travel, and tourism for the progress and prosperity of the millions living in the two countries.

Literature review indicates publications on CBC do not consider cross-border cooperation between conflict regions for example between Pakistan and India over border dispute. Further, this conceptual paper will add two most important objectives to current three CBC objectives, particularly for bordering countries with conflict regions such as SAARC region, where India and Pakistan are the key countries which could demonstrate good example of bilateral CBC in SAARC region by conducing (i) peaceful dialogue and discussion to resolve border conflicts and disputes (ii) disarmament for peace and prosperity between the bordering countries of SAARC for sustainable peace and sustainable development.

Heusala and Koistinen (2018) identified three key factors that will be applied in this paper to promote territorial success between both countries: (i) defining clear and common goals and objectives, (ii) promoting political transparency to commit for decisions linked with bilateral CBC projects, and (iii) promoting connectivity and bilateral communications. This research paper suggests a bilateral CBC between both countries based on the four levels of commitment presented by Castanho et al. (2018) and De Sousa (2012) as: (a) awareness raising co-cooperation – (b) mutual aid co-cooperation –(c) functional co-cooperation, and (d) common management of public resources.

The aim of this chapter is to: (i) examine the significance and relationship between bilateral cross-border cooperation (CBC) required for peace, disarmament and three pillars of sustainable development for achieving 17-SDGs in conflict regions bordering the neighbouring countries, with the aim for peace between India and Pakistan in SAARC region for socio-economic, progress and prosperity of the millions of people living in South Asia. (ii) Evaluate the success or failure of SAARC strategies that have been adopted for CBC for promoting trade and sustainable development. (iii) Propose a Public-Private Partnerships (PPPs) framework that could be adopted in India and Pakistan and border SAARC region for bilateral CBC and achieving the UN 17-SDG. This paper attempts to provide a platform for bilateral CBC for peace dialogue, disarmament and sustainable development for creating socio-economic development opportunities by bilateral trade, travel, tourism, business and employment opportunities in India and Pakistan, and empowering the local cross-border communities for their mutual benefit and sustainable future.

This chapter is structured as follows. The first section of the chapter introduces the importance and significance of bilateral CBC for achieving all or some of the United Nations 17-SDGs. Section two provides the literature review on CBC for sustainable development as a peace dividend for social transformation and economic progress and prosperity, specifically in case of India and Pakistan and global context in general. Section three discusses the development opportunities and socio-economic mutual benefits from bilateral CBC to India and Pakistan in particular, and SAARC countries in general. Section four presents recommendations for policy implications for Bilateral CBC between India and Pakistan and proposes a PPPs framework necessary for bilateral cross-border and cross-sector to build trust and promote trade, travel and tourism. Discussion in section five, and Section six provides conclusion and future research directions to advance the knowledge in the field of bilateral trade and CBC for peace and effective working of regional bodies such as SAARC for achieving 17-SDGs and economic prosperity to transform the region.

BACKGROUND

Cross-Border Cooperation (CBC)

Cross-Border Cooperation (CBC) is based on a background that is full of blood, hostility and hatred. Gordon (2009) explains the history of CBC with an example that today's European integration emerged from the bones and ashes of hundreds of years of war between France and Germany. The understanding and cooperation initiated only when the war-weary characters realised that partnership rather than rivalry was the only path to progress. Researchers agree that now Europe seems to have achieved the optimal position where regional cooperation is appreciated as a more valued approach in managing local, regional and national issues, and complementing each other with dialogue and expertise to solve mutual problems.

Cross-Border Cooperation (CBC) is best described as collaboration with neighbouring countries sharing land or sea borders in order to cooperate to reduce poverty, inequality among people and improve living standards for sustainable development of the regions (DeSousa, 2012; Timothy, 2009). European Union key objective has been CBC model where bordering countries in balanced partnership, have equal say in program decision making process for sustainable development to meet common goals. The projects under the CBC program receive funding if implemented by partnering countries on both sides with the aim for mutual benefit and sustainable development of the region; for example, in EU, South-Eastern

Europe, upper Adriatic and Baltic countries (De Sousa, 2012; Dimitrov, Petrakos, Totev, & Tsiapa,2014; Gerfert, 2009; Lepik, 2009).

In a different context, Kurowska-Pysz and Szczepańska-Woszczyna (2017) defined Cross-border cooperation as a unique case of inter-organizational partnership that is based on territorial, economic and social issues, in the shared borderland regions of two or more countries. Kurowska-Pysz and Szczepańska-Woszczyna (2017) discussed from their research that effective success of CBC depends on various players that are identified as three groups of factors: (i) people, agencies and institutions – quality of communication and personal relationships; (ii) cross-border planning, procedures and support mechanisms; and (iii) environment (historical resemblance and geographical immediacy and local level in neighbouring countries.

Cooperation can be of three types beyond borders (Verheugen & Barnier, 2000, pp.13-14). These should be linked with the border objectives of CBC between India and Pakistan, goals of SAARC regions, underpinning the three pillars of sustainable development and the United Nations 17-SDGs.

(a) **Cross-border Cooperation***:* Direct cooperation with the neighbours in all areas of life between regional and local authorises, along the border areas involving all stakeholders living around the borders (government, people, local businesses, farmers, educational institutions, artists and academics etc). They should have equality in decision making irrespective of the geographical size of the country, population, and its economic importance. Competencies and expertise on both side of the border should be harnessed to its full potential for CBC in planning, development and implementation stage and finally evaluation of the programs within the plans, to meet the set objectives of CBC, SAARC and 17-SDG. Srinivasan (2012), has analysed the direct link between cross-border cooperation for infrastructure development which has the potential to reduce poverty in the SAARC region with improved access to markets for trade, travel, health and education services and increase in productivity and economic growth for the group of eight (G-8) SAARC countries.

(b) **Inter-regional Cooperation:** Cooperation between regional and local authorities in a single sector such as small business, agriculture, border security cooperation, manufacturing, service sector, educational institutions, research and national institutions, banking and finance, tourism etc. Other SAARC countries in the region such as Bangladesh, Sri Lanka, Bhutan, and Nepal could be invited on a joint platform for political, economic, health, environment and social development programs.

(c) **Trans-national Cooperation***:* Cooperation between the SAARC countries for specific subjects is required, for example on regional development, trade, travel and tourism; at central government, national, local and states bordering with the countries such as the regional state of Kashmir, Punjab, Rajasthan and Gujarat share the border with Pakistan. Similarly states of West Bengal, Assam, Tripura and Meghalaya borders with Bangladesh; and eastern Ladakh region and Arunachal Pradesh with China.

Sustainable Development Goals

Although theoretical relationship between bilateral CBC for sustainable peace for achieving three pillars of sustainable development, economic growth, social equity, environmental protection, and prosperity of crossborder nations has been established, yet research on bilateral CBC for sustainable peace and meeting 17-SDGs can be applied and established in case of India and Pakistan and amongst the SAARC countries. United Nations, all 17-SDGs are based on cooperative partnership for all countries to achieve the five Ps-framework: (i) people, (ii) planet, (iii) prosperity, and (iv) peace and (v) partnering, and ensure their sustainability, for economic development, growth, equity, progress and prosperity of all the people and nations (Van Tulder, 2018).

Long-term bilateral CBC is necessary for achieving the UN 17-SDGs as a peace dividend for social transformation and economic progress and prosperity, specifically in case of India and Pakistan and the wider SAARC regional in general. However, the 17-SDGs very explicitly highlight the important role of partnership (i.e. goal number 17) to help progress towards SDGs 2030 agenda. All stakeholders from grassroots level, people, businesses, educational institutions, local, regional and national governments need to be involved in bilateral CBC. Further, where multiple stakeholder's collaboration and cooperation are involved, going a step further to Cross-Sector Partnerships (CSPs) (Van Tulder & Keen, 2018) for solving wicked problem by achieving (i) peace and disarmament, (ii) socio-economic transformation, and (iii) economic progress and prosperity (United Nations- SDGs) between the bordering nations and accelerate the pace of change and progress.

Asian Countries and CBC

In an Asian perspective, regional associations that reflect the organisation and operation of CBC include the examples of ASEAN (Association of Southeast Asian Nations) and SAARC (South Asian Association for Regional Cooperation). Kurowska-Pysz and Szczepańska-Woszczyna (2017) argue that hostilities and partnerships in this region are still premature, ASEAN being performing better than South Asian group of eight (G-8) countries under SAARC. However, both associations still lack confidence in their cooperative mechanisms. Moreover, it is not essential to assume that neighbouring members of a regional association should be naturally easy to cooperate than the far away ones.

It is generally accepted that neighbours are often hostile enemies and such enemies look for overcoming their enemies with powerful allies placed in more distant regions, it is more accepted in Asian countries with reference to the examples of Thailand and Myanmar as active members of ASEAN (Kurowska-Pysz & Szczepańska-Woszczyna, 2017). Thailand and Myanmar are traditional rivals and have engaged in conflict and competition for centuries. Similarly, tensions have been around between Malaysia and Indonesia as well as Singapore and Malaysia. ASEAN was established in 1967 during difficult times and with members experiencing tensions with immediate neighbours, it was a challenge to establish and make it work. The model chosen for cooperation within ASEAN was based on consensus. This model of consensus was also mapped with the Asian-way committing to non-interference and mutual respect permitting the flow of cooperation amongst tensed neighbours, improving with informal mechanisms (Kurowska-Pysz & Szczepańska-Woszczyna, 2017).

In South Asia, the CBC is more complex as India and Pakistan have experienced political, military and economic rivalry since the partition and independence from the United Kingdom in August 1947. This hostility has been destructive for SAARC that makes the rivalries within ASEAN seem much humbler. SAARC was established in 1985 and there is no argument about the unfortunately limited success, if any, in its performance in managing regional issues. The model of consensus that was mapped with the Asian-way for ASEAN needs to be redesigned and applied for SAARC. This chapter aims to find and deliver solutions for CBC between India and Pakistan, the discussion on problems and solutions of SAARC is beyond the scope of this research. Srinivasan (2012) has stressed that there is infrastructure deficit in South Asia and the urgent need for cross-border infrastructure development between the SAARC countries which not only integrates the regions, but also as a strategy for poverty reduction in the subcontinent, which generates employment opportunities, cross-border trade, travel and accelerates economic growth and living standards for millions living below poverty line in bordering villages of the two nations, without any access to clean drinking water, sanitation, electricity, healthcare and education.

India and Pakistan in particular, and South Asian countries in general should have a written charter of bilateral CBC goals for facilitating friendly relationship and for promoting socio-economic development in border areas and between SAARC countries to address numerous common challenges of border security, infrastructure and human development. Gordon (2009, p. 85) specified the failure of SAARC due to 'dysfunctional regionalism'. Various wicked problems include poverty, illiteracy, access to primary health, food and energy security, homelessness, unemployment, infrastructure bottlenecks, safety and security of citizens, climate change security. Only through CBC and peace dialogue, millions of dollars can be diverted from current level of defense expenditures in India and Pakistan and SAARC member countries, towards achieving peace for sustainable development expenditure, to solve various socio-economic problems faced by millions living in poverty in the two countries and SAARC region at large (Gordon, 2009).

Verheugen and Barnie (2000) suggestions that CBC model of EU should be adapted by India and Pakistan for successful infrastructure development projects under bilateral CBC between and within the SAARC region. A public-private-partnerships (PPPs) arrangement, establish subsidiaries, cross border development programs at joint, regional and local level as well as independent sources of financing development projects is required. Din (1988) focused on the need for diplomatic activities through partnership, dialogue, bilateral trade, travel and tourism, education and mass communication as four effective agents for sustainable peace and progress.

SOCIO-ECONOMIC BENEFITS FROM CBC: INDIA, PAKISTAN AND SAARC

In this 21th century and 72 years since independence in August 1947, CBC in context of India and Pakistan for Kashmir peace dialogue and disarmament for sustainable development and growth is critical. South Asian Association for Regional Cooperation was established in 1985, and only in 2004, South Asian Free Trade Area (SAFTA) was recognised as a slow transition towards a common market. However, this dream of a common market such as the EU has not yet realised in South Asia given the old rivalries and embedded nationalism, due to historical rivalry and political conflicts between India and Pakistan since 1947 partition over Kashmir, Bangladesh-Pakistan partition in 1971, and Afghanistan-Pakistan and influx of millions of refugee cross-border, at the detriment of the progress of the South Asian countries and millions living under the poverty line in the SAARC member countries.

Since the election of the Prime Minster Imran Khan in 2018, with his positive outlook for 'New Pakistan' and relationship with neighbouring country –India, is 'not to dwell in the past, but look to the future'. The focus of PM Khan is on socio-economic development, peace and prosperity for the people of Pakistan and India for peace and prosperity of the millions of people living in the Indian sub-continent via bilateral trade, travel and tourism. Further, the PM of Pakistan inaugurated in 2018, developing the cross-border spiritual tourism destination and opening the Kartarpur pilgrim corridor to the Sikh Temple (Mecca for the Sikhs) in Pakistan, to celebrate the 550th birth anniversary of the first Sikh Guru Nanak Ji. This will attract Sikh pilgrims from cross-border in India and around the world to travel to Pakistan for Sikh spiritual tourism. Further, cross-border development of spiritual tourism corridor between India and Pakistan can be a peace vehicle for socio-economic transformation and sustainable development of trade and employment opportunities along the border areas of India and Pakistan (Medhekar & Haq, 2019; Hall & Page, 2012).

This proposed spiritual tourism corridor initiative, along with recent return of the captured Indian Pilot in Feb 2019, by PM of Pakistan is a great step towards the CBC for peace, prosperity for sustainable-economic development of the two countries. If this first initiative is successful then through commitment for CBC via peace dialogues and not by raising arms against each other, one can move the Himalayan mountains to achieve sustainable peace necessary for achieving 17-SDGs, similar to the ASEAN, and the EU regions, which will result in socio-economic prosperity and inclusive growth of millions living below the poverty line and promote bilateral-trade, travel, tourism, business, and create investment and employment opportunities between the two countries and within the SAARC region.

However, unfortunately the current fundamentalist Indian government in power and some of the other aligned political parties are not for resolving issues between the two countries with cross-border cooperative peace dialogue. They are still aiming for political short-term gains, Kashmir issue, and living in the past conflicts, rather than CBC for peaceful dialogue for long-term peace for economic development and prosperity. A bilateral- CBC between the two countries can be achieved only with peace dialogue, with the aim to solve various socio-economic problems for sustainable development of the bordering areas.

There are few examples of bilateral CBC between India-Nepal, India-Bhutan electricity cooperation, but very slow and limited efforts are made due to regional barriers, cross-border conflicts; to fully harness the bilateral cross-border cooperation for electricity generation, distribution and trade, with the growing population demand urbanisation and access to larger market share for economic development and welfare of the people in the South Asian region (Singh, Jamasab, Nepal & Toman, 2018). Figure 1 illustrates the eight SAARC member countries, having centuries old historical, political, social, economic, cultural, linguistic and familial relationships.

Cooperation amongst the group of eight (G8-SAARC) countries can be very useful and beneficial to all, and open millions of opportunities for technical, socio-economic cooperation and partnering for improving healthcare, education, research and development, disaster management, supply of water and electricity, food shortage, trade, travel and tourism. Removing barriers to CBC and strengthening bilateral CBC for trade could be a solution for numerous wicked problems such as poverty and illiteracy faced by millions in India and Pakistan, and the other six South Asian neighbouring countries related to poverty, water and electricity, shortage, food security, healthcare, education, access to clean drinking water, sanitation, housing for homeless and joint defense petrol to solve crossborder terrorism, human and drug trafficking. Efforts must be made to remove several political and historical barriers

Figure 1. Group of Eight SAARC Countries
Source: SAARC, 2019

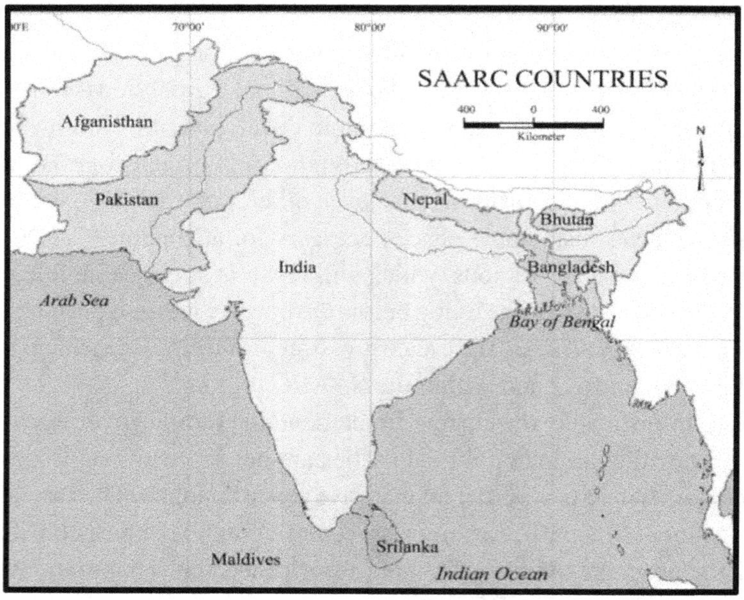

mainly between India and Pakistan which reflect the regional level 21st century political climate, where the bilateral CBC is limited to national level (government to government), rather than at grassroots people-to-people, artists, scholars and business-to-business private sector level in bordering areas.

It is nearly 72 years after independence in 1947, and there is short-term political goals and mistrust between the politicians and bureaucracy of the two countries; A peace dialogue over Kashmir border dispute since partition, has never been required more, than now in the 21st century between the two countries. Following Indonesia, India has second largest followers of Islam in the world (176 million =14.4% of total population) and third Pakistan 168 million (PEW Research Centre, 2017). In the long-run, CBC leads to mutual benefit for the millions of people living below poverty line in both countries, local business, public and private sector organisations. Individuals and educational institutions also benefit through bilateral trade, travel, tourism development, infrastructure investment, research collaborations, exchange of scholars, students, artists. It will create innumerable people–to-people and business-to-business opportunities having positive impact of peace dividend to meet the UN-17 sustainable development goal (UNSDG, 2019). Unless active participation and dialogue for peace and disarmament is pursued between the two largest countries India and Pakistan in the group of G-8 SAARC, economies, various regional and bilateral CBC programs will not take-off. That is, all embracing and successful South Asian Regional Cooperation will be unachievable, inefficient and ineffective to achieve 17-SDG, related to zero hunger, poverty, human development, infrastructure development, for the progress and prosperity of the millions of South Asian people.

SOLUTIONS AND RECOMMENDATIONS

Public–private-partnerships (PPPs) between India and Pakistan and SAARC region, through bilateral CBC, to achieve not just the three EU objectives of CBC and sustainable development three pillars of economic growth, social equity, and environmental protection; but additional 2 objective of bilateral dialogue for permanent cross-border peace and disarmament for achieving UN 17-SDGs, as proposed by this paper is required. It is paramount that bilateral CBC for countries with border conflict, for mutual benefit of the two countries is necessary, for sustainable management of cross-border trade, travel, tourism, agriculture, business, small and medium enterprises and agricultural resources.

An effective platform is adopted from three factors presented by Heusala and Koistinen (2018) applied to promote territorial success between India and Pakistan as explained below:

(i) **Clearly Defined and Common Objectives***:* For a successful CBC, both countries need to have objectives for CBC that are clear, transparent and similar. Over the years the goals and objectives for CBC not only changed among the two countries but also within. For example, the Left-Wing Congress Government of India had a different plan compared to the Right Wing Bharatia Janta-Party. Similarly, in the past, a military led government of Pakistan had a different vision compared to the democratic Pakistan People's Party. The current governments of both countries need to sit, discuss and negotiate peacefully the goals for CBC rather than assume or expect the other to be compliant.

(ii) **Political Transparency***:* Both countries need to resolve and set the political transparency within their own countries and then bring the agenda on a table. Both countries have several right, left and central political parties that must be aligned within the CBC policies. The combined CBC policies can then be passed on and shared, in fact there is a lot that India and Pakistan could learn from each other in political development, which benefits the citizens of the nation.

(iii) **Connectivity and Bilateral Communications***:* This paper suggests that the completion of the first two steps will lead towards connectivity and bilateral communication. The need is for both governments to specify the departments and people that will be in touch at various stages for different activities and measure the progress of the CBC programs.

The following recommendations are provided for bilateral CBC between India and Pakistan, once permanent peace over Jammu and Kashmir border dispute is settled between the two countries through bilateral peaceful dialogue. Hence, without the bilateral cooperation of the two countries, suggested recommendations are difficult to plan, and implement for achieving bilateral peace, disarmament and UN 17-SDGs, which will just remain a dream for authors on paper.

- Inter-regional social and economic development programs for inclusive growth which contribute to social and economic cohesion between India and Pakistan and other six SAARC countries (Afghanistan, Bhutan, Bangladesh, Nepal, SriLanka, and Maldives)
- Establish an economic development fund for the G8-SAARC countries for providing scholarships and conducting educational, research and development training program by academic and scholars, for promoting cooperation and peace for mutual benefit from bilateral trade and prosperity of the millions of people living in the regions.
- Establish a database of technical, social-economic and scientific expertise for mutual benefit of the region.
- Establish a list of key private sector business list of entrepreneurs who can invest through CBC under the umbrella of SAARC and create local job opportunities within the region such as TATA and Birla.
- Establish a SAARC single market with common currency, such as the European Union and free trade zones and supply-chains in border areas.
- Establish CBC programs to solve cross-border problems of security and claims of cross-border terrorism on land and sea.
- Cooperation for developing border areas infrastructure- tele-communication and transport supply chain channels such as, road, rail, water transport, shopping malls and hotels, are essential for sustainable new cross-border cooperative economic projects related to trade, travel and tourism.
- Encouraging diversity of economic activities and networking to prevent depopulation due to fear of cross-border terror and isolation.
- Cross-border cooperation to invest in human capital, physical capital, invention and innovation, and health infrastructure to provide quality education, employment opportunities, clean drinking water and sanitation, waste recycling, agriculture logistics, and infrastructure facilities in bordering regions.

- Encouraging partnerships programmes at cross-border grassroots local and regional levels for social and economic cooperation for promoting and solving every day cross-border conflict, local, environmental, agricultural, and socio-economic problems.
- Organising cross-border events such as festivals, conferences, trade fairs, cultural and sporting events and programs to encourage CBC in business, trade, travel and tourism related activities.
- Cross-border cooperation for conserving natural, environmental, spiritual and cultural heritage sites which is common history shared by both the nations and promote travel and tourism between the two countries.
- Cross-border cooperation for joint exercises with three wings of the armed forces, including border security and coastal guards to protect the two countries borders and SAARCC region.
- Supporting CBC for joint cultural events, by famous artist, singers and film stars should be encouraged under freedom of cultural democracy by creating a cross-border market for cultural services, as suggested by Wróblewski and Kasperek (2019). Recent example is where the Indian government prevented popular and famous artists from neighbouring Pakistan to travel and acting in Indian Bollywood cinemas and some were deported, leaving a bitter taste amongst the Indian fans.
- Neutral legal and institutional arrangements at national, regional and local bilateral cross-border level between neighbouring states bordering the countries, are required to facilitate and (not hinder) the smooth functioning of the various projects within the programs for CBC for funding, planning, implementation, monitoring and evaluation. For example, bilateral, cross-border working committees, protocol, treaties, business and investment contracts and bilateral-agreements at all levels for neighbourly cooperation and friendships for establishing good relations for promoting friendship, peace, cross-border local community initiatives to promote trade, travel and tourism for social cohesion, cultural exchange, improve health and education, economic development and prosperity.
- Finally, to have cross-border cooperation by public-private-partnership between all the stakeholders local, regional and national level to provide a peaceful, business and people friendly and attractive environment for private investment opportunities. This will create jobs, encourage trade, travel and tourism and provide a foundation to establish gateway flourishing cities of peace, trust, friendship and trade at the border areas.

Figure 2 provides a framework for PPPs between India and Pakistan for bilateral -CBC extending to cross-sector PPPs between the key stakeholders to plan, implement,

Figure 2. PPPs for Bilateral CBC between India and Pakistan
Source: Figure developed for this paper

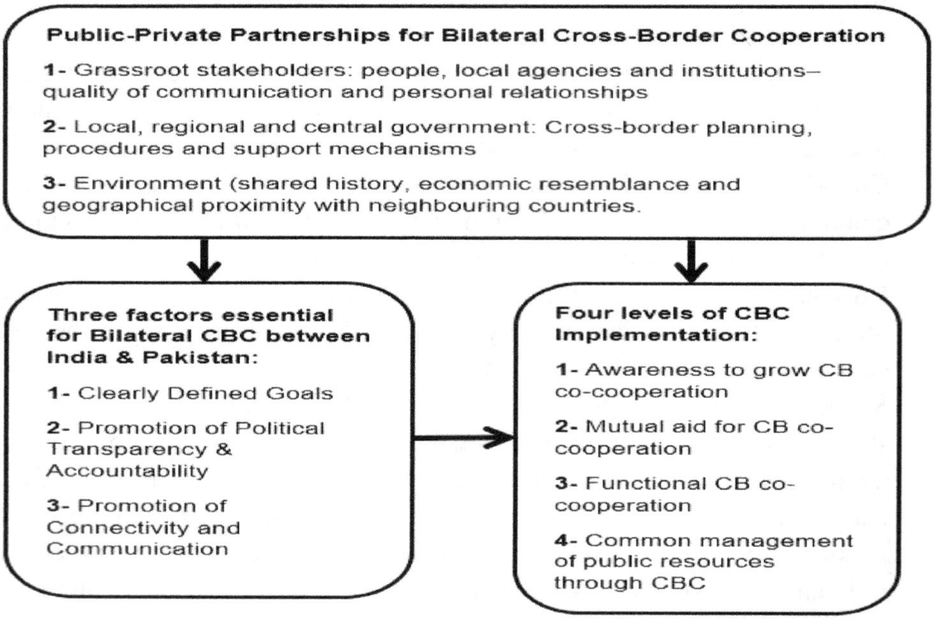

and evaluate projects and program in a transparent manner; starting from grassroots people living at the bordering villages, local council, regional and national level for the sustainability of people, planet, prosperity, peace and partnership (Van Tulder, 2018). Therefore, the success of bilateral CBC depends on the commitment and willpower for promoting peace dialogue for bilateral CBC, for trade, travel and tourism, to achieve United Nations 17-SDGs for millions living in South Asian region.

The proposed PPPs framework adopts the three factors provided by Heusala and Koistinen (2018), essential for bilateral-CBC between two countries extending to various sectors of the economy: (i) clearly defined goals, (ii) promotion of political transparency, and (iii) promotion of connectivity and communication. These three factors are directly correlated with the four levels of CBC implementation plan: (i) awareness to grow co-cooperation, (ii) mutual aid co-cooperation, (iii) functional co-cooperation, and (iv) common management of public resources in bordering areas (Castanho et al., 2018; De Sousa, 2012).

DISCUSSION

SAARC is not functional mainly because of lack of commitment and willpower between the governments of the two nations to promote peace for cross border SBC for trade, travel and tourism between the two countries who should take the lead within the SAARC region. Historical barriers since the partition of 1947, should be eliminated by the new generations of leaders via political will and CBC and commitment towards peace and prosperity through CBC, for defense security to eradicate terrorism and conflict across national borders, socio-economic progress, prosperity to promote trade, travel and tourism between India and Pakistan and the six other SAARC member countries.

According to Verheugen and Barnier (2000), CBC is most successful where from bottom-up approach regional and local administrative bodies and stakeholders take the collective and joint initiative and responsibility to plan, implement and evaluate the CBC strategies and programmes for sustainable long-term fruitful and peaceful bilateral CBC for local, regional and national development in terms of promoting peace, disarmament, trade, travel, and tourism between the two countries and SAARC region at large. An analysis of the actual and potential strengths, weaknesses, opportunities, and threats (SWOT), should be undertaken every 5 years to address problems and promote CBC for mutual benefit of both the country's and SAARC region at large with maritime borders with island of SriLanka and Maldives.

Based on the above analysis, this paper adopts the four levels of commitment presented by Castanho et al. (2018) and De Sousa (2012) for bilateral CBC between India and Pakistan as listed below:

(i) **Awareness Raising Co-cooperation**: This must be managed by the top government officials including both Prime Ministers activists and academics who research on peaceful CBC for economic development, progress and prosperity. The national leaders must teach their respective nations about the needs and benefits of bilateral CBC. The several media channels can also play an important role to create and diffuse the awareness. The governments of both countries need to have political will and specify media agencies tasked to work together to create the awareness and culture of friendship and trust among both nations to encourage trade and travel which will benefit the citizens of both the nations.

(ii) **Mutual Aid Co-cooperation**: The agencies and departments of both countries must be specified and trained for mutual aid cooperation that could be for natural disasters, social clashes or even economic crisis. The public private partnerships as explained earlier could also support this activity.

(iii) **Functional Co-cooperation**: This is the ministerial level responsibility where certain ministers must take the challenge for the completion of specific bilateral CBC activities, plans and programs. Imran Khan, the current Prime Minster of Pakistan, has personally constructed some task force teams with similar and direct goals and targets for solving bilateral concerns and promote bilateral CBC trade and travel for mutual benefit of the two nations. The governments of both countries are advised to create a combined office with cross-border intellectuals to monitor, assess and advise the performance of these activities with the manifesto of effective and sustainable CBC.

(iv) **Common Management of Public Resources**: Finally, the people of both countries such as students, academics, scholars, scientists, performing artists, and businesses must create and develop their own people-to-people personal contacts and friendship for successful implementation of any bilateral CBC plans, programs and activities. Several platforms based on social circles, sports activities, environment campaigns, water sharing, forest and fisheries resource management, music events, spiritual gatherings, and social clubs could be the way to engage common people managing the public resources for bilateral CBC success.

The homogeneity of the bordering local and regional states must be considered between India and Pakistan with shared race, language, social, culture, music, linguistic and economic history and family connections across with the Indian bordering states of the state of Gujarat, Rajasthan, Punjab and Kashmir with Pakistan side of the border. Some of these regions are deserts, mountainous and remote villages which are less developed, developed rural farming lands and more develop regions of bordering towns and cities.

Cross-Sector, Public-Private Partnerships and commitment for bilateral trade and CBC with regional, local and national partners for trade, business, travel and tourism will help the regions to development, attract private investment, develop sustainable transport and communication channels as the centuries old Grant Trunk Road, between India and Pakistan and greater SAARC regions. This will have a significant impact on improving business competitiveness, socio, political and economic trade relationships at all levels- people, educational institutions, artists, business, local and regional government. Further, it is important to be transparent and accountable with moral and ethical standard and formal process to ensure the evaluation and accomplishment of the goals of bi-lateral CBC (Bowen, et al., 2017; Biermann, Kanie & Kim, 2017).

FUTURE RESEARCH DIRECTIONS

The future research direction of this paper identifies empirical research based on qualitative and quantitative data collected from CBC based buyers and suppliers of trade, travel and tourism in both countries. People living in border areas of conflict zones and small and large business can be interviewed to know their perception on CBC and the benefits from cooperation versus the costs of conflict and non-cooperation between India and Pakistan. The public and private planners of CBC could be contacted for direct interviews to get insights into opportunities and weaknesses regarding bilateral CBC between India and Pakistan. The business and personal beneficiaries of bilateral CBC between both countries could be contacted by passing on surveys to realise and assess the costs and benefits of the partnership. The results and findings from such future studies on bilateral CBC can be generalized to other conflict zones to realise the potential benefits from cross-border cooperation

CONCLUSION

This unique paper has studied the situation between India and Pakistan and have suggested bilateral CBC and PPPs framework as a working solution, where the initiative should be taken from the bottom-up approach at grassroots level- people to people, local government of bordering villages, regional/ states sharing the common border and finally the central/national government. This is to be applied to all G-8 SAARC nations. The chapter explains the meanings and applications of bilateral-CBC in current world situation where European states and ASEAN present a perfect and a workable example of success.

Then the case of SAARC is examined which has shown no credible success over the years, mainly due to lack of political will for peaceful dialogue to end the mistrust for CBC to promote trade, travel and tourism between the two countries and SAARC region in general and operate as a South Asian trading block and common market. Based on SAARC case analysis, the situation faced by India and Pakistan was elaborated with all the weaknesses and opportunities to reap the benefits from bilateral CBC, by first establishing peace and disarmament, for meeting the national goals which must align with SAARC, and UN 17-SDGs and promote bilateral trust, trade, travel, and tourism, harnessing its full resource potential to improv lives of millions living below poverty line in the region, for bilateral CBC and integration of G-8 SAARC countries to work efficiently.

This paper concludes with numerous key recommendations and offers a working platform based on clearly defined and common goals, promotion of political transparency, accountability, and promotion of connectivity and communication for mutual benefit, which is possible only if bilateral peaceful talks are held over Kashmir border dispute and this problem solved permanently, so that trust can be established between governments, and people for implementing the suggested bilateral CBC achieving the 17-SDGs. The discussion offers an implementation plan for India and Pakistan and countries in conflict wanting to improve cross-border cooperation for bilateral relationships based on three factors that are correlated, with the four levels of bilateral CBC implementation: awareness to grow co-cooperation, mutual aid co-cooperation, functional co-cooperation and common management of public resources for the benefit of the two countries, in order to bring about peace, prosperity and inclusive growth to achieve, sustainable development goals for millions living in the two countries.

REFERENCES

Biermann, F., Kanie, N., & Kim, R. E. (2017). Global Governance by Goal-Setting: The Novel Approach of the UN Sustainable Development Goals. *Current Opinion in Environmental Sustainability*, *26*, 26–31. doi:10.1016/j.cosust.2017.01.010

Bowen, K. J., Cradock-Henry, N., Koch, F., Patterson, J., Häyhä, T., Vogt, J., & Barbi, F. (2017). Implementing the "Sustainable Development Goals": Towards Addressing Three Key Governance Challenges – Collective Action, Trade-offs, and Accountability. *Current Opinion in Environmental Sustainability*, *26-27*(2), 90–96.

Bufon, M. (2002). Experiences of Cross-Border Cooperation in the Upper Adriatic. *Regional & Federal Studies*, *12*(4), 177–196. doi:10.1080/714004771

Castanho, R., Loures, L., Fernández, J., & Pozo, L. (2017). Cross-Border cooperation (CBC) in Southern Europe- An Iberian case Study. The Eurocity Elvas-Badajoz. *Sustainability*, *9*(3), 1–16. doi:10.3390u9030360

Castanho, R., Loures, L., Fernández, J., & Pozo, L. (2018). Identifying critical factors for success in Cross Border Cooperation (CBC) development projects. *Habitat International*, *72*, 92–99. doi:10.1016/j.habitatint.2016.10.004

Chaudhary, A., & Jacob, S. (2019). Pakistan suspends trade with India. Retrieved from https://www.bloomberg.com/news/articles/2019-08-07/pakistan-suspends-bilateral-trade-with-india

De Sousa, L. (2012). Understanding European Cross-border Cooperation: A Framework for analysis. *Journal of European Integration*, *35*(6), 669–687. doi:10.1080/07036337.2012.711827

Dimitrov, M., Petrakos, G., Totev, S., & Tsiapa, M. (2014). Cross-Border Cooperation in South-Eastern Europe. *Eastern European Economics, 41*(6), 5–25. doi:10.1080/00128775.2003.11041063

Din, K. H. (1988). Tourism for Peace: Desires and attainability. In L. J. D'Amore, & J. Jafari (Eds.), *Tourism – A Vital Force for Peace (75-81): Proceedings for the First International Conference of the International Institute of Peace through Tourism* (IIPT), Montreal, Canada.

European Commission. (EC) (2019). Cross Border Cooperation. Retrieved from https://ec.europa.eu/neighbourhood-enlargement/neighbourhood/cross-border-cooperation

Gerfert, S. (2009). Cross-Border Cooperation: Transforming Borders. Retrieved from https://essay.utwente.nl/60149/1/BSc_S_Getfert.pdf

Gordon, S. (2009). Regionalism and cross-border cooperation against crime and terrorism in the Asia-Pacific. *Security Challenges, 5*(4), 75–102.

Hall, C. M., & Page, S. (2012). Developing Tourism in South Asia: India, Pakistan and Bangladesh – SAARC and Beyond. Tourism in South and Southeast Asia, chapter 14, pp. 197-224.

Haq, F., & Medhekar, A. (2015). Spiritual Tourism between India and Pakistan: A Framework for Business Opportunities and Threats. *World Journal of Social Sciences, 5*(2), 190–200.

Haq, F., & Medhekar, A. (2017). Is Spiritual Tourism an Innovation in Tourism for India and Pakistan. In R. Benlamri, & M. Sparer (Eds.), *Business and Economics: Leadership, Innovation and Entrepreneurship as Driving Forces of the Global Economy* (pp. 519–530). Switzerland: Springer International. doi:10.1007/978-3-319-43434-6_44

Haq, F., & Medhekar, A. (2019). Is Spiritual Tourism a Peace Vehicle for Social Transformation and Economic Prosperity in India and Pakistan? In N. Alexandru-Mircea, & M.-O. Nedelea (Eds.), *Marketing Peace for Social Transformation and Global Prosperity* (pp. 189–211). IGI Global. doi:10.4018/978-1-5225-7464-4.ch010

Heusala, A. L., & Koistinen, J. (2018). 'Rules of the game in cross-border cooperation': Legal-administrative differences in Finnish–Russian crime prevention. *International Review of Administrative Sciences, 84*(2), 354–370. doi:10.1177/0020852315625786

International Institute for Sustainable Development (IISD). (2019). Sustainable Development. Retrieved from https://www.iisd.org/topic/sustainable-development

Krätke, S. (2002). Cross-Border Cooperation and Regional Development in the German-Polish Border Area. In M. Perkmann, & N. L. Sum (Eds.), Globalisation, Regionalism and Cross-Border Regions. Chapter 6, pp. 125-147. International Political Economy Series. London, UK: Palgrave Macmillan. doi:10.1057/9780230596092_6

Kurowska-Pysz, J., & Szczepańska-Woszczyna, K. (2017). The analysis of the determinants of sustainable cross-border cooperation and recommendations on its harmonization. *Sustainability*, *9*(12), 2226. doi:10.3390u9122226

Lepik, K. L. (2009). Euroregion as Mechanism for Strengthening Cross-Border Cooperation in the Baltic Sea Region. *Trames*, *13*(3), 265–284. doi:10.3176/tr.2009.3.05

Medeiros, E. (2010). Old vs recent cross-border cooperation: Portugal–Spain and Norway–Sweden. *Royal Geographical Society*, *42*(4), 434–443.

Medeiros, E. (2018). Should EU cross-border cooperation programmes focus mainly on reducing border obstacles? *Documents d'Analisi Geografica*, *64*(3), 467–491. doi:10.5565/rev/dag.517

Medhekar, A., & Haq, F. (2019). Promoting Kashmir as an Abode of Peace Tourism Destination by India and Pakistan. In A.-M. Nedelea, & M.-O. Nedelea (Eds.), *Marketing Peace for Social Transformation and Global Prosperity* (pp. 22–49). IGI Global. doi:10.4018/978-1-5225-7464-4.ch002

PEW Research Centre. (2017). World's Muslim population more widespread than you might think. Retrieved from https://www.pewresearch.org/fact-tank/2017/01/31/worlds-muslim-population-more-widespread-than-you-might-think/

Prokkola, E. K. (2008). Resources and barriers in tourism development: Cross-border cooperation, regionalization and destination building at the Finnish-Swedish border. *International Journal of Geography*, *186*(1), 31–46.

Seung-Hyun, L., Shenkar, O., & Li, J. (2008). Cultural distance, investment flow, and control in cross-border cooperation. *Strategic Management Journal*, *29*(10), 1117–1125. doi:10.1002mj.685

Singh, A., Jamasab, T., Nepal, R., & Toman, M. (2018). Electricity Cooperation in South Asia: Barriers to cross-border trade. *Energy Policy*, *120*(c), 741–748. doi:10.1016/j.enpol.2017.12.048

South Asian Association for Regional Cooperation. (2019). SAARC. Retrieved from http://saarc-sec.org/

Srinivasan, P. V. (2012). Regional Cooperation and Integration through Cross-Border Infrastructure Development. Asian Development Bank. *South Asia Working Paper Series No. 14.*

Sugunakararaju, S. R. T. P., & Akhtar, S. (2015). India-Pakistan Relations: Challenges and Opportunities. *Journal of the Humanities and Social Sciences*, *20*(12), 7–12.

Timothy, D. J. (2009). Cross-Border Partnership in Tourism Resource Management: International Parks along the US-Canada Border. *Journal of Sustainable Tourism*, *7*(3-4), 182–205. doi:10.1080/09669589908667336

UNSDP. (2019). Sustainable Development Goals Knowledge Platform. Retrieved from https://sustainabledevelopment.un.org/sdgs

Van Tulder, R. (2018). *Business & The Sustainable Development Goals: A Framework for Effective Corporate Involvement*. Rotterdam, The Netherlands: Rotterdam School of Management, Erasmus University.

Van Tulder, R., & Keen, N. (2018). Capturing Collaborative Challenges: Designing Complexity-Sensitive Theories of Change for Cross-Sector Partnership. *Journal of Business Ethics*, *150*(2), 315–332. doi:10.100710551-018-3857-7 PMID:30996500

Verheugen, G., & Barnier, M. (2000). Practical guide to cross border corporation (3rd ed.). Association of European Border Regions: European Commission. Retrieved from https://www.aebr.eu/files/publications/lace_guide.en.pdf

Wróblewski, L., & Kasperek, A. (2019). Euroregion as an Entity Stimulating the Sustainable Development of the Cross-Border Market for Cultural Services in a City Divided by a Border. *Sustainability*, *1*(8), 2232. doi:10.3390u11082232

ADDITIONAL READING

Bandyopadhyay, R., Morais, D. D., & Chick, G. (2008). Religion and identity in India's heritage tourism. *Annals ofTourism Research*, *35*(3), 790–808. doi:10.1016/j.annals.2008.06.004

Kumar, A., & Singh, P. (2015). Cultural Heritage Tourism of Ayodhya-Faizabad. *The Geographer*, *62*(2), 66–74.

Levy, S. E., & Hawkins, D. E. (2010). Peace through tourism: Commerce based principles and practices. *Journal of Business Ethics*, *89*(1), 569–585.

Qureshi, R. B. (2003). Lineage, shrine, qawwali, and study circle: Spiritual kinship in transnational Sufism. *Religious Studies and Theology*, *22*(1), 63–84. doi:10.1558/rsth.v22i1.63

SAARC-Chamber of Commerce & Industry. (2019). South Asian Association for Regional Cooperation. Retrieved from https://saarcchamber.org/

Singh, S. (2018). SAARC, Power Asymmetry and Bilateral Conflicts in South Asia. Retrieved from https://www.youngbhartiya.com/article/saarc-power-asymmetry-and-bilateral-conflicts-in-south-asia

UN-ESCAP. (2019). Retrieved from https://www.unescap.org/announcement/un-meeting-highlights-tremendous-potential-border-zones-eastern-south-asia-promoting

KEY TERMS AND DEFINITIONS

Cross-Border Cooperation (CBC): A form of international cooperation exercised bilaterally or multilaterally through peace dialogue between countries or regions across shared borders by land or sea and non-shared borders to achieve common goals and objectives and United Nations 17-Sustainable Development Goals for mutual benefit of economic development opportunities.

Peace Dividend: A slogan used to express benefits derived from diverting and allocating scarce public resources/money from defence expenditure, to development expenditure, in order to promote peace between nations and reap economic benefit from peace initiatives.

Socio-Economic Transformation (SET): A process where the major contribution to income, output, employment and gross domestic product of the economy is generated from sectors – other than agriculture, such as manufacturing, small scale industries, information and communication technology, capital intensive industries and the service sectors.

Sustainable Development: The development, that meets the present needs, without compromising the ability of the future generations to meet their needs and wants (IISD, 2019). Sustainability is the foundations for international cooperation, to meet the 2030 agenda for SDGs.

Sustainable Development Goals (SDGs): These goals relate to transforming our world global 17- SDGs agenda for 2030, was adopted in 2015. All countries developed and developing such as India and Pakistan along with the six south Asian countries must achieve in a global partnership. For example, South Asian countries need to eradication poverty, hunger, universal access, provide clean drinking water and sanitation, green energy, improvement in health, education, reduce inequality, increase economic growth and prosperity, preserve rivers, forests and tackle climate change with cross border partnership.

Wicked Problems: Wicked problem include social, cultural, economic, environmental, and political problems that is difficult or impossible to solve. These, problem whose solution requires collaboration and cooperation where large number of people to change their mindsets and behavior. Therefore, many standard examples of wicked problems come from the areas of public planning and policy, such as poverty, hunger, climate change, illiteracy, healthcare, waste management, food security, terrorism and human trafficking.

Chapter 11
Tourism, Emigration, and Cooperation:
A Strategy for Growth and Sustainable Development in a Community of Portuguese-Speaking Member States

Rossana Andreia Santos
https://orcid.org/0000-0002-0221-880X
University of Madeira, Portugal

ABSTRACT

This chapter argues that tourism activities, emigration, and cooperation projects can spur growth and sustainable development in rural areas, in general, helping to reduce the existing asymmetries of development, phenomenon that reaches Portugal and other Member States of the Community of Portuguese-speaking Member States (CPLP). The results of a study developed in Portugal evidence that the potential return of a segment of Portuguese emigrants, settled around the world, can contribute to growth and sustainable tourism development in rural areas of Portugal. In this scope, the existence of a Portuguese-speaking cultural heritage allied to the CPLP Strategic Tourism Cooperation Plan can also have a critical role in growth and sustainable development in CPLP.

INTRODUCTION

The state of the art of tourism economic literature reveals that studies carried out in developing countries and rural areas evidence that tourism expenditure creates

DOI: 10.4018/978-1-7998-2513-5.ch011

more employment and income than any other sector of the economy, as well as generate and maintain employment in other sectors of the economy that support or provide tourism visitors and businesses. In this scope, in countries or regions where economic development is a priority the return of emigrants can contribute significantly to tourism growth and sustainable development. According with Organization for Economic Cooperation and Development, emigrants can be a source of external innovation through transfer of financial and social capital, as well as knowledge and professional experience. In this scope, the results of a study developed in Portugal evidence that Portuguese emigrants, with ages of 29-39 years old and with a house in a rural area, have greater propensity to return, invest and have a job in the area of tourism in Portugal, as well as have more training and professional experience in this area.

The phenomenon of emigration motivated by the improvement of living conditions also affects all Portuguese-speaking Member States, either as countries of destination, as countries of origin, or even in the dual origin and destination condition (see CPLP, 2011). Contextually, the existence of a Portuguese-speaking cultural heritage and its relationship with direct investment abroad and migration flows also lead us to argue that tourism development, through cooperation projects, can function as a strategy for growth and sustainable development in Community of Portuguese-Speaking Member States (CPLP). Thus, this chapter aims to argue that tourism, emigration and cooperation can impact positively on growth and sustainable development in rural areas of CPLP.

TOURISM AS A STRATEGY TO GROWTH AND SUSTAINABLE DEVELOPMENT

In order to argue that tourism can contribute to growth and sustainable development of rural areas (or low density areas), should be highlighted that these areas have several problems related with economic decline, large increase in unemployment, emigration, desertification, adverse impacts of the restructuring of agriculture and the loss of cultural identity (see for example Cavaco, 2003; Labrianidis et al., 2003; Sharpley & Vass, 2006). Contextually, according with metadata of Organization for Economic Cooperation and Development and Portuguese Statistical Institute, rural areas are those with a population of 2000 inhabitants or less. Considering that it is not the purpose of this study to differentiate typologies from rural areas, but to identify all rural areas, it is argued in this study that economic growth is fundamental to the sustainable development of these territories. In this scope, several authors have argued that rural space is no longer confined only to agricultural activities and land use, but also extends to multisectoral activities (see for example Diniz, 1999;

Ferrão 2000; Henriques, 2002; Figueiredo, 2003; Oliveira, 2005; Batista, 2006; Gonçalves, 2007). For this reason, and considering the geographic space under study, the potential of tourism to growth and sustainable development of rural areas is emphasized in this section.

Based on the existent literature it is revealed that, during the 80s increasing employment in rural areas of the countries of the Organization for Economic Cooperation and Development (OECD) was due largely to network growth in the services sector (Bryden & Bollman, 2000; Kilkenny & Partridge, 2009; King & Strachan, 1980a; 1980b, as cited by King, 1984).Therefore, the increase of employment in the tertiary sector has proved to be the key variable for explaining immigration or low emigration (see King & Strachan 1980a, 1980b, cited by King, 1984). However, not all activities of the tertiary sector demonstrate the same ability to generate employment. The state of the art on tourism economic literature reveals that a number of studies, conducted in developing countries and rural areas, show that tourism expenditure creates more employment and income than any other sector of the economy, as well as it generates and maintains employment in other sectors of the economy that support or provide visitors and tourist businesses (see Bergstrom et al., 1990; Fleischer and Felsenstein, 2000; Balaguer and Cantavella-Jorda, 2002; Mahony and Zyl, 2002; Vanegas and Croes, 2003; Lipman 1997, as cited by Hughes and Shields, 2007; Mazumder, 2009; Chen and Yang, 2010; Haddad et al., 2013; Lee et al., 2013; Snyman, 2013; Klytchnikova and Dorosh, 2014; Fodranov et al., 2015; Hyojin and Byung-Gook, 2015; Stephen, 2015; Crompton et al., 2016; Yesavdar et al., 2016; Croes and Rivera, 2017; Kim and Miller, 2017; Ruzic and Demonja, 2017; Sánchez et al., 2017; Veretekhina et al., 2017; Yashalova et al., 2017; Ferrari et al, 2018; Hjerpe, 2018; Pascariu and Ibanescu, 2018; Suresh, K. et al., 2018; Tohmo, 2018; Cannonier and Burke, 2019; Hasanlj, Y. et al., 2019; Hsu, 2019; Laterra et al., 2019).

In this scope, the multiplier effects of tourism expenditure are one of the most well researched areas in the tourism economic literature and most empirical studies use the input-output technique to assess the total economic impact of tourism expenditure (see for example Taylor et al., 1993, cited by Saayman and Saayman, 2006; Cernat and Gourdon, 2007; Fesenmaier et al., 1989, Heng and Low, 1990, Johnson and Moore, 1993, cited by Lejarraja e Walkenhorst, 2007; Mazumder, 2009; Crompton et al., 2016; Veretekhina et al. 2017; Kronenberg et al., 2018; Pascariu and Ibanescu, 2018; Tohmo, 2018). In addition, sustainability principles applied to tourism activities can ensure its suitable management under economic and social conditions, while preserving the environment (Cunha, 1997; Gonçalves, 2007). Tribe (2015) characterizes the sustainable development of tourism as the level of development in which the load capacity of destination is not exceeded - avoiding considerable or irreversible changes, and sustainability in the long term. In fact, several authors identify the strategic planning regarding tourist destinations as a crucial process in tourism - aiming efficient coordination and integration between resources, products and services (Beerli and Martin, 2004; Getz, 1986; Inskeep, 1991; Mason, 2015; Ruschmann, 2008).

However, the magnitude of the tourism expenditure multiplier depends on a number of internal factors, inherent in the countries and regions themselves, to explain the modest effects of tourism on local development. Moreover, not all rural areas that lack employment opportunities and income are candidates to promote tourism as a strategy for economic development (Fleischer and Felsenstein, 2000). It is necessary that rural areas have quality resources and know how to take advantage of them. In such case, tourism can be one activity capable of contributing to the revitalization of local economies, diversification of activities that are tributaries, development of other economic sectors (by the multiplier effect), creation and qualification of employment, income generation (see for example Mazumder, 2009; Balaguer and Jordá, 2010; Stephen, 2015; Suresh et al., 2018; Cannonier and Burke, 2019; Hasanlj et al. 2019), improvement of transport infrastructure (see Castanho et al., 2017a; Vulevic et al., 2018; Naranjo Gómez et al., 2019), of services (which also benefit the local society) and the creation of local government revenue (see Reeder and Brown, 2005). Contextually, an inland development policy will also have to be based on large investments in infrastructure and services essential to investment and human resource allocation (Kilkenny and Partridge, 2009). Therefore, tourism should be only a component of a broader rural development program, with close collaboration between the public sector, the private sector, communities and civil society, in order to ensure the objectives of its policy (Mahony and Zyl, 2002).

PORTUGUESE EMIGRATION AND THE SUSTAINABLE DEVELOPMENT

The study of the mobility of the rural population in Portugal, from the mid-1950s to the present, with the aim of identifying the local conditions and attraction of the rural or the most deprived areas, allows us to conclude that these are economic objectives, linked to employment and income opportunities, which still urge the Portuguese to leave, even temporarily, their regions of origin (see for example Murteira, 1965; Ferreira, 1976; Rocha-Trindade, 1976; Leeds, 1983; Arroteia, 1985; 2001; Althoff, 1985; Ferrão, 1996; Baganha and Góis, 1999 ; Portela and Nobre, 2001; Dias, 2008; Arroteia and Fiss, 2007; Gonçalves, 2007; Peixoto, 2007). The phenomenon of emigration motivated by the improvement of living conditions also affects all Portuguese-speaking Member States (CPLP), whether as destination countries, as countries of origin, or even in the dual condition of origin and destination, in addition to the fact that some of these states have port of departure to port of arrival, and vice versa, such as the cases of Brazil and Portugal (CPLP, 2011). Therefore, the type of return migration which is addressed here refers to the movements of workers and relatives of the more developed countries or regions for the regions that provide labor from rural areas (see King et al., 1986). It is intended to argue that the permanent return of Portuguese emigrants can contribute to sustainable development.

According with the Organization for Cooperation and Economic Development (2008) emigrants can bring knowledge and professional experience they have acquired abroad, return with financial capital in the form of accumulated savings during their stay abroad, and with social capital gained from their experience during emigration. In this scope, Bovenkerk (1974, cited by King, 1986) describes factors that allow return migration as an innovative force, namely: (i) the concentration of migrants who may have a greater or lesser effect on change; ii) the length of absence, that should be long enough to absorb certain experiences and values and small enough to apply the new skills and attitudes; iii) the social class, because the return of professionals or graduate students has a higher economic and cultural impact than the untrained; iv) the differences between emigration and immigration countries or regions; v) the nature of the training, that is, the potential for innovation tends to be higher when training is generic rather than highly specialized, so that it can be used in the original environment; and vi) the organization of return, because if it is spontaneous and unplanned it will have little impact on local development.

In Portugal, past evidence reveals that the impact of the return of Portuguese emigrants in rural development did not occur due to the existence of external barriers such as the lack of a migration policy to take care of the human and professional enhancement of emigrants, a return policy to report about the socio-economic local alternatives of rehabilitation and regional development policy that could stimulate them (Portela and Nobre, 2001; Cepeda, 1988; Silva et al., 1984). In addition, the cautious risk management (a behaviour which is rooted in peasant culture) and the non-existent or limited entrepreneurship capacity had constituted internal barriers to the occurrence of the development of the places of origin of the Portuguese emigrants (Portela and Nobre, 2001; Cepeda, 1988; Silva et al., 1984). In the present study it is conclude that, despite the importance of the demographic volume of the return of Portuguese emigrants throughout only one quarter of century (1976/2001), the research of its impact on sustainable development is very scarce, and furthermore most of this studies belongs to the 80`s decade (see also Neto and Neto, 2011).

In fact, in the context of studies addressing the impact of return migration on sustainable development, this study represents a first approach of the impact of tourism development, through the return of Portuguese emigrants as potential tourism promoters, on sustainable development. It will be demonstrated that are the Portuguese emigrants in active age (29-39 years old) and with a house in a rural area (or with smallest index of centrality) that have greater propensity to return, invest and have a job in the area of tourism in Portugal, as well as have more training and professional experience in this area. Contextually, the study provide evidence from the expectations and perceptions of the locals - Portuguese emigrants, who expressed their views on the future of sustainable planning of their places of origin. Thus, in countries or regions where economic development in rural areas is a priority, the return of emigrants can greatly contribute to the search for local development solutions, since to the impact on consumption can be joined the impact on production, because they are also the people who return, and not just the savings and consumption models. In this context, Pina (2011) clarifies that linguistic proximity significantly influences foreign direct investment and migratory flows. However, the Organization for Cooperation and Economic Development (2008) also states that emigrants will want to return to their origins only if economic conditions are attractive and if there are new opportunities.

METHODOLOGICAL APPROACH

The main issue that have motivated this study is the impact of tourism and return migration on rural areas. As argued in previous sections, rural areas have several problems related with economic decline, large increase in unemployment, emigration, desertification, adverse impacts of the restructuring of agriculture and the loss of cultural identity. At national level, these territories have a population of 2000 inhabitants or less and are the same as the places of origin of emigrants (or the most needed). Thus, recognizing that return migration can contribute to growth and sustainable development and that tourism is able to boost this process, in April 2008 began a study in Portugal, funded by the Foundation for Science and Technology, in order to assess the contribution of the potential return of Portuguese emigrants for the development of tourism in rural areas (Santos, 2013). The population target of this study are the locals of rural areas in Portugal (or the Portuguese emigrants). The fact that the number and characteristics of this target population is not known, it was intended to obtain relevant information from as many Portuguese emigrants as possible, leading to the option of an unrestricted sample (Santos, 2013).

The data collection process started July 1, 2011, and ended on October 31 of the same year, totalling at the end 5,157 filled and valid questionnaires. The data were obtained through the application of a questionnaire survey to emigrants. For the preparation of the questionnaire, nominal scales, checklists and ratio scales were used. Data analysis was carried out by means of a quantitative descriptive analysis (frequencies and crossings) and tests of correlation of variables, as well as a qualitative analysis through the application of Student's t-tests and ANOVA

(Analysis of Variance) tests (Kruskal Wallis and Mann Whitney). One of the ways of administering the survey was by mail, having been sent questionnaires to 4,000 households of Portuguese emigrants in the various countries of emigration. From the 4,000 questionnaires sent by mail, 54 were returned and, concerning those delivered, a response rate of 9.32% was obtained. The identification of regional publications associated with the districts and counties with the largest number of Portuguese emigrants' houses of origin allowed to obtain listings with the full names and contacts of their subscribers. In this way, it could be also identified the addresses of Portuguese emigrants in the countries of emigration and sent them 4000 questionnaires by post. During the same period from 1st July until 31st October, the internet and the social network of Facebook also did the administration of the questionnaire, allowing gathering more 4,800 filled and valid questionnaires. Until 31st July, the administration of the questionnaire was made in the press and in digital electronic portals aimed at Portuguese communities abroad, as well as by sending e-mails to emigrants associations and official bodies directly related to emigration. In addition to giving continuity to the administration of the questionnaire on the internet, during the month of August it was proceeded to its disclosure on the social network Facebook, through the official pages of administrators themselves singers of Portuguese music.

In the past two months, the questionnaire management strategy was extended to the creation and maintenance of an own study page in the Facebook (in www.facebook.com/emigrantesportugueses). During this period, with the goal of informing the Portuguese emigrants about the forms of participation in the study, the page was disclosed, several times a day, through the Portuguese radio and television, through channels of the International and Africa Radio, as well as International RTP channel (RTPI). In addition, the disclosure was also made in all digital newspapers, which co-operated in the administration of the questionnaire to Portuguese emigrants; and through e-mails sent to the Director-General of Consular Affairs and Portuguese Communities, Consulates/Embassies, associations and Benfica and Porto Houses abroad. It is also referred the divulgation by the researcher in the Facebook, administrator of the page of the study, in several groups of Portuguese emigrants, in Portugal theme related profiles (and other selected by the greatest number of fans), as well as by contact with some emigrants, administrators of group pages in Facebook, through their mailboxes.

RESULTS AND DISCUSSION

In this section, it is intend to demonstrate that Portuguese emigrants can contribute to boost tourism growth and sustainable development in rural areas of the Portuguese-

Table 1. County of house in Portugal (Source: Own Elaboration).

County of house	No.	%
Highest centrality index	1,109	21.5
Smallest index of centrality	3,989	77.4
Doesn't Know/ Doesn't Answer	59	1.1
Total	5,157	100.0

speaking Member States (CPLP). This assumption is based on the results obtained in a study applied to the Portuguese case, which show that the areas with the highest levels of emigration in Portugal are the most deprived and, at the same time, the places of origin of Portuguese emigrants (Santos, 2013). On the other hand, Portuguese emigrants, with 29-39 years old and with a house in those areas, can boost tourism growth and development by their greater propensity for return, investment and employment in tourism in rural areas (Santos, 2013). Thus, recognizing that linguistic proximity significantly influences migration flows and foreign direct investment, as well as the existence of a Portuguese-speaking cultural heritage that can be exploited for tourism, it is argued that Portuguese-speaking emigrants can also contribute to the development of tourism in rural areas of the CPLP countries.

The results of the mentioned study, on the evaluation of the contribution of the potential return of the Portuguese emigrants to the development of the tourism in rural territories, give empirical support to that argumentation (Santos, 2013). Firstly, it was found that the majority of emigrants have at least one house in a county with lowest index of centrality or deprived areas (77.4%), and that only 21.5% have a house in counties with higher index of centrality (Table 1). The counties of house location of emigrants were organized into two groups, according to the respective index of centrality. To this effect, it was considered that the counties with the highest index of centrality are up to *rank* 50 (INE, 2004). The index of centrality in urban centers, based in the areas of influence and functional marginality, allows the identification of the areas with a lower capacity of polarization, which are the most deprived areas. In this sense, it takes into account the number of functions provided by an urban centre as well as an associated weighting to reflect the degree of specialization of the function and the number of functional units that the urban centre holds (INE, 2004).

To verify if there are any differences between the groups analysed – the emigrants with a house in a county with lowest index of centrality and the emigrants with a house in a county with highest centrality index – it was applied ANOVA test. However, it not fulfilled the necessary assumptions. It has opted for the Kruskal Wallis test or Mann-Whitney test. It was concluded that there are no differences between the

Table 2. The Pearson correlation test (Source: Own Elaboration).

		P7 County of house in Portugal
P21 Desire to return and settle in Portugal	Pearson Correlation	-0.007
	Sig. (2-tailed)	0.710
	No.	2,806
P28 Desire to have a job in the tourism sector in Portugal	Pearson Correlation	-0.037
	Sig. (2-tailed)	0.050
	No.	2,806
P49 Have sufficient capital to invest in a business in Portugal	Pearson Correlation	0.059**
	No.	5,157

*. Correlation is significant at the 0.05 level (2-tailed).

**. Correlation is significant at the 0.01 level (2-tailed).

groups analysed, with the exception of variables "professional experience" and "professional training", where there are differences, however, negligible (values very close to 0) (Table 8). The results obtained from the Pearson correlation test made it possible to conclude that the county of house that the emigrants have in Portugal negatively influence their desire to return (r = -0.007) and there will to have a job in the area of tourism (r = -0.037), as well as positively influence having sufficient capital to invest in a business there too (r = 0.059) (Table 2). However, emigrants with a house in a county with the lowest index of centrality are those that most wish to return and settle in Portugal (39.4%) (Table 3).

Table 3 Municipality of house in Portugal vs. Desire to return and settle in Portugal (Source: Own Elaboration).

%	P21 Desire to return and settle in Portugal				Total
	Yes	Maybe	No	Doesn't Know / Doesn't Answer	
Highest centrality index	9.3%	4.5%	2.7%	1.2%	17.7%
Smallest centrality index	39.4%	24.9%	10.4%	7.2%	81.8%
Doesn't Know/ Doesn't Answer	0.4%	0.0%	-	0.1%	0.5%
Total	49.0%	29.4%	13.0%	8.5%	100.0%

Table 4. County of house in Portugal vs. Most important factors for returning and settle in Portugal (Source: Own Elaboration).

%	P22 If you decide to return to Portugal, what could be more important to you?								
	A	**B**	**C**	**D**	**E**	**F**	**G**	**H**	**I**
Highest centrality index	18.2%	19.4%	16.3%	18.6%		17.1%	10.5%	15.5%	16.0%
Smallest centrality index	81.0%	79.9%	83.3%	80.9%	81.3%	82.3%	89.3%	83.8%	84.0%
Doesn't Know/Doesn't Answer	0.8%	0.7%	0.4%	0.5%	0.7%	0.6%	0.3%	0.7%	-

A: Have a job opportunity; B: Have income opportunities; C: Have a rural lifestyle; D: Live near my family of Portugal; E: Exist infrastructures for living and investing in a business at the place of origin; F: Exist infrastructures for living and investing in a business at the place of origin; G: Have a house in the place of origin; H: Be able to exercise a paid activity, on their own, in the tourism sector; I: None

Table 5. County of house in Portugal vs. Sufficient capital to invest in a business in Portugal (Source: Own Elaboration).

%	P49 Have sufficient capital to invest in a business in Portugal				Total
	Yes	**Maybe**	**No**	**Doesn't Know/Doesn't Answer**	
Highest centrality index	4.2%	7.2%	5.4%	4.7%	21.5%
Smallest centrality index	12.9%	24.4%	28.7%	11.3%	77.4%
Doesn't Know/Doesn't Answer	0.1%	0.3%	0.2%	0.5%	1.1%
Total	17.2%	31.9%	34.3%	16.6%	100.0%

In relation to the most important factors of return for those emigrants, in active age and with a house in a county with lowest index of centrality, are, fundamentally, to have a house in the place where they were born (89.3%), engage in a remunerated activity, of their own, in the tourism (83.8%) and have a rural lifestyle (of origin) (83.3%) (Table 4). These data also suggest that, most likely, the house which they regard as "own" can be the property of their direct relatives. Although these emigrants are those who more deny having the capital to invest in a business in Portugal, are also at the same time, the ones that most confirm to have it (12.9%) (Table 5).

It is also highlighted that among these emigrants, in active age and with a house in a county with the lowest index of centrality (77.4%), there is still a significant proportion who do not know or did not respond to these issues related to their propensity for the return, investment, and employment in the tourism in Portugal. For them, tourism is also the area where they more would like to invest in Portugal, after livestock (84.4%) and transport (84.9%) (Table 6). In this context, compared

Table 6. County of house in Portugal vs. area/s where emigrants would like to invest in Portugal (Source: Own Elaboration).

		Highest centrality index	Smallest centrality index	Doesn't Know Doesn't Answer
P26 Area/s where emigrants would like to invest in Portugal	a) Agriculture	18.1%	81.2%	0.7%
	b) Forestry (forest)	16.6%	82.9%	0.6%
	c) Fisheries	20.2%	78.8%	1.0%
	d) Livestock	15.6%	84.4%	-
	e) Hunting	26.3%	73.7%	-
	f) Extractive industry (mining, oil, wood and paper)	23.2%	75.9%	0.9%
	g) Manufacturing	18.2%	81.0%	0.9%
	h) Construction	20.7%	78.7%	0.6%
	i) Energy production	18.8%	80.8%	0.4%
	j) Trade	18.2%	81.2%	0.5%
	l) Tourism (hotels, restaurants, transportation, cultural services, etc.)	15.5%	83.9%	0.6%
	m) Transport	14.7%	84.9%	0.4%
	n) Financial Activities	20.2%	78.5%	1.4%
	o) Other	17.6%	82.4%	-

with emigrants with a house in counties with a higher index of centrality (15.5%) also stand out significantly (83.9%).

The analysis of the knowledge that the emigrants have acquired during their stay in the country of emigration leads us also to observe that although most have few formal knowledge in the area of hospitality and/or tourism, are again the emigrants with a house in counties with smaller index of centrality that record more (new) knowledge (course, training and professional experience) in that area. In this case, between the emigrants in active age, was observed that those who are between the ages of 29-39 years are who more refer to have their own house in Portugal (Table 7).

Finally, in the perspective of emigrants with a house in a county with lowest index of centrality, who are between the ages of 29-39 years, they would like to control their own working hours in Portugal to have a "rural" lifestyle (of origin), to practice agriculture (mainly for self-consumption) and have a job in tourism business (66.5%). During the low season of tourist demand, they could continue to work, instead of benefiting from State support, mainly to reconcile tourism with other economic activity (61.0%). The results also revealed that the practice of agriculture for self-

Table 7. Age vs. Property of house in Portugal (Source: Own Elaboration).

%		P18 Age			Total
		Less than 18 years	Between 18 and 28 years old	Between 29 and 39 years	
P5 Property of house in Portugal	Own	1.1%	12.0%	22.3%	35.4%
	Rented	-	0.6%	2.3%	2.9%
	Of relatives	1.7%	21.7%	38.3%	61.7%
	Total	2.9%	34.3%	62.9%	100.0%

consumption, in their place of origin, is justified, because they usually use simple techniques, do not use insecticides and have others farmlands elsewhere (62.5%).

STRATEGIC TOURISM COOPERATION OF CPLP

According with Castanho et al. (2019) sustainable planning is crucial for growth and long-term sustained development, as well as to achieve sustainable cities, and projects and strategies of cooperation also have a critical role. This also explain why other authors highlight cooperation as an ideal framework for tourism development and as an indispensable instrument (see for example Jesus and Franco, 2016; Mottiar, 2016; Navarro et al, 2017; Costa and Lima, 2018; Candelo et al., 2019; Del Vas and Frias, 2019; Pilving et al., 2019; Wilke et al., 2019). In this regard, the Constitutive Declaration of the Community of Portuguese-Speaking Countries (CPLP), signed in July 1996, have established a commitment among Member States to strengthen the ties of solidarity and cooperation that unite them, combining initiatives to promote economic and social development of its peoples and for the greater and broader affirmation and dissemination of the Portuguese Language (CPLP, 2017). Contextually, cooperation in the tourism sector between Community of Portuguese-Speaking Countries (CPLP) began in the 1990s with the aim of promoting activity as an important vector for Member States' socio-economic development (CPLP, 2017).

In 2016, the Heads of State and Government of the Community of Portuguese-Speaking Countries, approved the CPLP's New Strategic Vision for the period 2016-2026, highlighting the desirability of strengthening the role of Community cooperation in the tourism sector (CPLP, 2017). In this context, the CPLP Strategic Tourism Cooperation Plan (PECTUR-CPLP) was prepared, a strategy for joint action for the coming years, determined by the resolution of the VII CPLP Conference of Tourism Ministers held in Maputo in 2013 (CPLP, 2017). The coordination of the

PECTUR-CPLP is hold by Permanent Technical Secretariat, a structure already provided for in the Rules of Procedure of the Ministers of Tourism. The implementation of the actions of the PECTURCPLP, in each Member State, take place under the coordination of the relevant Ministry which oversees the tourism sector, and with liaison of the Permanent Technical Secretariat and the CPLP Executive Secretariat (CPLP, 2017).

There are driving factors facilitating transnational tourism cooperation, which include geo-driving force, economic driving force and organizational controlling force (Tao, 2011). However, although political regions can cooperate in terms of tourism, they do not always become destinations (Studzieniecki, 2016). In this context, culture is central to tourism and the contemporary economy, because it makes places interesting, being a key prerequisite for the promotion of successful tourism (Walmsley, 2003). Capucho and Francisco (2010: 240) state that "culture, as an increasingly searched good by citizens and because it generate economic flows and wealth, is an important resource that must integrate local and regional development strategies, given the recognition that culture generates important external economies of human capital (through the creation of direct, indirect and induced employment) and as a catalyst for other activities such as tourism".

In this scope, the maritime expansion of the XV and XVI centuries led the Portuguese language to spread over several continents, with particular focus on South America, Africa and Asia. Thus, Portuguese has become the official language of Angola, Brazil, Cape Verde, Guinea-Bissau, Mozambique, São Tome and Principe and Timor, while some native speakers remain in other small territories, such as Goa (India) and Macau (China) (Esperança, 2009). The contact with the peoples found resulted in a strong exchange of products, customs, techniques, as well as deeper interpenetration through miscegenation (CPLP, 2011). This long historical process now results in a cultural identity shared by those eight countries, attached by a common past and a language that, enriched in its diversity, recognizes itself as one. Nevertheless, along with a shared history, culture and language, it also coexists with healthy historical, cultural and linguistic singular features that distinguish every one of its members (CPLP, 2011).

Contextually, the CPLP Strategic Tourism Cooperation Plan (PECTUR-CPLP) has the following general objectives for the period 2016-2026: "i) promote cooperation between CPLP Member States on the promotion and development of tourism; ii) support CPLP Member States to develop, implement, monitor and evaluate public tourism development policies in their respective countries; iii) support CPLP Member States in implementing actions that promote the achievement of the Sustainable Development Goals, in addition to other tourism-related Multilateral Conventions and Agreements, especially those concluded within the framework of the World Tourism Organization (CPLP, 2017:4)". In such case, Portuguese-speaking cultural tourism can be one activity capable of contributing to growth and sustainable development in Community of Portuguese-speaking Member States.

CONCLUSION

The literature review of this chapter was crucial to understanding the contribution of some variables, such as tourism, return migration and cooperation, to growth and sustainable development in rural areas of Community of Portuguese-speaking Member States. More specifically, the present study intends to demonstrate how the return of Portuguese emigrants, settled around the world, can influence tourism growth and development in rural areas, since to the impact on consumption can be joined to the impact on production, because they are also the people who return, and not just the savings and consumption models.

Contextually, through the use of an exploratory methodology it was possible to assess the Portuguese emigrants expectations and perceptions, as potential tourism promoters, in relation to the development of tourism in rural areas in Portugal. Therefore, it was possible to verify that Portuguese emigrants who wish to return with financial capital to invest and have a job in tourism businesses are aged with 29-39 years old and owns a house in a rural county. In addition, the final section presents the Strategic Tourism Cooperation Plan (2016-2026) of the Community of Portuguese-speaking Member States in order to contribute to tourism development in this region through the cooperation of all its members.

As a final remark, the identified expectations and perceptions are based on Portugal case study area and their populations. Thus, for remaining territories in Community of Portuguese-Speaking Member States similar studies should be carried out to properly define growth and sustainable development in this region.

ACKNOWLEDGMENT

This study is a result of the Research Group CITUR - Madeira - Centre for Tourism Research, Development and Innovation.

REFERENCES

Althoff, C. (1985). *Os Jovens de Origem Portuguesa em Hamburgo e a sua Atitude Face a Portugal e à Cultura Portuguesa*. Porto, Portugal: Secretaria de Estado da Emigração- Centro de Estudos.

Arroteia, J. (1985). *Atlas da Emigração Portuguesa*. Porto, Portugal: Secretaria de Estado da Emigração - Centro de Estudos.

Arroteia, J. (2001). As Comunidades Portuguesas no Mundo. *Janus*, 136–137.

Arroteia, J., & Fiss, R. (2007). Traços da Comunidade Portuguesa em Pelotas. *População e Sociedade,* (14), 171-191.

Baganha, M., & Góis, P. (1999). Migrações Internacionais de e para Portugal: O Que Sabemos e para Onde Vamos? *Revista Crítica de Ciências Sociais*, (52/53), novembro 1998/ fevereiro 1999, 229-280.

Balaguer, J., & Jordá, M. (2010). Tourism as a long-run economic growth factor: The Spanish case. *Applied Economics*, *34*(7), 877–884. doi:10.1080/00036840110058923

Batista, F. (2006). O Rural depois da Agricultura. In C. Cavaco, & L. Fonseca (Eds.), *Desenvolvimento e Território: Espaços Rurais Pós-Agrícolas e Novos Lugares de Turismo e Lazer* (pp. 85–106). Lisboa, Portugal: Centro de Estudos Geográficos da Universidade de Lisboa.

Beerli, A., & Martin, J. (2004). Factors influencing destination image. *Annals of Tourism Research, 31*(3), 657–681. doi:10.1016/j.annals.2004.01.010

Bergstrom, J., Cordell, K., Ashley, G., & Watson, A. (1990). Economic Impacts of Recreational Spending on Rural Areas: A Case Study. *Economic Development Quarterly*, *4*(1), 29–39. doi:10.1177/089124249000400104

Bryden, J., & Bollman, R. (2000). Rural Employment in Industrialized Countries. *Agricultural Economics*, *22*(2), 185–197. doi:10.1111/j.1574-0862.2000.tb00017.x

Candelo, E., Casalegno, C., Civera, C., & Büchi, G. (2019). A ticket to coffee: Stakeholder view and theoretical framework of coffee tourism benefits. *Tourism Analysis*, *24*(3), 329–340. doi:10.3727/108354219X15511864843830

Cannonier, C., & Burke, M. (2019). The economic growth impact of tourism in small islands developing states—Evidence from the Caribbean. *Tourism Economics*, *25*(1), 85–108. doi:10.1177/1354816618792792

Capucho, J., & Francisco, J. P. (2010). Cultura, Competitividade Territorial e Desenvolvimento Sustentável: Algumas Considerações sobre o Caso do Vale do Côa. In *Proceedings of IV Congresso de Estudos Rurais- Turismo, Património e Desenvolvimento Rural* (pp. 232-248), Aveiro, Portugal: Universidade de Aveiro.

Castanho, R., Vulevic, A., Cabezas, J., Fernández-Pozo, L., Goméz-Naranjo, J., & Loures, L. (2017). Accessibility and connectivity – Movement between cities, as a critical factor to achieve success on cross-border cooperation (CBC) projects. A European analysis. *Sustainable Cities and Society*, *32*, 181–190. doi:10.1016/j.scs.2017.03.026

Castanho, R. A., Kurowska-Pysz, J., & Naranjo Gómez, J. (2019). How to reach the Eurocities? A retrospective review of the evolution dynamics of urban planning and management on the Iberian Peninsula territories. *Sustainability Journal: Sustainable Cross-Border Cooperation: Common Planning, Policies, Strategies. Methods, and Activities*, *11*(602), 6–23.

Cavaco, C. (2003). Habitares dos Espaços Rurais. *Revista da Faculdade de Letras-Geografia*, 1 série, XIX, 47-64.

Cepeda, F. (1988). *Emigração, Regresso e Desenvolvimento no Nordeste Interior Português*. (Unpublished doctoral dissertation). University of Trás-os-Montes and Alto Douro, Vila Real.

Cernat, L., & Gourdon, J. (2007). *Is the Concept of Sustainable Tourism Sustainable? Developing the Sustainable Tourism Benchmarking Tool*. Retrieved from http://mpra.ub.uni-muenchen.de/4178/1/MPRA_paper_4178.pdf

Chen, K., & Yang, H. (2010). Appraising the economic impact of the opening up to mainland Chinese tourist arrivals' policy on Taiwan with a tourism—CGE model. *Asia Pacific Journal of Tourism Research*, *15*(2), 155–175. doi:10.1080/10941661003629961

Costa, T., & Lima, M. (2018). Cooperation in tourism and regional development. *Tourism & Management Studies*, *14*(4), 50–62. doi:10.18089/tms.2018.14405

CPLP. (2011). Intervenção do SE no Seminário da Sociedade Alemã para os Países Afrincanos de Língua Portuguesa: As Migrações no Mundo Lusófono. Retrieved from https://www.cplp.org/Files/Filer/cplp/Domingos_Simoes_Pereira/Discursos_DSP/D2/migracoes.pdf

CPLP. (2017). Plano Estratégico de Cooperação em Turismo da CPLP 2016-2026. Retrieved from https://www.cplp.org/Files/Filer/1_CPLP/Turismo/2017-07-19-PECTUR-DA-CPLP-(Vers%C3%A3o-Final)_FINAL.PDF

Croes, R., & Rivera, M. (2017). Tourism's potential to benefit the poor: A social accounting matrix model applied to Ecuador. *Tourism Economics*, *23*(1), 29–48. doi:10.5367/te.2015.0495

Crompton, J., Ji, Y., & Dudensing, R. (2016). Sources of variation in economic impact multipliers. *Journal of Travel Research, 55*(8), 1051–1064. doi:10.1177/0047287515617298

Cunha, L. (1997). *Economia e Política do Turismo*. Lisboa, Portugal: McGraw-Hill.

Dias, O. (2008). *A Integração dos Retornados no Interior de Portugal: O Caso do Distrito da Guarda*. Retrieved from http://www.aps.pt/vicongresso/pdfs/150.pdf

Diniz, F. (1999). *Desenvolvimento Rural, Que Perspetivas? O Caso do Alto Trás-os-Montes e Douro*. Zamora: Fundação Rei Afonso Henriques.

Esperança, J. (2009). *Uma Abordagem Eclética ao Valor da Língua: O Uso Global do Português*. Lisboa, Portugal: ISCTE-IUL/Instituto de Camões.

Fernandes, J. (1991). *A Arquitetura – Sínteses da Cultura Portuguesa*, Imprensa nacional Casa da Moeda, Portugal: Comissariado para a Europália 91.

Ferrão, J. (1996). Três Décadas de Consolidação do Portugal Demográfico. In A. Barreto (Ed.), *A Situação Social em Portugal, 1960-1995* (pp. 165–190). Lisboa, Portugal: Instituto de Ciências Sociais da Universidade de Lisboa.

Ferrão, J. (2000). Relações Entre Mundo Rural E Mundo Urbano: Evolução Histórica, Situação Atual e Pistas para o Futuro. *Sociologia, Problemas e Práticas* (33), 45-54.

Ferrari, G., Mondejar, J., & Secondi, L. (2018). Tourists' expenditure in Tuscany and its impact on the regional economic system. *Journal of Cleaner Production, 171*, 1437–1446. doi:10.1016/j.jclepro.2017.10.121

Ferreira, E. (1976). *Origens e Formas de Emigração: O Impacte da Emigração sobre o Desenvolvimento*. Lisboa, Portugal: Iniciativas Editoriais.

Figueiredo, E. (2003). *Um Rural para Viver e Outro para Visitar- O Ambiente nas Estratégias de Desenvolvimento para as Áreas Rurais* (Unpublished doctoral dissertation). Universidade de Aveiro, Aveiro.

Fleischer, A., & Felsenstein, D. (2000). Support for rural tourism- does it make a difference? *Annals of Tourism Research, 27*(4), 1007–1024. doi:10.1016/S0160-7383(99)00126-7

Fodranov, I., Kubickova, V., & Michalkova, A. (2015). Measuring societal value of tourism: A new approach. *Tourism (Zagreb), 63*(4), 423–434.

Getz, D. (1986). Models in tourism planning: Towards integration of theory and practice. *Tourism Management, 7*(1), 21–32. doi:10.1016/0261-5177(86)90054-3

Gonçalves, M. (2007). *Desenvolvimento em Meio Rural. Contributos da Emigração e do Regresso. Aplicação ao Concelho de Boticas na Região Barrosã.* (Unpublished doctoral dissertation). Open University, Portugal.

Haddad, E., Porsse, A., & Rabahy, W. (2013). Domestic tourism and regional inequality in Brazil. *Tourism Economics*, *19*(1), 173–186. doi:10.5367/te.2013.0185

Hasanlj, Y., Baizakov, S., & Salihova, S. (2019). Assessment of the impact of tourism sector on the economy of Azerbaijan, Kazakhstan and Iran using input-output models. In *Proceedings of the International Scientific Conference on Economic and Social Development – Socio Economic Problems of Sustainable Development*, Baku, Azerbaijan. Academic Press.

Henriques, A. (2002) Globalização e Integração Diferenciadora dos Espaços Rurais. In J. Reis, & M. Baganha (Eds.), A Economia em Curso: Contextos e Mobilidades (153-171). Porto, Portugal: Afrontamento.

Hjerpe, E. (2018). Outdoor recreation as a sustainable export industry: A case study of the boundary waters wilderness. *Ecological Economics*, *146*, 60–68. doi:10.1016/j.ecolecon.2017.10.001

Hsu, P. (2019). Economic impact of wetland ecotourism: An empirical study of Taiwan's Cigu Lagoon area. *Tourism Management Perspectives*, *29*, 31–14. doi:10.1016/j.tmp.2018.10.003

Hughes, D., & Shields, M. (2007). Revisiting Tourism Regional Economic Impact: Accounting for Secondary Household Employment. *The Review of Regional Studies*, *37*(2), 186–206.

Hyojin, K., & Byung-Gook, K. (2015). Economic impacts of the hotel industry: An input-output analysis. *Tourism Review*, *70*(2), 132–149. doi:10.1108/TR-11-2014-0056

Inskeep, E. (1991). *Tourism planning: an integrated and sustainable development approach.* New York: Van Nostrand Reinhold.

Jesus, C., & Franco, M. (2016). Cooperation networks in tourism: A study of hotels and rural tourism establishments in an inland region of Portugal. *Journal of Hospitality and Tourism Management*, *29*, 165–175. doi:10.1016/j.jhtm.2016.07.005

Kilkenny, M., & Partridge, M. (2009). Export Sectors and Rural Development. *American Journal of Agricultural Economics*, *91*(4), 910–929. doi:10.1111/j.1467-8276.2009.01320.x

Kim, S., & Miller, C. (2017). An economic model comparison of EMSI and IMPLAN: Case of mistletoe marketplace. *Tourism Economics*, *23*(5), 1124–1130. doi:10.1177/1354816616656420

King, R. (1984). Population Mobility: Emigration, Return Migration and Internal Migration. In A. Williams (Ed.), *Southern Europe Transformed- Political and Economic Change in Greece* (pp. 145–178). Italy, Portugal and Spain: Harpercollins College Div.

King, R. (1986). Return Migration and Regional Economic Development. In R. King (Ed.), *Return Migration and Regional Economic Problems* (pp. 1–37). Australia: Croom Helm.

King, R., Strachan, A., Mortimer, J., & Gastarbeiter, J. (1986). Go Home. Return migration and economic change in the Italian mezzogiorno. In R. King (Ed.), Return Migration and Regional Economic Problems. (pp. 38-68). London, UK: Ed. Croom Helm.

Klytchnikova, I., & Dorosh, P. (2014). Tourism sector in Panama: Regional economic impacts and the potential to benefit the poor. *Natural Resources Forum*, *32*(2), 70–79. doi:10.1111/1477-8947.12019

Kronenberg, K., Fuchs, M., & Lexhagen, M. A. (2018). Multi-period perspective on tourism economic contribution - a regional input-output analysis for Sweden. *Tourism Review*, *73*(1), 94–110. doi:10.1108/TR-03-2017-0044

Labrianidis, L., Kalantaridis, C., David, S., Herdzina, K., Mattsson, L., Ferrão, J., & Piasecki, B. (2003). *The Future of Europe's Rural Periphery, The Role of Entrepreneurship in Responding to Employment Problems and Social Marginalization*. Brussels, Belgium: European Commission.

Laterra, P., Nahuelhual, L., Gluch, M., Sirima, X., Bravo, G., & Monjeau, A. (2019). How are jobs and ecosystem services linked at the local scale? *Ecosystem Services*, *35*, 207–218. doi:10.1016/j.ecoser.2018.11.011

Lee, C., Lee, M., & Yoon, S. H. (2013). Estimating the economic impact of convention and exhibition businesses, using a regional input-output model: A case study of the Daejeon Convention Center in South Korea. *Asia Pacific Journal of Tourism Research*, *18*(4), 330–353. doi:10.1080/10941665.2012.658414

Leeds, E. (1983). Industrialização e Emigração em Portugal: Sintomas Inevitáveis de uma Doença Estrutural. *Análise Social,* XIX (77-78-79) (3° 4° 5°), 1045-1081.

Lejarraja, I., & Walkenhurst, P. (2007). *Diversification by Deepening Linkages with Tourism*. Washington, DC: International Trade Department, The World Bank.

Mahony, K., & Zyl, J. (2002). The Impacts of Tourism Investment on Rural Communities: Three Case Studies in South Africa. *Development Southern Africa*, *19*(1), 83–103. doi:10.1080/03768350220123891

Mason, P. (2015). *Tourism impacts, planning and management*. UK: Routledge. doi:10.4324/9781315781068

Mazumder, M., Ahmed, E., & Al-Amin, A. (2009). Does tourism contribute significantly to the Malaysian economy? Multiplier analysis using I-O technique. *International Journal of Business and Management*, *4*(7), 146–159. doi:10.5539/ijbm.v4n7p146

Mottiar, Z. (2016). The importance of local area as a motivation for cooperation among rural tourism entrepreneurs. *Tourism Planning & Development*, *13*(2), 203–218. doi:10.1080/21568316.2015.1076509

Murteira, M. (1965). *Emigração e Política de Emprego em Portugal*. Retrieved from http://analisesocial.ics.ul.pt/documentos/1224164168X2aIG3gp6Nd78YV7.pdf

Naranjo, J., Castanho, R., Cabezas-Fernández, J. & Loures, L. (2019). Evaluación de las áreas de servicio de la alta velocidad ferroviaria en la España peninsular desde un enfoque SIG multi-método. *Revista de Estudios Andaluces*, (37), 184-208.

Navarro, M., Iglesias, M., & Vinzón, L. (2017). Key variables for developing integrated rural tourism. *Tourism Geographies*, *19*(4), 575–594. doi:10.1080/14616688.2017.1336785

Neto, F., & Neto, J. (2011). Satisfaction with life among adolescents from returned Portuguese immigrant families. *Journal of Social Research & Policy*, *2*(2), 27–46.

Oliveira, J. (2005). *A Educação em Meio Rural como Paleta de Possibilidades para o Desenvolvimento Local: Contributos da Escola do 1º Ciclo do Ensino Básico e do Jardim de Infância* (Unpublished doctoral dissertation). Universidade do Minho, Braga.

Pascariu, G., & Ibanescu, B. (2018). Determinants and implications of the tourism multiplier effect in EU economies. Towards a core-periphery pattern? *Amfiteatru Economic*, *20*(S12), 982–997. doi:10.24818/EA/2018/S12/982

Peixoto, J. (2007). Dinâmicas e Regimes Migratórios: O Caso das Migrações Internacionais em Portugal. *Analise Social*, *XLII*(183), 445–469.

Pilving, T., Kull, T., Suškevics, M., & Viira, A. (2019). The tourism partnership life cycle in Estonia: Striving towards sustainable multisectoral rural tourism collaboration. *Tourism Management Perspectives*, (31), 219-230.

Pina, J. (2011). *O Valor Económico da Língua Portuguesa - Ciclo de Conferências do OLP.* Retrieved from http://observatorio-lp.sapo.pt/pt/temas-de-actualidade/o-valor-economico-da-lingua-portuguesa

Portela, J., & Nobre, S. (2001). Entre Pinela e Paris: Emigração e Regressos. *Analise Social*, *36*(161), 1105–1146.

Reeder, R., & Brown, D. (2005). Recreation, Tourism, and Rural Well-Being, Retrieved from http://www.ers.usda.gov/publications/err7/err7.pdf

Rocha-Trindade, M. (1976). Comunidades Emigrantes em Situação Dipolar: Análise de Três Casos de Emigração Especializada para os E.U.A., para o Brasil e para França. *Análise Social, 12*(48), (4), 983-997.

Ruschmann, D. (2008). *Turismo e planejamento sustentável: a proteção do meio ambiente*. São Paulo, Brazil: Papirus Editora.

Ruzic, P., & Demonja, D. (2017). Transformations in business & economics. *Economic Impacts of Rural Tourism in Rural Areas of Istria*, *16*(3), 31–40.

Saayman, M., & Saayman, A. (2006). Estimating the Economic Contribution of Visitor Spending in the Kruger National Park to the Regional Economy. *Journal of Sustainable Tourism*, *14*(1), 67–81. doi:10.1080/09669580608668592

Sánchez, V., Fernandez, M., & Lara, J. (2017). Economic impact of a religious and tourist event: A holy week celebration. *Tourism Economics*, *23*(6), 1255–1274. doi:10.1177/1354816616675996

Santos, R. (2013). *O regresso dos emigrantes portugueses e o desenvolvimento do turismo em Portugal*. (Unpublished doctoral dissertation). University of Aveiro, Aveiro.

Sharpley, R., & Vass, A. (2006). Tourism, Farming and Diversification: An Attitudinal Study. *Tourism Management*, *27*(5), 1040–1052. doi:10.1016/j.tourman.2005.10.025

Silberberg, T. (1995). Cultural Tourism and Business Opportunities for Museums and Heritage Sites. *Tourism Management*, *16*(5), 361–365. doi:10.1016/0261-5177(95)00039-Q

Silva, M., Amaro, R., Clausse, G., Conim C., Matos, M., Pisco, M. & Seruya, L. (1984). *Regresso, Emigração e Desenvolvimento Regional em Portugal.* Lisboa, Portugal: Instituto de Estudos para o Desenvolvimento.

Snyman, S. (2013). Household spending patterns and flow of ecotourism income into communities around Liwonde National Park, Malawi. *Development Southern Africa, 30*(4-5), 640–658. doi:10.1080/0376835X.2013.832149

Stephen, P. (2015). Potential Economic contribution of regional tourism development in China: A comparative analysis. *International Journal of Tourism Research, 17*(3), 303–312. doi:10.1002/jtr.1990

Suresh, K., Tiwari, A., Uddin, G., & Ahmed, A. (2018). Tourism, trade, and economic growth in India: a frequency-domain analysis of causality. *Anatolia – International Journal of Tourism and Hospitality Research, 29*(3), 319-325.

Tohamy, S., & Swinscoe, A. (2000). *The Economic Impact of Tourism in Egypt*, Retrieved from http://www.eces.org.eg/MediaFiles/Uploaded_Files/%7B02ADE2E4-F995-4CDE-82CE 32BB9A4A15E9%7D_ECESPVP5e.pdf

Tohmo, T. (2018). The economic impact of tourism in Central Finland: A regional input-output study. *Tourism Review, 73*(4), 521–547. doi:10.1108/TR-04-2017-0080

Tribe, J. (2015). *The economics of recreation, leisure and tourism.* UK: Routledge. doi:10.4324/9781315769233

Vanegas, M., & Croes, R. (2003). Growth, Development and Tourism in a Small Economy: Evidence from Aruba. *International Journal of Tourism Research*, (5): 315–330.

Vas, G., & Frías, M. (2019). Aplicación de los procesos de cooperación como instrumento para la configuración de un destino turístico a escala regional y local. *Investigaciones Turísticas*, (17): 103–125.

Veretekhina, S., Shinkareva, O., Kozhaev, J., Telepchenkova, N., Kuznetsova, E. & Plekhanov, N. (2017). Evaluation methodology of the multiplier effect for the Region as the result of the cluster formation. *Eurasian Journal of Analytical Chemistry*, (12), 533-547.

Vulevic, A., Macura, D., Djordjevic, D., & Castanho, R. (2018). Assessing accessibility and transport infrastructure inequities in administrative units in Serbia's Danube corridor based on multi-criteria analysis and GIS mapping tools. *Transylvanian Review of Administrative Sciences, 53*(53 E), 123–142. doi:10.24193/tras.53E.8

Walmsley, D. (2003). Rural Tourism: A Case of Lifestyle-Led Opportunities. *The Australian Geographer, 34*(1), 61–72. doi:10.1080/00049180320000066155

Wilke, E., Costa, B., Freire, O., & Ferreira, M. (2019). Interorganizational cooperation in tourist destination: Building performance in the hotel industry. *Tourism Management, 72*, 340–351. doi:10.1016/j.tourman.2018.12.015

Williams, A. (1984). Introduction. In A. Williams (Ed.), *Southern Europe Transformed- Political and Economic Change in Greece* (pp. 1–32). Italy, Portugal and Spain: Harpercollins College Div.

Yashalova, N., Akimova, M., & Aleksandrovich, R. (2017). Prospects for regional development of industrial tourism in view of the analysis of the main economic indicators of Russian tourism industry. *Economic and Social Changes-Facts Trends, 10*(2), 195–213.

Yesavdar, U., Belgibayav, A., & Mersakylova, G. (2016). The role of developing direction of international tourism in Kazakhstan. *Bulletin of the National Academy of Sciences of the Republic of Kazakhstan*, (2), 180-185.

ADDITIONAL READING

Asian Development Bank. (2019). *Promoting Regional Tourism Cooperation under CAREC 2030: A Scoping Study. Philipines*. Asian Development Bank.

Benckendorff, P., & Durlacher, D. (2013). *International Cases in Sustainable Travel & Tourism*. Oxford: Goodferllow Publishers.

Castanho, R. (2017). *Sustainable Urban Planning in transboundary areas: analysis of critical factors for territorial success*. (Unpublished doctoral dissertation). University of Extremadura (UEx), Badajoz.

Cavaco, C. (2006). *Desenvolvimento e Território- Espaços "Rurais" Pós-agrícolas e Novos Lugares de Turismo e Lazer*. Lisboa: Centro de Estudos Geográficos da Universidade de Lisboa.

Cresswell, T., & Merriman, P. (2012). *The Geography of Mobilities: Practices, Spaces, Subjects*. England: Ashgate.

Gursoy, D., & Nunkoo, R. (2019). *The Routledge Handbook of Tourism Impacts – Theoritetical and Applied Perspectives*. New York: Routledge.

Hall, M. (2005). *Tourism- Rethinking the Social Science of Mobility*. England: Prentice Hall.

Martins, L. (2005). *Espaços de Lazer e Turismo no Noroeste de Portugal*. Porto: Edições Afrontamento.

Wood, M. (2017). *Sustainable Tourism on a Finite Planet – Environmental, Business and Policy Solutions* (1st ed.). New York: Routlege. doi:10.4324/9781315439808

KEY TERMS AND DEFINITIONS

Community of Portuguese Language Countries: An international organization and political association of Lusophone nations across four continents, where Portuguese is an official language.

Cooperation: A joint action between individuals or organizations for a purpose or common goal.

Emigrantion: The act of leaving one's place of origin (the homeland) with the intention of settling in a foreign country.

Growth: Increased economic capacity of a country or region.

Return Migration: The movements of workers and relatives of the more developed countries or regions for the regions that provide labor from rural areas.

Rural Area: Geographic area with 2000 inhabitants or less (Portuguese Official Statistical Institute).

Sustainable Development: Involves the articulation between the various dimensions of sustainability, including economic, environmental, sociocultural and institutional.

Tourism: The activities that people carry out during their travels and stays in places other than their own, for a period of time less than one consecutive year, for leisure, business and other purposes (World Travel and Tourism Organization).

Chapter 12
Cooperation Strategies Towards Sustainability in Insular Territories:
A Comparison Study Between Porto Santo Island, Madeira Archipelago, Portugal and El Hierro Island, Canary Archipelago, Spain

Sérgio António Neves Lousada
University of Madeira, Portugal

Rui Alexandre Castanho
WSB University, Poland

ABSTRACT

Nowadays, the high environmental sensitivity and economic constraints, as well as future prospects for development, require a strong sustainable energy policy. Such policies should be based on the local resource valorization – which gains more emphasis in ultra-peripheral territories as the case of the Madeira and Canary Archipelagos. In fact, renewable energy sources become more competitive from the economic point of view – however, with high environmental and social benefits in both Archipelagos. Thus, the local policies of Porto Santo Island will be inspired on the neighbor archipelago (Canary Islands), more specifically in the El Hierro Island – which is one of the worldwide leaders in sustainability issues. Contextually, the work enables a view through the cooperation perspective, highlighting sustainability strategies in Porto Santo Island (Madeira, Portugal) and El Hierro Island (Canary, Spain). Therefore, it will address diverse forms of energy production through natural resources with influence on spatial planning.

DOI: 10.4018/978-1-7998-2513-5.ch012

INTRODUCTION

The contemporary age was primarily marked by the accelerated growth of cities which were widespread throughout the world, through the impulses and transformations arising from capitalism, even in underdeveloped nations with non-significant industrialization (Silva & Barroso & Rodrigues & Costa & Fontana, 2014). In this sense, the cities are constituted by a system of interconnection between people, companies, trades, transport, communication, and services, and up to 2015, about 50% of the world population was resident in urban areas, with the trend of growth to 75% up to 2050 (UN World Urbanization Prospects, 2012). It should be noted that megacities emerged in the 21st century, which gather about 10% of the world population, and most of them have severe concentrations of poverty and socio-environmental problems (UN World Urbanization Prospects, 2014).

Regarding the accelerated growth of cities, Johnson (2008) states that the growing and complex agglomeration of people tends inevitably to make the places more confusing and disorganized. For Rodríguez-Bolívar (2015), the rapid shift to an excessively urban population causes societies and their respective governances to encounter unprecedented challenges such as: unemployment, education, sustainable development, energy and the environment, security, public services and others. It is only in the middle of the 20st century that the global edition of legal regulations for urban planning was initiated, in order to regulate the agenda and promote social peace in urban areas (Humbert, 2017).

Figure 1. Urban and rural populations of the world 1950-2050. Source: UN, 2018.

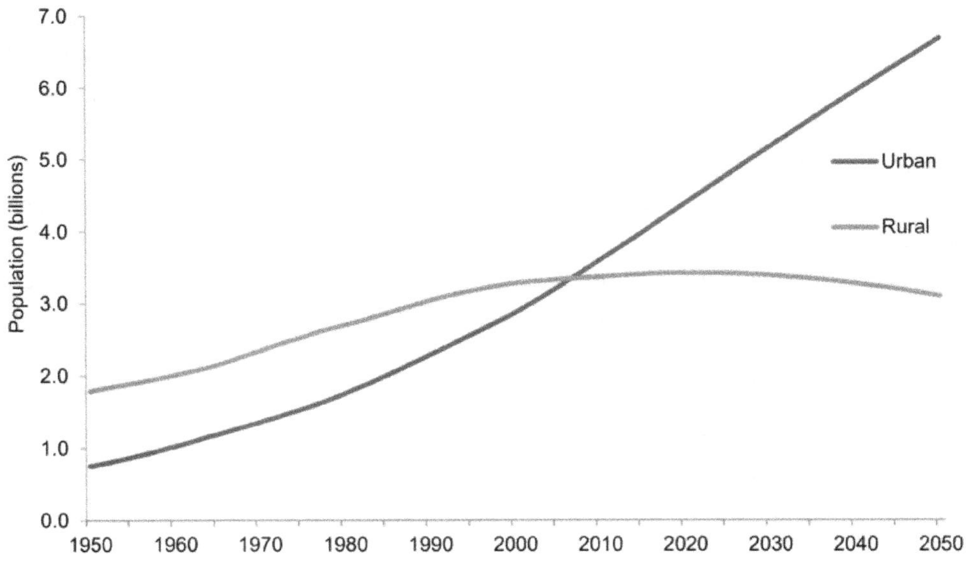

According to Mendes (2014), a revolution is currently happening and it is causing a great deal of tension over the cities. This is stated because *"although cities occupy 2% of the Earth's surface, urban residents consume more than three quarters of the world's natural resources, produce equivalent amounts of waste, use the oceans and soil as dumpbins, and are the Main responsible for greenhouse effect and gas emissions, which threatens to be the greatest danger of the planet Earth (Fernandes, 2016 citing Marceau, 2008 and Girardet, 2004) "*.

In this context, the United Nations Industrial Development Organization (UNIDO, 2015) corroborates the affirmation that although the Earth has always suffered from natural changes, for the first-time, the human activity is the main aggravating factor of this process and presents potentially serious consequences. The UNIDO (2015) highlights that considerable volumes of fossil fuels are used every day in the form of gasoline, petroleum, coal and natural gas, where its burning generates the release of carbon dioxide, and that together the release of other gases coming from human activity such as methane and nitrous oxide, the natural "greenhouse effect" that makes the planet Earth an uninhabitable place. Therefore, the sharp speed at which the changes are taking place threatens the social and environmental systems that fail to adjust at the same pace, increasingly promoting the occurrence of extreme meteorological phenomena (UNIDO, 2015).

Therefore, it is evident the importance of finding smarter ways to manage urban growth, and innovation is one of the most important elements for the development of societies, both at the economic and social level (Pardo & Nam, 2011). For Jenks & Burton & Williams (1996), the link between urban areas and the concept of sustainability is one of the most debated guidelines by international environmental preservation bodies, that is, the discussion of future development linked to efficient management of resources present, both in social and economic order. It is clear that *"sustainable development is a much broader concept, than simple protection of the environment, includes concern for quality of life, equity among people in the present, equity between generations and Social and ethical dimensions of human well-being (Fernandes, 2016 citing the European Commission, 1996). "*

According to Letaifa (2015), for this there are several urban development projects with the aim of transforming into smart cities, that is, transforming the socioeconomic environment into a place where people, private and public initiatives can give access to resources and services more efficiently. In this context, *"the initiatives to make a smart city have emerged as a model to mitigate and remedy the current urban problems and make cities better places to Live (Fernandes, 2016)"*. It is noted that the development of smart cities is not just a process of acquiring or selling technologies, because the construction of these cities requires a development process with a favorable environment and directed towards implementation in the urban areas (Mendes, 2014).

In this sense, several models have been proposed by several institutions (Pinto, 2017):

1. **IBM Model**: The model presented by *IBM* (*International Business Machines*) infers that cities should be prepared for their growth, so that transport, public safety, education, health and government services are more efficient and intelligent. This model suggests that this transformation should be done by advanced technology and systems designed for the best functioning of the city. Finally, the *IBM* proposal can be summarized by improving efficiency in the main areas mentioned above: minimizing traffic congestion, increasing security in order to reduce crime and response time emergency, educational enhancement and access to health;
2. **Siemens Model**: The model proposed by *Siemens* suggests that cities should have smarter and more efficient structures in order to have an evident objective, performance indicators and the integration of connected domains. It is noted that the concept of intelligent city of Siemens also provides for the integration of social and political projects, as well as the known six categories of evaluation of European Smart Cities: intelligent life, environment intelligent mobility, intelligent governance, intelligent citizen and intelligent economy. Finally, this methodology suggests some key considerations for all cities that want to become intelligent: commitment, well-defined objective, integrated cross-border program, commitment of the citizen and all the parties interested, integrating the use of informational and communicative technologies, deep analysis of the cost-efficiency of implementation of this practice;
3. **Microsoft Model**: The *CityNext* model proposed by *Microsoft* has as its primary objective to respond to urban growth and its problems, in addition to allowing the modernization of infrastructures and the quantification of necessary natural resources. In this sense, *Microsoft* has elaborated this model based on the premise that there are opportunities for cities to become safer, smarter, healthier, more efficient, with high schooling and more sustainable, providing better quality of life for the citizens who inhabit it. The company relies on the application of the cloud information store, where cities can connect privately or publicly, with privacy, security, interoperability and control. The system would work, roughly, as the current social media, which enable dialogue between people, companies and governmental entities;
4. **Sidewalk Labs Model**: This model created by *Sidewalk Labs* focuses primarily on sharing information. This methodology aims to present answers to the main urban problems such as: transport congestion, public health crises, exacerbated use of fossil fuels and atmospheric pollution. The essence of the model refers

to people, opportunities, interactivity, sharing of information and values, diversity and coordination.

Therefore, it is evident that all the above models tend to present different technological solutions, for the same problems, since they are presented with greater urgency of resolution.

As previously discussed, one of the main problems preventing sustainable development is the use of energy sources based on fossil fuels such as petroleum, coal, natural gas, etc. In this context, it is essential to find new alternatives for energy supply that cause less damage to the environment and are renewable, such as the use of wind energy, photovoltaic or solar energy and hydroelectric power. According to UNIDO (2015), renewable energy sources constantly produce low greenhouse gas (GHG) emissions. According to the UNIDO (2015), the use of renewable means has the following advantages:

1. They can contribute to social and economic development, since in favorable conditions it allows to reduce costs compared to the use of non-renewable energy;
2. They can help you achieve faster access to energy;
3. They can contribute to the supply of energy in a safer way;
4. Lower GHG emission compared to non-renewable sources.

Finally, it is important to know the knowledge of each of the renewable energy production methodologies in order to carry out the feasibility study of implementation in each region, since each one has particularities, advantages and disadvantages tend to interfere considerably in the cost-efficiency ratio.

BACKGROUND

As discussed above, it is necessary to advance knowledge of renewable methodologies so that the feasibility study of implementation is carried out. Therefore, before conducting the characterization of the practices adopted in the island of Porto Santo and in the island of El Hierro, it will be present the main characteristics of the means of production of renewable energy.

Hydro-Electric Power

Energy production by hydroelectric plants basically consists of harnessing the potential gravitational energy of water in a reservoir, which can be a river, natural

Figure 2. Energy matrix in the years 1973 and 2006. Source: ANEEL, 2008 and IEA, 2008.

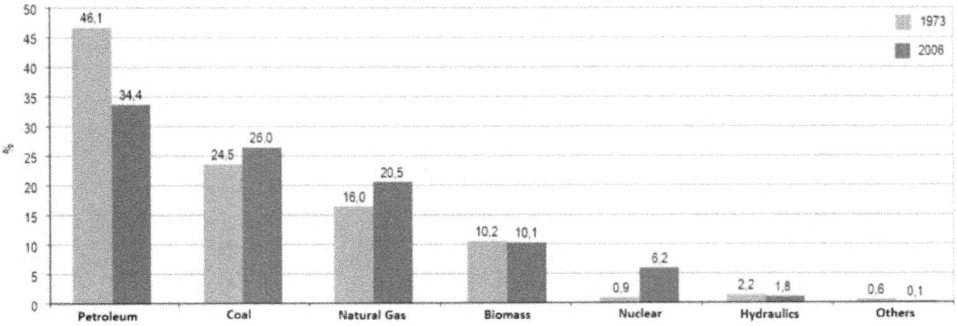

lake, artificial lake or obstructed canals with dams. In this sense, the water captured in the lake or reservoir is conducted to the powerhouse by means of channels, metal pipes or tunnels, and after passing through the hydraulic turbine is returned to the origin through an escape channel (Caus & Michels, 2014). According to the National Electric Energy Agency (ANEEL, 2008), to produce hydroelectric power, it is necessary to integrate the river flow, the amount of water available in a certain period and the difference in the level of relief, which can be natural or artificial. Finally, the electric power is generated when the water passes through the turbine causing it to rotate, and as it is coupled into the generator, it transforms the mechanical power into electrical power (Caus & Michels, 2014).

It is highlighted that *"water is also one of the few sources for energy production that does not contribute to global warming – the main environmental problem of today. And it is also renewable: by the effects of solar energy and the force of gravity, liquid becomes vapor that condenses into clouds, which return to the terrestrial surface in the form of Rain (ANEEL, 2008)* ". However, despite this great advantage, the use of hydroelectric power plants from 1973 to 2006 had a reduction of 2.2% to 1.8%, and the generation of electricity had a reduction of 21% to 16%, according to Figures 2 and 3:

The construction phase of large hydroelectric plants has social consequences (displacement of people), as well as direct and indirect effects on the environment such as: deviations from water courses, alteration of slopes, implementation of Interference of aquatic ecosystems, among others (UNIDO, 2015). Another factor that may explain the low utilization of hydroelectric power plants refers to the characteristics of water distribution on the terrestrial surface (ANEEL, 2008).

However, *"small-scale hydroelectric power can be important at the regional level, especially when it is profitable (UNIDO, 2015)"*. In this sense, it is again

Figure 3. Generation of electricity in the world by fuel type in 1973 and 2006. Source: ANEEL, 2008 and IEA, 2008.

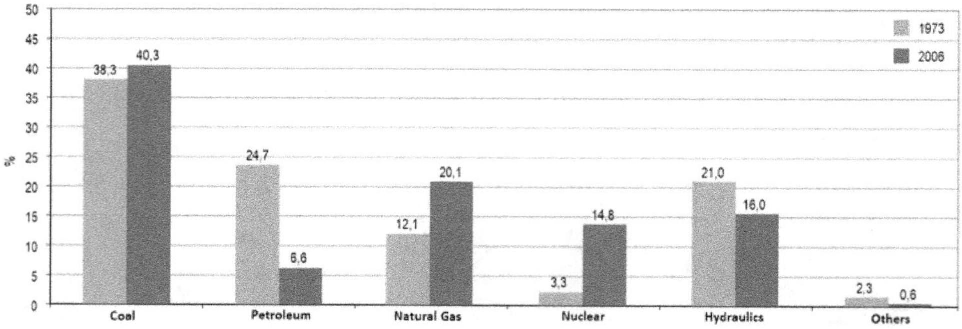

evidenced the need to carry out a study of economic, social and environmental viability according to the reality of each region.

Biomass Energy

Biomass is understood as *"any organic matter that can be transformed into mechanical, thermal or electrical energy (ANEEL, 2008)"*. For UNIDO (2015), among the possibilities of supplying biomass energy are the municipal and rural solid waste, industrial and agricultural waste, forests and energy plantations.

According to ANEEL (2008), biomass is one of the sources for energy production that has the highest potential for growth nowadays, being considered one of the main alternatives for the diversification of the energy matrix and the consequent reduction of use of fossil fuels. In this sense, it is said that *"the yield and costs of biomass energy depend on local conditions, such as the availability of land and biomass residues and the production technology (UNIDO, 2015)"*.

It is noted that in regions with less development, the most employed biomass is of forest origin, and the processes of obtaining energy are characterized by low efficiency. About large-scale production, the biomass used is agricultural and has efficient electrical power technologies (ANEEL, 2008).

In this sense, biomass conversion technologies, as well as biomass plantations, require improvements in order to achieve technical and economic viability (UNIDO, 2015). According to ANEEL (2008), each technique originates a derivative and is at different levels in the technological aspect. Among the methodologies used is the direct combustion by stoves, boilers, furnaces or pyrolysis/carbonization that consists of heating the biomass between 300 ° C and 500 ° C until the extraction of the volatile material (ANEEL, 2008).

Table 1. Installed power in the last ten years. Source: ANEEL, 2008 and WWEA, 2008.

Year	Power (MW)	Growth(%)
1997	7475	-
1998	9663	29,30
1999	13696	41,70
2000	18039	31,70
2001	24320	34,80
2002	31164	28,10
2003	39290	26,10
2004	47693	21,40
2005	59033	23,80
2006	74153	25,60
2007	93849	26,60
Total growth (%)		1255,50

Finally, it is crucial to note that *"the variation in mitigation costs for energy forms derived from biomass, such as electricity, heat, biogas or transport fuels, not only depends on the cost of biomass production, but also on the aspects of certain fuel conversion technologies (UNIDO, 2015).* "

Wind Energy

According to Picolo & Bühler & Rampinelli (2014), the displacement of the air masses (wind) brings a huge potential to convert this kinetic energy to electricity generation. In this context, *"wind energy is basically that obtained from the kinetic energy (of the movement) generated by the migration of the air masses caused by the temperature differences existing on the surface of the planet (ANEEL, 2008)".* The conversion of the kinetic energy of the air mass into electric energy occurs through the contact of the wind with the propellers coupled into a generator. Thus, when rotating the propellers give rise to the mechanical energy that triggers the rotor of the aerogenerator, in order to convert into electric energy (ANEEL, 2008).

It is pointed out that *"the concern with issues such as impacts on the environment and global warming have generated a need for changes in electricity generation in several countries of the world (Picolo & Bühler & Rampinelli, 2014)".* Based on this premise, it is noted that the technological evolution of the energy sector has led to the development of even more powerful equipment, where *"[...] for example, the diameter of the turbines was 20 meters, which resulted in an average power of 50*

Table 2. Installed power in 2007. Source: ANEEL, 2008 and WWEA, 2008.

Ranking	Country	Power	% related to the total
1º	German	22247,40	23,70
2º	US	16818,80	17,90
3º	Spain	15145,10	16,10
4º	India	7850,00	8,40
5º	China	5912,00	6,30
6º	Denmark	3125,00	3,30
7º	Italy	2726,10	2,90
8º	France	2455,00	2,60
9º	UK	2389,00	2,50
10º	Portugal	2130,00	2,30
25º	Brazil	247,10	0,30
Total		93849,10	100,00

kW (kilowatts). Today, these diameters reach 100 meters, which allows obtaining, in a single turbine, 5000 kW (ANEEL, 2008) ".

Wind energy installed in a large network can contribute up to 20% of annual electricity production, requiring special mechanisms for storage, reserve or cargo management (UNIDO, 2015). In addition, the feasibility study of implementation should consider the air density, the intensity, direction and speed of the wind, these being linked to the geographic aspects such as vegetation, relief, and thermal interactions between terrestrial surface and Atmosphere (ANEEL, 2008). Another problem involving this technology is the fact that it causes the population to move away from the wind farms due to the noise of the turbines, the landscape visual effects and the interference in wildlife (UNIDO, 2015).

Despite all the issues addressed, *"the worldwide Installed capacity of wind energy increased 1255% between 1997 and 2007, from 7500 to 93800 MW (ANEEL, 2008)"*, according to Table 1.

According to ANEEL (2008) citing WWEA (2008), in 2007 there was the installation of approximately 20000 MW of wind power generation across the globe, the largest producers, see Table 2.

Finally, it is emphasized the importance of performing the feasibility study of implementation according to local characteristics, in order to mitigate the socio-environmental impacts caused by this technology.

Figure 4: Installed power of photovoltaic cells in the world (MW). Source: ANEEL, 2008 and IEA, 2007.

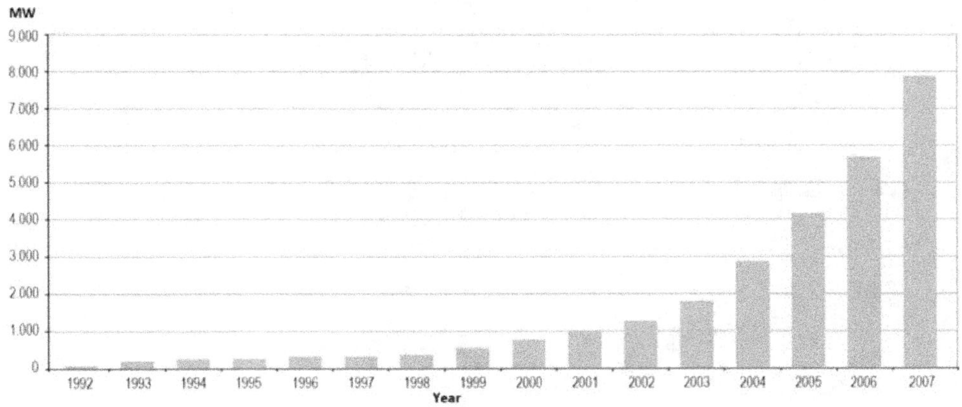

Solar energy

Solar energy is the direct conversion of sunlight into electricity and heat and can be obtained through photovoltaic technology (PV) and solar thermal energy. The PV technology is already considered competitive by being used as an independent energy source and away from electrical utility networks, but it is not competitive in much of the network connection applications (UNIDO, 2015).

One of the main problems related to solar energy is the high cost of solar panels, being less attractive for short-term investments. It is also said that *"PV devices do not contaminate in normal operation, in some systems it is necessary to use toxic materials, so that there may be risks in the phases of manufacturing, use and disposal (UNIDO, 2015)"*. But, *"[...] the cost of PV systems is expected to improve considerably through research and economies of scale (UNIDO, 2015)."*

In this context, it is evident that the participation of solar energy is little expressive in the world scenario. However, from 1996 to 2006 there was a significant increase of 2000% in its use, reaching in 2007, 7800 MW (ANEEL, 2008), as shown in Figure 4.

Porto Santo Framing

The island of Porto Santo is located in the Madeira archipelago, between the parallels 32° 59' 40" N and 33° 07' 35" N of latitude and meridians 16° 16 ' 35 "W and 16th 24 ' 35" W of longitude referring to Greenwich, being the smallest of the inhabited islands of the archipelago. The island has 42.5 km^2, 11 km long and 6 km of maximum width (Oliveira *et al.*, 2014).

Figure 5: Madeira archipelago. Source: Google earth, 2019a.

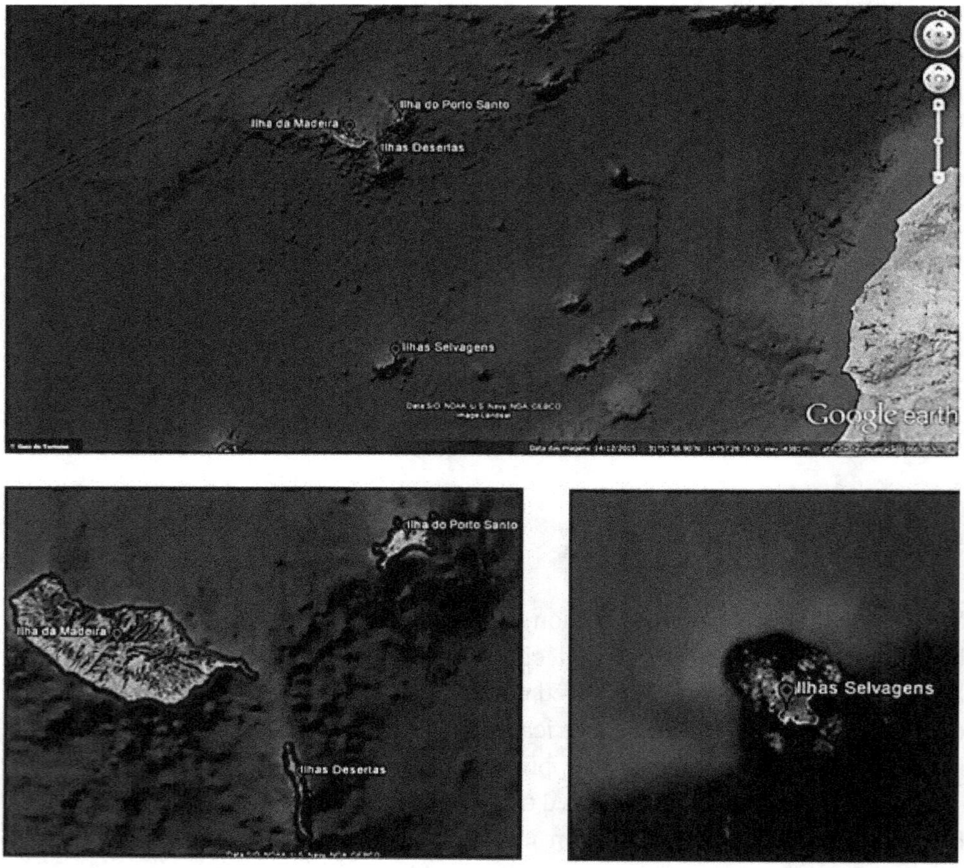

About demography, *"the population residing in the autonomous region of Madeira was 267785 inhabitants, of which 5483 reside on the island of Porto Santo, representing 2% of the population of the archipelago (Oliveira et al., 2014 citing Censos, 2011)"*. The population is characterized by seasonality and can reach 300% of the fixed population during the summer.

Referring to the electricity producer system of the island of Porto Santo, *"[...] consists of thermal and renewable production, which results in an installed total power of 21.01 MW, in which 17.73 MW are owned by EEM and the remaining 3.28 MW are owned by private entities (Gouveia, 2018) "*.

According to Gouveia (2018), the electric system of Porto Santo is composed of a thermal plant in the site of Penedo, known as Central Nova, belonging exclusively to the company of electricity of Madeira (EEM). The plant produces approximately 17.73 MW of power, with a contribution of 84.7% of thermal sources in 2017 (EEM,

Figure 6: Energy emission by primary energy source in 2017. Source: EEM, 2017.

2017). It is saved that the thermal production is driven by diesel oil (Pincha, 2019), and is therefore not of a renewable nature.

For photovoltaic solar energy, the use of PV technology represents the second largest contribution to the energy supply of the island of Porto Santo (11.3%), where the production period is found, primarily, between 10 and 18 hours, with emphasis between 12 and 16 hours (Gouveia, 2018). It is said that *"this energy is available throughout the island, being provided by two photovoltaic parks, located in Calheta and Vila Baleira, and by 18 micro and mini productions centers, distributed throughout the island. It should be noted that this type of energy came to the island of Porto Santo, only in 2009, having conquered the level of renewable energy with greater contribution to REE, soon in 2010 (Gouveia, 2018) "*.

Regarding wind energy, this is the technology that presents the smallest contribution (4%) for the electric network of the island of Porto Santo, because it has the lowest installed power (Gouveia, 2018). In this sense, *"the production of wind origin was significantly low [...] due to a lower available resource (EEM, 2017)"*.

In this context, the distribution of electrical potential by type of technology employed in the island of Porto Santo is shown in Figure 6.

As mentioned above, the seasonal population of the island of Porto Santo, mainly in summer, infers in variations in energy consumption over the months, reaching

Figure 7: Monthly emission (GWh) and Monthly peaks (MW). Source: EEM, 2017.

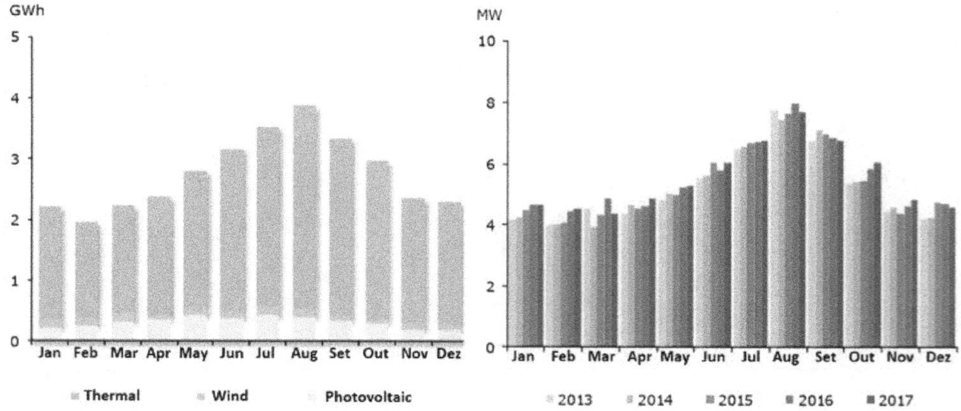

maximum emission and consumption values during the month of August, according to the Figure 7.

Another problem encountered refers to the use of fossil fuels in automobiles, where *"without water and without any source of energy itself, the island needs to import regularly from Madeira gasoline and diesel to the about 1000 vehicles that there circulate [...] (Lavrador, 2019) "*.

Finally, the island of Porto Santo becomes self-reliant using thermal energy (diesel burning), photovoltaic solar energy and wind energy, being, therefore, largely dependent on the use of fossil fuels.

El Hierro Framing

The island of El Hierro is located in the Canary Islands and has an approximate population of 10995 inhabitants (Godina & Rodrigues & Matias & Catalão, 2015) and 268.71 km^2 of area. Even though it is the best island in the Canary Islands, the consumption of fossil fuels for electricity generation accompanied the patterns of the other islands of the archipelago, that is, very high consumption of diesel fuel.

However, from the implementation of the *Gorona del Viento project,* the energy reality of the island of El Hierro became a world reference in terms of renewable and sustainable energy production. The project *Gorona del Viento* is an *"innovative project designed to affront the energy consumption on the island El Hierro the basis of renewable energies (Agudelo & Martin, 2016)"*. The singular factor of this project is the use of a hydroelectric-wind system, in order to allow the alternation of the energy source and its complementation.

Figure 8: Canary archipelago. Source: Google earth, 2019b.

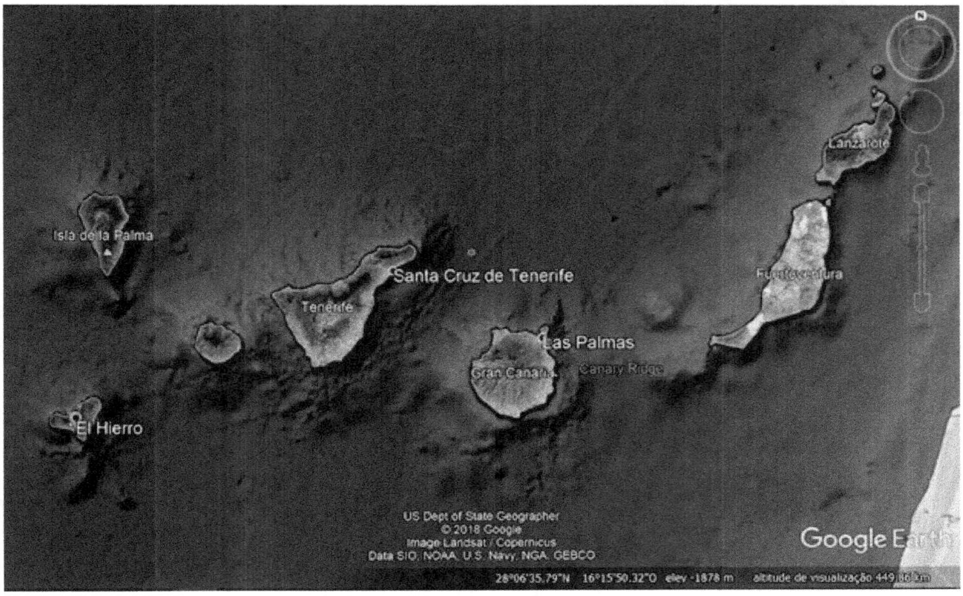

As shown in the online portal of the *Red Eléctrica de España*, the electrical supply system consists of hydroelectric power, wind energy and thermal energy (diesel). This platform allows the real-time verification of the consumption and

Figure 9: El Hierro energy production (MW) at 25/08/2019. Source: REE, 2019.

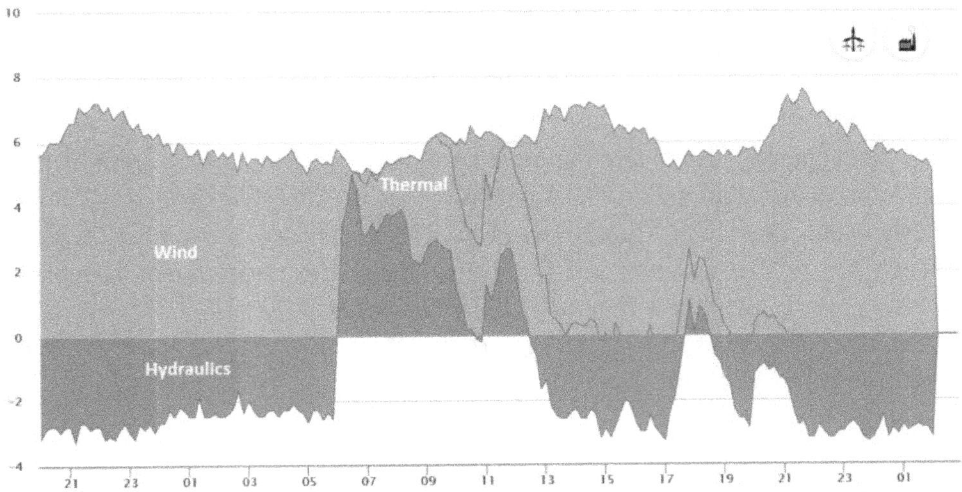

Figure 10: Renewable energy production (MW) in 100% at 21/08/2019. Source: REE, 2019.

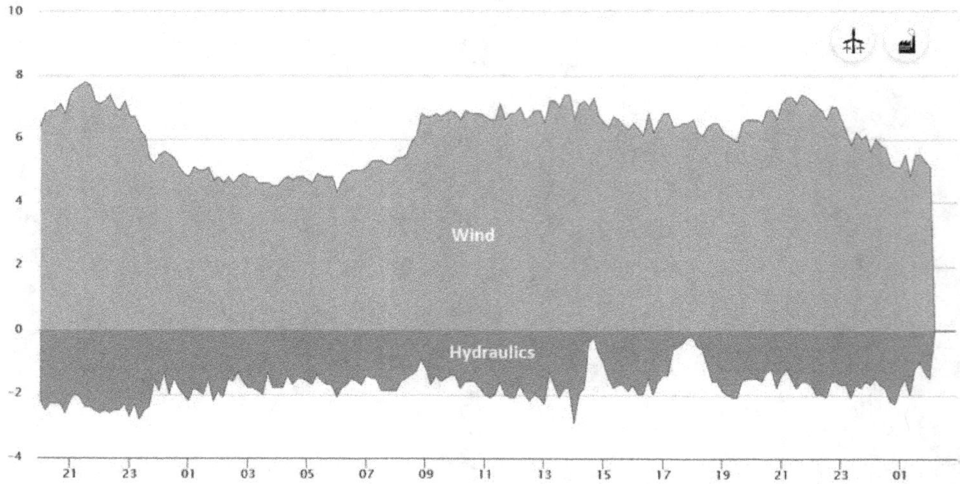

electrical production of the island of El Hierro, besides presenting the percentage of contribution of each energy source mentioned above, as shown in Figure 9.

It is noted that the production of energy of El Hierro is done through the variation and complementation of the three sources mentioned, having periods of peak between 21:00 to 22:00 and 14:00 to 15:00. It is also evident that during the periods of lower consumption there is a much higher contribution of the thermal (diesel) and hydroelectric sources, being replaced by wind energy again when consumption tends to increase. Finally, it is verified that during most of the time the production of hydroelectric power is negative, that is, it is consuming the energy from the wind source for the operation of the pumping systems of the hydroelectric power plant, in order to create a cycle Sustaining.

Another key point to be presented is the fact that there are days when electricity generation is 100% renewable from the wind farm, as shown in Figure 10.

In this context, it is evident the great sustainable potential of this project that has become a world reference. For Agudelo & Martin (2016), in 2050, 100% of the electricity generated in the Canary Islands will be from renewable sources, in order to reach 20% in 2020 and 58% in 2030. Thus, *"the energy revolution plans to pass from the current 338 MW of renewable power installed to the 11944 MW [...] With intermediate objectives of 1011 MW in 2020, 3254 MW in 2030 and 6933 MW in 2040 (Agudelo & Martin, 2016) ".*

COMPARATIVE ANALYSIS BETWEEN THE ISLANDS

As presented in the respective framings of the islands, Porto Santo presents a considerable deficiency when using primarily (84.7%) renewable sources for the energy supply of the island. On the other hand, El Hierro, even with the population approximately twice as large as Porto Santo, presents an efficient system based fundamentally on the collaboration of the wind source (predominant as an energy source) with the hydroelectric source (where the whole operation is sustained by wind energy and serves as an auxiliary source). Therefore, *"the island of El Hierro was able to cover its electricity demand with 100% renewable energy for 18 consecutive days, in the period between January 25th and February 12th (Público.es, 2018 citing Red electric de Espanã)"* in 2018.

It should be noted that the island of Porto Santo uses only wind energy, photovoltaic energy and thermal energy from the burning of diesel, while El Hierro has wind energy, thermal energy also from the burning of diesel and a central installed after the implementation of the *Gorona del Viento* project, in order to differentiate itself from the other Canary Islands that are fundamentally dependent on fossil fuels.

In addition to the population corresponding to approximately double Porto Santo, El Hierro has a territorial extension six times greater. This shows that the territorial utilization capacity for the implementation of wind farms is greater than that of Porto Santo, but tends to allow a larger population and consequently greater energy consumption. Analyzing from another perspective, Porto Santo would need less effort (because it has lower consumption) to become self-sustainable with renewable energies, primarily depending on government incentives and ambitious projects such as *Gorona del Viento.*

PERSPECTIVES FOR THE FUTURE

Porto Santo

As evidenced earlier, the island of Porto Santo has a great potential to become a smart and sustainable island. To this end, it is paramount to implement projects of a sustainable nature and renewable energy production. As the island of Porto Santo still has a vast use of fossil fuels to supply public areas and residences, this reveals itself as the biggest challenge to be overcome.

For the island of Porto Santo, we proceeded to implement the Plan of Action for Sustainable Energy, a project aimed at improving energy sources and sustainable public policies. In this context, *"as a vision for the future, the energy policy of the municipality of Porto Santo, concreted in the actions that are part of this action plan*

Table 3. Investment breakdown. Source: Oliveira, 2014.

Investment (thousand euro)				
Sectors	**County**	**Companies and public/private communities**	**Citizens**	**Overall**
County services, residential, commerce and services, street lighting, primary and secondary sectors	857	4068	756	5681
Transports	435	1398	960	2793
Local electricity generation	2	2509	339	2848
Land use planning	1155	15	0	1170
Public procurement for products and services	0	0	0	0
Work with citizens and stakeholders	103	3	0	106
Others	100	0	0	100
Overall	**2652**	**7993**	**2055**	**12698**

for sustainable Energy, will be oriented towards environmental sustainability, quality of life and local economic competitiveness, through the promotion of efficiency, energy valorization of internal natural resources, market boosting of sustainable energy products and services, and management tools and Energy monitoring [...] (Oliveira et al., 2014) ".

Still according to Oliveira (2014), the investment to be made up to 2020 consists in the financing of 12.7 million euros, being 20.9% by the municipality of Porto Santo, 16.2% by the citizens and 62.9% by companies and public-private initiatives. In this sense, the allocation of investments can be verified in table 3.

It is expected that with the implementation of the project, the increase of 87% of the contribution of renewable energy sources, the reduction of 27.4% of the consumption of fossil fuels and the consequent reduction of 32.9% of the CO2 emissions (Oliveira, 2014) is estimated. Another practice that can contribute largely to the end of the use of fossil fuels in Porto Santo is the governmental facilitation and incentive to obtain photovoltaic solar panels in the residences, in order to allow electrical production in the possible commercialization of the electricity produced in surplus form. The marketing can be made to the municipality itself directly or through tax exemption.

About to the problem of the consumption of fossil fuels in automobiles on the island of Porto Santo, comes in mid-2015 the project Smart fossil Free Island *"with the aim of valuing as a tourist destination, combining the politically correct to the need To protect the environment, aiming to attract an increasingly avid audience for all that is green and sustainable, so much so that there are more European funds to make all these improvements possible (Lavrador, 2019)"*. In this context, EEM together with automobile companies such as *Renault*, have joined in order to create partnerships to facilitate the replacement of cars with electric combustion, because *"not only because they end up with the need to transport to the small fuel island, as they avoid pollution when they burn (Lavrador, 2019)."* According to Lavrador (2019) quoting Rui Rebelo, CEO of EEM, it is sought by the Madeiran Electric to leave the current 15% of renewable energy to 25% in 2020, and to 60% in 2025.

El Hierro

Despite the incredible achievement of keeping for 18 days with only renewable energy sources, the island of El Hierro can still present improvements and aspire to be 100% renewable in all time. According to Aragón (2019), in centers disconnected from the electricity grid, in the year 2018 there was the burning of 12000 liters of fossil fuel, being completely inconsistent with the proposal of the island. The burning of these 12000 liters of fuel equals the emission of 26000 kilos of carbon dioxide. In this sense, it applies to the same recommendation made to Porto Santo, which consists of the facilitation and governmental incentive to obtain photovoltaic solar panels, with the possibility of commercialization of surplus energy to the municipality itself.

According to Aragón (2019) quoting Montserrat Gutiérrez, currently there are feasibility studies for the implementation of biomass energy, in order to achieve total energy sustainability and offer a better destination to the forest and agricultural residues of El Hierro. In this context, *"biomass facilitates the reuse of waste, mainly forestry and agricultural, to obtain thermal energy (Aragón, 2019)"*.

Another factor that can contribute to the desired reach by El Hierro, is to adhere to the proposed project for Porto Santo, which consists in the complete substitution of automobiles to combustion by electric. It is evident that by the greater number of inhabitants and consequently of automobiles, this process tends to be more lengthy for El Hierro in relation to Porto Santo, however, as the island is in a truly advanced process in the sustainable aspect, It will make it easier to achieve the objective of being an island 100% renewable energy. Finally, as mentioned in the El Hierro framework, the island became a reference for the Canary Archipelago itself, which has promising forecasts for short, medium and long term.

CONCLUSION

The theme of sustainable development has never been so evident and present in the public debate, since with the worrying forecasts of global warming and the greenhouse effect, it will affect mankind in a drastic way. Based on these assumptions, the island of El Hierro has become a global benchmark in the requirement to use renewable energies. Despite being on a very small scale, the sustainable practices adopted on the island presented significant results and can serve as a model for the island of Porto Santo, which also aims to obtain the *status* of Sustainable Island but is in initial phase of adaptation. In addition to the great feat of remaining 18 days fueled only with renewable energies, El Hierro tends to become, in the not too distant future, an island 100% stocked with renewable energies, with low emission of atmospheric pollutants, low emission of Forestry and agricultural waste and a model to be followed across the globe.

It is clear that the application of these methodologies on larger scales, such as countries of continental dimensions, tends to be a much more complex and lengthy process, obviously due to the high territorial extent that will increase the cost, time of implementation, Much more complex projects and excessively large consumption. However, the application at the municipal level or by parishes tends to be a major step to start reducing the consumption of fossil fuels throughout the country. Finally, it is evident the great importance of initiatives of this genus as the project *Gorona del Viento*, in El Hierro, and the Sustainable Action Plan applied to Porto Santo. The investment made by the public-private partnership tends to benefit both citizens and companies, municipalities and especially the environment.

Funding: This study was conducted under the project "Projeto Turismo: caraterização, impacto e sustentabilidade do turismo da Madeira" (M1420-01-0145-FEDER-000007), co-financed by the Madeira Program 14-20, Portugal 2020 and the European Union, through the European Regional Development Fund, which belongs to the Research Group CITUR - Madeira - Centre for Tourism Research, Development and Innovation.

REFERENCES

Agudelo, I. G. C., & Martin, S. D. (2016). *Gorona del Viento, Futuro Energético en Canarias*. La Laguna: Grado en Contabilidad y Finanzas.

ANEEL. (2008). *Atlas de Energia Elétrica do Brasil* (3rd ed.). Brasília: Agência Nacional de Energia Elétrica.

Aragón, E. (2019). La isla del Hierro aspira a ser 100% renovable. Disponível em: https://www.energynews.es/la-isla-del-hierro-aspira-a-ser-100-renovable/

Comissão Europeia. (1996). *Cidades europeias sustentáveis*. Luxemburgo: Serviço das Publicações Oficiais das Comunidades Europeias.

EEM. (2017). *Caracterização da Rede de Transporte de Distribuição em AT e MT*. Empresa de Eletricidade da Madeira. Disponível em: http://www.eem.pt

Fernandes, M. T. D. S. P. (2016). Cidades Inteligentes: Um novo paradigma urbano – Estudo de caso da cidade do Porto. Dissertação para obtenção do grau de Mestre em Gestão pela Universidade Católica Portuguesa, Porto.

Girardet, H. (2004). *Cities, People, Planet* (1st ed.). Wiley Academy.

Godina, R., Rodrigues, E. M. G., Matias, J. C. O., & Catalão, J. P. S. (2015). *Sustainable Energy System of El Hierro Island*. International Conference on Renewable Energies and Power Quality, La Coruña, Spain. ISSN 2172-038X, n. 13, April.

Google earth. (2019a). *Madeira archipelago.*

Google earth. (2019b). *Canary archipelago.*

Gouveia, L. M. C. (2018). *Projeto de Ligação Elétrica Entre a Ilha da Madeira e a Ilha do Porto Santo. Dissertação para obtenção do título de Mestre em Engenharia Eletrotécnica-Telecomunicações*. Funchal: Universidade da Madeira.

Humbert, G. L. H. (2017). *Curso de direito urbanístico e das cidades. 1*. Rio de Janeiro, Brazil: LMJ Mundo Jurídico.

International Energy Agency. (IEA, 2007). Disponível em: www.iea.org

International Energy Agency. (IEA, 2008). Disponível em: www.iea.org

Jenks, M., Burton, E., & William, K. (1996). *The Compact City: A Sustainable Urban Form?* Disponível em: https://books.google.pt/books?hl=pt-PT&lr=&id=MliRAgAAQBAJ&oi=fnd&pg=PP1&dq=The+Compact+City:+A+Sustainable+Urban+Form%3F+&ots=vXYYkX2ibh&sig=uLIT71fXS_jLG2BO7SyKpq5_zfw&redir_esc=y#v=onepage&q=The%20Compact%20City%3A%20A%20Sustainable%20Urban%20Form%3F&f=false

Johnson, B. (2008). Cities, systems of innovation and economic development. Innovation: Management. *Policy & Practice*, *10*(2-3), 146–155. doi:10.5172/impp.453.10.2-3.146

Lavrador, A. (2019). É inteligente, é nossa e está no meio do Atlêntico. Disponível em: https://observador.pt/2019/06/05/e-inteligente-e-nossa-e-esta-no-meio-do-atlantico/

Letaifa, S. (2015). How to strategize smart cities: Revealing the SMART model. *Journal of Business Research*, *68*(7), 1414–1419. doi:10.1016/j.jbusres.2015.01.024

Marceau, J. (2008). Introduction: Innovation in the city and innovative cities. Innovation. *Management Policy & Practice.*, *10*(2-3), 136–145. doi:10.5172/impp.453.10.2-3.136

Mendes, J. L. R. S. (2014). Smart cities: revitalização urbana no centro histórico de Braga. Disponível em: http://hdl.handle.net/11067/1559

Oliveira, F. M., Pestana, E., Vasconcelos, F., Brito, R., Freitas, S., & Mendonça, V. (2014). *Plano de Ação para a Energia Sustentável do Município do Porto Santo.* Município do Porto Santo.

Pardo, T., & Nam, T. Smart city as urban innovation: Focusing on management, policy, and context. In: *Proceedings of the 5th International Conference on Theory and Practice of Electronic Governance.* ACM, 2011

Picolo, A. P., Bühler, A. J., & Rampinelli, G. A. (2014). Uma abordagem sobre a energia eólica como alternativa de ensino de tópicos de física clássica. *Revista Brasileira de Ensino de Física*, *36*(4), 4306. doi:10.1590/S1806-11172014000400007

Pincha, J. P. (2019). O Porto Santo começa a dizer adeus ao petróleo. Disponível em: https://www.publico.pt/2019/05/27/local/noticia/porto-santo-quer-dizer-adeus-petroleo-1874091

Pinto, M. C. C. (2017). Smart Cities: Cidades Inteligentes em Portugal e o contributo dos SIG para o seu desenvolvimento. Dissertação para obtenção do grau de Mestre em Sistemas de Informação Geográfica e Ordenamento do Território pela Universidade do Porto, Porto.

Público.es (2018). La isla de El Hierro se abastece de energia 100% renovable durante 18 días seguidos. Disponível em: https://www.publico.es/sociedad/renovables-isla-hierro-abastece-energia-100-renovable-18-dias-seguidos.html

Raisanen, O. (2019). Canary islands. Disponível em: https://www.bugbog.com/european_cities/spain_travel_guide/canary-islands/

Red Eléctrica de Espanã. (2019). Demanda de energía eléctrica em tiempo real. Red Eléctrica de España. Disponível em: https://demanda.ree.es/visiona/canarias/el_hierro/total

Rodríguez-Bolívar, M. P. (2015). Transforming City Governments for Successful Smart Cities. Disponível em: http://link.springer.com/book/10.1007/978-3-319-03167-5

Silva, J. A., Barroso, R. C., Rodrigues, A. J., Costa, S., & Fontana, R. L. (2014). *A urbanização no mundo contemporâneo e os problemas ambientais*. Cadernos de Graduação – Ciências Humanas e Sociais. 2(2), 197-207. Disponível em https://periodicos.set.edu.br/index.php/cadernohumanas/article/view/1723/964

United Nations Industrial Development Organization – UNIDO. (2015). Programa de Capacitação em Energias Renováveis: Energia e Mudanças Climáticas – Módulo Teórico. Observatório de Energias Renováveis para a América Latina e o Caribe.

Wikipedia. (2019a). Madeira archipelago. Disponível em: https://commons.wikimedia.org/wiki/File:Madeira_archipelago.png

World Urbanization Prospects, U. N. (2012). Disponível em: https://esa.un.org/unpd/wpp/publications/Files/WPP2012_HIGHLIGHTS.pdf

World Urbanization Prospects, U. N. (2014). Disponível em: https://population.un.org/wup/Publications/Files/WUP2014-Highlights.pdf

World Urbanization Prospects, U. N. (2018). Disponível em: https://population.un.org/wup/Publications/Files/WUP2018-Highlights.pdf

KEY TERMS AND DEFINITIONS

Canárias: The Canary Islands are an archipelago belonging to Spain, located in the Atlantic Ocean, near Morocco.

El Hierro Island: The island of El Hierro is the island with the smallest territorial dimension that makes up the Canary archipelago.

Energy: The energy is the source of power for the operation of a mechanism, in this work, the term is related to electricity and its various forms of production.

Indicators: The indicators refer to the processing data of some activity, so that it allows to verify the performance, efficiency and problems of operation.

Insular Territories: Independent territory that is composed of an island or an archipelago.

Madeira: Madeira is a Portuguese archipelago located in the Atlantic Ocean, close to Morocco. The term is commonly used to reference the island of Madeira, the main and largest island of Madeira archipelago.

Porto Santo Island: The island of Porto Santo is one of the islands that compose the archipelago of Madeira.

Portugal: Portugal, or Portuguese Republic, is a sovereign country located in the Iberian Peninsula in southwestern Europe.

Regional Development: Regional development is about providing assistance or assistance to regions with less economic development.

Spain: Spain, or Kingdom of Spain, is a sovereign country located in the Iberian Peninsula in southwestern Europe.

Sustainability: The concept of sustainability can be understood as the development of a particular region, taking into account social, economic and environmental aspects.

Territorial Planning: It is a public policy instrument that enables regional development in a sustainable way.

Chapter 13
The Mercosur Waterway as a Cooperation Strategy Between Brazil and Uruguay

Antonio Paulo Cargnin
https://orcid.org/0000-0002-1212-0793
State Government of Rio Grande do Sul, Federal University of Rio Grande do Sul, Brazil

Bruno de Oliveira Lemos
State Government of Rio Grande do Sul, Brazil

Aldomar Arnaldo Rückert
Federal University of Rio Grande do Sul, Brazil

Joanna Kurowska Pysz
WSB University of Dąbrowa Górnicza, Poland

ABSTRACT

This chapter analyzes the territorial policies for the implementation of the Mercosur Waterway. The study contributes to the existing gap regarding the repercussions of the territorial policy of the Mercosur Waterway. The context is set around the Brazil/Uruguay border within its relations to South America and Mercosur. Authors analyze the cooperation in the scope of Mercosur with its developments and obstacles. The Border Strip between Brazil and Uruguay is analyzed, and the Mercosur Waterway as a Brazil-Uruguay integration strategy is commented. Commercial relations between southern Brazil and Uruguay are closely connected to their productive basis dependent on production, commodities, and imports, where cargos are not regular. The strategic meaning of the Waterway still needs to be reinforced in an integration context since efforts have not yet been sufficient so that it could be prioritized in the strategic agenda of the countries.

DOI: 10.4018/978-1-7998-2513-5.ch013

INTRODUCTION

Proximity between Brazil and Uruguay has gained strength in the end of the 1980's, as their political systems were redemocratized and both countries started to prioritize their relations with the South Cone and South America. In this context, the creation of the Southern Common Market (Mercosur) had an important role, contributing to define the South Cone as a region of commercial flow and relative political integration among the countries, different from the Andean region, which is marked by militarization and disputes.

The border between Brazil and Uruguay stretches along 1.068,4 kilometers, of which 749 km are rivers, channels and lakes, and 320 km are land (PUCCI, 2010, p.27). In the last few decades, although not continuously, the region has been object of public policies and governmental programs from both sides of the border as for instance, the Program for the Promotion and Development of the Border Strip (PDFF), in effect in Brazil from 2008 to 2011, and the Border Integration Policies Program, created by the Uruguayan government from 2006.

Presently, territorial policies have receded due to the political and economic context, and the current measures have been especially aimed at the infrastructure area. These measures are structured by the Initiative for the Integration of South-America (IIRSA), managed by South-American Council for Infra-structure and Planning (Cosiplan), political and strategic organization which is part of IIRSA, created in August 2009.

The Mercosur Waterway structuring project is a constituent part of the IIRSA-Cosiplan portfolio. It corresponds to project 27, which is classified as Multimodal Transportation in the System Merin and Patos Lagoon (*Transporte Multimodal en Sistema Laguna Mérin y Laguna dos Patos),* originating from the Agreement between the Federative Republic of Brazil and the Oriental Republic of Uruguay about River and Lake Transportation in the Waterway Uruguay-Brazil *(Acuerdo entre la República Federativa de Brasil y la República Oriental del Uruguay sobre Transporte Fluvial y Lacustre en la Hidrovía Uruguay-Brasil),* signed on 30th July 2010 in Santana do Livramento, Rio Grande do Sul, Brazil. It consists of the reactivation of river and lake transportation of cargo as well as passengers through the Waterway formed by Merin Lake, Patos Lagoon and their tributaries. The project consists of works of dredging, signaling, combined studies, construction of ports in Uruguayan territory and also measures for the regulation of immigration, customs and sanity, among others (Cosiplan/IIRSA, 2018).

Although most of the Merin Lake is located in Brazilian territory, it is set on the border between the two countries, and the Waterway can benefit the flow of local production, stimulating the integration between Brazil and Uruguay. To present the analysis of cooperation in the cross-border region between Brazil and Uruguay, the regional context and a brief history of the process of rapprochement of cooperation between the two countries in Mercosur are necessary as well as a short explanation of the Brazilian Border Strip where part of the Waterway is situated.

This article carries out an analysis of the territorial policies for the implementation of the Mercosur Waterway in the scope of the cooperation process between Brazil and Uruguay in the last decades. The Waterway gained strategic meaning since the redemocratization of both countries in the last decades. The hypothesis is that the region has no trade flows to justify the priority of the project. Initially, the context is set around the border between Brazil and Uruguay within its relations to South America and Mercosur. Next, the cooperation in the scope of Mercosur with its developments and obstacles is analyzed. Cooperation between Brazil and Uruguay has been increasing in the form of bilateral initiatives. Following, the Brazilian Border Strip between Brazil and Uruguay is analyzed and, finally, the Mercosur Waterway as a Brazil-Uruguay integration strategy is commented and evaluated. The study seeks to contribute to the existing gap of scientific articles regarding repercussions of the territorial policy of the Mercosur Waterway.

COOPERATION MODEL BETWEEN BRAZIL AND URUGUAY IN THE CONTEXT OF SOUTH AMERICA

Even though Brazil and Uruguay have historical relations that surpass their borders, proximity between them is relatively new and is set in the context of the redemocratization of political systems in the region between the years of 1980 and 1990. This process happened during a period when borders were opening, which characterized a phenomenon known as globalization; at the same time, liberalism started to rule the relation between the countries. Brazilian-Uruguayan relation is inserted in this perspective and develops especially from Mercosur negotiations, which started officially on 26th March 1991, when the Assuncion Treaty was signed by the governments of Argentina, Brazil, Paraguay and Uruguay, as shown on Figure 1.

In general, Brazilian membership to the cooperation model in Plata Basin from 1980's is set with certain advantage over its neighbors. Caetano (2011, p. 162), analyzing the occupation of this territory, states that there was geopolitical intelligence both in the occupation of the sources of the great rivers and in the development of persistent undertakings of foreign policy tending to obtain beneficial associations with neighbors. This strategy launched the basis for the Brazilian leadership in South America.

After a period of liberal thought prevalence characteristic of the 1990's, there was a reevaluation of Brazilian diplomacy during the 2000's, when the country adopted a more pragmatic posture in its foreign policy, strongly influenced by the United

States measures against terrorism (ROSEIRA, 2011, p. 144). This disposition was more evident along the northern border of the country, where the fight against drug trafficking through the Colombian Plan generated friction among Colombia and its neighbors Ecuador and Venezuela. This context resulted in less influence from the United States in the Southern Cone, and this was one of the elements which allowed a greater cooperative development among the countries in the region (PAGLIARI, 2009, p. 234).

In the period from 2003 to 2010, there was a pursuit for the expansion of the relations among Brazil and its South American neighbors, with the aim of establishing alliances among emergent countries with identical objectives, such as Argentina, and promoting the region to a more proactive stance in the international system[1].

Between 2010 and 2016, the cooperation among Brazil and other South American countries is directed to set up a South American unity. The cooperation aimed at the strengthening of the Brazilian position in the global context, which reflects the co-existence of idealism and realism in the Brazilian foreign policy. The first, since cooperation with other countries in the region is a priority for Brazilian foreign policy; the latter, as it can be noticed that this cooperation aims at a regional leadership on the part of Brazil for its global insertion (CERVO, 2006, p.28).

This Brazilian pursuit for the consolidation of the South American identity happens especially through the prioritization of Mercosur. This strategy allows the country to act as a promoter of South American integration, thus increasing its influence in the region. It is in this sense that the proximity of Brazil and the countries in the Southern Cone is much more consistent when compared to the Brazilian Andean neighbors. In summary, apart from specific aspects, it may be claimed that Brazil has an important role in the Southern Cone and Andean Region, differing in the sense that, while in the first tensions receded and there was an increase in integration and mutual confidence[2], resulting in greater proximity and reduction in conflicts, in the second there is still a rivalry pattern signaled by processes of safety and militarization[3] (PAGLIARI, 2009; TOKATLIAN, 2008).

Thus, the relations between Brazil and its neighbors from the South Cone since the 1980's has integration characteristics, marked by an end in tensions and by the decrease in weapon purchasing by the countries, reaching its highest point with the formation of Mercosur, which, although in a crisis, has contributed to the creation of a peace and cooperation zone between its affiliated countries. These internal differences between the Andean Arch countries and the South Cone have an influence in the expansion of the integration, with a higher stability in the latter, benefiting its process.

To Pagliari (2009, p.122), in the case of the Andean countries, instabilities are worsened by social problems, drug trafficking related crime and insurgencies, impairing integration measures. Tokatlian (2008, p.65) also points out the differences

Figure 1. Map of South American Trade Block – funding countries.
Source: Https://www.mercosur.int/pt-br. Elaboration: authors

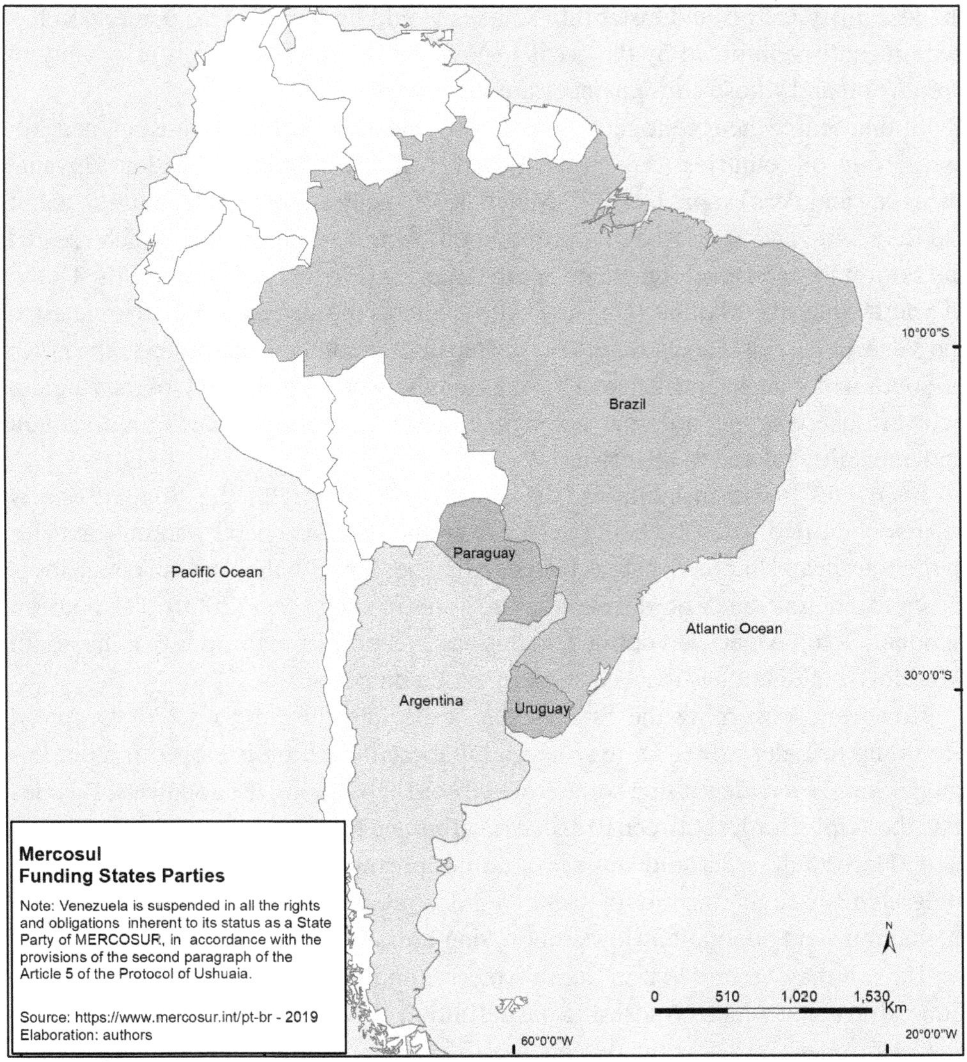

between the Andean Region and the South Cone in its relations with the United States. While the first notices the displacement of the North-American influence area, that presents itself in a more concrete way in the Caribbean and Central America, the second lives a less visible prominence of the Washington power. This scenery in the South Cone allowed more solid multilateral measures, which were affected in the Andean region by a strong presence of the United States.

Therefore, there is a perception, among those who devise the Brazilian foreign policy, that the threats to the country are concentrated in the northern border[4], where the insecurity factors and instability sources would be found[5]. This perception has been recently reinforced by the crisis in Venezuela, which has been increasing in proportion and whose consequences are yet unpredictable.

In this sense, the recent geopolitical crisis meant a decline in this perspective, as a group of countries (Argentina, Brazil, Chile, Colombia, Ecuador, Guyana, Paraguay and Peru) signed, on 22nd March 2019, the Presidential Declaration about the Renewing and Strengthening of the South America Integration, which created the Forum for the Development of South America (Prosul), substituting the Union of South American Nations (Unasur). Although this movement is directly related to the Venezuelan crisis and strengthens the tensions among the countries to the north of South America, its influence in the relations between Brazil and Uruguay cannot be overlooked, as the latter has not signed the Declaration for having a divergent understanding related to the crisis.

Even with these instabilities, the Brazilian border with the South Cone is relatively unified – despite being yet far from the stage reached by some countries in the European Union – whereas the Brazilian border with the Andean countries is closer to a definition of border-separation, as defined by Lafer (2000). The Andean region in South America is defined, in this way, very far from the idea that the South American continent has reached stability based on peace.

However, concerning the South Cone, especially in the border of Uruguay, according to Lafer (2000), it may be said that the definition is closer to a border-cooperation, even identifying some isolated conflicts among the countries. Besides that, the Triple Border between Brazil, Argentina and Paraguay is a constant attention zone. Nevertheless, these divergences do not prevent the building of a relatively integrated space in the South Cone region, presenting important commercial interactions and population flows, improving cross-border cooperation.

Thus, it may be said that in South America and more specifically in the South Cone, the region which is closest to the definition of border-cooperation, dealt with by Celso Lafer (2000), is the one between Brazil and Uruguay. In this region, the good relations between the two countries and the movement across borders on a daily basis contribute to state actions which go beyond its borders.

COOPERATION IN THE SCOPE OF THE SOUTHERN COMMON MARKET (MERCOSUR): DEVELOPMENTS AND OBSTACLES

Mercosur has been fostered by the proximity between Brazil and Argentina during the 1980's, when both countries returned to democracy. It has been characterized by developments and declines resulting from its affiliated countries' policies, as well as from different political-economic contexts in the world. Nowadays, the following countries are affiliated to Mercosur: Argentina, Brazil, Uruguay and Paraguay. Venezuela joined Mercosur on 12th August 2012, and its process should have been concluded in 2016; however, it was suspended from the condition of member state for failing to comply with terms in the Membership Treaty. The associated states (under membership process) are Bolivia, Chile, Colombia, Ecuador, Guyana, Peru and Surinam.

The first multilateral initiative to organize this cooperation had already been taken in Latin America in the second half of the XX century. One of the first was the creation of the Latin American Free Trade Association (LAFTA) in 1960, characterized by a developing drive and by the policy of substituting imports for industrialization. It was supported by the Economic Commission for Latin America (ECLA) and the United Nations (UN), and it shaped a free trade zone with high taxes for imports. Another initiative was the Latin American Integration Association (ALADI-LAIA) in 1980, which resulted from the failures of LAFTA, adjusting deadlines and processes for the settlement of the free-trade zone put forward by the previous block (GINESTA, 1999, p. 54). The adjustments proposed by ALADI allowed governments in Brazil and Argentina to promote the bilateral integration process, which presented itself as a more immediate anticipation of the establishment of Mercosur (PEÑA, 2007, p.24).

Another significant fact, according to Onuki (2006, p.302), happened during the military regime, when the Three Party Agreement for Technical-Operational Cooperation was signed (along with Paraguay), which allowed the shared use of the Itaipu power plant (between Brazil and Paraguay) and Corpus (between Paraguay and Argentina), as well as the regulation of sailing conditions on Paraná River in 1979.

Considering the context of redemocratization, we may highlight the co-signing of the presidents of Brazil and Argentina of the Economic Cooperation and Integration Programme (PICE) in 1986, still in the model of substitutions of imports and protectionism, promoting bilateral relations and increasing cross regional trade. However, the signing of the Integration, Cooperation and Development Treaty by the governments of Brazil and Argentina, on 29th November 1988, was decisive to trigger the creation of the common market. The aim of this treaty was to shape a common market in the maximum period of 10 years, eliminating tax-related and non-tax-related obstacles.

It is also important to highlight the signing of the Buenos Aires Minutes, in July 1990. The Minutes represented the shift from the interventionism and industrialism pattern of the integration to one of a more commercialist and liberal characteristic, predicting reduction and even elimination of tariff barriers as well as the creation of common taxes (ALMEIDA, 2011, p.4).

Nevertheless, it was just from the signing of the Assunción Treaty, on 26th March 1991, having as affiliated countries Brazil, Argentina, Paraguay and Uruguay, that the creation of the Southern Common Market (Mercosur) came into effect. Among the main motivations were the growth of commercial exchange and the commonality of interests around the implementation of economic liberalization policies in several countries in Latin America (ONUKI, 2006, p.305). The central objective of Mercosur, passed by the congresses of each country, was establishing a common market through the development of a customs union (PEÑA, 2007, p.17).

However, Mercosur cannot be actually considered a common market, but an imperfect customs union, due to obstacles to enforce a common external tariff, with the adoption of individual measures from each affiliated country. The existence of a common external tariff implies a customs union with standardization of procedures. For such, it is necessary to create a common customs code, which provides definitions, procedures and standard penalties in all affiliated countries (GINESTA 1999, p.40).

It is important to say that, during the shaping of Mercosur, Latin American countries were going through a shift from a substitution of imports model to an economic opening. These liberalization policies were successful during the initial phase of the block, with greater increase in the commerce among the countries, which was hindered as from the world economic crisis in 1998, and in Brazil in 1999. This emphasis in the commercial aspect was partially reverted during the 2000's. Nevertheless, the regionalism that followed the receding of liberal propaganda wave in the 1990's could not accommodate one of the main problems in the block either, which consists of not being able to provide a common project of development.

After the initial boost, Mercosur integration process went through different phases, but it has always received criticism for its lack of efficiency and achievement of initially set objectives. Despite supposedly different points of view, most scholars recognize the obstacles in establishing a common market in a region with countries of great social and economic diversity, significant differences in legal system, lack of strong financing instruments and mainly the adoption of unilateral decisions such as economic plans and regulations and border policies. (GINESTA, 1999; ONUKI, 2006; ALMEIDA, 2011; SICA, 2007; TOKATLIAN, 2008; JIMENEZ, 2009; CERVO e BUENO, 2010; VEIGA e RIOS, 2011).

In its initial phase, which was characterized by the democratization of the affiliated countries and by economic liberation spread in South America during the 1990's, there was an increase in commercial exchange and mainly facilitation for global companies to act in an opening market. However, even with greater liberalism, the cooperation agenda, and especially the commercial flow, were hindered by unilateral decisions.

From the 2000's, with the establishment of the new regionalism in South America and with the receding of the liberal wave, there was a greater pragmatism in the foreign policy in Brazil, most important country in the block, which prioritizes the relations with the countries in South America and Mercosur in order to confront the countries in the north hemisphere. There was a decrease in the importance of the commercial sense of the integration and an increase in the geopolitical aspects. Even so, essential commercial agreements for the evolution of the agenda were left behind. Besides that, there were few developments in the period concerning political-institutional issues, as it happened with the liberal regionalism in the 1990's. Thus, it may be claimed that the Brazilian inflection during the 1990's did not have satisfactory results, culminating in a bilateralism of Brazil towards its neighbors (LEMOS, 2013, p. 97).

Peña (2007) draws an optimistic picture of the integration process in the 2000's, claiming that the Montevideo summit sets a new phase in Mercosur, directed to decisions that seek consolidation of the customs union, among which the creation of the Mercosur Structural Convergence Fund (FOCEM); the improvement of the institutional structure, still defined by inter-governmentalism, of the integration process by the creation of the Mercosur Parliament; and the decision to incorporate new affiliated countries, proposing full membership of Venezuela to the block. The Agreement for the Residence of Nationals of the Mercosur Affiliated Countries and of Bolivia and Chile (associated states) allowed the legalization of residence of immigrants from the states that are part of Mercosur in other countries of the block, approved by Mercosur in 2002 and valid in Brazil from 2009, also demonstrates a greater emphasis of policies for social issues in the block (Peña, 2007, p.33-34).

However, there are deficits in the integration process in issues such as the lack of supra-nationality and noncompliance to the block norms, also the lack of macroeconomic articulation in the affiliated states remain worsened by protective measures from the Argentinean governments that affect exportation of Brazilian products, as well as by constant attempts to sign a free-commerce treaty between Uruguay and United States, which goes against the block policy of negotiating joint commercial deals (ALMEIDA, (2011-2012, p.103). These issues have become recurrent recently, when even Brazil has carried out parallel bilateral deals.

The strategy based on bilateral actions has become frequent, especially in the relations of the United States with other countries, also affecting South America (LOPES and CARVALHO, 2010). This strategy has been widespread among members of Mercosur, as in Brazil's performance in the free trade agreement signed between Brazil and Chile on 21st November 2018.

Another relevant aspect which impacts Mercosur greatly is the present situation in Venezuela. It joined the block in 2012, and it should have become a full functioning member in 2016. However, the country has been through an economic, social and political crisis, which resulted in its suspension from the block in December 2016 for noncompliance to the Protocol of accession, and it also suffered penalties in 2017 for breaking the block's democratic clause.

Thus, regarding the relation between Brazil and Uruguay, Mercosur has contributed to the proximity process, as it intensified the circulation of people and goods between Brazil and Uruguay and supported pacification in the region. However, its measures are restricted to projects financed by the Mercosur Structural Convergence Fund (FOCEM) and specific actions of bilateral cooperation.

FOCEM was signed in 2004 by the states that are part of Mercosur and deals with the financing of structural convergence programs for competitiveness development, social cohesion and strengthening of the institutional structure and the integration process. The programs supporting social cohesion should contribute to social development, especially in the border zone, and might include projects concerning human health, poverty and unemployment reduction.

Inspired by the European Regional Development Fund (ERDF), FOCEM, however, is not part of a supranational regional development program in the scope of Mercosur. This fund aims at decreasing inequalities among the countries affiliated to the block, which should take initiative to suggest projects to be financed by the fund. In other words, FOCEM does not deal first and foremost in regional scope, but in the internal and national scope of Mercosur. This situation may be explained by an intra-governmental characteristic of the Mercosur integration process, where an expansion in the direction of a supranational scope does not happen as in the European Union.

From an infra-structure standpoint, the Initiative for the Integration of Regional Infrastructure in South-America (IIRSA) was one of the institutions which supported the cooperation actions the most. This is the case of the Mercosur Waterway, which is in the IIRSA project portfolio[6].

It should be pointed out that, since the beginning, the works linked to IIRSA have been financed by different development banks, having received support from the Inter-American Development Bank (IDB), Andean Development Corporation (CAF), Financial Fund for the Development of the River Plate Basin (FONPLATA) and from the National Economic and Social Development Bank (BNDES).

BORDER STRIP: LEGISLATION, CHARACTERISTICS AND COMMERCIAL RELATIONS BETWEEN BRAZIL AND URUGUAY

The Brazilian Border Strip is extended along more than 15,000 kilometers of land border, covering more than 27% of the national territory in 11 states and 588 municipalities in the federation, as shown in Figure 2. In Rio Grande do Sul state, it comprises 61% of the territory (182 municipalities). Currently, the Brazilian

Border Strip is regulated by federal law number 6.634, from 2nd May 1979, which establishes as essential to national security an internal strip of 150 kilometers. It is called Border Strip, emphasizing activities of national interest that claim the attention of the national State.

By this law, it is forbidden, unless with prior authorization from the National Security Council, to carry out actions such as the disposal and concession of public lands; to build bridges, international roads or landing field; to establish industries of interest to national security; to install companies dedicated to the exploitation and use of mineral resources and to the colonization or rural allotments; and participation of a foreign person as legal entity which holds real rights in rural land. Established companies engaged in activities linked to national security must have at least 51% of its capital belonging to Brazilian citizens, at least two-thirds of Brazilian workers and have in its administration mostly Brazilians. This law was regulated by federal decree number 85.064, from 26th August 1980.

Law number 6.634-79 does not prohibit investments in the border region, but it imposes the condition of state approval. The only restrictions to investments in the law refer to the establishment of foreign companies linked to areas related to national security.

Article 20, § 2 of the Brazilian Constitution states that "the strip of up to 150 kilometers in width, along the land borders, designated as Border Strip, is considered essential to the defense of the national territory, and its occupation and use will be regulated by law" (BRAZIL, 2019). The constitution, written in 1988, predicts a greater concern with the border defense, not predicting the possibility of border integration, although it claims that economic, political, social and cultural integration with other countries in Latin America is fundamental. On the other hand, the law regulation of these 150 kilometers enables specific development policies to the Brazilian Border Strip.

From the point of view of the national State, it can be observed that the greater concern with issues related to the defense of the territory, being treated as "national security zone", is a factor which hindered the elaboration of territorial policies for the regions far from the country's political-economic center.

Historically, the Brazilian Federal Government State acts in the Border Strip mainly through plans, programs and federal actions to help municipalities located in these areas. Among these we can point out the Program for Financial Aid to the Municipalities in the Border Strip, in effect until 1995, and the Program for the Support of Development in the Border Strip (PDFF), effective until 2011.

PDFF, as a part of the strategy of the Regional Development National Policy (PNDR), discussed in Brazil from the 2000's and implemented by the federal decree number 6.047, from 22nd February 2007, was concentrated on the Border Strip region. The integration of the border area was treated as a guideline of the National

Figure 2. Map of Brazilian municipalities in the Brazilian Border Strip.
Source: MI/Brazil. Elaboration: authors

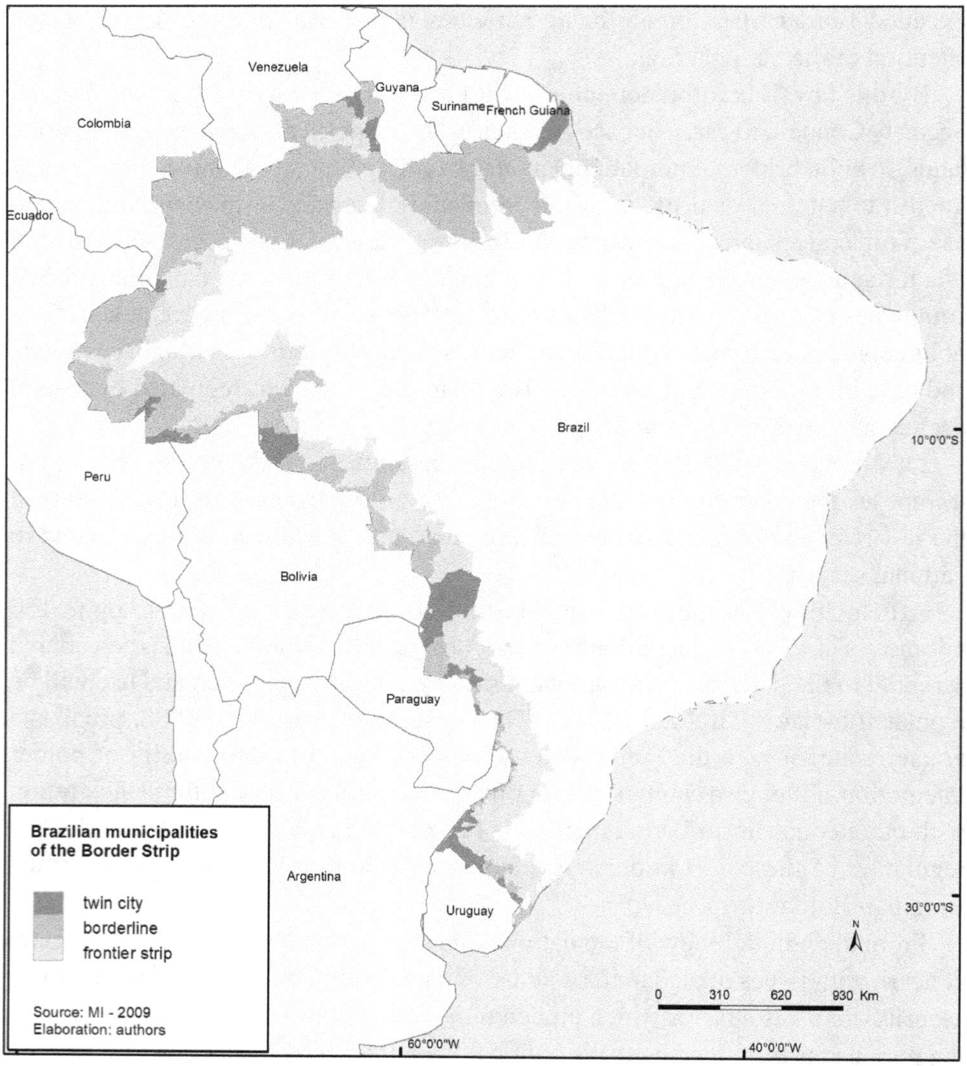

Policy for Regional Development, with the aim of incorporating these portions of the territory to the national economic dynamics and also to the neighboring regions. In the national Multi-annual Plan (PPA) from 2012-2015, the programs supporting PNDR were extinct, and the inexistence of a Regional Development Fund was nearly the end of a regional policy in the country, once the initiatives were limited to the preparation of documents or to discussion forums.

The theme was back in the agenda with the federal decree number 9.810, from 30th May 2019, which again established the National Policy for Regional Development. In the scope selected for federal operation remains the region understood as Border Strip. However, the decree does not go further to define instruments for the financing of public policies towards the region.

Even with these plans and programs, it can be observed that the zone understood as Border Strip is underdeveloped economically, marked by obstacles in accessibility to services and public goods. Among the factors leading to this situation is the dynamics in the Brazilian colonization, which was concentrated in the coast and the almost sole concern with the security in these areas.

In 2010, the Permanent Commission for the Development and Integration of the Border Strip – CDIF – was created. The task of this commission was to coordinate regional centers of integration of the Border Strip for the preparation of Plans for Development and Integration of the Border (PDIFs) in Brazilian states, for the further creation of the Border Plan Brazil. In Rio Grande do Sul, the southernmost Brazilian state bordering with two countries, the Regional Center for the Integration of the Border Strip in Rio Grande do Sul (Center – RS) was created in July 2011. However, activities in these commissions are fragile and have limited articulation with government planning.

Uruguay does not have a border strip regulated by law. While in Brazil there are recurrent discussions about the relaxation of the Border Strip, suggesting the decrease to 50 kilometers, in Uruguay its creation is on its way, and the proposal from the Livestock Farming, Agriculture and Fishing Ministry of Uruguay (MGAP) is a strip of up to 50 kilometers wide, aiming at the sovereignty and sanity security, opposing "speculative foreign exploitation" of the land (PUCCI, 2010, p.38).

Although it does not have a Border Strip regulated by law, Uruguay already has had a program dedicated to its border region created in 2006, and coordinated by the Direction of Territorial Coordination of the Ministry of Social Development (MIDES), which organized several bi-national seminars called *Politicas de Integración de Frontera: Espacio de Vida Diverso e Complejo (*Border Integration Policies: Complex and Diverse Living Space*)* until 2009 in the Uruguayan border cities. This program was inserted in a context of strengthening of local capacities, of social participation and the administrative decentralization supported by the Uruguayan government of Tabaré Vásquez (2005-2010) (LEMOS, 2013, p.115).

The border region between Brazil and Uruguay is characterized by an extensive territory, having little economic activity and low demographic density. The existence of six twin cities is highlighted: Chuí-*Chuy*; Jaguarão-*Rio Branco*; Aceguá-*Aceguá*; Santana do Livramento-*Rivera*; Quaraí-*Artigas*; and Barra do Quaraí-*Bella Unión*, as shown in Figure 5. These centers have some importance in shopping tourism due to the existence of duty free shops.

Figure 3. Origin of imports and destination of exports in Uruguay in 2018. Source: Central Bank of Uruguay. Elaboration: authors

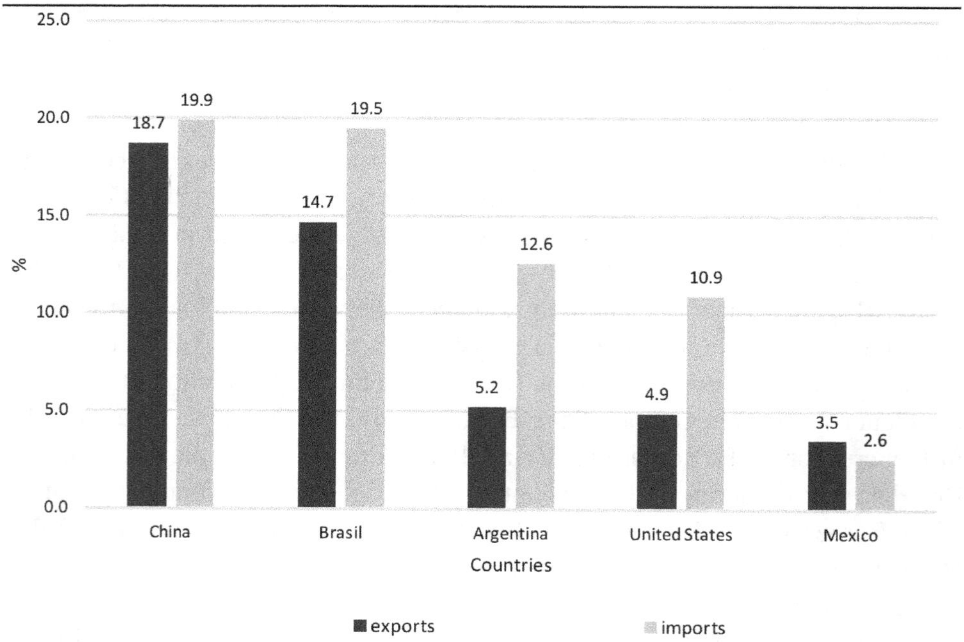

The economic activities developed in both sides of the border are similar, especially extensive livestock farming and rice fields. Also important are the forest exploitation, fruit farming, olive growing and milk production.

On the point of view of commercial relations, the main destination of Uruguayan exports is China, with 18.7%; followed by Brazil, with 14.4%, as shown in Figure 3. The same countries are also the main origin of imports, with 19.9% and 19.5% respectively. China has been gaining increasing importance for the Mercosur countries, competing with United States.

The main Uruguayan exports in 2018 are livestock and products of animal origin (34.4%), especially meats and derivate, which are 21.7% of the total. Among the products of vegetal origin, the most important are grains (12%), wood and derivate (12.1%). In imports, petroleum and derivate (10.9%), machines and equipment (9.8%), food and beverages (8.9%) and cars and transport material (5.3%) are highlighted.

Uruguay exports primary products of smaller added value to Brazil, due to the economic structure of this southeastern country in South America. This structure is the result of a focus on the farming sector since the redemocratization in 1985, following an interpretation that the world market for farming products would be opening (FREGA et al, 2008, p.236). This condition was strengthened by the

Figure 4. Origin of imports and destination of exports in Brazil in 2018. Note: Main origins and destination and Uruguay. Source: MDIC. Elaboration: authors

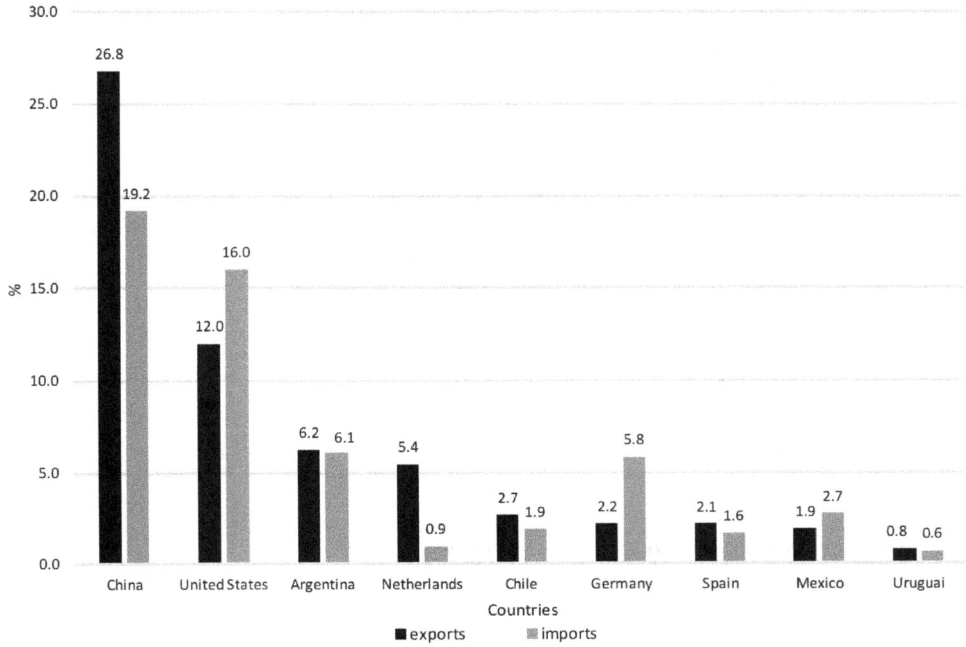

setting of Mercosur, since Brazil gained importance in its industrial products with the block, while Uruguay had a more significant importance in its farming sector (SICA, 2007, p.64).

Although Brazil has a more diversified industrial structure, in the same way the base of its exports are the *commodities*. About 50% of its exports are based on minerals and vegetal origin products (especially grains). Concerning imports, machines and appliances, electrical material and chemical products prevail, representing 43% of the total. As shown in Figure 4, the main partners are China – with 26% of exports and 19.2% of imports; United States – with 12% and 16%; and Argentina with 6.2% and 6.1%, respectively.

A relevant aspect is the evolution of commercial balance between Brazil and Uruguay. As soon as the customs union of Mercosur came into effect in 1995, Uruguay had a positive commercial balance in relation to Brazil. The recent increase of the commercial balance favoring Brazil is mainly due to the higher added value of manufactured goods exported from Brazil to Uruguay, which had a substantial increase during the first decade of 2000.

Uruguayan economy lost importance for the foreign commerce in Brazil from the year 1999, when Brazilian currency devaluated after the increase of intrazone commerce in the beginning of the Mercosur customs union. The Uruguayan economic crisis from 1999 to 2002 strengthened its decrease in participation. The increasing degree of interrelations among the economies in Mercosur, which triggered the increase in GDP of affiliated countries and the range of intrazone commerce, was asymmetric, increasing the incidence of the biggest countries in the block – Brazil and Argentina – over the smallest – Uruguay and Paraguay. It may be said that the Uruguayan economy has a considerable dependence in relation to Brazil, and the opposite is not true. It is based on this dependence that relations between the two countries are expanded, while Brazil seeks to exercise leadership in South America.

This expansion in bilateral relations between the two countries led to the creation of the Bilateral Commission of Strategic Planning and Production Integration (CBPE) in March 2010, by the presidents of Brazil and Uruguay. The commission sought industrial and productive complementation, with integration and cooperation in the energy area and greater integration of physical structure, especially concerning investments in ports, bridges and railways (SIMÕES, 2011, p.112).

MERCOSUR WATERWAY AS BRAZIL-URUGUAY INTEGRATION STRATEGY

Navigation in the Waterway complex in south Brazil, as well as in Plata Basin, is not a recent practice; it has been important since the Spanish and Portuguese colonization process. However, after the redemocratization of the South Cone countries, emphasized from the 1980's, and with the opening of the world economy, phenomenon known as globalization, the process gained its present status.

A first aspect to be observed is the difference in cargo and draught in ports. Concerning cargo, grains transportation is among the greatest volumes in both countries, while other kinds of cargo vary according to specificities in import and export quotas in the countries, highlighting petroleum and derivate and automotive vehicles. Concerning draught, Rio Grande port reaches 14 meters, depending on dredging conditions, which enables mooring of larger scale ships. In the same way, the Montevideo port has a draught reaching 14 meters, with the advantage of having low dredging density due to natural conditions. Buenos Aires port is also 10 meters deep, but its location makes it permanently dependent on dredging.

Considering individual strategies of competitiveness and different characteristics, redemocratization in the countries has led to proximity aiming at cooperation and organization to face the global market. In 2000, this perspective led to the adoption of a common strategy of infrastructure valuation by a group of countries, the initiative called IIRSA signed by twelve countries: Argentina, Bolivia, Brazil, Chile, Colombia, Ecuador, Guyana, Paraguay, Peru, Surinam, Uruguay and Venezuela.

IIRSA was influenced by the concept of Open Regionalism, understood as an integrated geo-economic space, where the reduction of obstacles and infrastructure bottlenecks become the fundamental condition for the competitive integration of the countries in South America, protecting the economies from the global market (FERNANDES and FILHO, 2017).

In the first decade of 2000, IIRSA was strengthened by the endorsement of the South American Union of Nations (Unasur), created in 2008 with the aim of integrating Mercosur and the Andean Community. Since its origin, IIRSA's main directing concept is the axis of integration and development, structured by a project portfolio that, since August 2009, has been managed by South-American Council for Infra-structure and Planning (Cosiplan), institution created by South American Union of Nations (Unasur).

Through an agreed agenda since 2004, IIRSA had put together a project portfolio for the period of 2005-2010, which was renewed by Cosiplan in 2011. These projects were structured around ten Integration and Development Axes, among which is the Mercosur-Chile Axis, where the Mercosur Waterway is inserted[7]. Analyzing the Brazilian case, an aspect to be pointed out is that the project portfolio was not drawn in an Axis Integration strategy, being formed by a group of pre-existing projects, mostly long expected by infrastructure institutions.

Thus, the Mercosur Waterway structuring project is a constituent part of the IIRSA-Cosiplan portfolio. It corresponds to project 27, which is classified as Multimodal Transportation in the System Merin Lake and Patos Lagoon (*Transporte Multimodal en Sistema Laguna Mérin y Laguna dos Patos),* originating from the Agreement between the Federative Republic of Brazil and the Oriental Republic of Uruguay about River and Lake Transportation in the Waterway Uruguay-Brazil *(Acuerdo entre la República Federativa de Brasil y la República Oriental del Uruguay sobre Transporte Fluvial y Lacustre en la Hidrovía Uruguay-Brasil),* signed on 30 July 2010 in Santana do Livramento, Rio Grande do Sul, Brazil. It consists of the reactivation of the river and lake transportation of cargo as well as passengers, through the Waterway formed by Merin Lake, Patos Lagoon and their tributaries.

The project aims to develop waterway transport of cargo as well as passengers. It consists of works of dredging, signaling and marking, cartographic and bathymetric surveys in the Merin Lake and construction of ports in Uruguayan territory. Besides that, it involves measures for the control of customs related to migration and sanity of farming products. It includes the subprojects of Dredging of the River Tacuari (MCC 157); Dredging, marking and signaling of the System Merin and Patos Lakes (MCC 158); Port Terminal and Dredging of River Tacuari (MCC 160); and Dredging of Merin Lake (MCC 85).

According to the project file of the project bank IIRSA/Cosiplan[8], the bi-national project is estimated at US$ 20.8 billion. Its execution involves works based on the necessity of improving connections, presently restricted to highway modal, which may be an option for the transportation of great volume cargo, relieving the existing transport system. Moreover, it has an environment sustainability component, as it removes gas emissions from the environment, besides bringing a decrease in a great number of accidents. Originally, the project was predicted to finish in 2019, however, economic instability and recent politics, especially in Brazil, meant the delay and possibly even the interruption of the project.

According to data from the Department of Transport Infrastructure (DNIT, 2019), the Mercosur Waterway has 1.860 km of navigable ways. From 2010, after the signing of the Agreement between Brazil and Uruguay for the joint exploitation of river and lake transport of cargo and passengers in the Uruguay-Brazil Waterway, it started to be considered in a regional integration context. Since then, the efforts for the adaptation of infrastructure have begun, in aspects such as dredging, terminal constructions and adaptations, signaling and interconnections with other modes. However, the agreement that allows free access of companies that work with cargo to the markets of both countries was signed in 2010 but came into effect only in 2015.

The Mercosur Waterway is located in the southernmost part of Brazil and is formed by rivers Jacui, Taquari, Cai, Sinos, Gravatai, Camaquã and Jaguarão, which are connected to the Patos Lagoon through Guaiba Lake, reaching Rio Grande, as shown in Figure 5. From there, it stretches towards Uruguay through São Gonçalo Channel and Merin Lake, where it goes along rivers Jaguarão, Cebollati and Tacuari. Merin Lake is the main integration point, and 74% of its surface is in Brazilian territory.

In river Jacui, in the region of the valley of rivers Taquari, Cai and Pardo, there are dams and locks that allow navigation in the Waterway: Amarópolis, Dom Marco, Fandango, Bom Retiro do Sul and Rio Branco, the latter considered to be the first lock built in Latin America – from 1958 on. Besides these locks, built to regulate navigation in the rivers, there is a lock, in the municipality of Capão do Leão in São Gonçalo Channel, which prevents the salinization of Merin Lake (DNIT, 2019).

The handling of cargo through the Waterway is about 4.5 million tons a year. Fertilizers and compost, fuel, mineral oils, organic chemical products, grains, specially soy and wheat, cellulose and mineral coal are some of the main transported goods. Presently, ships which are 90 meter long, 15.5 meter of breadth and 2.5 meter draught can navigate (DNIT, 2019).

The main infrastructure of the Waterway is Rio Grande Port, which is significantly busy, it is important for the waterway system in Brazil and Mercosur, reaching nearly 43 million accumulated cargo in 2018, as shown in Figure 6. This number is affected by the export quotas moving through the port, in great part commodities in bulk.

Concerning the movement of containers, Rio Grande Port is among the twenty busiest ports, with nearly 700 thousand TEUs[9] in 2016, according to data from the port supervision. In the same year, the biggest port in Latin America in movement

Figure 5. Location of the Mercosur Waterway. Source: SEPLAG/RS. Elaboration: authors

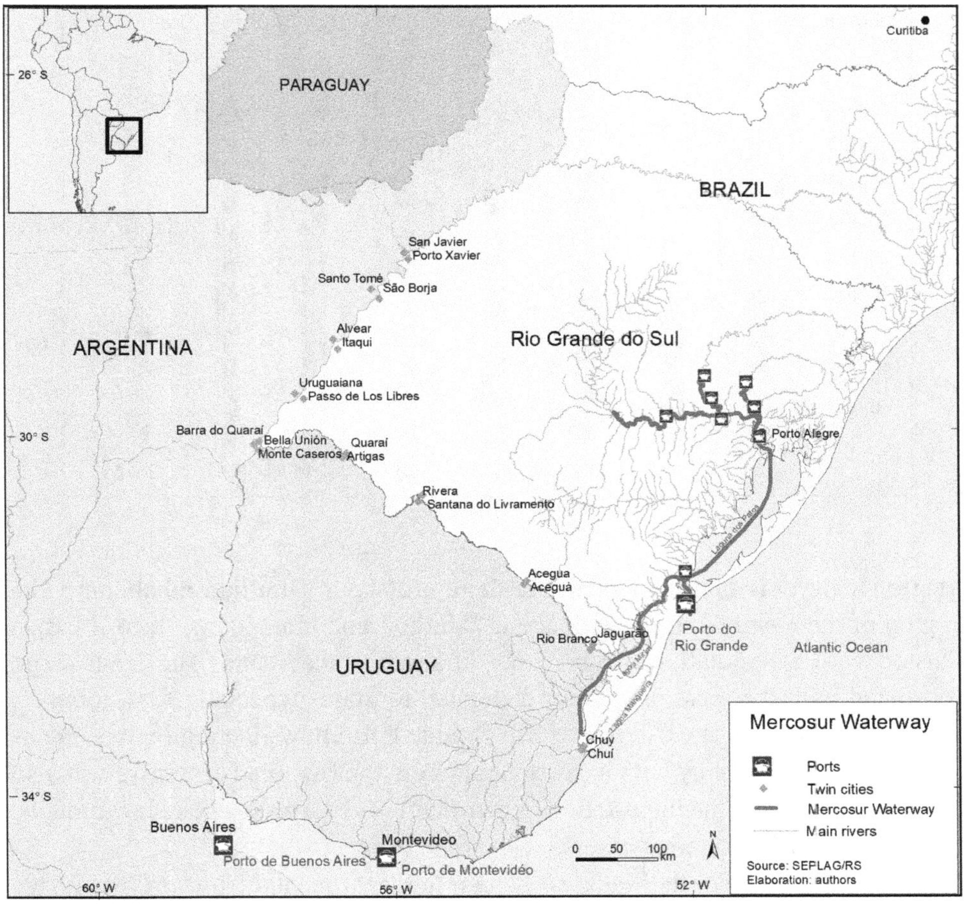

of this kind of cargo is Santos Port, with 3.6 million TEUs; Buenos Aires Port is in the ninth position with 1.4 million TEUs; and Montevideo Port is nineteenth, with 850 thousand TEUs (CEPAL, 2019).

However, the Mercosur Waterway is not fully functional throughout its length and has been treated in a context of promotion of development in the region and integration of the countries. Only after 2015 full access to companies was granted, as predicted in the agreement signed in 2010.

The Waterway has the limitation of low demographic densities and limited economic dynamics, especially on the Uruguayan side. On the Brazilian side, the border is formed by 309 municipalities in the state of Rio Grande do Sul. Even without a direct contact area, the proximity with the Metropolitan Region of Porto

Figure 6. Evolution of cargo movement in Rio Grande Port.
Source: SUPRG/RS. Elaboration: authors

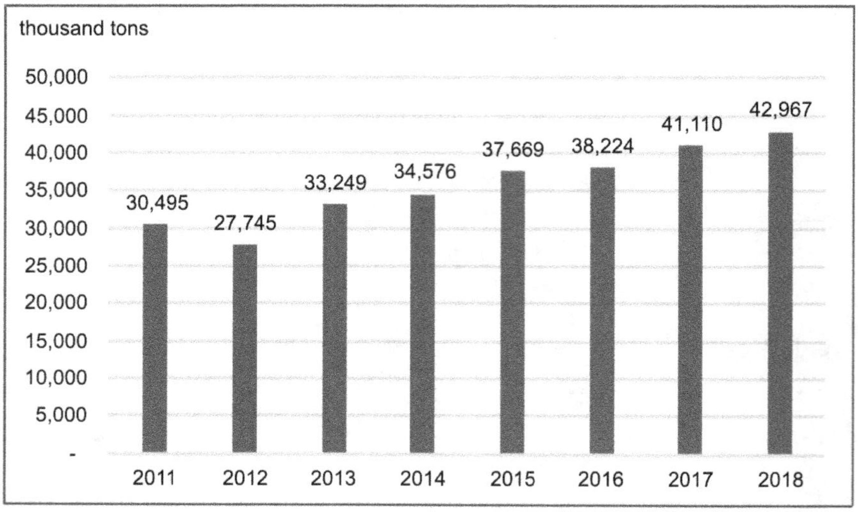

Alegre (RMPA) is highlighted, where there are about 4 million inhabitants; the Region of the *Serra Gaúcha*, with about 750 thousand inhabitants; the *Sul* Urban Cluster, with a population of about 600 thousand inhabitants. The main cargo associated with the local production is related to grains (specially soy), tobacco, meat and derivate. The existence of Rio Grande Port allows the region to serve as grain outlet, occasionally with harvest inputs from the Brazilian center west. It also serves as entrance to the importation of petroleum and derivate, chemical products, automotive vehicles, among others.

In the Uruguayan side the Waterway borders the departments of *Rocha, Cerro Largo* and *Treinta y Tres* which, as in almost all the country, have very low demographic density. Together, these three departments have a little more than 300 thousand inhabitants, according to data from the National Institute of Statistics from Uruguay (INE). On the point of view of production, the prevalence is breeding of cattle and sheep, production of milk and derivate, farming of grains and forestry. In the *Cerro Largo* department, the breeding of cattle and sheep is predominant, while in *Treinta y Tres,* livestock farming is associated with rice fields. However, one of the greatest cargo potential is in *Rivera* Department, which has one of the largest areas destined to the exploitation of forests in the region.

COOPERATION AGENDA BETWEEN BRAZIL AND URUGUAY

Formal recent cooperation relations between Brazil and Uruguay have happened in the scope of the called New Agenda for Border Cooperation and Development, carried out by the Ministry of Foreign Affairs from the year 2002[10]. The Agenda has been focused on supporting the adoption of bilateral actions with the aim of improving the life of inhabitants living in the border region between the two countries. Many of the themes in the Agenda are of a technical cooperation aspect, treated in the scope of national agencies of technical cooperation; in Brazil, the Technical Cooperation Agenda (ABC), linked to the Ministry of Foreign Affairs; and by the Uruguayan Agency of International Cooperation, in Uruguay, link to the Presidency of the Republic.

The New Agenda for Border Cooperation and Development was composed as the highest instance for cooperation and border integration between Brazil and Uruguay, originating from the demands of the Brazilian-Uruguayan border region and from the political proximity between the two Nation-States. Issues such as smuggling, workers, students and citizens illegality, as well as hospital treatment on both sides of the border are pressing in the region, demanding actions from the national and local authorities.

In 2012, in the scope of the New Agenda, the Brazil-Uruguay High Rank Group (GAN) was created with the aim of devising and following projects in strategic areas of bilateral relations, with subgroups dealing with themes such as production integration; science, technology and innovation; communications and information; transport infrastructure integration; free circulation of goods and services; and free circulation of people. The group has been meeting from July 2013, when the Action Plan for the Sustainable Development and the Brazil-Uruguay Integration was structured. This document covers 40 actions of strategic character in the short, medium and long terms.

Several agreements were signed in the Group's scope. The result of a second meeting held in Montevideo on 16th May 2014 may be highlighted, in the occasion, agreements were signed for the facilitation of bilateral commerce; production integration (Maritime and Offshore Agreement); free circulation of people (in effect since 7th July 2017); and facilitation for the circulation of workers.

Among the most recent actions, in the area of physical integration, is the project for the construction of a second international bridge over Jaguarão river, which aims at improving international traffic of cargo and passengers transport between Brazil and Uruguay; the restoration of the historical and architectural heritage of *Barão de Mauá* Bridge between the cities of Jaguarão (Brazil) and Rio Branco (Uruguay), which was opened in 1930 and declared historical heritage of Mercosur in 2015;

and the coordination act between the two countries for the physical and institutional structuring of the Mercosur Waterway.

After 2016, resulting from political and economic instability, the actions of the New Agenda receded, whereas technical cooperation actions between the two countries were kept active. The efforts for cooperation started from the second half of the 1970's, when the Agreement for Scientific and Technical Cooperation was signed on June 12th, 1975. According to the Brazilian Cooperation Agency, actions that stand out are in the area of education – such as the integration of languages, farming, health and sanitary surveillance, public defenders, meteorology, nutrition, heritage, environment and public security. These are actions of common qualification to develop joint activities in the border area.

Most technical efforts of cooperation, developed specially from 2000, are projects or activities related to border routines, both in the social area and in the innovation and local development. In the scope of this article, the most important actions are in environmental qualification and sustainability in Merin Lake, connection link of the Mercosur Waterway.

FINAL CONSIDERATIONS

The cooperation relations between Brazil and Uruguay have developed in a peaceful way, with a group of mainly bilateral actions being developed, especially in the local scale, in other words, on the border line mainly in twin cities. Among the most important are cooperation efforts in education and health care, with joint actions aiming at providing training and access to services for the population who have work and housing relations, especially in twin cities.

The evolution of cooperation agreements and commercial relations in this context show that the difference in size of the economies of both countries render unequal commercial relations in favor of Brazil. Besides that, contributing to the inequality is the higher complexity of the Brazilian economic structure, grounded on a more diverse industrial sector, while the Uruguayan one is based on an economy of a more agro-industrial basis.

Concerning Mercosur, it can be observed that the actions taken for its strengthening, even in different economic and geopolitical contexts, are yet far from reaching a common integration project. This may be said about public policies and cooperation relations. Direct actions relevant to the border region between Brazil and Uruguay are still mostly taken via a bilateral cooperation agenda. Except for the Mercosur Structural Convergence Fund (FOCEM), which, even if from time to time only, has already supported projects and represents a concrete instrument with the possibility of development of integration actions.

Concerning the project portfolio undertaken by IIRSA/Cosiplan, it must be pointed out that it presents a great weakness on the point of view of a real integration strategy. In general, it can be said that it is a group of projects developed by the governments in the countries, just put together under a common portfolio.

Concerning the Mercosur Waterway, it may be observed that, although it was considered an integration strategy in the cooperation agreement between the two countries, it is not a priority for any of them. Moreover, by analyzing the economic structure of both countries in the Waterway region, it may be concluded that there is not a sufficient volume of cargo to justify such an investment. This way, the Waterway can only be justified under an integration regional development perspective, but recent facts in the international political scope in Brazil, as well as in several other Latin American countries, seem unpromising for this approach. However, the new free trade agreement between Mercosur and the European Union, signed on June 28th, 2019, can bring new perspectives for the future of the Waterway.

REFERENCES

Almeida, P. R. de. (2011-2012). A diplomacia da era Lula: balanço e avaliação. Revista Política Externa, Paz e Terra, São Paulo, v.20, n.3. Dez./Jan./Feb., 2011-2012.

ARGENTINA. MINISTÉRIO DOS TRANSPORTES. (2019). Institutional site. Available in: https://www.argentina.gob.ar/puerto-buenos-aires/el-puerto

Aveiro, T. M. M. (2006). *Relações Brasil-Uruguai: a Nova Agenda para a Cooperação e o Desenvolvimento Fronteiriço*. Masters dissertation. Brasília: UNB. Available at http://www.funag.gov.br/ipri/btd/index.php/10-dissertacoes/595-relacoes-brasil-uruguai-a-nova-agenda-para-a-cooperacao-e-o-desenvolvimento-fronteirico

BRASIL. (2012). MINISTÉRIO DA INTEGRAÇÃO NACIONAL. *Programa de Desenvolvimento da Faixa de Fronteira. Institutional site*. Available in http://www.mdr.gov.br/desenvolvimento-regional-e-urbano/publicacoes

BRASIL. (2019). *Constituição da República Federativado Brasil*. 1988. Available in http://www.planalto.gov.br/ccivil_03/constituicao/constituicao.htm

BRASIL. AGÊNCIA BRASILEIRA DE COOPERAÇÃO (ABC). (2019). Projetos de cooperação Uruguai. Institutional site. Available in: http://www.abc.gov.br/Projetos/CooperacaoSulSul/Uruguai

BRASIL. DEPARTAMENTO NACIONAL DE INFRAESTRUTURA DE TRANSPORTES (DNIT). (2019). Hidrovia do Mercosul. Available in http://www.dnit.gov.br/hidrovias/hidrovias-interiores/hidrovia-do-Mercosul

BRASIL. MINISTÉRIO DAS RELAÇÕES EXTERIORES. (2019). Institutional site. Available in http://www.itamaraty.gov.br

Caetano, G. (2011). *El Uruguay internacional y la región: apuntes históricos y desafíos vigentes. In: Brasil-Uruguai: os próximos 20 anos*. Brasília, Fundação Alexandre de Gusmão. Available in: http://funag.gov.br/biblioteca/index.php?route=product/product&product_id=216

Cervo, A. L., & Bueno, C. (2010). História da política exterior do Brasil. Brasília, Editora da Universidade de Brasília. 3rd. ed.

Cervo, A. L. (2006). A ação internacional do Brasil em um mundo em transformação: conceitos, objetivos e resultados (1990-2005). In H. Altemani, & A. C. Lessa (Eds.), Relações internacionais do Brasil. v. 1. São Paulo, Editora Saraiva.

COMISSÃO ECONÔMICA PARA A AMÉRICA LATINA E O CARIBE (CEPAL). (2019). *Ranking de portos: os Top 20 na América Latina e no Caribe em 2016. Institutional site*. Available in https://www.cepal.org/pt-br/infografias/ranking-portos-os-top-20-america-latina-caribe-2016

CONSELHO SUL-AMERICANO DE INFRAESTRUTURA E PLANEJAMENTO (Cosiplan) – INTEGRAÇÃO SUL-AMERICANA (IIRSA). (2018). *Institutional site*. Available in http://www.iirsa.org/Page/Detail?menuItemId=45

de Almeida, P. R. (2011). O desenvolvimento do Mercosul: progressos e limitações. Brasília: 2011.

Fernandes, M. S., & Filho, L. L. D. (2017). *Planejamento territorial da IIRSA: conceitos e projetos*. Natal, *Revista de Geopolítica*, v., n.1, 2017. Available in http://www.revistageopolitica.com.br/index.php/revistageopolitica/article/view/167

Foucher, M. (1991). *Fronts et frontières: un tour du monde geopolitique*. Paris, France: Fayard.

Frega, A. (2008). *Historia del Uruguay en el siglo XX (1890-2005)*. Montevidéu, Ediciones de la Banda Oriental.

Ginesta, J. (1999). *El Mercosur y su contexto regional e internacional*. Porto Alegre: UFRGS.

Ginesta, J. (2004). *La regionalización en la Unión Europea y en el MERCOSUR: el caso uruguayo*. Rosario. *VI Encuentro de las Regiones del MERCOSUR*. October 14 and 15. Available in: http://www.cedep.ifch.ufrgs.br/Textos_Elet/pdf/LA%20Regiona.pdf

Guichonnet, P., & Raffestin, C. (1974). *Géographie des frontières*. Paris, France: PUF.

Jimenez, M. L. O. (2009). *El derecho del MERCOSUR y el derecho internacional a la lucha por independencia. Revista Electrónica de Estudios Internacionales,* n. 18. Available in: http://www.reei.org/index.php/revista/num18/articulos/derecho-mercosur-derecho-internacional-lucha-independencia

Lafer, C. (2000). Brasil: dilemas e desafios da política externa. *Revista Estudos Avançados, 14*(38), pp. 260-267. Paz e Terra. São Paulo: jan./abr. 2000. Available in: http://www.scielo.br/scielo.php?script=sci_arttext&pid=S0103-40142000000100014

Lemos, B. de O. (2013). *A nova agenda para cooperação e desenvolvimento fronteiriço entre Brasil e Uruguai: repercussões territoriais nas cidades-gêmeas de Sant'ana do Livramento e Rivera.* Porto Alegre. (Masters dissertation). UFRGS. Available in: https://lume.ufrgs.br/handle/10183/28461. June 19, 2019

Lopes, R. R., & Carvalho, C. E. (2010) *Acordos Bilaterais de Comércio como Estratégia de Inserção Regional e Internacional do Chile.* Rio de Janeiro, *Contexto Internacional, 32*(2). Available in: http://www.scielo.br/scielo.php?script=sci_arttext&pid=S0102-85292010000200011

Onuki, J. (2006). O Brasil e a construção do Mercosul. In: H. Altemani, & A. C. Lessa (Eds.), Relações internacionais do Brasil. V. 1. São Paulo, Brazil: Saraiva.

Pagliari, G. de C. (2009). *O Brasil e a segurança na América do Sul.* Curitiba: Editora Giruá.

Peña, F. (2007). Los grandes objetivos del MERCOSUR: zona de libre comercio, unión aduanera y mercado común. In R. A. Barbosa (org.), Mercosul: quinze anos. São Paulo, Brazil: Fundação Memorial da América Latina: Imprensa Oficial do Estado de São Paulo.

Pucci, A. S. (2010). *O Estatuto da fronteira Brasil-Uruguai.* Brasília: Fundação Alexandre de Gusmão. Available in: http://funag.gov.br/biblioteca/download/685-O_estatuto_da_fronteira_brasil_uruguai.pdf

RIOGRANDEDOSUL.SECRETARIADACOORDENAÇÃOEPLANEJAMENTO. (2006). Estudo de Desenvolvimento Regional e Logística do Rio Grande do Sul. v. 1-5. Porto Alegre, Secretaria da Coordenação e Planejamento.

Roseira, A. M. (2011). *Nova ordem sul-americana: reorganização geopolítica do espaço mundial e projeção internacional do Brasil*. Thesis. São Paulo, Brazil: USP. Available in: http://www.teses.usp.br/teses/disponiveis/8/8136/tde-14122012-094017/pt-br.php.

Scheibe, E. F. (2018). *IIRSA and the role assigned to the La Plata Basin region in South American physical integration*. In A. P. Cargnin et al., *Territorial Planning and La Plata Basin Borders*. Porto Alegre, Letra 1. Available in https://editoraletra1.com.br/epub/9788563800350/

Sica, D. (2007). Mercosur: Evolución y perspectivas. In: R. A Barbosa (org.), Mercosul: quinze anos. São Paulo, Fundação Memorial da América Latina, Imprensa Oficial do Estado de São Paulo.

Simões, A. J. F. (2011). *Brasil e Uruguai sob o signo da solidariedade e do pragmatismo*. In: *Brasil-Uruguai: os próximos 20 anos*. Brasília, Fundação Alexandre de Gusmão. Available in: http://funag.gov.br/biblioteca/index.php?route=product/product&product_id=216&search=Brasil-Uruguai%3A+os+pr%C3%B3ximos+20+anos

Tokatlian, J. G. (2008). *O Cone Sul e suas relações internacionais: um espaço de cooperação para a América do Sul*. São Paulo, *Revista Política Externa, Paz e Terra 17*(1).

URUGUAY. ADMINISTRAÇÃO NACIONAL DE PUERTOS (ANP) (2019). *Institutional site*.

Veiga, P. da M., & Rios, S. P. (1977). Tratado de Cooperação para o Aproveitamento dos Recursos Naturais e o Desenvolvimento da Bacia da Lagoa Mirim (Tratado da Bacia da Lagoa Mirim). Divisão de Atos Internacionais do Ministério das Relações Exteriores do Brasil.

Veiga, P. da M., & Rios, S. P. (2011). *O Brasil como vetor de integração sul-americana: possibilidades e limites*. São Paulo, Brazil. *Revista Política Externa, Paz e Terra, 20*(2).

Veiga, P. da M., & Rios, S. P. (2013). *Estratégia Nacional de Segurança Pública nas Fronteiras (ENAFRON)*. Secretaria Nacional de Segurança Pública do Ministério da Justiça. Presentation. Available in https://www2.camara.leg.br/atividade-legislativa/comissoes/comissoes-permanentes/credn/audiencias-publicas/2011/acompanhar-e-esclarecer-as-acoes-e-dificuldades-encontradas-para-prover-a-devida-protecao-as-fronteiras-brasileiras-1/apresentacao-enafron

ENDNOTES

1 It is in this context that the South American Community of Nations (CASA) was created in 2002. 12 South American countries were part of it, bringing together Mercosur, Andean Community of Nations, Chile, Guyana and Surinam. CASA was later called South American Union of Nations (Unasur), and it brought forward the consolidation of the development and achievement of the constituent blocks.

2 In the South Cone, this proximity increased from the break in the hostility between Brazil and Argentina, since the solving of the Itaipu-Corpus conflict and the Nuclear Cooperation Agreement. In 1985, there is the Iguazu Declaration, which seeks to coordinate efforts aiming at a greater bilateral integration. The Integration, Cooperation and Development Treaty in 1988 highlight the objective of shaping a common market with other countries in the region. This process originates the Southern Common Market (Mercosur).

3 Some of the conflicts contributing to this situation in the Andean sub-region are pointed out by Pagliari (2009, p.230): Colombia, Venezuela and Chile develop a process of increase in their military force; more evident presence of the United States military; borderline rivalry especially between Venezuela and Colombia; there is also rivalry between Chile and Bolivia and Chile and Peru. Besides, the last international war in South America occurred in this sub-region, between Peru and Ecuador in the warzone border of the river Cenepa, in 1985.

4 This perception led Brazil to the creation of the SIVAM – Amazon Survaillance System in 2002, with the aim of obtaining data to support defense, monitor air traffic control, and border surveillance, environment and monitoring issues, dealing with drug trafficking and arms smuggling.

5 The main threat for safety in the South Cone border region refers to the Triple Border between Brazil, Paraguay and Argentina, where organized crime may be found.

6 Initiated in 2000, IIRSA is an initiative taken by the 12 countries in South America which aims at supporting the South-American integration through the physical integration of the countries.

7 A more detailed analysis about IIRSA may be found in Scheibe (2018).

8 Available at: http://cosiplan.org/proyectos/detalle_proyecto_api.aspx?h=27. June 04, 2019.

9 *Twenty Foot Equivalent Unit* (TEU) is a standard measure of container capacity, considering an intermodal container standard of 20 feet, equal to one TEU.

10 A more detailed analysis about this theme may be found in Lemos (2013).

Chapter 14
Guarani Aquifer System Transboundary Management

Luciana Cordeiro de Souza Fernandes
UNICAMP, Brazil

ABSTRACT

This chapter presents the Guarani Aquifer System (GAS), its location and its characteristics, and discusses its management, since it is located in four countries, Argentina, Brazil, Paraguay, and Uruguay. The GAS is a transboundary aquifer, which goes beyond political boundaries, watersheds, and hydrogeological provinces. After briefly highlighting the technical aspects of the GAS, an overview of the groundwater management legislation of each country will be offered, with emphasis on Brazil. International Environmental Law and international treaties and agreements involving this territory will also be discussed, to present the characteristics of the Guarani Aquifer Agreement formulated by these four MERCOSUR countries, which, although not in force, provides for the protection of this environmental good. Finally, it is proposed to create an urban environmental planning tool to protect the GAS recharge areas, innovating the legal system to unite environmental law with urban law in search for GAS protection. This special environmental zoning tool will be called ZEA.

INTRODUCTION

Fresh water, a vital element found in nature in three physical states: solid, liquid and gaseous. In its liquid state, it is contained in surface and groundwater reservoirs as rivers, streams, lakes and in the so-called aquifers.

DOI: 10.4018/978-1-7998-2513-5.ch014

Within the aquifers, groundwater is considered invisible, because it is found within the subsoil, collected in its fissures, pores and fractures of rocks, in other words, distant from human vision and susceptible to exploitation. Within these groundwater reservoirs the water which is found was stored millions, thousands, hundreds, dozens of years or including months within the subsoil, depending on the soil formation in the geological history of the planet. This water made up the water cycle once the evaporated water from the surface condensed and turns back to its liquid state infiltrating within the soil recharging the aquifers. In this process the groundwater and surface water, it is interdependent, teaches Rebouças, A. C. (2002)

Hirata, R.; Suhogusoff, A.V.; Marcellini, S.S.; Villar, P.C., Marcellini, L. (2019, p. 4) date and note that groundwater is critical for the global water safety, because within the aquifers a 97% of fresh liquid water of the planet can be found, which makes it the largest fresh water reservoir of humanity.

According to estimations of the UNESCO, the worlds aquifers which participate more actively within the mechanism of renovation of the worlds water, store close to 10,3M km^3 of the total volume of the planets water (34,6M km^3) and its contribution to the river flow is 13.000 km^3 per year-1. At the same time, the total water demand, human and industrial consumption and land irrigation within the year 2000 were estimated between 4.000 and 5.000 km^3 per year-1. The Phi/UNESCO 2003 estimates that between 600 and 700 km^3 per year-1 are extracted from the wells to supply the 50% of the world's freshwater consumption, 40% of the industrial demands and 20% for agriculture of land irrigation. Generally, the lack of constructive and operative quality of large part of wells, favors the idea of that the use is unreliable as a generator for water production (SOUZA, 2009).

Meanwhile, recent studies by Hirata, R.; Suhogusoff, A.V.; Marcellini, S.S.; Villar, P.C., Marcellini, L. (2019, p. 8), claim that the estimated overall groundwater collection of the world, exceeds since 2010 1.000.000 Mm^3, which places it in a key position with a higher level of abstraction on the ground. Groundwater plays a fundamental role in several countries, being present within the populations water supply, irrigation and industry.

These data justify the necessity of adopting preventive tools which promote management of the quality of its water through an adequate land planning. All at once, the surface is the key element for this protection, declares Souza (2009).

Due to the importance of aquifers within the global water supply, the focus of this study will be the known Guarani Aquifer System.

Figure 1. Spatial localization of the Guarani Aquifer System in South America. Source: ECOA, 2017.

THE GUARANI AQUIFER SYSTEM.

The Guarani Aquifer System (SAG) is transboundary, as mentioned before. It is considered the largest aquifer of the world in territorial extension, located in South America in part of the territories of Argentina, Brazil, Paraguay and Uruguay, because of its hydrogeological and hydro chemical properties and it is the main groundwater reservoir of this region (OEA, 2009).

In Figure 1 can the spatial projection of the location of this South American aquifer be observed, which covers a total area of 1.087.879 km^2, according to the executed upheavals of the project of environmental protection and sustainable development of the Guarani Aquifer System- PSAG, within the area of influence of 735.918 km^2 (61.65%) in Brazil; 36.170 km^2 in Uruguay (3,32%); 228.255 km^2 (20,98%) in Argentine, and 87.536 km^2 (8,05%) in Paraguay (OEA, 2009, p. 30).

In Brazil, SAG is distributed amongst the states of Goiás (39.367,72 km^2), Mato Grosso (7.217,57 km^2), Mato Grosso do Sul (189.451,38km^2), Minas Gerais

(38.585,20 km^2), Paraná (119.524,47 km^2), Rio Grande do Sul (154.680,82km^2), Santa Catarina (44.132,12 km^2) and São Paulo (142.958,48 km^2). (OEA, s/d, p. 25)

The project of environmental protection and sustainable development of the Guarani Aquifer System (SAG) was carried out between 2003 and 2009 in an integrated way, in which the four countries participates through the institution of four pilot projects within the cities of Ribeirão Preto (Brazil), Concórdia-Salto (Argentine/Uruguay); Rivera-Santana (Uruguay/Brazil) and Itapúa (Paraguay).

The project was structured in seven components:

- Expansion and reinforcement of the current basis of scientific and technical knowledge about the SAG.
- Development and combined instrumentation of a management framework for SAG, based on a strategic program of the parts.
- Promotion of public participation and of the interested agents of the social communication and environmental education.
- Evaluation and accompaniment of the project and dissemination of the results.
- Precautions taken for the management of subterranean water and for the mitigation of prejudices according to the characteristics of the region within critical areas – (¨hot spots¨).
- Consideration of the potential of the usage of clean geothermal energy of the SAG.
- Coordination and management of the project (CPRM, 2008).

Some conclusions of the two conducted studies by the PSAG were already divulged and among these, the following are highlighted: a) confirmation of the existence of SAG as an extensive set of rock strata (geological formations); b) SAG is present within the subsoil of four countries, but also shows some natural differences related to the original estimated areas; c) the waters of SAG represent natural heterogeneity despite the internal continuity of the aquifer; d) There is vulnerability in the upwelling and recharging area, meaning that they are areas which are susceptible to increase the pollution of its water; e) The need for changes of land uses, mainly in areas of recharge that could open spaces to specific strengths of cooperation and dialogue between countries; f) The diverse uses to which the waters are applied and the tendency to increase the use of its water can be accentuated by the effects caused by climate change in the region; g) the project promoted an integrated analysis for the knowledge of the local, state, provincial, national and regional interests; h) there still exists a decompensation between the legal system and the application of rules; i) Although in the four countries exist legal and institutional bases which are able to increase the development and environmental protection of SAG, these legal regulations need to be reviewed and adapted (OEA, 2009, p. 30-31).

In this way, we can conclude that,

At international level an important legal outcome of the GEF-Program is the agreement for continuing regional cooperation on SAG management and protection through: assuming direct responsibility for continuation of the main activities, with each country responsible for providing (in coordination with the others) the necessary tools and resources – SISAG database management (Argentina), groundwater monitoring and modelling (Brasil), capacity building and dissemination (Paraguay) and coordination of activities and office-base (Uruguay); continuation of the activities initiated in the pilot projects – with Concordia/Salto being coordinated by Argentina, Rivera/Santana by Uruguay, Riberão Preto by Brasil and Itapúa by Paraguay – although there has been reluctance or difficulty to retain the services of the Pilot Project Facilitator scritical to continuity and effectiveness, and an option here (which needs urgent consideration) would be to appoint someone accountable from within (as opposed to outside) existing line agencies).(FOSTER, S.; HIRATA, R.; VIDAL, A.; SCHMIDT, G.; GARDUÑO, H ., 2009, p. 13)

This project was created with the purpose to support these countries with the creation and implementation of a common institutional legal framework and technical management and preservation of the Guarani Aquifer System, proving the capacity of cooperation between four countries due to the importance of this source for the water supply within the most diverse uses of this territory.

The extensive area underlain by the SAG has a present population of about 15 million (although including large cities in its proximity this figure increases to about 90 million), a mainly sub-tropical climate, and abundant (but often polluted) surface water resources which experience occasional droughts. Thus the need for reliable potable water-supply sources and industrial supplies (of low-treatment cost) is likely to grow significantly, especially in some climate-change scenarios (which imply increased water demand due to ambient temperature increase and more frequent and intense surface-water droughts).(FOSTER, S.; HIRATA, R.; VIDAL, A.; SCHMIDT, G.; GARDUÑO, H ., 2009, p. 8)

According to resent studies, the use of water from SAG has turned out to be more extensive, with a substantial increase of their operation in the four countries, especially in Brazil, being the only source of supply in some regions.

The current resource exploitation exceeds 1.0 km^3 /a, 93.6% in Brazil (of which about 80% is in São Paulo State), 2.8% in Uruguay, 2.3% in Paraguay and 1.3% in Argentina. Some 80% of the total is used for public water supply, 15% for industrial *processes and 5% by geothermal spas (Foster et al., 2009). Although this water extraction is essential, it should be considered that it is still a small fraction of its full capacity (SINDICO et al, 2018, p. 50).*

Meanwhile, as is already mentioned, the studies demonstrated the vulnerability of some areas of SAG, especially in areas of recharge which require more protection to prevent the tributaries from contamination of their waters through the soil, areas which can be identified in figure 2., emphasizing the researchers Foster, S., Hirata, R., Vidal, A., Schmidt, G., and Garduño, H. (2009, p. 10). The conceptual revised model of the hydrology of SAG has important implications in terms of the definitions of an efficient and sustained strategy for the managed development of groundwater resources in areas of management of resources (which can be useful for the whole aquifer system).

The only parts of the SAG which exhibit significant vulnerability to groundwater pollution from anthropogenic activities on the land-surface are the main recharge area – comprising the aquifer outcrop and adjacent areas where the basalts are highly-fractured or 'windows' through the basalt exist. The degree of groundwater pollution vulnerability here will vary with water-table depth, and the degree of consolidation of the sandstone units or fracturing of the overlying basalts, and although not 'extreme' is likely to be in the 'moderate to high range'. (FOSTER, S.; HIRATA, R.; VIDAL, A.; SCHMIDT, G.; GARDUÑO, H., 2009, p. 9).

As a result of PSAG, a Strategic Program of Action (PEA) was created for the protection of the land and sustainable management of the Guarani Aquifer System (SAG) as an instrument of planning on short and long terms for the management in the four countries. The PEA has as its aim, to promote the coordinated and sustainable management about the resources with a description for implementation supported by the OEA (2009, p. 252-341); and concerning the legal question, the dices of the PSAG favored the creation of an international agreement for the management of the Guarani integrating the part of international environmental law.

THE INTERNATIONAL ENVIRONMENTAL LAW

Historically, the Industrial Revolution started a continuous process of environmental degradation which reached its peak during the second half of the twentieth century. After this, during the decade of 1970, the international scientific community agreed to join strengths to identify the diverse impacts of the contamination on environmental resources and to find a way to prevent them. Regarding the groundwater, the studies

Figure 2. General delineation of resource management zones for the Guarani Aquifer System (Foster, S., Hirata, R., Vidal, A., Schmidt, G., and Garduño, H. 2009, p. 11). Source: GWP World Bank, 2009.

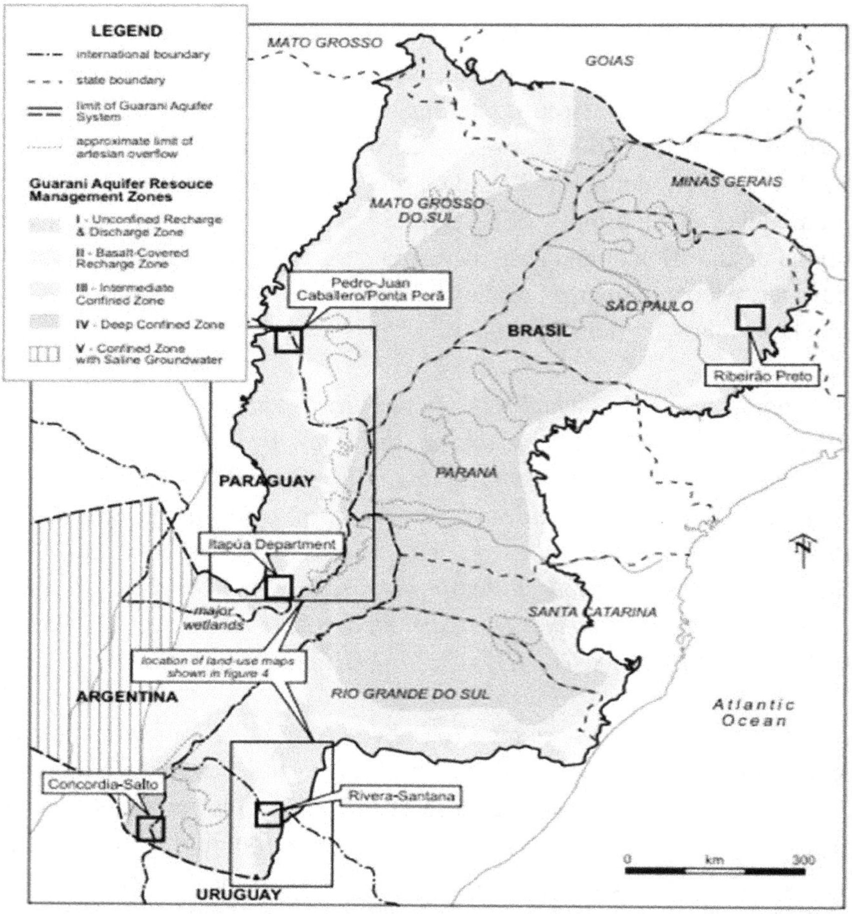

were more intensive in the end of the twentieth century because of multiple sources of contamination and pollution which compromised the aquifers, act which has also been seen in Brazil. In this way, countries which are nowadays organized in institutions of states cannot renounce the existence of a recognized territory as their own without knowing the physical boundaries. Meanwhile rivers and cross-border aquifers don't change the color of their water when they cross a geographical border, when they pass the sovereign area of another country, indicated Soares (2003a, p. 14).

Therefore, the need for an International Environmental Law, which, through agreements and international treaties, is able to offer protection to the cross-border environmental goods, apart from bringing peace to possible conflicts between sovereign states about these natural resources.

Regard the issue of cross-border waters, the "Convention on the Law of the Non-navigational Uses of International Watercourses", adapted by the General Assembly of the United Nations in 21.05.1997, by means of resolution number 51/229 and by the resolution of the International Law Commission of the United Nations on Groundwater Systems, approved during these same dates other important legal decrees which stand out on international or cross-border waters, claims Soares (2003b, p. 110).

The author (2003b, p. 111- 113), highlights that in 1992, consequently, before the convention of 1997, there had already been treaties and international conventions which abandoned the traditional concept of international rivers and lakes excelling the "Convention on the Protection and Use of Transboundary Watercourses and International Lakes" signed in Helsinki on the 17.03.1992, which introduced to the International Environmental Law the concept of "cross-border waters".

Accordingly, we note that since 2002, this has been a subject of the Commission on International Right of the United Nations (ILC) who searched to codify a law about transboundary aquifers to create a legal regulation which is appropriate to the management of aquifers considering its importance as a source of fresh water.

In a rather short period of 6 years, the ILC was able to adopt a set of 19 draft articles at its session in 2008. It sent the draft articles together with the commentaries thereto to the 63rd session (2008) of the UN General Assembly. (STEPHAN, 2009, p.6)

Being that,

As of January 2006, a total of 68 transboundary aquifers had been identified (Fig 4); 29 located in South America, 18 in Central America, 17 in North America and four in the Caribbean. Evaluation of the results shows that some of the largest aquifers in South America are transboundary systems. (STEPHAN, 2009, p.10), the locations might be observed in figure 3.

It should be noted, as our study brings the subject up to the question of the Guarani Aquifer System, perhaps other aquifers also need a regulation of international environmental rights through an agreement and/or international treaties like the one made at SAG, although this one is not in force yet.

Figure 3. Transboundary Aquifers of the World (UNESCO, 2009, p.44). Source: Atlas of transboundary aquifers. Global maps, regional cooperation and local inventories. 2009.

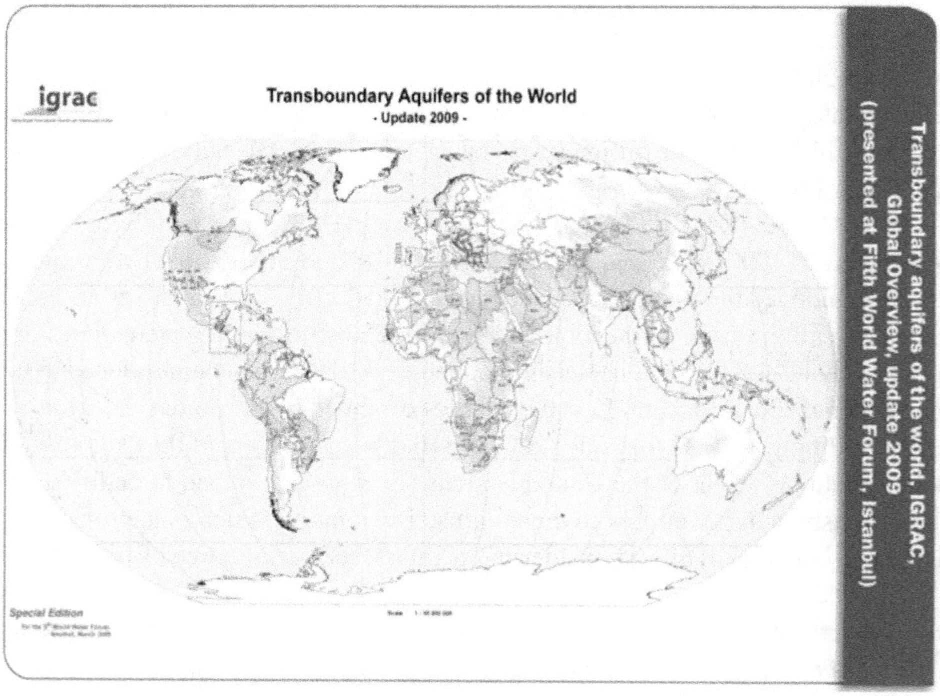

INTERNATIONAL AGREEMENT ON MANAGEMENT OF THE GUARANI AQUIFER SYSTEM

The cross-border management of water resources is generally characterized by the previous existence of conflicts, like it has already occurred in different locations on the planet. Meanwhile, the Agreement of the Guarani Aquifer, signed by Argentine, Brazil, Paraguay and Uruguay, is one of the few agreements signed in a context of precaution and prevention, basic principles of environmental law.

Although history shows that at the transboundary Basin of Plata have occurred several conflicts related to surface waters, it is a fact that till today, there have not been any conflicts related to the use of shared groundwaters between these countries and that the PSAG has been an instrument which united researchers and the political power, making the creation of an International Agreement among the Member States possible based on Resolution 63/124 of the National Assembly of the United Nations which treats the right of Transboundary Aquifers approved in

2009, as for Resolution 1803 also of the General Assembly which refers to permanent sovereignty of natural resources.

Hereby, the "Agreement of the Guaraní Aquifer" was signed on the second of October 2010 in San Juan, Argentinian Republic, between the four countries. It declares that the Guarani Aquifer System is a transboundary water resource which integrates the sovereign territorial domain of the Republic of Argentine, the Federal Republic of Brazil, the Republic of Paraguay and the Oriental Republic of Uruguay which are the only owners of this resource and which, from here on forward, will be called "Members".

Among other aims, it is attempted to broaden the levels of cooperation for a higher scientific level on the Guarani Aquifer System and the responsible management of their water resources. In addition, the above-mentioned agreement is not yet in force, depending on the ratification on the part of Paraguay.

The obligations of the Member States are to exchange technical information about studies, activities and work, which consider the sustainable advantages of the water resources of SAG. This stems from an important strategy of planning with the celebration of the agreement.

The environmental information is also an important tool of cooperation ad prevention within the environmental management. The agreement of the Guarani Aquifer System reaches an international status because it includes, within articles 8 to 11, the obligation of the Members to inform the rest about all activities and work which they pretend to carry out. With this, the Member, when reaching the information, will judge if the presented project might cause him sensitive damage within his environmental area or environment. It will be indicated within the conclusions to the other member. During the negotiations and consultations, the implementation of the activity or work will be evaluated, or the project will stop being executed in case of a negative outcome. From this action, the exchange of environmental information between Members will be the key piece for continuing success of the shared management of SAGs resources for present and future generations

This Agreement also includes the expectation of creating an integrated commission by the 4 Members, which will coordinate the cooperation between them for the implementation of the principles and objectives of this Agreement with its own regulations, and which in dispute situations must try to search for a solution, with the Members, in a friendly way. And when these disputes cannot be solved with the provided procedures within the previous articles, the Members can turn to the arbitral proceedings.

However, it should be reiterated that this agreement is not yet accomplished, because the ratification of Paraguay is still pending to be approved. Argentina approved the agreement through Law 26/780 on the 31st of October of 2012; Uruguay agreed through Law 18/913 on the 12th of June 2010 and in Brazil it was ratified by means of Decree 52/2017 published by the Senate Federal Journal on the 23rd of February 2017 and took effect in March 2017.

In this way, each country possesses its own legislations to manage SAG within its territories with diverse similar issues as we will see in the following.

OVERVIEW OF THE WATER LEGISLATION IN SAG TERRITORIES

Many governments have introduced legislation to regulate groundwater development and to constrain activities that might compromise groundwater availability and quality. This trend reflects increasing competition and conflict between groundwater users and increasing threat of groundwater pollution. Initially, this legislation was piecemeal, relating to specific water uses or problems as they arose. Subsequently, realization that negative impacts on groundwater may also affect surface water is bringing about the greater integration of legal provisions on water resources. (Nani, M.; Foster, S.; Dumars, C.; Garduño, H.;Kemper, K.; Tuinhof, A, 2004, p. 1).

In relation to the water legislation, the authors in question suggest that

aims to regulate the relationship between persons (physical and legal) and between the people and the state administration on water resources; it includes all legal provisions on development, use, protection and management of groundwater resources, which may be either scattered in various enactments or integrated into a comprehensive water law. (Nani, M.;Foster, S.; Dumars, C.; Garduño, H.;Kemper, K.; Tuinhof, A, 2004, p. 2).

Table 1 shows the legislation of the four countries regarding groundwater control and management in different legal regulations

It should be noted that, however Brazil has a political geographical Division that possesses 27 Federal Units (UF) on a National level, -26 Stats and a Federal District – and that by Federal Constitution (art.26, I) these hold the domain of groundwater, hardly 12 states made a specific legislation about groundwater, which are: São Paulo, Minas Gerais, Santa Catarina, Rio Grande do Sul, Distrito Federal, Goiás, Mato Grosso, Mato Grosso do Sul, Alagoas, Pernambuco, Maranhão e Pará. The rest verify the existence of laws, decrees, regulations, entrances related to surface water, which together with the State Policies for Water Resources are managed, lack from specific legal certificates. (SOUZA-FERNANDES & OLIVEIRA, 2018).

When verifying that SAG is located in Brazil on part of the territory of 8 states, - São Paulo, Paraná, Rio Grande do Sul, Santa Catarina, Mato Grosso, Mato Grosso

Table 1. Dominance and legislation of the four countries (adapted by authors) Source: OEA, 2009

	DOMAIN	LEGISLATION
ARGENTINA	- Constitution: water property of the provinces. - According to the Civil Code of 1968 groundwater is public domain, but some provincial legislations still consider it private - The main inherence (water property related to land) is well established	- A federal law of water doesn't exist. - The provincial laws refer more to the institutions than to the management of water and water policies.
BRAZIL	In the Federal Constitution of 1988 (CF/88), water is a good of common use of the village – diffuse good (art. 225). Meanwhile within the Federal Law 9433/1997 water is considered a public domain (art. 1°, I). According to CF/88, the competence to legislate general norms about water is the Union (22, IV), and it includes between goods of the surface water union which go to more than one state, serve as a limit with other countries or extend to foreign territory (art. 20, III), and the goods of two States of groundwater (art. 26,I). Still, the groundwater is considered as mineral water and not mineral of the States (Decree 227/1967). **Obs:** The river headwaters are considered particular by the Code of Waters (arts. 8° e 103) and the Civil Code (art.1290), however, these legal devices can be considered unconstitutional as all water forms part of the water cycle.	There are decree, laws, resolutions and certificates which try to set discipline on surface and groundwater resources. In this general matter we have: - Decree n. 24.643/1934 – Water Code – arts. 96 a 101- concerning groundwater (Not completely received Decree CF/88); - Decree-law 2848/1940 – Criminal Code (arts. 270 and 271) considering the cases of poisoning, corruption or the pollution of drinking water a crime; - Law 6938/1981 – National Environmental Policy (general rules for the environmental protection) - Federal Constitution of 1988 (arts. 225, 20, III and IX; 22, IV; 23, XI; 26, I) and 170, VI); - Law 9433/1997 – National Policy on Water Resources; - Law 9984/2000 – Creation of the National Agency of Water– ANA – Management board of federal waters; - Law 10406/2002 – Civil Code – arts. 1288 to 1296
PARAGUAY	- Constitution: it is interpreted that water is public domain, but according to the civil and rural code also water of private domain exists.	- A Law Decree of 1948 regulates the public Waters, but is not accomplished - A law of Water does not exist, but there are services of water and sanitation, the environmental impact assessment and protection of wild areas - For some time, a Project for Water Codes has been discussed. Today there are three versions of this project
URUGUAY	Surface water as groundwater, with an exception of river water, integrated in the water cycle, make a single resource, subordinated to the general interest, which takes part in public domain, like public water domain.	Las leyes y los decretos del Poder Ejecutivo son de aplicación nacional por tratarse de un estado unitario. - Code of Waters law 14589 of 1978 comprises surface and groundwater; - Law 16466 of 1994 (Environmental Impact) - Law 16858 of 1997 (of Riego) - Law 17823 of 2000 (Environmental Protection) - Management Plan of the Infrabasaltic Guarani Aquifer – Decree 214/2000 - Penalties for contravention of the Water Code (fines) Decree 123/1999

do Sul, Minas Gerais e Goiás – of these, only the state of Paraná didn't fulfill its constitutional duties of making a specific law on groundwater, and in none of these legislations exists the concern recharging areas of the Guarani Aquifer System, according to Souza-Fernandes & Oliveira (2018).

In this matter, we highlight researcher Foster, S., Hirata, R., Vidal, A., Schmidt, G., e Garduño, H. (2009, p. 13),

In most respects an adequate legal basis (at national and/or sub-national level) exists for the management and protection of groundwater resources in the 'Guarani countries', with the notable exception of clearly specified powers for groundwater protection in recharge areas by exerting influence over: agricultural policy as a key driver of rural land-use, municipal decision-making on urban land-use.

TERRITORIAL PLANNING IN THE GUARANI AQUIFER RECHARGE AREAS: AN URBAN ENVIRONMENTAL PROPOSAL.

As we have seen in Figure 2., the Guarani Aquifer System possesses large recharge areas, mainly in brazil, which, working as a sponge, allow the pollution to reach the aquifer, because the contamination of groundwater can be caused in two different ways: one, by the transportation of pollution of rainwater which filters quickly till reaching the levels under the subsurface; or when the polluting substances already affected the aquifers and they move sideways, warns Silva (2003, p.16).

For this,

The land use must be managed and suitable to the competences of the villages, which is the best way to protect the aquifers, according to recommended studies, the land use must give related to the aquifer, defining a protected area, in which the area of vulnerability of the aquifer will be respected, forcing to redirect it in a way that it can use the land which is related to other existing activities (businesses, industry, residences, etc.), mainly, prioritizing the disposal or so it will not be occupied by polluting activities – purpose to the pollution of land and groundwater. This might give the idea to redirect the Municipal General Plan and enable the effective environmental prevention.

There is also a need to analyze the ecosystem for prevention, protection and conservation of groundwater. We must always keep the interdependence and the existing indescribability between ground and surface water resources in mind. The heterogeneity is the most important element of hydrogeology. In nature, homogeneity does not exist.

We must always take into consideration the interdependence and inseparability between groundwater and surface water resources. Heterogeneity is the most important element of hydrogeology. In nature there is no homogeneity. (SOUZA, 2009, p. 199).

On this approach, the General Plan is the instrument for action of the urban function of the municipalities – in Brazil, villages compete this function of land use planning (Art. 30 CF/88) – and they create a general and global plan which has the task to systematize physical, economic and social development of the municipal territory, betting on the welfare of the local community. This is a plan because it establishes the aims which must be included. Till the deadline, activities which should be executed and reached, must be implemented. It is the General Plan, because it sets the guidelines for urban development of the Municipality. (SILVA, 1992).

This choice is based on the constitutional competences of Brazil of which the municipality assigns the land management and planning in a way where this becomes a participant within the process of prevention and precaution of groundwater in recharge zones of SAG.

Therefore, it is within the municipality where land exists and is being used for most different means has the power to order the land uses. It is within the municipalities where different initiatives and companies install themselves and it is also where life happens (SOUZA, 2009, p. 201).

Still, the municipality must previously know its geological characteristics and its hydrogeological potential, as for identifying the recharge areas for its aquifers, in the way where the boundaries of its territory are made considering the planning of land uses with constraints of highly polluting activities in these areas.

In this way, the proposed boundaries titled 'special environmental zoning – ZEA´, could become the technical and political framework of the management of groundwater because we know that there is no way to separate groundwater from the land, either groundwater from the surface water and for this it is proposed to give visibility to the protection and conservation of hydrological resources in a complete and integrated way within the territories of SAG.

However, when the study of PSAG demonstrated that Brazil possess an extensive area of recharge, as can be identified in figure 2, it is shown that the other countries of SAG also overlap these areas, being able to zone proposals to be adopted within the other territories of SAG, as vulnerable areas of the planet to promote an integrated management of the land and groundwater in accordance to their legal arrangements.

CONCLUSION

After all exposed, we verify the great importance of groundwater for many different uses on the entire planet. The Largest aquifer in territorial extension is found in South America: The guarani Aquifer System, which covers part of Argentine,

Brazil, Paraguay and Uruguay, being their waters key pillars for these countries, mainly in Brazil.

Through the project of environmental protection and sustainable development of the Guarani Aquifer System, a strategic plan of action has been developed which enabled the creation of an international agreement of the Guarani Aquifer, to foster the shared management of this cross border aquifer with important tools that must be implemented and are not yet in force, because it depends on the ratification of Paraguay.

Despite the inexistence of this regulation of international environmental law, studies show that SAG possesses vulnerable areas to recharge, which, functioning as a sponge, take the land pollution to the subsoil by infiltration till reaching the levels under the surface. Meanwhile, this agreement does not consider the protection of these recharge areas, neither the legal structure where the 4 countries participate.

In this way, the creation of an urban environmental tool is essential for the management of these areas through the use and planning of land according it has been proposed within this paper, although its concise is titled especial environmental zoning – ZEA.

This zoning or delimitation doesn´t allow the activities with a potential pollution to be installed within these areas and will indicate that under this, there is an aquifer which needs to be protected.

This tool, which we propose, can be replicated for other vulnerable areas of different aquifers of the planet with specific legal plans of other countries as paradigm.

ACKNOWLEDGEMENT

Project FAPESP nr. 19973/2017.

This research has also been possible thanks to the European Social Fund the Youth Employment Plan of the Government of Extremadura, which made it possible to hire technical research support at the University of Extremadura.

REFERENCES

BRASIL. (2017). *Decreto legislativo nº 52/2017*. Retrieved from https://www2.camara.leg.br/legin/fed/decleg/2017/decretolegislativo-52-3-maio-2017-784714-acordo-152560-pl.html

CPRM. (2008). *Projeto de Proteção Ambiental e Desenvolvimento Sustentável do Sistema Aquífero Guarani – PSAG.* Retrieved from https://www.cprm.gov.br/publique/Noticias/Projeto-de-Protecao-Ambiental-e-Desenvolvimento-Sustentavel-do-Sistema-Aquifero-Guarani---PSAG-938.html?from%5Finfo%5Findex=3061

ECOA. (2017). *Aquífero Guarani: como se formou esse imenso oceano que está sob nossos pés?* Retrieved from https://ecoa.org.br/aquifero-guarani-como-se-formou-esse-imenso-oceano-que-esta-sob-nossos-pes/

Foster, S.; Hirata, R.; Vidal, A.; Schmidt, G.; & Garduño, H. (2009). The Guarani Aquifer Initiative –Towards Realistic Groundwater Management in a Transboundary Context. Sustainable Groundwater Management Lessons from Practice. Case Profile Collection Number 9. Washington D.C.: World Bank, 1-28.

Hirata, R.; Suhogusoff, A. V.; Marcellini, S. S.; Villar, P. C., & Marcellini, L. (2019). A revolução silenciosa das águas subterrâneas no Brasil: uma análise da importância do recurso e os riscos pela falta de saneamento. Brasília, D. F.: Trata Brasil.

Nani, M., Foster, S., Dumars, C., Garduño, H., Kemper, K., & Tuinhof, A. (2004). Groundwater Legislation & Regulatory Provision from customary rules to integrated catchment planning. Sustainable Groundwater Management: Concepts and Tools GWMATE Briefing Note Series. Note 4. Washington, D.C.: World Bank, 1-6.

ORGANIZAÇÃO DOS ESTADOS AMERICANOS - OEA. (2009). Aquífero Guarani: programa estratégico de ação =Acuífero Guaraní: programa estatégico de acción. Ed. bilíngue– Brasil; Argentina; Paraguai; Uruguai: Organização dos Estados Americanos (OEA), janeiro 2009.

ORGANIZAÇÃO DOS ESTADOS AMERICANOS – OEA. (s/d). *Síntese Hidrogeológica do Sistema Aquífero Guarani*. Série Manual e Documentos Técnicos do Projeto de Proteção Ambiental e Desenvolvimento Sustentável do Sistema Aquífero Guarani. Montevideo: OEA.

Rebouças, A. C. (2002). Água Doce no Brasil e no Mundo. In *Águas Doces no Brasil. Capital Ecológico, uso e conservação* (pp. 1–37). São Paulo, Brazil: Ed. Escrituras.

Silva, J. A. (1992). *Curso de Direito Constitucional Positivo* (8th ed.). São Paulo, Brazil: Malheiros.

Silva, R. B. G. (2003). *Águas Subterrâneas: um valioso recurso que requer proteção*. São Paulo, Brazil: DAEE.

Sindico, F., Hirata, R., & Manganelli, A. (2018). The Guarani Aquifer System: From a Beacon of hope to a question mark in the governance of transboundary aquifers. *Journal of Hydrology: Regional Studies*, *20*, 40–49.

Soares, G. F. S. (2003a). *A proteção internacional do Meio Ambiente*. Barueri, SP: Manole.

Soares, G. F. S. (2003b). *Direito Internacional do Meio Ambiente. Emergências, obrigações e responsabilidades* (2nd ed.). São Paulo, Brazil: Atlas.

Souza, L. C. (2009). *Águas subterrâneas e a legislação brasileira*. Curitiba: Juruá.

Souza-Fernandes, L. C., & Oliveira, E. (2018). Coletânea da legislação brasileira de águas subterrâneas. 5 v. São Paulo: IAS.

Stephan, R. M. (2009). *Transboundary aquifers. Managing a vital resource*. Paris, France: UNESCO.

UNESCO. (2009). *Atlas of transboundary aquifers. Global maps, regional cooperation and local inventories*. Paris, France: UNESCO.

Chapter 15
Nationalistic Independent Movements Within the European Union and Its Challenge to Create a Territorial Identity

Demi Wilhelmina Maria van Huisseling
https://orcid.org/0000-0003-0496-0394
Universidad de Extremadura, Spain

ABSTRACT

Throughout history, humanity has been known to move in groups as a way of surviving, to expand their identity and culture. In Europe this has led to international and civil wars in the past but changed with the creation of the European Union. This chapter analyzes the creation and demarcation of nations during the past, the territorial identity that was formed and the need of the EU to create a European Identity to overcome the threat of independent movements. Secessionist nationalistic movements have gained importance since the economic crisis which started in 2007 and have been rising in different regions and countries of the EU. The main question that needs to be solved in this chapter: How does the EU cope with the rise of new nationalistic movements? It can only be overcome with the creation of a European territorial identity.

DOI: 10.4018/978-1-7998-2513-5.ch015

INTRODUCTION: HISTORICAL SHAPING OF THE EUROPEAN COUNTRIES

Humankind has always had the tendency of living in groups in which they could search for protection, live and develop. They would establish communities at a territory in excellent conditions where they could create their civilization. The link with this territory would define them and here they establish a social and political life (for example Vikings, Egyptian or the Mesopotamian civilizations). They lived in a society divided by a system of hierarchy where they had different social classes, but they were also recognisable by their culture, architecture, temples, etc.

Evolution of the European States

The expansion of the European civilizations became clearer with the creation of the first maps during the fifteenth and sixteenth century. The different civilizations who settled and identified themselves with one territory expanded their territory to gain prestige. This has led to the creation of a firm society that became more organized, with a political structure (hierarchy) and which, at the same time, attracted more people.

According to the German writer and cartographer Johann Zahn, who wrote in 1696 about nations and their inhabitants, the most significant nations in Europe were Germany, Italy, Spain, France and England because of their clearly defined borders, but also because of the way of living of their inhabitants, their language and physical aspects (Leerssen, 2006, p. 63).

Although he wrote about nations, the definition of ´national character´ rose during the Enlightenment (18th century) with the principles of democracy. The North American demographic Revolution (1776) and the French Revolution (1789) set the origin of ´nationalism´.

The word ´nation´ comes to refer to the corporate identity of all political subjects of a given country. The realization that these people form, not a servile estate or a subaltern layer in society, but the general body politic, with a will and a mandate of its own, will call into play the concept of nation [...] the birth of democracy vests power, [...] in the united will of the people; and that people, following 1789, will proclaim its inclusiveness and emancipation by calling itself a nation (Leerssen, 2006, p. 89).

Although nationalism was meant to be represented by democratic ideas, it was brought to extremes and interpreted by many leaders during the following centuries as a principle of totalitarianism. After the French Revolution, according to Leerssen,

¨there was no space for differences by nation, region, class, etc. In France, everyone was part of the ´Republique française, une et indivisible´¨ (2006).

The nationalistic feeling, which developed during the following centuries, changed from cultural nationalism, the identity of inhabitants with their territory, to geopolitics, where xenophobia and ethnicity took over, and leaded to different (world) wars. However, after the fall of the empires of Germany, Russia and Austria, new states emerged with, in most cases, a government based on democracy, sovereignty. All these different nations decided that there couldn´t be any other war in Europe triggered by expansionism or nationalism.

EUROPEAN STATES SINCE THE CREATION OF THE EUROPEAN UNION[1].

After ending the twentieth centuries wars, Europe found itself divided into multiple new states, which were defined and put onto the map. West- and South European states were delimited as we know them today, but eastern states, which were part of the former Soviet Union and Germany, experienced more changes till the last decade of the twentieth century, until the fall of the Berlin Wall in 1991, and the end of the Balkan War in 1995.

The EU recognises the different (member) states within the Europe, and their frontiers but, as its objective has been from the beginning to open the intern borders to provide economic and social freedom for its citizens, it has created different agreements, so it´s inhabitants are free to work, travel and negotiate within it´s different countries (Schengen Agreement, 1985). On the one hand, European citizens are free to move through 26 of its countries, pay with one common coin (€) in 18 countries and share European symbols which unify them, but on the other hand, each member state of the EU preserves its own culture, language and sovereignty.

According to the Spanish writer Luis Moreno (2014) it is important to maintain cultural diversities within the EU member states and minority groups, but with an integrational process in terms of ¨political participation, governance and solidarity among large, small, rich and poor territories [...]. Territorial subsidiarity and democratic responsibility are two of its large political principals¨ (p. 45). In this way, inhabitants of one country, can identify themselves as, for example, Catalan, Spanish and European citizens. They identify themselves with the Catalan territory, their neighbours, the city they live in or where they work, but respond to the Spanish State in terms of politics, although they also have a regional policy, and see themselves as European citizens, because of the freedom they receive to travel around its member states, or subsidy they received for different projects, for example.

With the implementation of the Lisbon Treaty (2009) many national competences of Member States, were suppressed and became sovereign competences of the EU, which the Member States try to reach with common objectives. This means that European rights stay above the constitutional rights of each Member State. So, the first and most important level is the European Lisbon Treaty, then the, for example Spanish Constitution of 1978, and under this come the autonomy statutes which are the regional competences of each Autonomous Community (in the Spanish case). It is understood that every Member State has its own national goals and must try to resolve possible problems or challenges on its own. The EU will only intervene when at a local, regional or national level, the intervention could not be solved by these governments (Moreno, 2014, pp. 46-47). For example, when Catalonia has a conflict with the central government of Spain, they must try to resolve their issues first internally, before reaching out to the EU.

On the other hand, when a state wants to introduce changes within one of its regions on territorial level for example, they need to ask permission from the EU first. Territorial, Social and Economic cohesion were designated ¨as an area of ´shared competence´ between the EU and the member states¨ (Baun & Marek, 2014, pp. 57-58).

ADVERSARY PROCEEDINGS WITHIN THE EU AND THE RISE OF NATIONALISTIC MOVEMENTS

The success of the EU started to turn with the outbreak of the economic financial crisis (2007). The crisis has had repercussions on the integrity of the EU because of the growing social, economic and political inequalities it caused.

Europe wasn´t prepared for the crisis to share sovereignty on an international level and to support each country with monetary help. ¨Where they have had to intervene and rescue countries, others have felt ´abandoned´¨ (Zamarriego, 2017, p. 7). The same is applied to regions within countries. Regions with a higher GDP than others, which have contributed to the economy of their country instead of receiving help, have felt that they did not need their central government to survive and could stand on their own.

Within the 27 Member States, the EU regulates at least half of our daily life and, at the same time, within the realities of the (pluri)national states, there are important matters of decentralization happening, which transfer the socioeconomic regulation within a competitive environment to the smallest units (Calzada, 2017, p. 56).

Figure 1. Pro-independence movements in Europe (Henley, J., Sheehy, F., Swann, G. and Fenn C. 2017). Source: The Guardian, 2017

Other reasons for the raise of nationalistic movements during the twenty first century apart from the economic crisis and unemployment, are the fear of globalism, as people fear to lose their culture and roots with the disappearance of physical borders, the migrant crisis, which started in 2015 with the arrival of refugees to the continent (1,2 million people in 2015 (White book, 2017, p. 11) and the fear of terrorism (van Huisseling & Mora, 2018, pp. 35-36).

These regions where nationalism raises, go against the EU´s purpose, because they try to obtain their own sovereign state against the shared sovereignty of the EU with more social and territorial balance.

This figure 1, gives a clear view of most of the EU regions which present strong independent movements in 2017. They are mostly regions who have a desire to become independent states and as can be seen, they are, apart from a central region of Hungary, peripheral regions. However, not all their inhabitants agree with this independency, they do not form a majority, and therefore they still belong to their current States. The final decision to become independent lays on the Nation-State they belong to. If they truly leave their Member State, they would also have to leave the EU.

The regions which have caused higher conflicts over the last years to become independent have been Catalunya, Corsica, Scotland and Bavaria, which are known for their political independent parties and support of large part of their population who stand behind them.

Another example is the Brexit in Great Britain, where the whole country is in process of leaving the EU. With this movement, can be seen that not only regions within nations are willing independence, however, also a whole nation can create a nationalistic feeling against the European Union's policies and unity. The United Kingdom has held a referendum in 2016 within their population with the question if they wanted to become independent from the EU and a 52% of their population voted ´yes´. They will leave the EU in the fall of 2019 after a long process of negotiation with the European Parliament to reach an agreement. However, till the date of writing this article (august 2019), no deal has been reached. With this process can be seen that, once sharing different competences, sovereignty with other countries or other regions, it is very difficult to become a separate, independent state again.

At the same time, Scotland, region with certain autonomy and an own parliament within the United Kingdom, has shown a strong feeling of wanting the independence of the United Kingdom and stay within the EU. They have held a referendum in 2015 where a 45% of their population (total of 5,37 inhabitants in 2015) voted in favour of the independence, which was not enough, and with the Brexit they have tried to reach their independence again, when their prime minister Nicola Sturgeon, went to talk with the EU in Brussels. She did not succeed as other member states did not support this decision as they were also dealing with regions within their Nations who want independence, and if they agreed to give Scotland their independence, their regions would claim it too (Catalonia in Spain, Kosovo from Serbia etc.).

THE CASE OF CATALONIA (SPAIN)

General Facts About Catalonia

Catalonia, which is one of Spain´s 19 Autonomous Communities, is located in the north east of the country, southern from the Pyrenees and has a long coastline at the Mediterranean Sea, has an extension of 32.108 square km. Catalonia is divided into four provinces (Barcelona, Tarragona, Girona and Lleida). It has a population of 7.6 million inhabitants with the province of Barcelona as its most populated one with more than 5.6 million people in January 2019 (Idescat, 2019a). The other communities are mostly rural, with it´s population centred within the larger cities. Catalonia represents in 2018, a 16.27% of the total Spanish population (INE, 2019).

Figure 2. Sectorial Distribution of the active population in Catalonia 1800-2000 (in %). Source: Nadal and Parejo, 2005.

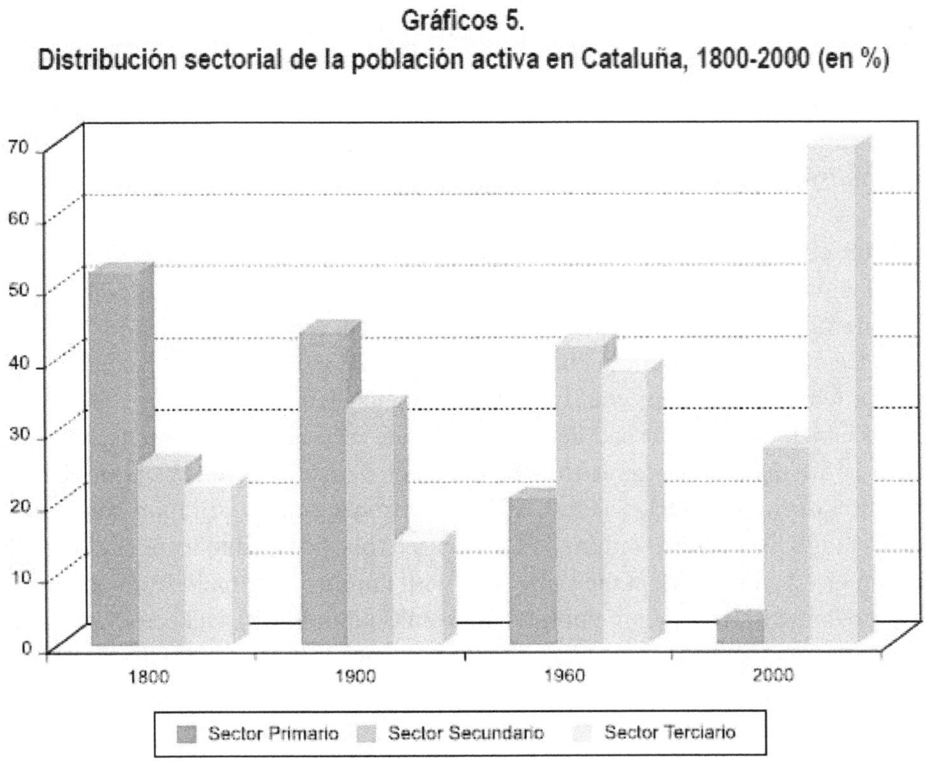

During the nineteenth and twentieth century, because of the industrial revolution, which was in Spain mostly centered in Catalonia, the economy of Catalonia grew, and with this, its population. Catalonia became an important region of Spain where agriculture was replaced with industry. Figure 2 shows these changes of economic sectors over the centuries.

The reason for Spain to center the industry in Catalonia was mostly due to its geographical location, close to France, where they could transport goods with terrestrial transport on the east side of the Pyrenees to the rest of Europe and on ships, because of the Ports which connect with the Mediterranean Sea and the rest of the world. Over the years, Barcelona became the second largest city of the country (after Madrid).

In 2018, with a GDP per capita of 32,121 against 25.900 per capita of Spain, Catalonia is one of the richest Communities of the country, and, also ahead of the GDP per capita of the EU with 30.900 (Idescat, 2019b).

Independent Movement of Catalonia

Catalonia has been on the international news for the past three years because large part of its population senses a strong feeling of wanting independence from Spain and desire to create the Republic of Catalonia. However, they do want to belong to the EU. The feeling has existed for a long time within large part of its population but became stronger since the creation of the first Catalan political party ¨*Lliga Regionalista*¨ in 1901 (till 1936) and regain forces since 2011 during the economic crisis.

Their cultural differences in comparation with the rest of Spain, play a role. Their language has been promoted since the fall of the dictatorial regime (during the dictature of Franco, Catalan and their symbols were prohibited). A study released by the Catalan Government in 2016 shows that ¨94 per cent of residents understood Catalan while 80 per cent could speak the language. This was from a population among which 35 per cent had been born outside of Catalonia¨. (Minder, 2017, p. 84). It is the main language learned and spoken at schools. When the minister of education of Spain (Wert) tried, in 2012, to introduce more common courses and classes taught in Spanish within the Catalan schools, he got into a conflict with the Catalan government and, at the same time with families originally from other parts of Spain, but with children in public schools in Catalonia who lacked of knowledge of the Spanish language, because they did not learn it at their schools. In the end, Catalan is on public schools still the mainly spoken language (Trujillo, 2016, p.104).

If being looked at the history of Catalonia, because of their geographical laying, they have had many conflicts with the rest of the Spanish territory, with the kingdom of Castilla, with France or later the Central State of Spain during the civil war and dictature of Franco. Catalonia has been for some years in the past, part of France with Andorra, the Balearic Islands and Valencia and have also more cultural aspects similar to them than to the rest of Spain. They have formed part of the Crown of Aragon, during the fourteenth century where the territory of Catalonia was called ¨principality of Catalonia¨. In 1479 this crown joined the Kingdom of Castilla when Isabel de Castilla married Fernando V of Aragon. However, they were now part of the mandate of Castilla, they kept being governed by 4 viceroys: Aragon, Catalonia, Valencia and Mallorca. This way, they kept their heterogeneity within their territories, politics and culture. During the seventeenth century, after the ´thirty year war of Europe´, Catalonia became part of France and with the ¨Peace Treaty´ signed in 1659 where new borders were established between Spain and France, part of Catalonia stayed n hands of France (Roussillon, Conflent, Vallespir and part of Sardinia) and the other territory became Spanish again. During the nineteenth century Catalonia again fell into the hands of the French when Napoleon conquered Catalonia. In 1812 when the Constitution of Cadiz was signed, Spain became Unified. From this can be seen, that Catalonia, Valencia and the Balearic Islands have been during large part of history a territory of unstable governments and kingdoms where they belonged to.

On economic level, and as explained before, Catalonia is one of the richest communities of Spain. During the economic crisis which started in 2007, Catalonia maintained its GDP in large parts of their territory, and mostly within their larger cities, while, at the same time, in the rest of Spain, it decreased. While many communities of Spain have lost job opportunities, population which moved to other parts of Spain or other countries, and received funds from the EU to support them, Catalonia has mostly contributed to the Spanish economy and received these people who have come to search for a job. This is one of the reasons for the growth of the independent movements in Catalonia, phrases like ¨Spain Steals from us, or Catalonia is being exploited¨ are often heard (Moreno, 2017).

Although the economic growth has mainly been produced in densely populated, larger cities and industrial areas, the independent movements have grown mostly in rural areas.

In Catalonia, on the 30th of September 2005, the Parliament of Catalonia approved the proposal of creating a new Statute to define Catalonia as a Nation. This proposal has had 150 votes in favor and only 15 against within their parliament. And, when they held a non-binding referendum among their population on the 18th of June 2006 where 48.8% of the Catalan population participated, 73.90% voted in favor, 20.76% against and 5,35% blank. Although the referendum was non-binding, they could not declare the independence either, because they didn´t reach a minimum of 50% of participants who went to vote this day.

After long discussions, in June 2010 these Statutes were declined by the Central Government of Spain because they were illegal within some of their articles. One of the main reasons to be declared illegal is because it is not for an Autonomous Community to decide to become a nation, but for the State. A total of 14 articles of the Autonomous Statue were compressed and 27 were redefined so they could not reach their independency (Trujillo, 2016, p.100).

From this moment, and with the results of the economic crisis which started in 2007, their nationalistic movement raised and on the 11th of September 2011, the day of Catalonia, a large demonstration took place in the center of Barcelona. Till 2017, these demonstrations became more frequent and were also seen ono national and international level where Catalan population demonstrated for independency. (Moreno, 2017, p. 132).

According to a study of Moreno (2017), held between 1985 and 2013, about how the population of Catalonia consider themselves, Spanish, Catalan or both, in 1985 only 9% of their population considers themselves only Catalan. In 2013 this number raised to 31%. From 12% of people who considered themselves in 1985 only Spanish, this number decreased to only 4% in 2013. The rest considered themselves more Catalan than Spanish (27% in 2013), more Spanish than Catalan (2% in 2013) or as Catalan as Spanish (33% in 2013). The increase of these numbers in favor or ´feeling Catalan´ increased according to Moreno (2017) due to the lack of negotiations between the Central Government of Spain (under the lead of President Rajoy of the Popular Party) and the Catalan Government. The president has demonstrated that he was not interested in decentralizing some of the fiscal competences of the Government of Catalonia (Basque Country and Navarra do have these competences).

If Catalonia really decided to become an independent state, they would have to leave the EU, they would have to create an own constitution, acquire a new bank with a new currency, government, etc. If they wanted to enter the EU again, they would have to apply.

David Cameron stated in 2015 at a conference with Mariano Rajoy, and approved by Angela Merkel the following:

If one part of a state secedes from that state, it is no longer part of the European Union and it has to take its place at the back of the queue, behind those other countries that are applying to become members [...]. Merkel said that European treaties must be respected and those treaties ´guarantee the sovereignty and territorial integrity of each state´ (Minder, 2017, p. 142).

However, in 2017, within the Government of Catalonia and their followers within the Catalan Population, raised the feeling of wanting independence and, although the Central Government of Spain tried to impede it, on the 1st of October, a referendum was held. An exact number of population who went to vote is not possible to be given due to the lack of control on who voted and who not, as some people voted several times as said on the media during the day, and other people who didn´t go to vote at all because they knew it was an illegal referendum and they didn´t want independence. The referendum was declared illegal and unconstitutional by the central government through the Council of Ministers, the States Prosecutors Office and the Constitutional Court. According to the most reliable data, although known that this is not to be considered reliable, a 43% of the Catalan population voted with a 90,2% in favor and 7,8% against the independency of Catalonia (Marco, 2017).

Charles Puigdemont, the president of Catalonia declared the Republic of Catalonia on the 27th of October, but also this was declared illegal by the Central government by applying the Article number 155 of the Spanish Constitution. The central government took over the regional government and made a call for new elections which would be held on the 21st of December 2017. Catalonia has entered from there on a long and difficult process to form a new government.

RELATION BETWEEN TERRITORY AND NATIONALISM.

Looking at the map of Spain and the localization of strong nationalistic movements within its territory, it can be concluded that they are located in the peripherical areas of the country. Basque Country and Catalonia. Galicia also has an independent movement, but it is not so strong on political means and supported by their inhabitants as the other two. However, they are all located in the north and limiting with the sea. Two at the Atlantic Ocean and the other at the Mediterranean Sea. Catalonia and Basque country are regions which experimented a process of industrialization during the nineteenth century because of their geographical situation as their territory is close to the rest of Europe too. This industrialization brought demographic and economic growth to the regions and with this, and over time, the creation of their national movements, which, according to Joana Trujillo (2016: p. 97) is called ¨peripherical nationalism¨. In the case of Galicia, they didn't develop industry and was characterized mostly by their agriculture and low economy. Their nationalism is characterized mainly by their language, cultural and social identity which has been different then the rest of Spain (Sabucedo & Fernández, 1998).

Table 1. GDP average EU 2015. Source: Own creation, from Eurostat 2017.

Regional GDP in European Union, 2015			
Region (NUTS 2013)	**GDP € MILLION**	**GDP per capita €**	**GDP per capita PPS, EU28 =100**
European Union	14714029	28900	100
Germany	3032820	42800	124
Bavaria	550446	43100	144
Spain	1075639	23200	90
Basque Country	66553	30800	119
Catalonia	204189	27600	107
Galicia	55821	20500	79
Italy	1645439	27100	96
Lombardi	357200	35700	127
Sicily	87383	17200	61
Trentino/South Tirol	18608	34600	123
United Kingdom	2580064	39600	108
Scotland	196980	36700	100
Wales	86352	27900	76
Northern Ireland	53262	28800	78

As can be seen on figure 1, most of the independent movements are located in peripherical areas of the countries they are part of (Scotland in the north of the United Kingdom, Sicily in the South and South Tirol in the north of Italy, Bavaria in the South East of Germany. These regions are mostly richer regions of their Member States or have a strong cultural or historical difference compared with the rest of their country.

In table 1, some of these regions are represented with their GDP per capita according to a report of Eurostat released in 2015. If we compare these different regions with the EU28 average and with the Member States they are part of, it can be concluded that they are in most cases one of the wealthiest regions of their countries with a GDP higher than average. If we take Basque Country (GDP per capita 119%) or Catalonia (GDP per capita 107%) for example and compare them to the average of Spain (GDP per capita 90%) we can see that they are above both national and EU GDP average. The GDP of Galicia, however, was only a 79%. As mentioned before, due to their lower economic development. They are a much more rural area of Spain than the rest. According to the GDP in Euros per million, Basque Country sums a 6,19% of the national GDP in euros per million and Catalonia an 18,98% of the total GDP in euros per million in Spain, representing 26,1% of the Spanish population living in Catalonia and 4,7% in the Basque Country. Galicia represents a 5.2% of the total GDP in euros per million in Spain and they represent a 5.8% of Spanish population (INE).

On the other hand, this population and economy are not equally distributed within each region, as it is concentrated within the larger cities where most of their inhabitants live, and industries and jobs are located. In Catalonia for instance, in the year 2011, only an 1.1% of the inhabitants of Catalonia lived in one of the 328 municipalities of Catalonia with less than 500 inhabitants each. On the contrary, a 53.9% of its inhabitants, lived in only 23 cities with more than 50.000 inhabitants. (Table 2).

At the same time, these 23 largest cities are located near the coast and around Barcelona where most of the industries are concentrated, and the smaller villages can be found in the inlands of the region.

This information is very important at the moment of studying the nationalistic movements of a region. Because when a whole region votes, and at the time of looking at the results, these dates are not taken into account. At the elections of Catalonia in December 2017, in Barcelona and Tarragona, 50-55% of their population, voted for non-independence parties, and on the opposite, only a 35% of the population in Girona and Lleida voted for these parties. And a 63 and 64% in favor.

On figure 3, 4 and 5, are the results of the regional elections in Catalonia in December 2017 shown, and where, people voted for and against independent parties. It can clearly be seen that on the periphery, near the coast line and close to the border

Table 2. Population and municipalities of Catalonia in 2001 and 2011. Source: Idescat. population census

	Population				Number of municipalities			
	2001	%	**2011**	%	**2001**	%	**2011**	%
Till 500	89.485	1,4	82.343	1,1	360	38,1	328	34,6
From 501 till 2.000	293.679	4,6	268.313	3,6	285	30,1	267	28,2
From 2.001 till 5.000	393.535	6,2	432.983	5,8	127	13,4	142	15,0
From 5.001 till 10.000	510.777	8,1	621.042	8,3	76	8,0	89	9,4
From 10.001 till 50.000	1.517.310	23,9	2.060.824	27,4	77	8,1	98	10,3
More then 50.000	3.538.324	55,8	4.054.338	53,9	21	2,2	23	2,4
Total	**6.343.110**	**100,0**	**7.519.843**	**100,0**	**946**	**100,0**	**947**	**100,0**

Figure 3. Results in percentage of the regional elections in Catalonia, December 2017. Source: El País.

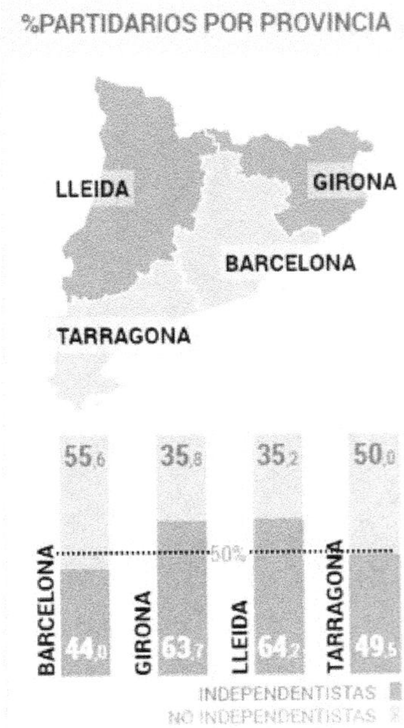

Figure 4. Results regional elections in Catalonia, December 2017. Source: El confidencial.

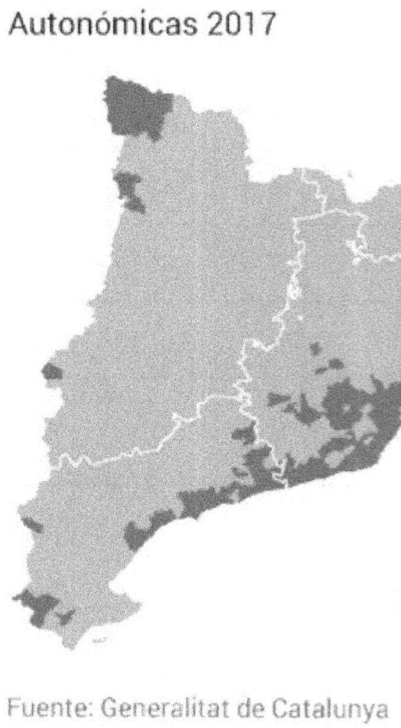

Figure 5. Results regional elections Catalonia, December 2017. Source: El confidencial.

with the Pyrenees and France, where, at the same time, the largest cities are located, most people voted for non-independent parties (see the blue spots within figure 4). And if looked at figure 5, according to population, can be seen that far more people in these densely populated areas voted in favor of non-independent parties. On the contrary, in rural areas, the independent parties gained more votes.

PROPOSALS: TERRITORIAL COHESION AS A REGIONAL LACE

According to the EU it is very important to preserve cultural diversity and wealth like languages and traditions of its different Member States. The EU defends the territorial identity of each nation, but also the creation of a European Identity. Only if its inhabitants consider themselves Europeans, they will defend its territory and work together on a common future.

People have always felt more identified with their nearest surroundings. Think about your village or the region you live in. This is where you know your neighbours, go to work, know your local government and create a feeling of ¨belonging to¨. According to a study of Roberta Capello about territorial identity, this sense of belonging to a system and interact with other people within it, creates solidarity. Solidarity is *the main ingredient for the creation of a collective identity* (Capello, 2018, p 491). This local identification is very important for the EU, but how could they create a European identity too, when it feels so far away from ones ´home´?

It is though, very important to create a feeling of similarity between the different societies within the EU by sharing their cultural historical and ethnical connections (Capello, 2018, p. 492). The information can be spread by the EU by organizing cultural events, information talks at schools and universities and by creating a European community where they feel being part of. The EU also funds different social and educational exchanges like the Erasmus+ programme.

A report of the European Commission about mid-term evaluation of the Erasmus+ programme (2014-2020) states that *the Erasmus+ programme fosters positive social/civic behaviour and a sense of feeling ´European´ (+19% compared to non-participants).* During the last years, more than 1,8 million inhabitants of the EU have taken part in it´s mobility programme and around 940 000 organizations have participated.

At the same time, it is also important that different states with common borders show good international cooperation where the inhabitants of both see the good flow of information, goods, but also of communication between both countries when extra control is needed and they might need to intervene in legal, questions like during the migrant crisis and possible threats caused by terrorism, which has recently happened in Europe (Sassen, 2013).

Further, it is important to create economic networks where an enterprise of a local market works together with others and creates a financial relationship to export their products. They establish a relationship and promote their local product (loyalty) on a national or international market where they share knowledge and create collective feelings and cross-border cooperation. The Euro-cities, which are created to create economic, political and social development through creating a good communication between them are an example of this cooperation. According to Castanho, R. A., Naranjo Gómez, J.M., & Kurowska-Pysz, J.;

"Although it is not possible to implement the Eurocity model in every border city, once it depends on many factors, some of its elements may be an inspiration to create new structures of cross-border cooperation in other parts of the world, especially in border cities [...] this is the basis for building various alliances and partnerships, also similar to the Eurocity model" (2019).

Less developed regions of the EU Member States are known to feel less European. With different economic funds which they receive from the Committee of Regions, like the Social and Territorial Cohesion Policies of the EU, these regions obtain financial resources to be invested in growth and job creation. When these enterprises receive funds that help them develop and create job opportunities, they feel that the EU helps them, and they acknowledge this. The Committee of Regions is besides, the one which stands closest to the citizens because it is represented in Brussel by politicians from the region where they live (van Huisseling and Mora, 2018).

CONCLUSION

Although nations and nationalism were meant to unify different states and their inhabitants in the past, during the eighteenth nineteenth and twentieth centuries they have been used to differentiate people and have led to several (world) wars. The EU, created to end these wars has had the objective to unify countries to create peace and create agreements on first economic, but later also on social and political level. The EU has achieved the opening of borders with the Schengen Agreement, to the implementation of one currency, the Euro and the Lisbon Treaty, among others.

However, during the first decade of the twentieth century, several nationalistic, independent movements have arisen within the EU, as can be seen with the United Kingdom who wants to leave the EU, or within different Member States. These movements have gained more importance and became stronger since the economic crisis which started in 2007, the migrant crisis since 2015 and the terrorist attacks which have increased fear within the European population.

In Spain, different regions also know strong independent movements, but during the last years, specially Catalonia has developed its feeling to become an independent republic. They have negotiated with the Spanish Government and held several referendums, but haven´t obtained their independence, mainly because it is against the Spanish Constitution for an Autonomous Community to declare their independence. This would need many more discussions, agreements and negotiations to be achievable. If they would leave Spain, they would also have to leave the EU, and need to start negotiating with them to become a new Member State. This is a subject still open for discussion as Catalonia would have to first, create a new democratic state with an own government, currency, etc. and accomplish the requirements of the EU which are written within the Copenhagen Treaty. Other states which are candidates to become part of the EU at the moment are Serbia, Albania, the north of Macedonia, Montenegro or Turkey.

The EU, created with the slogan *United in Diversity* is trying to reach a European Identity because it is fundamental for the unity of this organization that its inhabitants feel European so that they care about its politics, cultural and economic laces and together, work on a future. This identity can be reached by creating different educational programmes for example and to show people the importance of the EU by letting them know what the EU funds in each region, on agricultural, social and economic level, among others.

The lace between the territory where a person lives and to be able to share this with the EU, with other countries and inhabitants is very important and can be shared by for example the creation of local markets or cultural events, or by creating laces through becoming part of the Eurocities, before mentioned.

When people feel connected to their local environment, but also have a feeling of belonging to their Nation and the EU, when they have a territorial connection with these territories and are willing to share this and interact with others, separatist nationalism can be overcome.

ACKNOWLEDGMENT

The dissemination of this present chapter has been possible thanks to the financial support from the ´European Fund of Regional Development´ (ERDF) and the Government of Extremadura to the research group DESOSTE through the subsidies with reference GR18052.

This research has also been possible thanks to the European Social Fund and the Project of the Government of Extremadura to contract technical research support.

REFERENCES

Baun, M., & Marek, D. (2014). *Cohesion Policy in the European Union*. London, UK: Palgrave. doi:10.1007/978-1-137-47192-5

Calzada, I. (2017). Urbanidad postnacional más allá de los estados (pluri)nación(ales) en la UE: comparación de Escocia, Cataluña y el País Vasco, *University of Oxford, Debats*. 131(1) 51/64.

Capello, R. (2018). Cohesion Policies and the Creation of a European Identity: The Role of Territorial Identity. *Journal of Common Market Studies*, *56*(3), 489–503. doi:10.1111/jcms.12611

Castanho, R. A., Naranjo Gómez, J. M., & Kurowska-Pysz, J. (2019) How to Reach the Eurocities? A Retrospective Review of the Evolution Dynamics of Urban Planning and Management on the Iberian Peninsula Territories, Sustainability, 11(3). pp. 1-23.

European Commission. (2017). *Libro Blanco sobre el Futuro de Europa*. Comisión Europea.

European Commission. (2018). *Report from the Commission to the European Parliament, the Council, the European Economic Social Committee and the Committee of Regions. Mid-term evaluation of the Erasmus+ programme (2014-2020)*. European Commission.

European Communities. (1985). *Convention. The Schengen Agreement acquis*. Official Journal of the European Communities.

Eurostat. (2017, March 30) *2015 GDP per capita in 276 EU regions*. 52/2017 news release. Retrieved from https://ec.europa.eu/eurostat/documents/2995521/7962764/1-30032017-AP-EN.pdf/4e9c09e5-c743-41a5-afc8-eb4aa89913f6

Henley, J., Sheehy, F., Swann, G., & Fenn, C. (2017) *Beyond Catalonia: pro-independence movements in Europe*. Retrieved from https://www.theguardian.com/world/ng-interactive/2017/oct/27/beyond-catalonia-pro-independence-movements-in-europe-map

IDESCAT. (2011) *Población y municipios. Por tramos de población*. Retrieved from https://www.idescat.cat/pub/?id=aec&n=993&lang=es

Idescat. (2019a). Retrieved from https://www.idescat.cat/pub/?id=aec&n=245&lang=es

Idescat (2019b). Retrieved from https://www.idescat.cat/indicadors/?id=ue&n=10131&lang=es

INE. *Cifras oficiales de población resultantes de la revisión del Padrón municipal a 1 de nero*. Retrieved from https://www.ine.es/jaxiT3/Datos.htm?t=2853

Leerssen, J. (2006). *National Thought in Europe, A Cultural History*. Amsterdam, The Netherlands: Amsterdam University Press.

Marco, F. (2017). *De la Operación Cataluña al 155*. Madrid, indicios.

Minder, R. (2017). *The struggle for Catalonia, rebel politics in Spain*. London, UK: Hurst Company.

Moreno, L. (2014). *Europa sin Estados, Unión política en el (des) orden global*. Madrid, Spain: Catarata.

Nadal, J., & Parejo, A. (2005). Andalucía y Cataluña: Dos trayectorias económicas divergentes (Finales del siglo XVIII-comienzos del siglo XXI), *Colección Mediterráneo Económico: "Mediterráneo e Historia Económica"*, 7, pp. 184-205.

Sabucedo, J. M., & Fernádez, C. (1998). Universidad de Santiago de Compostela. Nacionalismos e Ideología. Un análisis psicosocial. *Psicología Política*, (17): 7–19.

Sassen, S. (2013). When territory Deborders Territoriality. *Territory, Politics, Governance: An International Journal of Policy, Administration and Institutions*, *1*(1), 21–45.

Trujillo, J. (2016). Un nacionalismo más allá de las fronteras: La transnacionalización del movimiento independentista catalán. *Anuari del conflicto social. Sección, 1*, 90–117.

Van Huisseling, D. W. M., & Mora Aliseda, J. (n.d.). *Movimientos secesionistas en la Unión Europea*. Mauritius: Editorial Académica Española

Zamarriego, L. (2017) *Los nacionalismos, de uno u otro signo, siempre tratan de escribir la historia a su manera*. Retrieved from https://ethic.es/entrevistas/los-nacionalismos-uno-u-signo-siempre-tratan-escribir-la-historia-manera/

ENDNOTE

1 European Union, from now on EU

Compilation of References

Acharya, A. (2018). *The end of American world order*. John Wiley & Sons.

Acs, Z., Audretsch, D., Braunerhjelm, P., & Carlsson, B. (2012). Growth and Entrepreneurship. *Small Business Economics*, *39*(2), 289–300. doi:10.100711187-010-9307-2

Adger, W. N., Arnell, N. W., & Tompkins, E. L. (2005). Successful adaptation to climate change across scales. *Global Environmental Change*, *15*(2), 77–86. doi:10.1016/j.gloenvcha.2004.12.005

Adorno, T. W. (1991). *The Schema of Mass Culture. The Culture Industry: Selected Essays on Mass Culture*. London, UK: Routledge.

AEBR - Association of European Border Regions. (2013). Retrieved from http://www.aebr.eu/en/news/news_detail.php?news_id=4 1 (accessed Mar. 24, 2013).

Agnew, J. (1993). Representing space: Space, scale & culture in social science. In J. Duncan, & S. Ley (Eds.), *Place / cultural representation* (pp. 251–271). London, UK: Routledge.

Agudelo, I. G. C., & Martin, S. D. (2016). *Gorona del Viento, Futuro Energético en Canarias*. La Laguna: Grado en Contabilidad y Finanzas.

Alexeeva-Talebi, V., Löschel, A., & Mennel, T. (2008). Climate Policy and the Problem of Competitiveness: Border Tax Adjustments or Integrated Emission Trading? ZEW *Discussion Papers*, No. 08-061.

Allen, W. (2013). "I am From Busia!": Everyday Trading and Health Service Provision at the Kenya–Uganda Border as Place-Making Activities. *Journal of Borderland Studies*, *28*(3), 291–306. doi:10.1080/08865655.2013.862756

Almeida, P. R. de. (2011-2012). A diplomacia da era Lula: balanço e avaliação. Revista Política Externa, Paz e Terra, São Paulo, v.20, n.3. Dez./Jan./Feb., 2011-2012.

Althoff, C. (1985). *Os Jovens de Origem Portuguesa em Hamburgo e a sua Atitude Face a Portugal e à Cultura Portuguesa*. Porto, Portugal: Secretaria de Estado da Emigração- Centro de Estudos.

Andrés, J., & Ferri, J. (2017). *Precio de la vivienda, empleo y PIB en España. Estudios sobre la Economía Española (09)*. FEDEA.

ANEEL. (2008). *Atlas de Energia Elétrica do Brasil* (3rd ed.). Brasília: Agência Nacional de Energia Elétrica.

Angulo-Guerrero, M., Pérez-Moreno, S., & Abad-Guerrero, I. (2017). How economic freedom affects opportunity and necessity entrepreneurship in the OECD countries. *Journal of Business Research*, *73*, 30–37. doi:10.1016/j.jbusres.2016.11.017

APPENDIX NO. 1 TO THE HANDBOOK FOR BENEFICIARIES OF THE INTERREG V-A POLAND-SLOVAKIA PROGRAM (State as of 31.12.2018), Retrieved from https://pl.plsk.eu/zapoznaj-sie-z-dokumentami. May 24, 2019.

Aragón, E. (2019). La isla del Hierro aspira a ser 100% renovable. Disponível em: https://www.energynews.es/la-isla-del-hierro-aspira-a-ser-100-renovable/

Arellano, M., & Bentolilla, S. (Eds). (2009). La burbuja inmobiliaria: causas y responsables. En Los orígenes inmobiliarios de la crisis actual, capítulo 7 en Antonio Cabrales et al. (Eds). Banco de España. Retrieved from http://www.bde.es

ARGENTINA. MINISTÉRIO DOS TRANSPORTES. (2019). Institutional site. Available in: https://www.argentina.gob.ar/puerto-buenos-aires/el-puerto

Arroteia, J., & Fiss, R. (2007). Traços da Comunidade Portuguesa em Pelotas. *População e Sociedade,* (14), 171-191.

Arroteia, J. (1985). *Atlas da Emigração Portuguesa.* Porto, Portugal: Secretaria de Estado da Emigração - Centro de Estudos.

Arroteia, J. (2001). As Comunidades Portuguesas no Mundo. *Janus*, 136–137.

Asselt, H., & von. (2010). Addressing competitiveness and leakage concerns in climate policy: An analysis of border adjustment measures in the US and the EU. *Energy Policy*, *38*(1), 42–51. doi:10.1016/j.enpol.2009.08.061

Audretsch, D. (2007). Entrepreneurship capital and economic growth. *Oxford Review of Economic Policy*, *23*(1), 63–78. doi:10.1093/oxrep/grm001

Audretsch, D., Heger, D., & Veith, T. (2015). Infrastructure and entrepreneurship. *Small Business Economics*, *44*(2), 219–230. doi:10.100711187-014-9600-6

Audretsch, D., & Keilbach, M. (2004a). Does entrepreneurship capital matter? *Entrepreneurship Theory and Practice*, *28*(5), 419–429. doi:10.1111/j.1540-6520.2004.00055.x

Audretsch, D., & Keilbach, M. (2004b). Entrepreneurship capital and economic performance. *Regional Studies*, *38*(8), 949–959. doi:10.1080/0034340042000280956

Audretsch, D., & Keilbach, M. (2007). The localisation of entrepreneurship capital: Evidence from Germany. *Papers in Regional Science*, *86*(3), 351–365. doi:10.1111/j.1435-5957.2007.00131.x

Audretsch, D., & Keilbach, M. (2008). Resolving the knowledge paradox: Knowledge-spillover entrepreneurship and economic growth. *Research Policy, 37*(10), 1697–1705. doi:10.1016/j.respol.2008.08.008

Aveiro, T. M. M. (2006). *Relações Brasil-Uruguai: a Nova Agenda para a Cooperação e o Desenvolvimento Fronteiriço*. Masters dissertation. Brasília: UNB. Available at http://www.funag.gov.br/ipri/btd/index.php/10-dissertacoes/595-relacoes-brasil-uruguai-a-nova-agenda-para-a-cooperacao-e-o-desenvolvimento-fronteirico

Ayuso, J., & Restoy, F. (2006). Precios de la vivienda y de los alquileres: Un enfoque de valoración de activos de equilibrio. *Journal of Empirical Finance, 0609*, 371–388. doi:10.1016/j.jempfin.2005.10.004

Ayyagari, M., & Kosová, R. (2010). Does FDI facilitate domestic entrepreneurship? Evidence from the Czech Republic. *Review of International Economics, 18*(1), 14–29. doi:10.1111/j.1467-9396.2009.00854.x

Bachtler, J., & Gorzelak, G. (2007). Reforming EU Cohesion Policy. *Policy Studies, 28*(4), 309–326. doi:10.1080/01442870701640682

Baganha, M., & Góis, P. (1999). Migrações Internacionais de e para Portugal: O Que Sabemos e para Onde Vamos? *Revista Crítica de Ciências Sociais*, (52/53), novembro 1998/ fevereiro 1999, 229-280.

Bai, L., & Stumpner, S. (2019). Estimating US consumer gains from Chinese imports, *Banque de France Working Paper No. 718.*

Balaguer, J., & Jordá, M. (2010). Tourism as a long-run economic growth factor: The Spanish case. *Applied Economics, 34*(7), 877–884. doi:10.1080/00036840110058923

Baltà, P. J. (2015). *Cross-Border Cooperation and Cultural Communities in Europe*. Brussels, Belgium: Centre Maurits Coppieters.

Banco Mundial. Retrieved from http://www.bancomundial.org

Barlevy, G. (2007). Economic theory and asset bubbles. *Economic Perspectives, 31*(3), 44–59.

Batista, F. (2006). O Rural depois da Agricultura. In C. Cavaco, & L. Fonseca (Eds.), *Desenvolvimento e Território: Espaços Rurais Pós-Agrícolas e Novos Lugares de Turismo e Lazer* (pp. 85–106). Lisboa, Portugal: Centro de Estudos Geográficos da Universidade de Lisboa.

Batista, T., Caballero, C., Ceballos, F., Carriço, C., Mateus, J., Lopes, H., ... Pinto-Gomes, C. (2013). IDE-OTALEX C. The First Crossborder SDI between Portugal and Spain: Background and Development. *Journal of Earth Science an Engineering, 6*(3), 393–400.

Baun, M., & Marek, D. (2014). *Cohesion Policy in the European Union*. London, UK: Palgrave. doi:10.1007/978-1-137-47192-5

Beerli, A., & Martin, J. (2004). Factors influencing destination image. *Annals of Tourism Research, 31*(3), 657–681. doi:10.1016/j.annals.2004.01.010

Bergstrom, J., Cordell, K., Ashley, G., & Watson, A. (1990). Economic Impacts of Recreational Spending on Rural Areas: A Case Study. *Economic Development Quarterly, 4*(1), 29–39. doi:10.1177/089124249000400104

Berkhout, F., Hertin, J., & Gann, D. M. (2006). Learning to Adapt: Organizational Adaptation to Climate Change Impacts. *Climatic Change, 78*(1), 135–156. doi:10.100710584-006-9089-3

Biermann, F., Kanie, N., & Kim, R. E. (2017). Global Governance by Goal-Setting: The Novel Approach of the UN Sustainable Development Goals. *Current Opinion in Environmental Sustainability, 26*, 26–31. doi:10.1016/j.cosust.2017.01.010

Binder, J. (2016). *Global project management: communication, collaboration, and management across borders*. Routledge. doi:10.4324/9781315584997

Boehnke, K., Rippl, S., & Fuss, D. (2015). Sustainable civil-society engagement: Potencials of a transnational civil society in French-German, Polish-German, and Czech-German border regions. *Sustainability, 7*(4), 4078–4099. doi:10.3390u7044078

Böhme, K., Finka, M., Gustedt, E., Schön, P., Sielker, F., & Zillmer, S. (2014). *Response to the European Consultation on the Future of the Europe 2020 Strategy*. Academy for Spatial Research and Planning.

Böhm, H. (2014). A comparison of governance forms for cross-border co-operation within the EU. *Journal of Cross-border Studies, 2014*, 9.

Böhringer, C., Balistreri, E. J., & Rutherford, T. F. (2012). The role of border carbon adjustment in unilateral climate policy: Overview of an Energy Modeling Forum study (EMF 29. *Energy Policy*, (34): 97–110.

Boldeanu, F. T., & Tache, I. (2016). The financial system of the EU and the Capital Markets Union. *European Research Studies, 19*(1), 59.

Bond, I., Odendahl, C., & Rankin, J. (2015). *Frozen: The politics and economics of sanctions against Russia*. Centre for European Reform.

Bonner, R. C., & Rozental, A. T. (2009). *Managing the united states-Mexico border: Cooperative solutions to common challenges. Full report of the binational Task Force on the United States-Mexico border*. Washington, DC: Woodrow Wilson Internat.

Boorsma, M., & Chiaravalloti, F. (2010). Arts marketing performance: An artistic-mission-led approach to evaluation. *The Journal of Arts Management, Law, and Society, 40*(4), 297–317. doi:10.1080/10632921.2010.525067

Bourdieu, P. (1994). *Distinction. A social Critique of the Judgement of Taste*. Cambridge, MA: Harvard University Press.

Bowen, K. J., Cradock-Henry, N., Koch, F., Patterson, J., Häyhä, T., Vogt, J., & Barbi, F. (2017). Implementing the "Sustainable Development Goals": Towards Addressing Three Key Governance Challenges – Collective Action, Trade-offs, and Accountability. *Current Opinion in Environmental Sustainability*, *26-27*(2), 90–96.

Branger, F., & Quirion, P. (2013). Climate policy and the 'carbon haven' effect. *Wiley Interdisciplinary Reviews: Climate Change*, *5*(1), 53–71.

BRASIL. (2012). MINISTÉRIO DA INTEGRAÇÃO NACIONAL. *Programa de Desenvolvimento da Faixa de Fronteira. Institutional site.* Available in http://www.mdr.gov.br/desenvolvimento-regional-e-urbano/publicacoes

BRASIL. (2017). *Decreto legislativo nº 52/2017.* Retrieved from https://www2.camara.leg.br/legin/fed/decleg/2017/decretolegislativo-52-3-maio-2017-784714-acordo-152560-pl.html

BRASIL. (2019). *Constituição da República Federativado Brasil.* 1988. Available in http://www.planalto.gov.br/ccivil_03/constituicao/constituicao.htm

BRASIL. AGÊNCIA BRASILEIRA DE COOPERAÇÃO (ABC). (2019). Projetos de cooperação Uruguai. Institutional site. Available in: http://www.abc.gov.br/Projetos/CooperacaoSulSul/Uruguai

BRASIL. DEPARTAMENTO NACIONAL DE INFRAESTRUTURA DE TRANSPORTES (DNIT). (2019). Hidrovia do Mercosul. Available in http://www.dnit.gov.br/hidrovias/hidrovias-interiores/hidrovia-do-Mercosul

BRASIL. MINISTÉRIO DAS RELAÇÕES EXTERIORES. (2019). Institutional site. Available in http://www.itamaraty.gov.br

Brenner, N. (2005). *New state spaces: urban governance and the rescaling of statehood.* New York: Oxford University Press.

Brunet-Jailly, E. (2004). Comparing Local Cross-border Relations under EU and NAFTA. *Canadian American Public Policy*, *58*, 1–59.

Brunet-Jailly, E. (2011). Special Section: Borders, Borderlands and Theory: An Introduction. *Geopolitics*, *16*(1), 1–6. doi:10.1080/14650045.2010.493765

Brunet-Jailly, E., & Dupeyron, B. (2017). Introduction: Borders, Borderlands, and Porosity. In *Borderlands. Comparing Border Security in North America and Europe* (pp. 1–17). Ottawa, Canada: Les Presses de l'Université d'Ottawa, University of Ottawa Press.

Bryden, J., & Bollman, R. (2000). Rural Employment in Industrialized Countries. *Agricultural Economics*, *22*(2), 185–197. doi:10.1111/j.1574-0862.2000.tb00017.x

Budnikevich, I. M. (2017) Implementation Of Partnership Marketing Concept In Corss-Border Cooprration Programs Of Bukovyna Cross-Border Area. *Ecoforum Journal*, 6(2).

Bueb, J., Hanania, L. R., & Le Clezio, A. (2016). Border adjustment mechanisms Elements for economic, legal, and political analysis. WIDER Working Paper (20).

Bufon, M. (2002). Experiences of Cross-Border Cooperation in the Upper Adriatic. *Regional & Federal Studies*, *12*(4), 177–196. doi:10.1080/714004771

Bufon, M. (2013). Researching Elements of Cross-Border Social Cohesion: The Case of Slovene Border Areas. *European Countryside*, *5*(2), 89–101. doi:10.2478/euco-2013-0006

Buis, H. (2009). The role of local government associations in increasing the effectiveness of city-to-city cooperation. *Habitat International*, *33*(2), 190–194. doi:10.1016/j.habitatint.2008.10.017

Busch, T. (2011). Organizational adaptation to disruptions in the natural environment: The case of climate change. *Scandinavian Journal of Management*, *27*(4), 389–404. doi:10.1016/j.scaman.2010.12.010

Caetano, G. (2011). *El Uruguay internacional y la región: apuntes históricos y desafíos vigentes. In: Brasil-Uruguai: os próximos 20 anos*. Brasília, Fundação Alexandre de Gusmão. Available in: http://funag.gov.br/biblioteca/index.php?route=product/product&product_id=216

Callahan, W. A. (2016). China's Belt and Road Initiative and the New Eurasian Order. Norwegian Institute of International Affairs, 22.

Calzada, I. (2017). Urbanidad postnacional más allá de los estados (pluri)nación(ales) en la UE: comparación de Escocia, Cataluña y el País Vasco, *University of Oxford, Debats.* 131(1) 51/64.

Candelo, E., Casalegno, C., Civera, C., & Büchi, G. (2019). A ticket to coffee: Stakeholder view and theoretical framework of coffee tourism benefits. *Tourism Analysis*, *24*(3), 329–340. doi:10.3727/108354219X15511864843830

Cannonier, C., & Burke, M. (2019). The economic growth impact of tourism in small islands developing states—Evidence from the Caribbean. *Tourism Economics*, *25*(1), 85–108. doi:10.1177/1354816618792792

Capello, R. (2018). Cohesion Policies and the Creation of a European Identity: The Role of Territorial Identity. *Journal of Common Market Studies*, *56*(3), 489–503. doi:10.1111/jcms.12611

Capello, R., Caragliu, A., & Fratesi, U. (2018). Measuring border effects in European cross-border regions. *Regional Studies*, *52*(7), 986–996. doi:10.1080/00343404.2017.1364843

Capucho, J., & Francisco, J. P. (2010). Cultura, Competitividade Territorial e Desenvolvimento Sustentável: Algumas Considerações sobre o Caso do Vale do Côa. In *Proceedings of IV Congresso de Estudos Rurais- Turismo, Património e Desenvolvimento Rural* (pp. 232-248), Aveiro, Portugal: Universidade de Aveiro.

Cargnin, A. P., Ruckert, A. A., & Lemos, B. (2018) Territorial planning and La Plata Basin borders. 2018.

Casarini, N. (2008). What Role for the European Union in Asia? An Analysis of the EU's Asia Strategy and the Growing Significance of EU-China Relations. *Current Politics and Economics of Asia*, *17*(1), 59–82.

Case, K. E., & Shiller, R. J. (2003). Is there a bubble in the housing market? Cowles Foundation Paper(1089), 299-362.

Castanho, R. A., Naranjo Gómez, J. M., & Kurowska-Pysz, J. (2019) How to Reach the Eurocities? A Retrospective Review of the Evolution Dynamics of Urban Planning and Management on the Iberian Peninsula Territories, Sustainability, 11(3). pp. 1-23.

Castanho, R., Cabezas, J., Fernández-Pozo, L., Vulevic, A., Gómez, N., Gallardo, J. M., & Loures, L. (2018). Common Regional Development Strategies on Iberian Territory. Envisioning New Horizons: Post 2020. – Enfoques En La Planificación Territorial Y Urbanística. 1ª Ed., Enero 2018, Thompson Reuters, pp. 293 – 304.

Castanho, R. A., Kurowska-Pysz, J., & Naranjo Gómez, J. (2019). How to reach the Eurocities? A retrospective review of the evolution dynamics of urban planning and management on the Iberian Peninsula territories. *Sustainability Journal: Sustainable Cross-Border Cooperation: Common Planning, Policies, Strategies. Methods, and Activities*, *11*(602), 6–23.

Castanho, R. A., Loures, L., Cabezas, J., & Fernández-Pozo, L. (2017). Cross-Border Cooperation (CBC) in Southern Europe—An Iberian Case Study. The Eurocity Elvas-Badajoz. *Sustainability*, *9*(3), 360. doi:10.3390u9030360

Castanho, R. A., Loures, L., Cabezas, J., & Fernández-Pozo, L. (2018). Identifying critical factors for success in Cross Border Cooperation (CBC) development projects. *Habitat International*, *72*, 92–99. doi:10.1016/j.habitatint.2016.10.004

Castanho, R. A., Naranjo Gómez, J. M., & Kurowska-Pysz, J. (2019). How to Reach the Eurocities? A Retrospective Review of the Evolution Dynamics of Urban Planning and Management on the Iberian Peninsula Territories. *Sustainability*, *11*(3), 602. doi:10.3390u11030602

Castanho, R. A., Vulevic, A., Cabezas, J., Fernández-Pozo, L., Goméz-Naranjo, J., & Loures, L. (2017). Accessibility and connectivity – Movement between cities, as a critical factor to achieve success on cross-border cooperation (CBC) projects. A European analysis. *Sustainable Cities and Society*, *32*, 181–190. doi:10.1016/j.scs.2017.03.026

Castaño, M., Méndez, M., & Galindo, M. (2015). The effect of social, cultural, and economic factors on entrepreneurship. *Journal of Business Research*, *68*(7), 1496–1500. doi:10.1016/j.jbusres.2015.01.040

Cavaco, C. (2003). Habitares dos Espaços Rurais. *Revista da Faculdade de Letras-Geografia*, 1 série, XIX, 47-64.

Cavanna, T. P. (2019). *Unlocking the Gates of Eurasia: China's Belt and Road Initiative and its Implications for US Grand Strategy (May 2019).* Texas National Security Review.

Caves, R. (1974). Multinational Firms, Competition and Productivity in Host Country Markets. *Economica*, *41*(162), 176–193. doi:10.2307/2553765

Cepeda, F. (1988). *Emigração, Regresso e Desenvolvimento no Nordeste Interior Português*. (Unpublished doctoral dissertation). University of Trás-os-Montes and Alto Douro, Vila Real.

Cernat, L., & Gourdon, J. (2007). *Is the Concept of Sustainable Tourism Sustainable? Developing the Sustainable Tourism Benchmarking Tool*. Retrieved from http://mpra.ub.uni-muenchen.de/4178/1/MPRA_paper_4178.pdf

Cervo, A. L. (2006). A ação internacional do Brasil em um mundo em transformação: conceitos, objetivos e resultados (1990-2005). In H. Altemani, & A. C. Lessa (Eds.), Relações internacionais do Brasil. v. 1. São Paulo, Editora Saraiva.

Cervo, A. L., & Bueno, C. (2010). História da política exterior do Brasil. Brasília, Editora da Universidade de Brasília. 3rd. ed.

Cetl, V., Tomas, R., Kotsev, A., de Lima, V. N., Smith, R. S., & Jobst, M. (2019). Establishing Common Ground Through INSPIRE: The Legally-Driven European Spatial Data Infrastructure. In *Service-Oriented Mapping. Lecture Notes in Geoinformation and Cartography*. Cham, Switzerland: Springer. doi:10.1007/978-3-319-72434-8_3

Chaudhary, A., & Jacob, S. (2019). Pakistan suspends trade with India. Retrieved from https://www.bloomberg.com/news/articles/2019-08-07/pakistan-suspends-bilateral-trade-with-india

Chen, K., & Yang, H. (2010). Appraising the economic impact of the opening up to mainland Chinese tourist arrivals' policy on Taiwan with a tourism—CGE model. *Asia Pacific Journal of Tourism Research*, *15*(2), 155–175. doi:10.1080/10941661003629961

Chilla, T., & Sielker, F. (2016). Measuring the Added-Value of the EUSDR – Challenges and Opportunities. Discussion Paper. University Of Erlangen-Nuremberg.

Chow, D. C. (2019). United States Unilateralism and the World Trade Organization. BU Int'l LJ, 37, 1.

Coleman, D., Rajabifard, A., & Crompvoets, J. (2016). *Spatial Enablement in a Smart World. Gilbertville*. GSDI Association Press.

COMISSÃO ECONÔMICA PARA A AMÉRICA LATINA E O CARIBE (CEPAL). (2019). *Ranking de portos: os Top 20 na América Latina e no Caribe em 2016. Institutional site*. Available in https://www.cepal.org/pt-br/infografias/ranking-portos-os-top-20-america-latina-caribe-2016

Comissão Europeia. (1996). *Cidades europeias sustentáveis*. Luxemburgo: Serviço das Publicações Oficiais das Comunidades Europeias.

Condon, M., & Ignaciuk, A. (2013). Border Carbon Adjustment and International Trade: A Literature Review. *OECD Trade and Environment Working Papers*. OECD Publishing.

CONSELHO SUL-AMERICANO DE INFRAESTRUTURA E PLANEJAMENTO (Cosiplan) – INTEGRAÇÃO SUL-AMERICANA (IIRSA). (2018). *Institutional site*. Available in http://www.iirsa.org/Page/Detail?menuItemId=45

Cosbey, A.; Susanne Droege, S.; Fischer, C., Reinaud, J.; Stephenson, J.; Weischer, L., & Wooders, P. (2012). A Guide for the Concerned: Guidance on the elaboration and implementation of border carbon adjustment. Entwined, *Policy Report.*

Cosbey, A. (2012). *It ain't easy: The complexities of creating a regime for border carbon adjustment* (pp. 1–8). Entwined. Issue Brief.

Costa, T., & Lima, M. (2018). Cooperation in tourism and regional development. *Tourism & Management Studies, 14*(4), 50–62. doi:10.18089/tms.2018.14405

CPLP. (2011). Intervenção do SE no Seminário da Sociedade Alemã para os Países Afrincanos de Língua Portuguesa: As Migrações no Mundo Lusófono. Retrieved from https://www.cplp.org/Files/Filer/cplp/Domingos_Simoes_Pereira/Discursos_DSP/D2/migracoes.pdf

CPLP. (2017). Plano Estratégico de Cooperação em Turismo da CPLP 2016-2026. Retrieved from https://www.cplp.org/Files/Filer/1_CPLP/Turismo/2017-07-19-PECTUR-DA-CPLP-(Vers%C3%A3o-Final)_FINAL.PDF

CPRM. (2008). *Projeto de Proteção Ambiental e Desenvolvimento Sustentável do Sistema Aquífero Guarani – PSAG.* Retrieved from https://www.cprm.gov.br/publique/Noticias/Projeto-de-Protecao-Ambiental-e-Desenvolvimento-Sustentavel-do-Sistema-Aquifero-Guarani---PSAG-938.html?from%5Finfo%5Findex=3061

Craglia, M., & Campagna, M. (2009). *Advanced Regional Spatial Data Infrastructures in Europe*. Luxembourg: Office for Official Publications of the European Communities.

Croes, R., & Rivera, M. (2017). Tourism's potential to benefit the poor: A social accounting matrix model applied to Ecuador. *Tourism Economics, 23*(1), 29–48. doi:10.5367/te.2015.0495

Crompton, J., Ji, Y., & Dudensing, R. (2016). Sources of variation in economic impact multipliers. *Journal of Travel Research, 55*(8), 1051–1064. doi:10.1177/0047287515617298

Cross-Border Cooperation Program Interreg V-A Poland-Slovakia 2014-2020, Available at https://pl.plsk.eu/zapoznaj-sie-z-dokumentami. June 16, 2019.

Cunha, L. (1997). *Economia e Política do Turismo.* Lisboa, Portugal: McGraw-Hill.

Dacko-Pikiewicz, Z., & Wróblewski, Ł. (2017). Spatial range of the iñuence of the philharmonic institutions in Katowice. *Forum Scientiae Oeconomia, 5*, 17–34.

Dale, G. (2016). *Karl polanyi: A life on the left.* New York: Columbia University Press.

Datta, S. K. (2014). *Inside ISI: The Story and Involvement of the ISI, Afghan Jihad, Taliban, Al-Qaeda, 9/11, Osama Bin Laden, 26/11 and the Future of Al-Qaeda.* Vij Books India Pvt Ltd.

Davidsson, P., & Honig, B. (2003). The Role of Social and Human Capital among Nascent Entrepreneurs. *Journal of Business Venturing, 18*(3), 301–331. doi:10.1016/S0883-9026(02)00097-6

Davis, S. (2011). The US military base network and contemporary colonialism: Power projection, resistance and the quest for operational unilateralism. *Political Geography, 30*(4), 215–224. doi:10.1016/j.polgeo.2011.04.003

de Almeida, P. R. (2011). O desenvolvimento do Mercosul: progressos e limitações. Brasília: 2011.

de Molina, M., & Luis, J. (2010). *La economía española en la crisis mundial.* Banco de España.

De Sousa, L. (2012). Understanding European Cross-border Cooperation: A Framework for analysis. *Journal of European Integration, 35*(6), 669–687. doi:10.1080/07036337.2012.711827

Decoville, A., & Durand, F. (2017). Challenges and Obstacles in the Production of Cross-Border Territorial Strategies: The Example of the Greater Region. *Transactions of the Associations of the European Schools of Planning Journal, 1*(1), pp. 65-78, Doi:10.24306/Traesop.2017.01.005

Desjardins, F. (2019). *The Economies Adding the Most to Global Growth in 2019.* Retrieved from https://www.visualcapitalist.com/economies-global-growth-2019/

Dias, O. (2008). *A Integração dos Retornados no Interior de Portugal: O Caso do Distrito da Guarda.* Retrieved from http://www.aps.pt/vicongresso/pdfs/150.pdf

Dimitrov, M., Petrakos, G., Totev, S., & Tsiapa, M. (2014). Cross-Border Cooperation in South-Eastern Europe. *Eastern European Economics, 41*(6), 5–25. doi:10.1080/00128775.2003.11041063

Din, K. H. (1988). Tourism for Peace: Desires and attainability. In L. J. D'Amore, & J. Jafari (Eds.), *Tourism – A Vital Force for Peace (75-81): Proceedings for the First International Conference of the International Institute of Peace through Tourism* (IIPT), Montreal, Canada.

Diniz, F. (1999). *Desenvolvimento Rural, Que Perspetivas? O Caso do Alto Trás-os-Montes e Douro.* Zamora: Fundação Rei Afonso Henriques.

Dołbzasz, S., & Raczyk, A. (2010). *Cross-border cooperation in Poland after EU accession* (p. 16). Warsaw, Poland.

Doménech, R. (2011). *El impacto económico de la construcción y de la actividad inmobiliaria.* BBVA Research.

Domínguez, B. G. (2009). Creación y destrucción de la burbuja inmobiliaria de España. En La primera crisis global: procesos, consecuencias, medidas. Revista ICE 850.

Domínguez, B. G. (2009). Creación y destrucción de la burbuja inmobiliaria de España. En La primera crisis global: procesos, consecuencias, medidas. Revista ICE N°: 850.

Dominguez, L., & Pires, I. (2014). *Cross-Border Cooperation Structures in Europe. Learning from the Past, Looking To the Future.* Brussels, Belgium: P. I. E. Peter Lang. doi:10.3726/978-3-0352-6452-4

Dörry, S., & Walther, O. (2015). Contested 'Relational Policy Spaces' In Two European Border Regions. *Environment & Planning A, 47*(2), 338–355. doi:10.1068/a130315p

Dühr, S. (2011). *Baltic Sea, Danube and Macro-Regional Strategies: A Model for Transnational Cooperation in the Eu?* Notre Europe.

Durà, A., Camonita, F., Berzi, M., & Noferini, A. (2018). *Euroregions, Excellence and Innovation across EU borders. A Catalogue of Good Practices*. Barcelona, Spain: Universidad Autónoma de Barcelona.

EC - European Commission. (2007). Directive 2007/2/EC of the European Parliament and of the Council of 14 March 2007 establishing an Infrastructure for Spatial Information in the European Community (INSPIRE). *Official Journal of the European Union, 50*, 1–14.

ECOA. (2017). *Aquífero Guarani: como se formou esse imenso oceano que está sob nossos pés?* Retrieved from https://ecoa.org.br/aquifero-guarani-como-se-formou-esse-imenso-oceano-que-esta-sob-nossos-pes/

EEM. (2017). *Caracterização da Rede de Transporte de Distribuição em AT e MT*. Empresa de Eletricidade da Madeira. Disponível em: http://www.eem.pt

Elliott, L., & Smith, H. (2013). *IMF 'to admit mistakes' in handling Greek debt crisis and bailout*. Retrieved From https://www.theguardian.com/business/2013/jun/05/imf-admit-mistakes-greek-crisis-austerity

Eriksen, T. H., & Nielsen, F. S. (2001). A History of Anthropology. London, UK: Pluto Press.

Esperança, J. (2009). *Uma Abordagem Eclética ao Valor da Língua: O Uso Global do Português*. Lisboa, Portugal: ISCTE-IUL/Instituto de Camões.

ESPON European Spatial Planning Observation Network. (2013). In *TRACC. Transport Accessibility at Regional/Local Scale and Patterns in Europe*. Brussels, Belgium: European Union. Retrieved from https://www.espon.eu/tracc

ESPON RESSI- Regional Strategies for Sustainable and Inclusive Territorial Development 2017: Regional Interplay and EU Dialogue Targeted Analysis Annex 2. Governance Regimes, Opportunities and Challenges for European Cities and Regions Version 30/11/2017.

ETUC. (2006). Climate Change and Employment: Impact on Employment in the European Union-25 of Climate Change and CO2 Emission Reduction Measures by 2030. Available at www.tradeunionpress.eu/Web/EN/Activities/Environment/Studyclimatechange/rapport.pdf, accessed 5 November 2018.

EUROPEAN COMMISSION. (2000). Fundusze Strukturalne 2000-2006, Ewaluacja ex-ante oraz wskaźniki dla programu Interreg, Dokument roboczy nr 7, Brussels, Belgium.

EUROPEAN COMMISSION. (2007). *Aid Delivery Methods* (p. 32). Guidelines on the Programming, Design, and Management of General Budget Support.

European Commission. (2017). *Libro Blanco sobre el Futuro de Europa*. Comisión Europea.

European Commission. (2018). *Report from the Commission to the European Parliament, the Council, the European Economic Social Committee and the Committee of Regions. Mid-term evaluation of the Erasmus+ programme (2014-2020)*. European Commission.

European Commission. (EC) (2019). Cross Border Cooperation. Retrieved from https://ec.europa.eu/neighbourhood-enlargement/neighbourhood/cross-border-cooperation

European Communities. (1985). *Convention. The Schengen Agreement acquis*. Official Journal of the European Communities.

EUROPEAN REGIONAL DEVELOPMENT FUND. Available at https://ec.europa.eu/regional_policy/en/. August, 1, 2014.

Eurostat. (2008). Retrieved from http://www.ec.europa.eu/eurostat

Eurostat. (2017, March 30) *2015 GDP per capita in 276 EU regions*. 52/2017 news release. Retrieved from https://ec.europa.eu/eurostat/documents/2995521/7962764/1-30032017-AP-EN.pdf/4e9c09e5-c743-41a5-afc8-eb4aa89913f6

Evangelidis, K., Agrianidis, A., Perakis, K., Papadopoulos, T., & Papatheodorou, K. (2018). Web-GIS Development of Geospatial Data Dissemination in EU Operational Programmes. *European Journal of Geography*, *9*(2), 21–36.

Faludi, A. (2010). *Cohesion, Coherence, Cooperation: European Spatial Planning Coming of Age?* Abingdon: Routledge. doi:10.4324/9780203842324

Fernandes, J. (1991). *A Arquitetura – Sínteses da Cultura Portuguesa*, Imprensa nacional Casa da Moeda, Portugal: Comissariado para a Europália 91.

Fernandes, M. S., & Filho, L. L. D. (2017). *Planejamento territorial da IIRSA: conceitos e projetos*. Natal, *Revista de Geopolítica*, v., n.1, 2017. Available in http://www.revistageopolitica.com.br/index.php/revistageopolitica/article/view/167

Fernandes, M. T. D. S. P. (2016). Cidades Inteligentes: Um novo paradigma urbano – Estudo de caso da cidade do Porto. Dissertação para obtenção do grau de Mestre em Gestão pela Universidade Católica Portuguesa, Porto.

Fernández Luna, M. (2016). Análisis económico de la crisis del sector inmobiliario en España (2007-2013). (Doctoral thesis). Universidad de Sevilla.

Ferrão, J. (2000). Relações Entre Mundo Rural E Mundo Urbano: Evolução Histórica, Situação Atual e Pistas para o Futuro. *Sociologia, Problemas e Práticas* (33), 45-54.

Ferrão, J. (1996). Três Décadas de Consolidação do Portugal Demográfico. In A. Barreto (Ed.), *A Situação Social em Portugal, 1960-1995* (pp. 165–190). Lisboa, Portugal: Instituto de Ciências Sociais da Universidade de Lisboa.

Ferrari, G., Mondejar, J., & Secondi, L. (2018). Tourists' expenditure in Tuscany and its impact on the regional economic system. *Journal of Cleaner Production*, *171*, 1437–1446. doi:10.1016/j.jclepro.2017.10.121

Ferreira, E. (1976). *Origens e Formas de Emigração: O Impacte da Emigração sobre o Desenvolvimento*. Lisboa, Portugal: Iniciativas Editoriais.

Figueiredo, E. (2003). *Um Rural para Viver e Outro para Visitar- O Ambiente nas Estratégias de Desenvolvimento para as Áreas Rurais* (Unpublished doctoral dissertation). Universidade de Aveiro, Aveiro.

Fischer, C., & Fox, A. K. (2012). *Journal of Environmental Economics and Management*, 64(2), September 2012, pp. 199-216

Fleischer, A., & Felsenstein, D. (2000). Support for rural tourism- does it make a difference? *Annals of Tourism Research*, *27*(4), 1007–1024. doi:10.1016/S0160-7383(99)00126-7

Fodranov, I., Kubickova, V., & Michalkova, A. (2015). Measuring societal value of tourism: A new approach. *Tourism (Zagreb)*, *63*(4), 423–434.

Fondo Monetario Internacional. (2008).

Foster, S.; Hirata, R.; Vidal, A.; Schmidt, G.; & Garduño, H. (2009). The Guarani Aquifer Initiative –Towards Realistic Groundwater Management in a Transboundary Context. Sustainable Groundwater Management Lessons from Practice. Case Profile Collection Number 9. Washington D.C.: World Bank, 1-28.

Foucher, M. (1991). *Fronts et frontières: un tour du monde geopolitique*. Paris, France: Fayard.

Frega, A. (2008). *Historia del Uruguay en el siglo XX (1890-2005)*. Montevidéu, Ediciones de la Banda Oriental.

Fuentes Castro, D. (2009). Una nota sobre el exceso de oferta de viviendas y la duración del ajuste del sector. Boletín Económico del ICE (2958), 15-24.

Funcas. (2007). Cuadernos de Información Económica nº 203.

Galindo, M., & Méndez, M. (2014). Entrepreneurship, economic growth, and innovation: Are feedback effects at work? *Journal of Business Research*, *67*(5), 825–829. doi:10.1016/j.jbusres.2013.11.052

Gänzle, S., & Kern, K. (2008). A 'Macro-Regional' Europe in the Making? Theoretical Approaches and Empirical Evidence (pp. 99–120). London, UK: Palgrave Macmillan. Added Value of the Regional Development Fund (ERDF) (No. 2008. Ce.16.0.at.016). Final Report. Zoetermeer.

García Montalvo, J. (2003). La vivienda en España: desgravaciones, burbujas y otras historias. Perspectivas del sistema financiero (78), 1-43.

Géphyres, E., & Radboud, P. (2010). *Ex-Post Evaluation of INTERREG 2000-2006 Initiative financed by the Regional Development Fund (Erdf). Panteia, Eure Consult S.A., Policy Research and Consultancy. – University Nijmegen no. 2008.ce.16.0.at.016). Final Report.* Zoetermeer: Panteia.

Gerfert, S. (2009). Cross-Border Cooperation: Transforming Borders. Retrieved from https://essay.utwente.nl/60149/1/BSc_S_Getfert.pdf

Getz, D. (1986). Models in tourism planning: Towards integration of theory and practice. *Tourism Management*, *7*(1), 21–32. doi:10.1016/0261-5177(86)90054-3

Ginesta, J. (2004). *La regionalización en la Unión Europea y en el MERCOSUR: el caso uruguayo.* Rosario. *VI Encuentro de las Regiones del MERCOSUR.* October 14 and 15. Available in: http://www.cedep.ifch.ufrgs.br/Textos_Elet/pdf/LA%20Regiona.pdf

Ginesta, J. (1999). *El Mercosur y su contexto regional e internacional.* Porto Alegre: UFRGS.

Girardet, H. (2004). *Cities, People, Planet* (1st ed.). Wiley Academy.

Godina, R., Rodrigues, E. M. G., Matias, J. C. O., & Catalão, J. P. S. (2015). *Sustainable Energy System of El Hierro Island.* International Conference on Renewable Energies and Power Quality, La Coruña, Spain. ISSN 2172-038X, n. 13, April.

Gómez Bujía, D. (2016). La crisis inmobiliaria española, motivaciones y perspectivas. Trabajo de fin de grado. Universidad da Coruña.

Gonçalves, M. (2007). *Desenvolvimento em Meio Rural. Contributos da Emigração e do Regresso. Aplicação ao Concelho de Boticas na Região Barrosã.* (Unpublished doctoral dissertation). Open University, Portugal.

Google earth. (2019a). *Madeira archipelago.*

Google earth. (2019b). *Canary archipelago.*

Gordon, S. (2009). Regionalism and cross-border cooperation against crime and terrorism in the Asia-Pacific. *Security Challenges*, *5*(4), 75–102.

Gouveia, L. M. C. (2018). *Projeto de Ligação Elétrica Entre a Ilha da Madeira e a Ilha do Porto Santo. Dissertação para obtenção do título de Mestre em Engenharia Eletrotécnica-Telecomunicações.* Funchal: Universidade da Madeira.

Guichonnet, P., & Raffestin, C. (1974). *Géographie des frontières.* Paris, France: PUF.

Haddad, E., Porsse, A., & Rabahy, W. (2013). Domestic tourism and regional inequality in Brazil. *Tourism Economics*, *19*(1), 173–186. doi:10.5367/te.2013.0185

Hale, G., Hobijn, B., Nechio, F., & Wilson, D. (2019). How Much Do We Spend on Imports?. *FRBSF Economic Letter*, 1.

Hall, C. M., & Page, S. (2012). Developing Tourism in South Asia: India, Pakistan and Bangladesh – SAARC and Beyond. Tourism in South and Southeast Asia, chapter 14, pp. 197-224.

Hansen, H. S., Reiter, I. M., & Schrøder, L. (2017). Lecture Notes in Computer Science: Vol. 10441. *A System Architecture for a Transnational Data Infrastructure Supporting Maritime Spatial Planning. Electronic Government and the Information Systems Perspective. EGOVIS 2017* (pp. 158–172). Cham, Switzerland: Springer.

Haq, F., & Medhekar, A. (2015). Spiritual Tourism between India and Pakistan: A Framework for Business Opportunities and Threats. *World Journal of Social Sciences*, *5*(2), 190–200.

Haq, F., & Medhekar, A. (2017). Is Spiritual Tourism an Innovation in Tourism for India and Pakistan. In R. Benlamri, & M. Sparer (Eds.), *Business and Economics: Leadership, Innovation and Entrepreneurship as Driving Forces of the Global Economy* (pp. 519–530). Switzerland: Springer International. doi:10.1007/978-3-319-43434-6_44

Haq, F., & Medhekar, A. (2019). Is Spiritual Tourism a Peace Vehicle for Social Transformation and Economic Prosperity in India and Pakistan? In N. Alexandru-Mircea, & M.-O. Nedelea (Eds.), *Marketing Peace for Social Transformation and Global Prosperity* (pp. 189–211). IGI Global. doi:10.4018/978-1-5225-7464-4.ch010

Hasanlj, Y., Baizakov, S., & Salihova, S. (2019). Assessment of the impact of tourism sector on the economy of Azerbaijan, Kazakhstan and Iran using input-output models. In *Proceedings of the International Scientific Conference on Economic and Social Development – Socio Economic Problems of Sustainable Development*, Baku, Azerbaijan. Academic Press.

Healey, P. (2007). *Urban Complexity and Spatial Strategies - Towards a Relational Planning For Our Times. (RTPI Library Series).* London, UK: Routledge.

Hedaa, L., & Törnroos, J. A. (2002). Towards a theory of timing. In R. Whipp, B. Adam, & I. Sabelis (Eds.), *Making Time Time & Management in Modern Organization* (pp. 31–45). New York: Oxford University Press.

Henley, J., Sheehy, F., Swann, G., & Fenn, C. (2017) *Beyond Catalonia: pro-independence movements in Europe*. Retrieved from https://www.theguardian.com/world/ng-interactive/2017/oct/27/beyond-catalonia-pro-independence-movements-in-europe-map

Henrikson, A. K. (2010). Border Regions as Neighborhoods. In D. Wastl-Walter (Ed.), *The Ashgate Research Companion to Border Studies* (pp. 85–102). Farnham: Ashgate.

Henriques, A. (2002) Globalização e Integração Diferenciadora dos Espaços Rurais. In J. Reis, & M. Baganha (Eds.), A Economia em Curso: Contextos e Mobilidades (153-171). Porto, Portugal: Afrontamento.

Herrero, A. G., & Xu, J. W. (2017). China's Belt and Road Initiative: Can Europe expect trade gains? *China & World Economy*, *25*(6), 84–99. doi:10.1111/cwe.12222

Herszenhorn, D., & Von Der Burchard, H. (2019) *EU scores at China summit with assist from Trump*. Retrieved from https://www.politico.eu/article/eu-china-summit-result-assist-donald-trump/

Heusala, A. L., & Koistinen, J. (2018). 'Rules of the game in cross-border cooperation': Legal-administrative differences in Finnish–Russian crime prevention. *International Review of Administrative Sciences*, *84*(2), 354–370. doi:10.1177/0020852315625786

Hill, L., O'Sullivan, C., & O'Sullivan, T. (2003). *Creative Arts marketing, Linacre House.* Oxford, UK: Jordan Hill.

Hirata, R.; Suhogusoff, A. V.; Marcellini, S. S.; Villar, P. C., & Marcellini, L. (2019). A revolução silenciosa das águas subterrâneas no Brasil: uma análise da importância do recurso e os riscos pela falta de saneamento. Brasília, D. F.: Trata Brasil.

Hjerpe, E. (2018). Outdoor recreation as a sustainable export industry: A case study of the boundary waters wilderness. *Ecological Economics*, *146*, 60–68. doi:10.1016/j.ecolecon.2017.10.001

Holmes, R. (2016). Fascism 2. *Anthropology Today*, *32*(2), 1–3. doi:10.1111/1467-8322.12235

Holzer, K., & Shariff, N. (2012). *The Inclusion of Border Carbon Adjustments in Preferential Trade Agreements: Policy Implications* (pp. 1–27). Milan, Rome: Trade and Climate Change.

Hornero, A. (2008). La crisis de las hipotecas subprime y el riesgo de credit crunch. *Revista de Economía Mundial*, (18): 195–204.

Horn, H., & Mavroidis, P. C. (2011). To B(TA) or Not to B(TA)? On the Legality and Desirability of Border Tax Adjustments from a Trade Perspective. *World Economy*, *34*(11), 1911–1937. doi:10.1111/j.1467-9701.2011.01423.x

Hsu, P. (2019). Economic impact of wetland ecotourism: An empirical study of Taiwan's Cigu Lagoon area. *Tourism Management Perspectives*, *29*, 31–14. doi:10.1016/j.tmp.2018.10.003

https://www.spiegel.de/international/germany/the-nsa-and-american-spies-targeted-spiegel-a-1042023.html

Huang, Y. (2019). US–China economic tensions: origins and global implications. *China International Strategy Review*, 1-12.

Hughes, D., & Shields, M. (2007). Revisiting Tourism Regional Economic Impact: Accounting for Secondary Household Employment. *The Review of Regional Studies*, *37*(2), 186–206.

Humbert, G. L. H. (2017). *Curso de direito urbanístico e das cidades. 1*. Rio de Janeiro, Brazil: LMJ Mundo Jurídico.

Hyojin, K., & Byung-Gook, K. (2015). Economic impacts of the hotel industry: An input-output analysis. *Tourism Review*, *70*(2), 132–149. doi:10.1108/TR-11-2014-0056

ICPDR – EUSDR PA4 & PA5 COORDINATIO. (2014). Joint Paper on Cooperation and Synergy for the EUSDR Implementation.

Idescat (2019b). Retrieved from https://www.idescat.cat/indicadors/?id=ue&n=10131&lang=es

IDESCAT. (2011) *Población y municipios. Por tramos de población.* Retrieved from https://www.idescat.cat/pub/?id=aec&n=993&lang=es

Idescat. (2019a). Retrieved from https://www.idescat.cat/pub/?id=aec&n=245&lang=es

INE. *Cifras oficiales de población resultantes de la revisión del Padrón municipal a 1 de nero.* Retrieved from https://www.ine.es/jaxiT3/Datos.htm?t=2853

Inskeep, E. (1991). *Tourism planning: an integrated and sustainable development approach.* New York: Van Nostrand Reinhold.

Instituto Nacional de Estadística. (2008).

Instituto Nacional de Estadística. Retrieved from http://www.ine.es

INTERACT Programme. (2012). INTERACT Handbook. – Practical Handbook for Ongoing Evaluation of Territorial Cooperation Programs. Updated Version. Retrieved from http://Wiki.Interact-Eu.Net/Display/Pc/Practical+Handbook+For+Ongoing+Evaluation

INTERACT. (2017). Added Value of Macro-Regional Strategies Project and Programme Perspective. Final Report of the Study. EU.

International Energy Agency. (IEA, 2007). Disponível em: www.iea.org

International Energy Agency. (IEA, 2008). Disponível em: www.iea.org

International Institute for Sustainable Development (IISD). (2019). Sustainable Development. Retrieved from https://www.iisd.org/topic/sustainable-development

INTERREG: The European Territorial Co-operation. Available Oct. 1, 2018.

Inwood, J. (2019). White supremacy, white counter-revolutionary politics, and the rise of Donald Trump. *Environment and Planning C. Politics and Space*, *37*(4), 579–596.

Jaschitz, M. (2013). Key factors for successful territorial cohesion: Cross-border cooperation–how can some EU instruments create a new geography. *European Journal of Geography*, *4*(4), 8–19.

Javorcik, B. (2004). Does foreign direct investment increase the productivity of domestic firms? In search of spillovers through backward linkages. *The American Economic Review*, *94*(3), 605–627. doi:10.1257/0002828041464605

Jenks, M., Burton, E., & William, K. (1996). *The Compact City: A Sustainable Urban Form?* Disponível em: https://books.google.pt/books?hl=pt-PT&lr=&id=MliRAgAAQBAJ&oi=fnd&pg=PP1&dq=The+Compact+City:+A+Sustainable+Urban+Form%3F+&ots=vXYYkX2ibh&sig=uLIT71fXS_jLG2BO7SyKpq5_zfw&redir_esc=y#v=onepage&q=The%20Compact%20City%3A%20A%20Sustainable%20Urban%20Form%3F&f=false

Jesus, C., & Franco, M. (2016). Cooperation networks in tourism: A study of hotels and rural tourism establishments in an inland region of Portugal. *Journal of Hospitality and Tourism Management*, *29*, 165–175. doi:10.1016/j.jhtm.2016.07.005

Jimenez, M. L. O. (2009). *El derecho del MERCOSUR y el derecho internacional a la lucha por independencia. Revista Electrónica de Estudios Internacionales,* n. 18. Available in: http://www.reei.org/index.php/revista/num18/articulos/derecho-mercosur-derecho-internacional-lucha-independencia

Johnson, B. (2008). Cities, systems of innovation and economic development. Innovation: Management. *Policy & Practice*, *10*(2-3), 146–155. doi:10.5172/impp.453.10.2-3.146

Johnson, C. (2019). *Tin Cans and Greyhounds: The Destroyers that Won Two World Wars.* Simon and Schuster.

Jones, E. (2015). The forgotten financial union. In The future of the euro, 44-69. doi:10.1093/acprof:oso/9780190233235.003.0003

Jones, K. (1998). Scale as epistemology. *Political Geography*, *17*(1), 25–28. doi:10.1016/S0962-6298(97)00049-8

Juran, J. M. (2003). *Juran on Leadership for Quality* (p. 24). Simon and Schuster.

Jyrama, A., & Ayvari, A. (2010). Marketing contemporary visual art. *Marketing Intelligence & Planning*, *28*(6), 723–735. doi:10.1108/02634501011078129

Kilkenny, M., & Partridge, M. (2009). Export Sectors and Rural Development. *American Journal of Agricultural Economics*, *91*(4), 910–929. doi:10.1111/j.1467-8276.2009.01320.x

Kim, S., & Miller, C. (2017). An economic model comparison of EMSI and IMPLAN: Case of mistletoe marketplace. *Tourism Economics*, *23*(5), 1124–1130. doi:10.1177/1354816616656420

King, R., Strachan, A., Mortimer, J., & Gastarbeiter, J. (1986). Go Home. Return migration and economic change in the Italian mezzogiorno. In R. King (Ed.), Return Migration and Regional Economic Problems. (pp. 38-68). London, UK: Ed. Croom Helm.

King, R. (1984). Population Mobility: Emigration, Return Migration and Internal Migration. In A. Williams (Ed.), *Southern Europe Transformed- Political and Economic Change in Greece* (pp. 145–178). Italy, Portugal and Spain: Harpercollins College Div.

King, R. (1986). Return Migration and Regional Economic Development. In R. King (Ed.), *Return Migration and Regional Economic Problems* (pp. 1–37). Australia: Croom Helm.

Kireev, A. A., & Yachin, S. E. (2019). Paradigms of Border Studies and the Metacultural Approach. *Journal of Borderland Studies*, *34*(3), 395–412. doi:10.1080/08865655.2017.1344563

Klatt, M., & Wassenberg, B. (2017). Secondary foreign policy: Can local and regional cross-border cooperation function as a tool for peace-building and reconciliation? *Regional & Federal Studies*, *27*(3), 205–218. doi:10.1080/13597566.2017.1350652

Klytchnikova, I., & Dorosh, P. (2014). Tourism sector in Panama: Regional economic impacts and the potential to benefit the poor. *Natural Resources Forum*, *32*(2), 70–79. doi:10.1111/1477-8947.12019

Kolb, B. M. (2005). *Marketing for Cultural Organizations: New strategies for attracting audiences to Classical Music, Dance, Museums, Theater and Opera*. London, UK: Thomson Learning.

Kolosov, V. A. (2015). Theoretical Approaches in the Study of Borders. Introduction to Border Studies (33-59). Vladivostok, Russia: Far Eastern Federal University.

Konrad, V. (2015). Toward a Theory of Borders in Motion. *Journal of Borderland Studies*, *30*(1), 1–17. doi:10.1080/08865655.2015.1008387

Konrad, V., & Nicol, H. T. (2011). Border Culture, the Boundary Between Canada and the United States of America, and the Advancement of Borderlands Theory. *Geopolitics*, *16*(1), 70–90. do i:10.1080/14650045.2010.493773

Kortum, S., & Weisbach, D. (2016). *Border Adjustments for Carbon Emissions: Basic Concepts and Design. Resources for the Future* (pp. 1–43). Discussion Papers.

Kowalczyk, A., & Nawrocki, T. (1999). Współpraca transgraniczna w „miastach podzielonych - na przykładzie miast Słubice-Frankfurt nad Odrą oraz Cieszyn-Czeski Cieszyn. In A. Mync, & R. Szul (Eds.), *Rola granicy i współpracy transgranicznej w rozwoju regionalnym i lokalnym* (pp. 188–202). Warsaw, Poland: Europejski Instytut Rozwoju Regionalnego i Lokalnego Uniwersytetu Warszawskiego.

Kraemer, K. L., Linden, G., & Dedrick, J. (2011). Capturing value in Global Networks: Apple's iPad and iPhone. *University of California, Irvine, University of California, Berkeley, y Syracuse University, NY.* http://pcic. merage. uci. edu/papers/2011/value_iPad_iPhone. pdf. Consultado el, 15.

Krätke, S. (2002). Cross-Border Cooperation and Regional Development in the German-Polish Border Area. In M. Perkmann, & N. L. Sum (Eds.), Globalisation, Regionalism and Cross-Border Regions. Chapter 6, pp. 125-147. International Political Economy Series. London, UK: Palgrave Macmillan. doi:10.1057/9780230596092_6

Kronenberg, K., Fuchs, M., & Lexhagen, M. A. (2018). Multi-period perspective on tourism economic contribution - a regional input-output analysis for Sweden. *Tourism Review*, *73*(1), 94–110. doi:10.1108/TR-03-2017-0044

Kucera, T. (2019). What European army? Alliance, security community or postnational federation. *International Politics*, 1–18.

Kurki, T. (2014). Borders from the Cultural Point of View: An Introduction to Writing at Borders. *Culture Unbound*, *6*(6), 1055–1070. doi:10.3384/cu.2000.1525.1461055

Kurowska-Pysz, J. (2015) The Circumstances of Knowledge Transfer within the Scope of the Cross-Border Czech-Polish Projects 2014-2020, Forum Scientiae Oeconomia, 3(3).

Kurowska-Pysz, J. (2019) Zarządzanie partnerstwami transgranicznymi organizacji uczących się, PWN, 2019.

Kurowska-Pysz, J., Castanho, R. A., & Naranjo Gómez, J. M. (2018) Cross-border cooperation: the barriers analysis and the recommendations. *Polish Journal of Management Studies*, pp. 134-147.

Kurowska-Pysz, J. (2015). Assessment of Trends for the Development of Cross-Border Cultural Clusters at an Example of Euroregion Cieszyn Silesia. *Forum Scientiae Oeconomia.*, *3*(1).

Kurowska-Pysz, J. (2016). Opportunities for cross-border entrepreneurship development in a cluster model exemplified by the Polish-Czech border region. *Sustainability*, *8*(3), 230. doi:10.3390u8030230

Kurowska-Pysz, J. (2019). *Zarządzanie partnerstwami transgranicznymi organizacji uczących się*. Warsaw, Poland: PWN.

Kurowska-Pysz, J., Castanho, R. A., & Naranjo, J. (2018). Cross-Border Cooperation – The Barriers Analysis and The Recommendations. *Polish Journal of Management Studies*, *17*(2), 134–147. doi:10.17512/pjms.2018.17.2.12

Kurowska-Pysz, J., Castanho, R., & Loures, L. (2018). Sustainable Planning of Cross-Border Cooperation: A Strategy for Alliances in Border Cities. *Sustainability*, *10*(5), 1416. doi:10.3390u10051416

Kurowska-Pysz, J., & Szczepańska-Woszczyna, K. (2017). The analysis of the determinants of sustainable cross-border cooperation and recommendations on its harmonization. *Sustainability*, *9*(12), 2226. doi:10.3390u9122226

Kuzmin, O., & Kravchenko, I. (2014). Cross-Border Cooperation of Enterprises: Essence and Significance.

Labrianidis, L., Kalantaridis, C., David, S., Herdzina, K., Mattsson, L., Ferrão, J., & Piasecki, B. (2003). *The Future of Europe's Rural Periphery, The Role of Entrepreneurship in Responding to Employment Problems and Social Marginalization.* Brussels, Belgium: European Commission.

Lafer, C. (2000). Brasil: dilemas e desafios da política externa. *Revista Estudos Avançados, 14*(38), pp. 260-267. Paz e Terra. São Paulo: jan./abr. 2000. Available in: http://www.scielo.br/scielo.php?script=sci_arttext&pid=S0103-40142000000100014

Laine, J. P. (2015). A Historical View on the Study of Borders. In Introduction to Border Studies (14-32). Vladivostok, Russia: Far Eastern Federal University.

Laterra, P., Nahuelhual, L., Gluch, M., Sirima, X., Bravo, G., & Monjeau, A. (2019). How are jobs and ecosystem services linked at the local scale? *Ecosystem Services*, *35*, 207–218. doi:10.1016/j.ecoser.2018.11.011

Lavrador, A. (2019). É inteligente, é nossa e está no meio do Atlêntico. Disponível em: https://observador.pt/2019/06/05/e-inteligente-e-nossa-e-esta-no-meio-do-atlantico/

Leal Maldonado, J., & Martínez del Olmo, A. (2017). Tendencias recientes de la política de vivienda en España. *Cuadernos de las relaciones laborales, 35*(1), 15-41.

Lee, C., Lee, M., & Yoon, S. H. (2013). Estimating the economic impact of convention and exhibition businesses, using a regional input-output model: A case study of the Daejeon Convention Center in South Korea. *Asia Pacific Journal of Tourism Research, 18*(4), 330–353. doi:10.1080/10941665.2012.658414

Leeds, E. (1983). Industrialização e Emigração em Portugal: Sintomas Inevitáveis de uma Doença Estrutural. *Análise Social,* XIX (77-78-79) (3° 4° 5°), 1045-1081.

Leerssen, J. (2006). *National Thought in Europe, A Cultural History*. Amsterdam, The Netherlands: Amsterdam University Press.

Lee, S., & Na, S. (2010). E-waste recycling systems and sound circulative economies in east asia: A comparative analysis of systems in Japan, South Korea, China and Taiwan. *Sustainability Journal, 2*(6), 1632–1644. doi:10.3390u2061632

Lehman, K., & Wickham, M. (2014). Arts-Marketing and Marketing Strategy Development: Modeling The Marketing Activities of Visual Artists across Their Career. *Academy of Taiwan Business Management Review, 9*(2), 133–141.

Lejarraja, I., & Walkenhurst, P. (2007). *Diversification by Deepening Linkages with Tourism.* Washington, DC: International Trade Department, The World Bank.

Lemos, B. de O. (2013). *A nova agenda para cooperação e desenvolvimento fronteiriço entre Brasil e Uruguai: repercussões territoriais nas cidades-gêmeas de Sant'ana do Livramento e Rivera.* Porto Alegre. (Masters dissertation). UFRGS. Available in: https://lume.ufrgs.br/handle/10183/28461. June 19, 2019

Lepik, K. L. (2009). Euroregion as Mechanism for Strengthening Cross-Border Cooperation in the Baltic Sea Region. *Trames, 13*(3), 265–284. doi:10.3176/tr.2009.3.05

Letaifa, S. (2015). How to strategize smart cities: Revealing the SMART model. *Journal of Business Research, 68*(7), 1414–1419. doi:10.1016/j.jbusres.2015.01.024

Lewis, P. J. (2001). *Project planning, scheduling and control* (3rd ed.). The McGraw Hill Companies.

Lima, F. (2012) *As dinâmicas territoriais no espaço de fronteira na fachada atlântica peninsular: a eurocidade Valença/Tuy*. Retrieved from http://ler.letras.up.pt/uploads/ficheiros/9963.pdf (accessed on 21 February 2017).

LISER. (2015). Opportunities of cross-border cooperation between small and medium cities in Europe. Report written in the scope of the Observatory of Territorial Development, in partnership with the Department of Spatial Planning and Development – Ministry of Sustainable Development and Infrastructure, Luxembourg Institute of Socio – Economic Research. Luxembourg.

Lisiński, M. (2016). Metody naukowe w metodologii nauk o zarządzaniu. *Przegląd Organizacji* 4.

Lopes, R. R., & Carvalho, C. E. (2010) *Acordos Bilaterais de Comércio como Estratégia de Inserção Regional e Internacional do Chile*. Rio de Janeiro, *Contexto Internacional, 32*(2). Available in: http://www.scielo.br/scielo.php?script=sci_arttext&pid=S0102-85292010000200011

López García, M. Á. (2011). *Precios de la vivienda, booms inmobiliarios y política impositiva: ¿podría España haber sido diferente?* Huelva: XIV Encuentro de Economía Aplicada.

López, T. J. (2009). Crisis in mobiliaria, crisis crediticia y recesión económica en España. En Papeles de Europa. Vol. 19-2009, (pp. 82-107).

López, T. J. (2009). Crisis inmobiliaria, crisis crediticia y recesión económica en España. En Papeles de Europa. Vol. 19-2009, (pp. 82-107).

Loures, L., Castanho, R. A., Vulevic, A., Naranjo Gómez, J., Cabezas, J., & Fernández-Pozo, L. (2018). *The Multivariated Effect of City Cooperation in Land Use Planning and Decision-making Processes - a European Analysis. Urban Agglomerations* (pp. 87–106). London, UK: InTech.

Mahony, K., & Zyl, J. (2002). The Impacts of Tourism Investment on Rural Communities: Three Case Studies in South Africa. *Development Southern Africa*, *19*(1), 83–103. doi:10.1080/03768350220123891

Ma, N., & Cheng, E. W. (2019). *The Umbrella Movement: Civil Resistance and Contentious Space in Hong Kong*. Amsterdam, The Netherlands: Amsterdam University Press B. V. doi:10.1515/9789048535248

Manzella, G. P., & Mendez, C. (2009). The turning points of EU cohesion policy, Working Paper Report to BARCA Report.

Marceau, J. (2008). Introduction: Innovation in the city and innovative cities. Innovation. *Management Policy & Practice.*, *10*(2-3), 136–145. doi:10.5172/impp.453.10.2-3.136

Marco, F. (2017). *De la Operación Cataluña al 155*. Madrid, indicios.

Markuszewska, I., Tanskanen, M., & Vila, J. (2016). Boundaries From Borders: Cross-Border Relationships in the Context of the Mental Perception of a Borderline – Experiences from Spanish-French and Polish-German Border Twin Towns. *Quaestiones Geographicae*, *35*(1), 105–119. doi:10.1515/quageo-2016-0010

Marston, S. A., Jones, J. P. III, & Woodward, K. (2005). Human geography without scale. *Transactions of the Institute of British Geographers*, *4*(30), 416–432. doi:10.1111/j.1475-5661.2005.00180.x

Martinez-Fernandez, C., Hinojosa, C., & Miranda, G. (2010). Green jobs and skills: the local labour market implications of addressing climate change. OECD/LEED Local Employment and Economic Development Program.

Mason, P. (2015). *Tourism impacts, planning and management*. UK: Routledge. doi:10.4324/9781315781068

Matthiesen, U., & Bürkner, H. (2002). Antagonistic structures in border areas: Local milieux and local politics in the polish – German twin city Gubin/Guben. *GeoJournal*, *54*(1), 43–50. doi:10.1023/A:1021136614586

Mayoral, M., de la Cruz, L., Osuna, J. A., Rodríguez, L., & Mora, P. (2015). *Estudio de Accesibilidad Viaria en el Área OTALEX-C / Estudo de Acessibilidade Rodoviária da Área OTALEX-C*. Retrieved from http://dl.dip-caceres.es/proyectos/otalex2/actividades.html

Mazumder, M., Ahmed, E., & Al-Amin, A. (2009). Does tourism contribute significantly to the Malaysian economy? Multiplier analysis using I-O technique. *International Journal of Business and Management*, *4*(7), 146–159. doi:10.5539/ijbm.v4n7p146

McCall, C. (2015). State Borders in Europe. In Introduction to Border Studies (180-197). Vladivostok, Russia: Far Eastern Federal University.

Medeiros, E. A. C. (2005). *Coesão territorial nas NUTS III de fronteira de Portugal Continental. A iniciativa Interreg III-A e o desenvolvimento regional. O caso da NUT III do Alentejo Central* (Unpublished master's thesis). Universidade de Lisboa, Portugal.

Medeiros, E. (2010). Old vs recent cross-border cooperation: Portugal–Spain and Norway–Sweden. *Royal Geographical Society*, *42*(4), 434–443.

Medeiros, E. (2018). Should EU cross-border cooperation programmes focus mainly on reducing border obstacles? *Documents d'Analisi Geografica*, *64*(3), 467–491. doi:10.5565/rev/dag.517

Medeiros, E. (2018). The role of European Territorial Cooperation (ETC) in EU cohesion policy. In *European Territorial Cooperation* (pp. 69–93). Springer. doi:10.1007/978-3-319-74887-0_5

Medhekar, A., & Haq, F. (2019). Promoting Kashmir as an Abode of Peace Tourism Destination by India and Pakistan. In A.-M. Nedelea, & M.-O. Nedelea (Eds.), *Marketing Peace for Social Transformation and Global Prosperity* (pp. 22–49). IGI Global. doi:10.4018/978-1-5225-7464-4.ch002

Meentemeyer, V. (1989). Geographical perspectives of space, time, and scale. *Landscape Ecology*, *3*(3-4), 163–173. doi:10.1007/BF00131535

Mendes, J. L. R. S. (2014). Smart cities: revitalização urbana no centro histórico de Braga. Disponível em: http://hdl.handle.net/11067/1559

Miao, J. (2015). Expectations and Realities: Managing the risks of the "Belt and Road" Initiative. *China Quarterly of International Strategic Studies*, *1*(03), 497–522. doi:10.1142/S2377740015500244

Minder, R. (2017). *The struggle for Catalonia, rebel politics in Spain*. London, UK: Hurst Company.

Ministerio de Economía y Hacienda. Gobierno de España. Retrieved from http://www.mineco.gob.es

Ministerio de Fomento. Gobierno de España. Retrieved from http://www.fomento.gob.es)

MINISTRY OF REGIONAL DEVELOPMENT. Effects of cross-border cooperation of Polish regions in 2004 -2006. Available at https://www.ewt.2007-2013.gov.pl/Wiadomosci/Documents/broszura_INTERREG_IIIA.pdf

Monjon, S., & Quirion, P. (2010). How to design a border adjustment for the European Union Emissions Trading System? *Energy Policy*, *38*(9), 5199–5207. doi:10.1016/j.enpol.2010.05.005

Moreno, L. (2014). *Europa sin Estados, Unión política en el (des) orden global*. Madrid, Spain: Catarata.

Mottiar, Z. (2016). The importance of local area as a motivation for cooperation among rural tourism entrepreneurs. *Tourism Planning & Development*, *13*(2), 203–218. doi:10.1080/21568316.2015.1076509

Mukheibir, P., Kuruppu, N., Gero, A., & Herriman, J. (2013). Overcoming cross-scale challenges to climate change adaptation for local government: A focus on Australia. *Climatic Change*, *121*(2), 271–283. doi:10.100710584-013-0880-7

Münnich, S. (2015). Readjusting imagined markets: Morality and institutional resilience in the German and British bank bailout of 2008. *Socio-economic Review*, *14*(2), 283–307. doi:10.1093er/mwv014

Murteira, M. (1965). *Emigração e Política de Emprego em Portugal*. Retrieved from http://analisesocial.ics.ul.pt/documentos/1224164168X2aIG3gp6Nd78YV7.pdf

Nabeeh, N. A., El-Ghareeb, H. A., & Riad, A. M. (2015). Integrating software agents and web services in service oriented architecture based cloud services discovery framework. *Journal of Convergence Information Technology*, *10*(1), 2015.

Nadal, J., & Parejo, A. (2005). Andalucía y Cataluña: Dos trayectorias económicas divergentes (Finales del siglo XVIII-comienzos del siglo XXI), *Colección Mediterráneo Económico: "Mediterráneo e Historia Económica"*, 7, pp. 184-205.

Nani, M., Foster, S., Dumars, C., Garduño, H., Kemper, K., & Tuinhof, A. (2004). Groundwater Legislation & Regulatory Provision from customary rules to integrated catchment planning. Sustainable Groundwater Management: Concepts and Tools GWMATE Briefing Note Series. Note 4. Washington, D.C.: World Bank, 1-6.

Naranjo, J., Castanho, R., Cabezas-Fernández, J. & Loures, L. (2019). Evaluación de las áreas de servicio de la alta velocidad ferroviaria en la España peninsular desde un enfoque SIG multi-método. *Revista de Estudios Andaluces*, (37), 184-208.

Naranjo, J. M. (2016). Impacts on the social cohesion of mainland Spain's future motorway and high-speed rail networks. *Sustainability*, *8*(7), 624–646. doi:10.3390u8070624

Naredo, J. M. (2009). La cara oculta de la crisis. El fin del boom inmobiliario y sus consecuencias. En Revista de economía crítica, 7 (pp. 118-133).

Navarro, M., Iglesias, M., & Vinzón, L. (2017). Key variables for developing integrated rural tourism. *Tourism Geographies*, *19*(4), 575–594. doi:10.1080/14616688.2017.1336785

Neto, F., & Neto, J. (2011). Satisfaction with life among adolescents from returned Portuguese immigrant families. *Journal of Social Research & Policy*, *2*(2), 27–46.

Nightingale, A. J. (2015). Challenging the romance with resilience: communities, scale and climate change. In W. Harcourt, & I. L. Nelson (Eds.), Practicing Feminist Political Ecologies. Moving Beyond Green Economy. Zed Books. Chicago Distribution Center.

Norton, M. A. (2019). *Testimony before the US-China Economic Security Review Commission Hearing on "An Emerging China-Russia Axis? Implications for the United States in an Era of Strategic Competition"*. Jeanne L. Wilson Shelby Cullom Davis Professor of Russian Studies.

OECD. (1968). Border tax adjustments law. Report of the Working Party adopted on December 2, 1970.

OECD. (1993). *OECD core set of indicators for environmental performance reviews. A synthesis report by the Group on the State of the Environment. OECD Environment Monographs 83*. Paris, France: OECD.

OECD. (2017). *The geography of firm dynamics: measuring business demography for regional development.* Paris, France: OECD. Retrieved from http://dx.dol.org/10.1787/9789264286764-en

Oliveira, J. (2005). *A Educação em Meio Rural como Paleta de Possibilidades para o Desenvolvimento Local: Contributos da Escola do 1º Ciclo do Ensino Básico e do Jardim de Infância* (Unpublished doctoral dissertation). Universidade do Minho, Braga.

Oliveira, F. M., Pestana, E., Vasconcelos, F., Brito, R., Freitas, S., & Mendonça, V. (2014). *Plano de Ação para a Energia Sustentável do Município do Porto Santo*. Município do Porto Santo.

Onuki, J. (2006). O Brasil e a construção do Mercosul. In: H. Altemani, & A. C. Lessa (Eds.), Relações internacionais do Brasil. V. 1. São Paulo, Brazil: Saraiva.

ORGANIZAÇÃO DOS ESTADOS AMERICANOS - OEA. (2009). Aquífero Guarani: programa estratégico de ação =Acuífero Guaraní: programa estatégico de acción. Ed. bilíngue– Brasil; Argentina; Paraguai; Uruguai: Organização dos Estados Americanos (OEA), janeiro 2009.

ORGANIZAÇÃO DOS ESTADOS AMERICANOS – OEA. (s/d). *Síntese Hidrogeológica do Sistema Aquífero Guarani*. Série Manual e Documentos Técnicos do Projeto de Proteção Ambiental e Desenvolvimento Sustentável do Sistema Aquífero Guarani. Montevideo: OEA.

OTALEX C. (2013). *Atlas OTALEX C*. Mérida: Dirección General de Transportes, Ordenación del Territorio y Urbanismo. Consejería de Fomento, Vivienda, Ordenación del territorio y Turismo.

OTALEX C. (2015). *OTALEX C. Historia de un Proyecto Transfronterizo / História de um Projecto Transfronteiriço, 1997 - 2015*. Retrieved from http://www.ideotalex.eu/OtalexC/paginas/Publicacion.jsp

Paasi, A., & Zimmerbauer, K. (2016). Penumbral Borders and Planning Paradoxes: Relational Thinking and the Question of Borders in Spatial Planning. *Environment & Planning A*, *48*(1), 75–93. doi:10.1177/0308518X15594805

Pagliari, G. de C. (2009). *O Brasil e a segurança na América do Sul*. Curitiba: Editora Giruá.

Paine, J. (2019). Democratic Contradictions in European Settler Colonies. *World Politics*, 1–44.

Pardo, T., & Nam, T. Smart city as urban innovation: Focusing on management, policy, and context. In: *Proceedings of the 5th International Conference on Theory and Practice of Electronic Governance*. ACM, 2011

Pascariu, G., & Ibanescu, B. (2018). Determinants and implications of the tourism multiplier effect in EU economies. Towards a core-periphery pattern? *Amfiteatru Economic*, *20*(S12), 982–997. doi:10.24818/EA/2018/S12/982

Peixoto, J. (2007). Dinâmicas e Regimes Migratórios: O Caso das Migrações Internacionais em Portugal. *Analise Social*, *XLII*(183), 445–469.

Peña, F. (2007). Los grandes objetivos del MERCOSUR: zona de libre comercio, unión aduanera y mercado común. In R. A. Barbosa (org.), Mercosul: quinze anos. São Paulo, Brazil: Fundação Memorial da América Latina: Imprensa Oficial do Estado de São Paulo.

Perkman, M. (2003). Cross-border regions in Europe. Significance and drivers of regional cross-border co-operation. *European Urban and Regional Studies*, *10*(2), 153–171. doi:10.1177/0969776403010002004

Perkowski, M. (2010). *Współpraca transgraniczna. Aspekty prawno-ekonomiczne*. Białystok: Fundacja Prawo i Partnerstwo.

Peterson, G. D. (2000). Scaling Ecological Dynamics: Self-Organization, Hierarchical Structure, and Ecological Resistance. *Climatic Change*, *44*(3), 291–309. doi:10.1023/A:1005502718799

PEW Research Centre. (2017). World's Muslim population more widespread than you might think. Retrieved from https://www.pewresearch.org/fact-tank/2017/01/31/worlds-muslim-population-more-widespread-than-you-might-think/

Peyrony, J., & Denert, O. (2012). Planning for Cross-Border Territories: The Role Played by Spatial Information. *Raumforschung und Raumordnung*, *70*(3), 229–240. doi:10.100713147-012-0156-0

Picolo, A. P., Bühler, A. J., & Rampinelli, G. A. (2014). Uma abordagem sobre a energia eólica como alternativa de ensino de tópicos de física clássica. *Revista Brasileira de Ensino de Física*, *36*(4), 4306. doi:10.1590/S1806-11172014000400007

Pilving, T., Kull, T., Suškevics, M., & Viira, A. (2019). The tourism partnership life cycle in Estonia: Striving towards sustainable multisectoral rural tourism collaboration. *Tourism Management Perspectives*, (31), 219-230.

Pina, J. (2011). *O Valor Económico da Língua Portuguesa - Ciclo de Conferências do OLP.* Retrieved from http://observatorio-lp.sapo.pt/pt/temas-de-actualidade/o-valor-economico-da-lingua-portuguesa

Pincha, J. P. (2019). O Porto Santo começa a dizer adeus ao petróleo. Disponível em: https://www.publico.pt/2019/05/27/local/noticia/porto-santo-quer-dizer-adeus-petroleo-1874091

Pinto, M. C. C. (2017). Smart Cities: Cidades Inteligentes em Portugal e o contributo dos SIG para o seu desenvolvimento. Dissertação para obtenção do grau de Mestre em Sistemas de Informação Geográfica e Ordenamento do Território pela Universidade do Porto, Porto.

Pires, I. (2008). *A integração dos mercados ibéricos: um processo dependente e territorialmente diferenciado?* Lisboa, Portugal: Centro de Estudos Geográficos, Universidade de Lisboa.

Portela, J., & Nobre, S. (2001). Entre Pinela e Paris: Emigração e Regressos. *Analise Social, 36*(161), 1105–1146.

Poschen, P. (2015). *Decent Work, Green Jobs, and the Sustainable Economy*. Sheffield, UK: Greenleaf.

Poschke, M. (2013). 'Entrepreneurs out of necessity': A snapshot. *Applied Economics Letters, 20*(7), 7. doi:10.1080/13504851.2012.727968

Preston, B., Brooke, C., Measham, T., Smith, T., & Gorddard, R. (2008). Igniting change in local government: Lessons learned from a bushfire vulnerability assessment. *Mitigation and Adaptation Strategies for Global Change, 14*(3), 251–283. doi:10.100711027-008-9163-4

Pringle, R. W. Jr. (2018). *The Costs of Hidden Involvements. Lindsey A. O'Rourke: Covert Regime Change*. Ithaca, NY: America's Secret Cold War Cornell University Press.

Priorities for 2014-2020. Available at http://ec.europa.eu/regional_policy/pl/policy/how/priorities. June, 16, 2018.

Probst, G., & Büchel, B. S. (1997). *Organizational learning: The competitive advantage of the future*. Prentice Hall.

Project Management Institute. (2000). *A Guide to the Project Management Body of Knowledge* (p. 10).

Prokkola, E. K. (2008). Resources and barriers in tourism development: Cross-border cooperation, regionalization and destination building at the Finnish-Swedish border. *International Journal of Geography, 186*(1), 31–46.

Prokop, M. (2003). Saudi Arabia: The politics of education. *International Affairs, 79*(1), 77–89. doi:10.1111/1468-2346.00296

Público.es (2018). La isla de El Hierro se abastece de energia 100% renovable durante 18 días seguidos. Disponível em: https://www.publico.es/sociedad/renovables-isla-hierro-abastece-energia-100-renovable-18-dias-seguidos.html

Pucci, A. S. (2010). *O Estatuto da fronteira Brasil-Uruguai*. Brasília: Fundação Alexandre de Gusmão. Available in: http://funag.gov.br/biblioteca/download/685-O_estatuto_da_fronteira_brasil_uruguai.pdf

Puyosa, I. (2019). Venezuelan Struggle Towards Democratization: The 2017 Civil Resistance Campaign. In *Civil Resistance and Violent Conflict in Latin America. Studies of the Americas* (pp. 85–110). Cham, Switzerland: Palgrave Macmillan. doi:10.1007/978-3-030-05033-7_5

Raisanen, O. (2019). Canary islands. Disponível em: https://www.bugbog.com/european_cities/spain_travel_guide/canary-islands/

Rebouças, A. C. (2002). Água Doce no Brasil e no Mundo. In *Águas Doces no Brasil. Capital Ecológico, uso e conservação* (pp. 1–37). São Paulo, Brazil: Ed. Escrituras.

Red Eléctrica de Espanã. (2019). Demanda de energía eléctrica em tiempo real. Red Eléctrica de España. Disponível em: https://demanda.ree.es/visiona/canarias/el_hierro/total

Reeder, R., & Brown, D. (2005). Recreation, Tourism, and Rural Well-Being, Retrieved from http://www.ers.usda.gov/publications/err7/err7.pdf

Regio, D. G. (n.d.). Draft implementing acts. List of ETC programmes. Retrieved from http://ec.europa.eu/regional _policy/what/ future/experts _documents_en.cfm#2

REGULATION. (EC) NO 1080/2006 OF THE EUROPEAN PARLIAMENT AND OF THE COUNCIL OF 5 JULY 2006 ON THE EUROPEAN REGIONAL DEVELOPMENT FUND, EUROPEAN TERRITORIAL COOPERATION. Available at http://ewt.slaskie.pl/article/1279787593. August, 1, 2019.

Reitel, B. (2007). Are Cross-Border Urban Spaces European Integration Patterns At Local Level? Analysis of the Management of Urban Areas astride the "French Border". – Borders of the European Union: Strategies of Crossing and Resistance.

Rentschler, R., & Shilbury, D. (2008). Academic assessment of arts management journals: A multidimensional rating survey. *International Journal of Arts Management*, *10*(3), 60–71.

Report from the Commission to the European Parliament, the Council, the European Economic and Social Committee and the Committee of the Regions Concerning the Governance of Macro-Regional Strategies. Brussels. 20.5.2014 Com (2014) 284 Final

Reports, U. S. C. B. C. (2018). *US Exports to China*. Retrieved from https://www.uschina.org/reports/us-exports/national

RIO GRANDE DO SUL. SECRETARIA DA COORDENAÇÃO E PLANEJAMENTO. (2006). Estudo de Desenvolvimento Regional e Logística do Rio Grande do Sul. v. 1-5. Porto Alegre, Secretaria da Coordenação e Planejamento.

Rocha-Trindade, M. (1976). Comunidades Emigrantes em Situação Dipolar: Análise de Três Casos de Emigração Especializada para os E.U.A., para o Brasil e para França. *Análise Social, 12*(48), (4), 983-997.

Rodríguez López, J. (2008). La situación del mercado de vivienda en España. Boletín Económico del ICE (2951), 11-23.

Rodríguez López, J. (2006). *Financiación de la vivienda en un contexto de tipos de interés crecientes*. Lleida: IX Semana de Estudios Urbanos.

Rodríguez, A. R. (2002). Análisis Comparado de las políticas de suelo y vivienda aplicadas en países europeos con fines sociales y ambientales. En el Congreso "La política de vivienda en España desde la perspectiva de otros modelos europeos", Ibiza (España), 30 de Noviembre de 2002. Instituto Juan de Herrera de la Escuela Técnica Superior de Arquitectura de Madrid y La Agencia de Ecología Urbana de Barcelona, que fue dirigido por José Manuel Naredo y Fernando Roch.

Rodríguez-Bolívar, M. P. (2015). Transforming City Governments for Successful Smart Cities. Disponível em: http://link.springer.com/book/10.1007/978-3-319-03167-5

Romania-Serbia, I. P. A. (2014). *CBC Programme 2014 – 2020*. Territorial Analysis SECOND DRAFT.

Romero, A. (2004). "Migraciones". En Tendencias Demográficas durante el siglo XX en España. Instituto Nacional de Estadística, 207-253.

Roseira, A. M. (2011). *Nova ordem sul-americana: reorganização geopolítica do espaço mundial e projeção internacional do Brasil*. Thesis. São Paulo, Brazil: USP. Available in: http://www.teses.usp.br/teses/disponiveis/8/8136/tde-14122012-094017/pt-br.php.

Rubio de Juan, M. A. (2006). *Flujos de inversión de no residentes en inmuebles residenciales. Flujos de inversión de residentes en inmuebles residenciales fuera de España*. Estudios y Publicaciones del Ministerio de la Vivienda en España.

Ruschmann, D. (2008). *Turismo e planejamento sustentável: a proteção do meio ambiente*. São Paulo, Brazil: Papirus Editora.

Ruzic, P., & Demonja, D. (2017). Transformations in business & economics. *Economic Impacts of Rural Tourism in Rural Areas of Istria*, *16*(3), 31–40.

Saayman, M., & Saayman, A. (2006). Estimating the Economic Contribution of Visitor Spending in the Kruger National Park to the Regional Economy. *Journal of Sustainable Tourism*, *14*(1), 67–81. doi:10.1080/09669580608668592

Sabucedo, J. M., & Fernádez, C. (1998). Universidad de Santiago de Compostela. Nacionalismos e Ideología. Un análisis psicosocial. *Psicología Política*, (17): 7–19.

Sack, R. D. (1980). *Conceptions of Space in Social Thought: A Geographic Perspective*. London, UK: Macmillan. doi:10.1007/978-1-349-16433-2

Sánchez Vera, P., & Riella, A. (2010). Globalización y perspectivas de la integración regional. Murcia: edit.um.

Sánchez, V., Fernandez, M., & Lara, J. (2017). Economic impact of a religious and tourist event: A holy week celebration. *Tourism Economics*, *23*(6), 1255–1274. doi:10.1177/1354816616675996

Santos, R. (2013). *O regresso dos emigrantes portugueses e o desenvolvimento do turismo em Portugal.* (Unpublished doctoral dissertation). University of Aveiro, Aveiro.

Sassen, S. (2013). When territory Deborders Territoriality. *Territory, Politics, Governance: An International Journal of Policy, Administration and Institutions, 1*(1), 21–45.

Scanlon, K., Lunde, J., & Whitehead, C. (2008). En respuesta a las viviendas y crisis financieras: Préstamos hipotecarios, productos de hipotecas y las políticas del gobierno. *Revista Internacional de Política de Vivienda, 11*(1), 23–49.

Scheibe, E. F. (2018). *IIRSA and the role assigned to the La Plata Basin region in South American physical integration.* In A. P. Cargnin et al., *Territorial Planning and La Plata Basin Borders.* Porto Alegre, Letra 1. Available in https://editoraletra1.com.br/epub/9788563800350/

Schrenk, M., & Pozarek, W. (2007). *Centrope MAP: Combining X-Border Information from Multiple Sources for Planning Purposes. Information Fusion and Geographic Information Systems. Lecture Notes in Geoinformation and Cartography* (pp. 96–110). Berlin, Germany: Springer.

Schroeder, J. E. (2005). The artist and the brand. *European Journal of Marketing, 39*(11/12), 1291–1305. doi:10.1108/03090560510623262

Schumpeter, J. (1934). *The theory of economic development.* Harvard University Press.

Scott, J. (1999). European and North American Contexts for Cross-Border Regionalism. *Regional Studies, 33*(7), 605–617. doi:10.1080/00343409950078657

Servicio Público de Empleo Estatal. Retrieved from http://www.sepe.es

Seung-Hyun, L., Shenkar, O., & Li, J. (2008). Cultural distance, investment flow, and control in cross-border cooperation. *Strategic Management Journal, 29*(10), 1117–1125. doi:10.1002mj.685

Shariatinia, M., & Azizi, H. (2017). Iran–China Cooperation in the Silk Road Economic Belt: From Strategic Understanding to Operational Understanding. *China & World Economy, 25*(5), 46–61. doi:10.1111/cwe.12213

Sharpley, R., & Vass, A. (2006). Tourism, Farming and Diversification: An Attitudinal Study. *Tourism Management, 27*(5), 1040–1052. doi:10.1016/j.tourman.2005.10.025

Shiell, T. (2014, April). Who Cares about Carbon Leakage? The Economics of Border Tax Adjustments under Incomplete Climate Treaties. Department of Economics Faculty of Social Sciences University of Ottawa. Working Paper, #1403. pp. 1-22.

Sica, D. (2007). Mercosur: Evolución y perspectivas. In: R. A Barbosa (org.), Mercosul: quinze anos. São Paulo, Fundação Memorial da América Latina, Imprensa Oficial do Estado de São Paulo.

Siddiqui, K. (2019). The US Dollar and the World Economy: A Critical Review. *Athens Journal of Business & Economics.*

Sielker, F. (2016). A Stakeholder-Based Eu Territorial Cooperation: The Example of European Macro-Regions. European Planning Studies. Doi: Http://Dx.Doi.Org/10.1080/09654313.2016.1221383

Silberberg, T. (1995). Cultural Tourism and Business Opportunities for Museums and Heritage Sites. *Tourism Management, 16*(5), 361–365. doi:10.1016/0261-5177(95)00039-Q

Silva, J. A., Barroso, R. C., Rodrigues, A. J., Costa, S., & Fontana, R. L. (2014). *A urbanização no mundo contemporâneo e os problemas ambientais*. Cadernos de Graduação – Ciências Humanas e Sociais. 2(2), 197-207. Disponível em https://periodicos.set.edu.br/index.php/cadernohumanas/article/view/1723/964

Silva, M., Amaro, R., Clausse, G., Conim C., Matos, M., Pisco, M. & Seruya, L. (1984). *Regresso, Emigração e Desenvolvimento Regional em Portugal*. Lisboa, Portugal: Instituto de Estudos para o Desenvolvimento.

Silva, J. A. (1992). *Curso de Direito Constitucional Positivo* (8th ed.). São Paulo, Brazil: Malheiros.

Silva, R. B. G. (2003). *Águas Subterrâneas: um valioso recurso que requer proteção*. São Paulo, Brazil: DAEE.

Simo, B. (2017) The Analysis Of Absorption Capacity Of Project Beneficiaries Contributing To Cross-Border Programmes Based On The Most Fundamental Criteria. *APSTRACT: Applied Studies in Agribusiness and Commerce, 10*(1033-2017-145), pp. 100-93.

Simões, A. J. F. (2011). *Brasil e Uruguai sob o signo da solidariedade e do pragmatismo*. In: *Brasil-Uruguai: os próximos 20 anos*. Brasília, Fundação Alexandre de Gusmão. Available in: http://funag.gov.br/biblioteca/index.php?route=product/product&product_id=216&search=Brasil-Uruguai%3A+os+pr%C3%B3ximos+20+anos

Sindico, F., Hirata, R., & Manganelli, A. (2018). The Guarani Aquifer System: From a Beacon of hope to a question mark in the governance of transboundary aquifers. *Journal of Hydrology: Regional Studies, 20*, 40–49.

Singh, A., Jamasab, T., Nepal, R., & Toman, M. (2018). Electricity Cooperation in South Asia: Barriers to cross-border trade. *Energy Policy, 120*(c), 741–748. doi:10.1016/j.enpol.2017.12.048

Slawinski, N., & Bansal, T. (2012). A matter of time: The temporal perspectives of organizational responses to climate change. *Organization Studies, 33*(11), 1537–1563. doi:10.1177/0170840612463319

Smith, N. (2000). Scale. In R. J. Johnston, D. Gregory, G. Pratts, & M. Watts (Eds.), *The Dictionary in Human Geography* (pp. 724–727). Oxford, UK: Blackwell.

Smith, R. G. (2003). World city topologies. *Progress in Human Geography, 27*(5), 561–582. doi:10.1191/0309132503ph447oa

Snyman, S. (2013). Household spending patterns and flow of ecotourism income into communities around Liwonde National Park, Malawi. *Development Southern Africa, 30*(4-5), 640–658. doi:10.1080/0376835X.2013.832149

Soares, G. F. S. (2003a). *A proteção internacional do Meio Ambiente*. Barueri, SP: Manole.

Soares, G. F. S. (2003b). *Direito Internacional do Meio Ambiente. Emergências, obrigações e responsabilidades* (2nd ed.). São Paulo, Brazil: Atlas.

Sohn, C., & Giffinger, R. (2015). A policy network approach to cross-border metropolitan governance: The cases of Vienna and Bratislava. *European Planning Studies, 23*(6), 1187–1208. doi:10.1080/09654313.2014.994089

Sohn, C., Reitel, B., & Walther, O. (2009). Cross-Border Metropolitan Integration in Europe: The Case of Luxembourg, Basel and Geneva. *Environment and Planning. C, Government & Policy, 27*(5), 922–939. doi:10.1068/c0893r

South Asian Association for Regional Cooperation. (2019). SAARC. Retrieved from http://saarc-sec.org/

Souza-Fernandes, L. C., & Oliveira, E. (2018). Coletânea da legislação brasileira de águas subterrâneas. 5 v. São Paulo: IAS.

Souza, L. C. (2009). *Águas subterrâneas e a legislação brasileira*. Curitiba: Juruá.

Spicer, A. (2006). Beyond the convergence-divergence debate: The role of spatial scales in transforming organizational logic. Organization Studies, (27), 10, 1,467-1,483.

Spirkova, D., & Ivanicka, K. (2009). Dynamics of Bratislava urban and housing development. In T. Panagoupolos (Ed.), *New models for innovative management and urban dynamics* (pp. 37–52). Faro, Portugal: University of Algarve.

Srinivasan, P. V. (2012). Regional Cooperation and Integration through Cross-Border Infrastructure Development. Asian Development Bank. *South Asia Working Paper Series No. 14.*

Staff, SPIEGEL. (2015). *SPIEGEL Targeted By US Intelligence.*

Steinbock, D. (2012). The Eurozone debt crisis: Prospects for Europe, China, and the United States. *American Foreign Policy Interests, 34*(1), 34–42. doi:10.1080/10803920.2012.653719

Stephan, R. M. (2009). *Transboundary aquifers. Managing a vital resource*. Paris, France: UNESCO.

Stephen, P. (2015). Potential Economic contribution of regional tourism development in China: A comparative analysis. *International Journal of Tourism Research, 17*(3), 303–312. doi:10.1002/jtr.1990

Storey, J. (2003). *Cultural Studies and the Study of Popular Culture*. Athens, GA: University of Georgia Press.

Stromer-Galley, J. (2019). *Presidential Campaigning in the Internet Age*. New York: Oxford University Press. doi:10.1093/oso/9780190694043.001.0001

Studzieniecki, T. (2005). Euroregions - new potential destinations. *Tourism Review*, *60*(4), 26–32. doi:10.1108/eb058463

Suárez, J. L. (2016). Proyección de las necesidades de vivienda en España. IESE Business School.

Sugunakararaju, S. R. T. P., & Akhtar, S. (2015). India-Pakistan Relations: Challenges and Opportunities. *Journal of the Humanities and Social Sciences*, *20*(12), 7–12.

Suresh, K., Tiwari, A., Uddin, G., & Ahmed, A. (2018). Tourism, trade, and economic growth in India: a frequency-domain analysis of causality. *Anatolia – International Journal of Tourism and Hospitality Research*, *29*(3), 319-325.

Szromnik, A. (2010). Marketing terytorialny. Oficyna Wydawnicza Wolters. Warsaw, Poland: Kluwer.

Tàbara, J. D., Cots, F., Pedde, S., Hölscher, K., Kok, K., Lovanova, A., & ... Frantzeskaki, NEtherington, J. (2018). Exploring Institutional Transformations to Address High-End Climate Change in Iberia. *Sustainability*, *10*(2), 161. doi:10.3390u10010161

Tallberg, J. (2008). Bargaining power in the European Council. *Journal of Common Market Studies*, *46*(3), 685–708. doi:10.1111/j.1468-5965.2008.00798.x

TG-WeB. (2018). *Position paper on territorial governance in the Western Balkans*. The Western Balkans Network on Territorial Governance.

Thrift, N. (1995). A hyperactive world. In R. J. Johnston, P. Taylor, & M. Watts (Eds.), *Geographies of global change: remapping the world in the late twentieth century* (pp. 18–35). Oxford, UK: Blackwell.

Timothy, D. J. (2009). Cross-Border Partnership in Tourism Resource Management: International Parks along the US-Canada Border. *Journal of Sustainable Tourism*, *7*(3-4), 182–205. doi:10.1080/09669589908667336

Tohamy, S., & Swinscoe, A. (2000). *The Economic Impact of Tourism in Egypt*, Retrieved from http://www.eces.org.eg/MediaFiles/Uploaded_Files/%7B02ADE2E4-F995-4CDE-82CE 32BB9A4A15E9%7D_ECESPVP5e.pdf

Tohmo, T. (2018). The economic impact of tourism in Central Finland: A regional input-output study. *Tourism Review*, *73*(4), 521–547. doi:10.1108/TR-04-2017-0080

Tokatlian, J. G. (2008). *O Cone Sul e suas relações internacionais*: *um espaço de cooperação para a América do Sul*. São Paulo, *Revista Política Externa, Paz e Terra 17*(1).

Torrero Mañas, A. (2010). La crisis financiera y sus efectos sobre la economía española. Universidad de Alcalá de Henares.

Tribe, J. (2015). *The economics of recreation, leisure and tourism*. UK: Routledge. doi:10.4324/9781315769233

Trujillo, J. (2016). Un nacionalismo más allá de las fronteras: La transnacionalización del movimiento independentista catalán. *Anuari del conflicto social. Sección*, *1*, 90–117.

UNCED. (1992). Programa 21. Documentos oficiales de la Cumbre de la Tierra. Río de Janeiro, Brazil: UN. Retrieved from https://sustainabledevelopment.un.org/milestones/unced

UNESCO. (2009). *Atlas of transboundary aquifers. Global maps, regional cooperation and local inventories*. Paris, France: UNESCO.

United Nations Industrial Development Organization – UNIDO. (2015). Programa de Capacitação em Energias Renováveis: Energia e Mudanças Climáticas – Módulo Teórico. Observatório de Energias Renováveis para a América Latina e o Caribe.

UNSDP. (2019). Sustainable Development Goals Knowledge Platform. Retrieved from https://sustainabledevelopment.un.org/sdgs

Urbano, D., & Aparicio, S. (2016). Entrepreneurship capital types and economic growth: International evidence. *Technological Forecasting and Social Change*, *102*, 34–44. doi:10.1016/j.techfore.2015.02.018

URUGUAY. ADMINISTRAÇÃO NACIONAL DE PUERTOS (ANP) (2019). *Institutional site*.

Van Hamme, G., & Pion, G. (2012). The relevance of the world-system approach in the era of globalization of economic flows and networks. *Geografiska Annaler. Series B, Human Geography*, *94*(1), 65–82. doi:10.1111/j.1468-0467.2012.00396.x

Van Huisseling, D. W. M., & Mora Aliseda, J. (n.d.). *Movimientos secesionistas en la Unión Europea*. Mauritius: Editorial Académica Española

Van Tulder, R. (2018). *Business & The Sustainable Development Goals: A Framework for Effective Corporate Involvement*. Rotterdam, The Netherlands: Rotterdam School of Management, Erasmus University.

Van Tulder, R., & Keen, N. (2018). Capturing Collaborative Challenges: Designing Complexity-Sensitive Theories of Change for Cross-Sector Partnership. *Journal of Business Ethics*, *150*(2), 315–332. doi:10.100710551-018-3857-7 PMID:30996500

Vanegas, M., & Croes, R. (2003). Growth, Development and Tourism in a Small Economy: Evidence from Aruba. *International Journal of Tourism Research*, (5): 315–330.

Varoufakis, Y. (2017). *Adults in the room: My battle with Europe's deep establishment*. Random House.

Vas, G., & Frías, M. (2019). Aplicación de los procesos de cooperación como instrumento para la configuración de un destino turístico a escala regional y local. *Investigaciones Turísticas*, (17): 103–125.

Veemaa, J. (2012). Internationalizing the spatial identity of cross-border cooperation. *European Planning Studies Journal*, *20*(10), 1647–1666. doi:10.1080/09654313.2012.713335

Veiga, P. da M., & Rios, S. P. (1977). Tratado de Cooperação para o Aproveitamento dos Recursos Naturais e o Desenvolvimento da Bacia da Lagoa Mirim (Tratado da Bacia da Lagoa Mirim). Divisão de Atos Internacionais do Ministério das Relações Exteriores do Brasil.

Veiga, P. da M., & Rios, S. P. (2011). *O Brasil como vetor de integração sul- americana: possibilidades e limites*. São Paulo, Brazil. *Revista Política Externa, Paz e Terra, 20*(2).

Veiga, P. da M., & Rios, S. P. (2013). *Estratégia Nacional de Segurança Pública nas Fronteiras (ENAFRON)*. Secretaria Nacional de Segurança Pública do Ministério da Justiça. Presentation. Available in https://www2.camara.leg.br/atividade-legislativa/comissoes/comissoes-permanentes/credn/audiencias-publicas/2011/acompanhar-e-esclarecer-as-acoes-e-dificuldades-encontradas-para-prover-a-devida-protecao-as-fronteiras-brasileiras-1/apresentacao-enafron

Veretekhina, S., Shinkareva, O., Kozhaev, J., Telepchenkova, N., Kuznetsova, E. & Plekhanov, N. (2017). Evaluation methodology of the multiplier effect for the Region as the result of the cluster formation. *Eurasian Journal of Analytical Chemistry*, (12), 533-547.

Verheugen, G., & Barnier, M. (2000). Practical guide to cross border corporation (3rd ed.). Association of European Border Regions: European Commission. Retrieved from https://www.aebr.eu/files/publications/lace_guide.en.pdf

Vulevic, A., Macura, D., Djordjevic, D., & Castanho, R. (2018). Assessing accessibility and transport infrastructure inequities in administrative units in Serbia's Danube corridor based on multi-criteria analysis and GIS mapping tools. *Transylvanian Review of Administrative Sciences*, *53*(53 E), 123–142. doi:10.24193/tras.53E.8

Walmsley, D. (2003). Rural Tourism: A Case of Lifestyle-Led Opportunities. *The Australian Geographer*, *34*(1), 61–72. doi:10.1080/00049180320000066155

Weber, R. H. (2015). Border tax adjustment – legal perspective. Springer. *Climatic Change*, *133*(3), 407–417. doi:10.100710584-015-1414-2

Weitzel, M., & Peterson, S. (2012). Border Carbon Adjustments: Not a Very Promising Climate Policy Instrument. Kiel Policy Brief. no 55.

Werpachowski, L. (2014). Regionalna współpraca transgraniczna na Śląsku Cieszyńskim. Doświadczenia i perspektywy, in Kasperek, A. (Ed.), Euroregion Śląsk Cieszyński – Těšínské Slezsko. Współpraca transgraniczna i międzyregionalna prowadzona w obszarze trójstyku polsko-czesko-słowackiego. Cieszyn-Katowice: Polska Akademia Nauk Oddział w Katowicach-Stowarzyszenie Rozwoju i Współpracy Regionalnej "Olza", pp. 15-25.

Wiesner, C. (2019). Inventing the EU: But as a Democratic Polity or a Balance of Powers? In *Inventing the EU as a Democratic Polity* (pp. 85–96). Cham, Switzerland: Palgrave Macmillan. doi:10.1007/978-3-319-94415-9_6

Wikipedia. (2019a). Madeira archipelago. Disponível em: https://commons.wikimedia.org/wiki/File:Madeira_archipelago.png

Wilbanks, T., & Kate, R. W. (1999). Global change in local places: How scale matters. *Climatic Change*, *43*(3), 601–628. doi:10.1023/A:1005418924748

Wilke, E., Costa, B., Freire, O., & Ferreira, M. (2019). Interorganizational cooperation in tourist destination: Building performance in the hotel industry. *Tourism Management*, *72*, 340–351. doi:10.1016/j.tourman.2018.12.015

Williams, A. (1984). Introduction. In A. Williams (Ed.), *Southern Europe Transformed- Political and Economic Change in Greece* (pp. 1–32). Italy, Portugal and Spain: Harpercollins College Div.

Winchester, N., Paltsev, S., & Reilly, J. (2010). Will border carbon adjustments work? MIT Joint Program on the Science and Policy of Global Change. Report no. 184, 1-22.

Wong, P., Ho, Y., & Autio, E. (2002). Entrepreneurship, innovation and economic growth: Evidence from GEM data. *Small Business Economics*, *24*(3), 335–350. doi:10.100711187-005-2000-1

Woolley, J. (2013). The creation and configuration of infrastructure for entrepreneurship in emerging domains of activity. *Entrepreneurship Theory and Practice*, *38*(4), 1042–2587.

World Bank. (2019). *World Bank national accounts data, and OECD National Accounts data files*. Retrieved from https://data.worldbank.org/indicator/NY.GDP.MKTP.KD.ZG

World Bank. Ecofys & Vivid Economics. (2016). State and trends of carbon pricing. Washington, DC: International Bank for Reconstruction and Development/The World Bank.

World Urbanization Prospects, U. N. (2012). Disponível em: https://esa.un.org/unpd/wpp/publications/Files/WPP2012_HIGHLIGHTS.pdf

World Urbanization Prospects, U. N. (2014). Disponível em: https://population.un.org/wup/Publications/Files/WUP2014-Highlights.pdf

World Urbanization Prospects, U. N. (2018). Disponível em: https://population.un.org/wup/Publications/Files/WUP2018-Highlights.pdf

Wróblewski, Ł. (2014). Wpływ kultury i przemysłów kultury na wizerunek Euroregionu Śląsk Cieszyński, in Kasperek, A. (Ed.), Euroregion Śląsk Cieszyński – Těšínské Slezsko. Współpraca transgraniczna i międzyregionalna prowadzona w obszarze trójstyku polsko-czesko-słowackiego, Cieszyn-Katowice: Polska Akademia Nauk Oddział w Katowicach-Stowarzyszenie Rozwoju i Współpracy Regionalnej „Olza", pp. 37-82.

Wróblewski, Ł., Dacko-Pikiewicz, Z., & Cuyler, A. (2017). The European Union consumer behaviour in the festivals market in Poland. *Polish Journal of Management Studies*, *16*(2), 302–314. doi:10.17512/pjms.2017.16.2.26

Wróblewski, Ł., Dziadzia, B., & Dacko-Pikiewicz, Z. (2018). Sustainable Management of the Offer of Cultural Institutions in the Cross-Border Market for Cultural Services - Barriers and Conditions. *Sustainability, 10*(9), 3253. doi:10.3390u10093253

Wróblewski, Ł., & Kasperek, A. (2019). Euroregion as an Entity Stimulating the Sustainable Development of the Cross-Border Market for Cultural Services in a City Divided by a Border. *Sustainability, 11*(8), 2232. doi:10.3390u11082232

Xiao, H., Cheng, J., & Wang, X. (2018). Does the Belt and Road Initiative Promote Sustainable Development? Evidence from Countries along the Belt and Road. *Sustainability, 10*(12), 4370. doi:10.3390u10124370

Xing, L. (2019). China's Pursuit of the "One Belt One Road" Initiative: A New World Order with Chinese Characteristics? In *Mapping China's 'One Belt One Road' Initiative* (pp. 1–27). Cham, Switzerland: Palgrave Macmillan. doi:10.1007/978-3-319-92201-0_1

Yashalova, N., Akimova, M., & Aleksandrovich, R. (2017). Prospects for regional development of industrial tourism in view of the analysis of the main economic indicators of Russian tourism industry. *Economic and Social Changes-Facts Trends, 10*(2), 195–213.

Yesavdar, U., Belgibayav, A., & Mersakylova, G. (2016). The role of developing direction of international tourism in Kazakhstan. *Bulletin of the National Academy of Sciences of the Republic of Kazakhstan*, (2), 180-185.

Yu, M. (2019). Introduction to the special issue on understanding the current China-US 'Trade War'. *China Economic Journal, 12*(2), 97–99. doi:10.1080/17538963.2019.1616919

Zafiropoulou, M., Theodosiou, A., & Papakonstantinou, A. (2015). *Discourse analysis report of official and political documents for Greece: Public discourse analysis of the Greek crisis: the case of Greek politicians' perceptions of the Germans and Readers' online comments about Chancellor Merkel's visits to Athens*, FRAGMEX Research Programme Report.

Zamarriego, L. (2017) *Los nacionalismos, de uno u otro signo, siempre tratan de escribir la historia a su manera.* Retrieved from https://ethic.es/entrevistas/los-nacionalismos-uno-u-signo-siempre-tratan-escribir-la-historia-manera/

Zhang, Y., & Feng, W. (2019). Deng Xiaoping and China's Reform and Opening-Up. In *Peaceful Development Path in China.* Singapore: Springer. doi:10.1007/978-981-13-1439-1_2

Zyikov, A. A., & Sevastianov, S. V. (2015). Transborder Relations. In Introduction to Border Studies (118-138). Vladivostok, Russia: Far Eastern Federal University.

About the Contributors

Julián Mora Aliseda in Regional Geographical Analysis. Some of the subjects or research lines executed at the University of Extremadura have been, or are the following: Spatial Planning, Town Planning, Sustainable Development, Strategic Planning and Cross-border Cooperation, etc. He participated as a member or main researcher within 64 Competitive R+D+I Research Projects, financed with public calls and other diverse ¨non-competitive¨ projects with administrations and other public and private entities. Regarding the scientific production, at a quantitative level, stands out the publication of 80 projects, as a supervisor, coordinator and/or writing the books, chapters of boos or articles within university magazines and 104 of papers published within congresses, conferences and Seminars.

José Cabezas is a professor and researcher in ecology and land management.

Antonio Cargnin is Director of Department of Governmental Planning (DEPLAN) of Secretariat of Planning, Budget and Management of State Government of Rio Grande do Sul – Brazil. Fellow Professor of Programa de Pós-Graduação em Geografia (POSGEA) at Universidade Federal do Rio Grande do Sul (UFRGS). Researcher of Laboratório Estado e Território (LABETER) - POSGEA/UFRGS.

Cristina Carriço since 2008 is senior technician in the Environment and Development Unit of CIMAC, a public service entity that groups the 14 municipalities of the Central Alentejo region. Working on cross-border cooperation projects where stands out OTALEX project. Involved in indicators group (environmental and sustainability), data harmonization between the portuguese regions of Alentejo and Centro and spanish Extremadura, and in the creation of Territorial Observatory. Nowadays managing the implementation of 1130 km of walking and cycling paths, the “Montado Great Route”, a project wich connect allthe municipalities of Central Alentejo.

Rui Alexandre Castanho holds an International Ph.D. on Sustainable Urban Planning in Transboundary Areas. Collaborates with the Environmental Resources Analysis Research Group (ARAM) - University of Extremadura (UEx); VALORIZA - Research Center for the Enhancement of Endogenous Resources, Polytechnic Institute of Portalegre (IPP), Portugal; ICAAM—Institute for Agrarian and Environmental Sciences, Évora, Portugal; and CITUR - Madeira - Centre for Tourism Research, Development and Innovation, Madeira, Portugal. He has Graduated in Green Spaces Engineering and Agricultural Engineering, and has a Master´s Degree in Planning, Audit and Control in Urban Green Spaces. Nowadays, he´s a Professor on the WSB University, Poland and the Coordinator of International Relations on the Research Institute on Territorial Cooperation and Inter-Organizational Cooperation.

Betina Cavaco de São Pedro has a Degree in Mathematics, Master in Local Development and PhD. Student in Territorial Planning. University of Extremadura.

Fernando Ceballos - Arquitecto, Ha desempeñado diversos cargos en la Administración Regional de la Junta de Extremadura desde hace más de 30 años, siempre en las temáticas de Ordenación del Territorio y Urbanismo.

Luciana Cordeiro de Souza-Fernandes - Doutora e Mestre em Direito – área de Direitos Difusos: Direito Ambiental - pela Pontifícia Universidade Católica de São Paulo. Especialista em Direito Processual Civil e em Direito Penal e Processual Penal. Professora de Direito da Faculdade de Ciências Aplicadas da Universidade Estadual de Campinas- FCA/UNICAMP e do Programa de Pós Graduação em Ensino e História das Ciências da Terra (PEHCT) do Instituto de Geociências da UNICAMP. Líder do Grupo de Pesquisa CNPQ Aquageo Ambiente Legal. Titular da Cadeira n. 9 da academia Jundiaiense de Letras Jurídicas. Advogada, Parecerista e Consultora Ambiental. Sócia Fundadora da Associação dos Professores de Direito Ambiental do Brasil – APRODAB. Foi Titular da Comissão Estadual de Logística, Infraestrutura e Desenvolvimento Sustentável da OABSP (2017-2019). Foi Assessora da Diretoria Jurídica da Companhia de Desenvolvimento Habitacional e Urbano do Estado de São Paulo (CDHU) na área de Direito Ambiental e Urbanístico. Foi Diretora de Habitação do Município de Jundiaí – SP. Representou o Brasil como Especialista Legal junto ao Projeto Sistema Aquífero Guarani em Montevidéu - Uruguai. Criou e coordenou, de 2007 a 2013, os cursos de Pós Graduação Lato Sensu em Direito Ambiental e em Direito Imobiliário no UNIANCHIETA. Autora das obras: "Águas e sua proteção" e "Águas subterrâneas e a Legislação Brasileira" pela Editora Juruá; do livro "Instituições de Direito" (no prelo) pela Editora Saraiva; co-organizadora das obras "I Simpósio de Direito Ambiental da APRODAB"; "Direito ambiental, recursos hídricos e saneamento"; "Geoparque Corumbataí. Primeiros passos de um projeto de desenvolvimento regional"; "Programa Aquífero Guarani"; e da "Coletânea de Legislação das Águas Subterrâneas do Brasil"- 5 volumes; e dos livros infantis de educação ambiental para água: "Clara: uma gotinha d'água" (traduzido para espanhol, inglês e francês), "Clara e a reciclagem", "Clara e as águas invisíveis", "Clara e a água do dia a dia" e "Clara e os rios voadores" (no prelo); além de inúmeros capítulos de livros e artigos em periódicos nacionais e internacionais com a temática água. Currículo lattes: http://lattes.cnpq.br/9687583143146959 E-mail: lucord@unicamp.br Site: https://www.aquageoambientelegal.com/

Paulo Ferreira is currently a professor at the Escola Superior Agrária de Elvas, Instituto Politécnico de Portalegre. He is also researcher at VALORIZA and CEFAGE-UÉ, with works mainly devoted to the analysis of the behavior of financial markets, an area where he has published several articles in scientific journals. He holds a degree in Economics and a PhD in Management, and is the author of other technical books.

Sema Yilmaz Genc is Assoc. Prof., Kocaeli University, Kocaeli Vocational School, Head of Department of Marketing and Advertising, Turkey

José Manuel Naranjo Gómez is PhD in Geodesy and Cartography (2015); an engineer in Geodesy and Cartography (2002) and Engineer Surveying (1999) by the University of Extremadura. He works as a professor for the University of Extremadura since 2002 and researches in the fields of sustainability, transport infrastructure and territorial accessibility.

Farooq Haq is an Associate Professor and the Chair of Marketing & International Business Program at the Canadian University Dubai. He received his PhD from Charles Darwin University in Australia in 2011. His research interests are in spiritual tourism, Islamic Marketing, halal branding and marketing of Islamic products and services. He has published in various journal articles, conference papers and book chapters in his areas of research.

Joanna Kurowska-Pysz has a Ph.D. in economics and management, WSB University in Dąbrowa Górnicza Poland · Faculty of Applied Sciences. Director of Research - Institute on Territorial and Inter-Organizational Cooperation, Akademia WSB / WSB University in Dąbrowa Górnicza, Poland Email: jkurowska@wsb.edu.pl https://www.researchgate.net/profile/Joanna_Pysz https://scholar.google.pl/citations?user=1KT3VGkAAAAJ&hl=pl http://orcid.org/0000-0002-3967-9263

Bruno Lemos - M. S. in Geography by Universidade Federal do Rio Grande do Sul (UFRGS). Geographer of technical-scientific career of Rio Grande do Sul State Government working at Secretaria do Planejamento, Governança e Gestão (SPGG). Researcher of Laboratório Estado e Território (LABETER), of Programa de Pós-Graduação em Geografia (POSGEA) at Universidade Federal do Rio Grande do Sul (UFRGS).

Luís Loures is a Landscape Architect and Agronomic Engineer, Vice-President of the Polytechnic Institute of Portalegre, who holds a Ph.D. in Planning and a Post-Doc in Agronomy. Since he graduated he has published several per reviewed papers at the national and international levels and he has been a guest researcher and lecturer both at Michigan State University (USA), and at University of Toronto (Canada) where he has developed part of his Ph.D. research with the Financial support from the Portuguese Foundation for Science and Technology (Ph.D. grant). During his academic career he had teach in several courses in different Universities including the University of Trás-os-Montes e Alto Douro, Letterkenny Institute of Technology – Ireland, and the University of Algarve, mainly regarding the fields of landscape architecture, urban and environmental planning and sustainability. Currently, He is a researcher both at the CIEO - Research Centre for Spatial and Organizational Dynamics – University of Algarve, and the C3I - Interdisciplinary Research Centre for Innovation - Polytechnic Institute of Portalegre, where he is a researcher on several financed research projects focusing several different investigation domains such as urban planning, landscape reclamation and urban redevelopment, and the use of urban planning as a tool for achieving sustainable development.

Sérgio António Neves Lousada is a Civil Engineering with a Ph.D. in Civil Engineering, area of knowledge in Hydraulics. He teaches at the University of Madeira, Faculty of Exact Sciences and Engineering in Civil Engineering course, major field of Hydraulics, Environment and Water Resources and secondary area of Construction. Nowadays he is course director of the 1st Cycle in Civil Engineering, according to the statement of the Scientific Council of the Faculty of Exact Sciences and Engineering at the University of Madeira. Develops, since 2012, research in Hydraulic sciences, particularly in the areas of Hydraulics, Urban Hydraulics and Marine and Fluvial Construction. He has published some articles, books and participated in events mainly in the areas of Hydraulics, Urban Planning and Land Management.

Anita Medhekar is an economist and holds a PhD from Deakin University. She has taught at undergraduate and post graduate levels in India, Indonesia and Australia. Currently, she is teaching at Central Queensland University, Rockhampton,

Australia. Her research interest are in micro and macroeconomics, international trade, development economics, public finance, South-Asia, health economics, tourism economics, spiritual tourism, trade and development for peace, public policy, and public and private partnerships. She has presented papers at numerous international conferences and has many publications to her credit as refereed conference proceedings, book chapters, and journal articles. http://orcid.org/0000-0002-6791-4056

Aldomar Rückert - Full Professor at Universidade Federal do Rio Grande do Sul, Porto Alegre, RS, Brasil. Undergraduate in Geography from Universidade Regional do Noroeste do Estado do Rio Grande do Sul (1978); Social Studies from Universidade Regional do Noroeste do Estado do Rio Grande do Sul (1974), Master Degree in Geography from Universidade Estadual Paulista Júlio de Mesquita Filho (1991) and Doctor in Sciences: Human Geography from Universidade de São Paulo (2002). CNPq Researcher since 2010. Experienced in Geography, focusing on Political Geography and Regional Planning, acting on the following subjects: State and territory; territorial policies, border regions; regional planning. Member of the scientific committees of CIST - Collège International des Sciences du Territoire - Universités Paris 1 Panthéon Sorbonne and 7 - Denis Diderot and Confins and L'Espace Politique journals. https://orcid.org/0000-0003-0616-6661

Rossana Santos is full time teacher at Superior School of Technologies and Management of University of Madeira. Currently, she is course director of the 1st cycle in Hotel Management and Administration. She holds a Ph.D. in Tourism and is integrated member of CITUR Madeira – Center for Research, Development and Innovation in Tourism. She has graduated in Tourism and has a Master's degree in Tourism Management and Development.

Yeşim Pınar Sarıca is an Associate Professor at Işık University, Management Department, Istanbul/Turkey. Her research areas are labour relations and social politics. She conducted funded scientific research projects on fields like employee and industrial relations in Turkey and microcredits for women. She has also worked as a short-term consultant with FSWW (the Foundation for the Support of Women's Work). She has several articles in national and international journals and is the author of books and book chapters in the field.

Asli Tasbasi is an Associate Professor of Economics and the Co-chair of the Social Policy Research Center at Işık University. Her research focuses on international economics, particularly on international trade and its environmental extensions. Her undergraduate, master's and Ph.D. degrees are from Istanbul University, Yildiz Technical University, and Marmara University, respectively. Awarded with a TUBITAK scholarship, she conducted research at the Department of Economics, Lund University, Sweden during her PhD studies. Dr. Taşbaşı also received a UNESCO grant for her research on international trade policy. She has authored several articles, book chapters and edited two books in the field.

Demi Wilhelmina Maria van Huisseling is Graduated in Geography and Spatial Planning at the University of Extremadura (UEx), Spain. She is specialized in European Studies and has coursed a Jean Monnet course on Constitutional Right of the European Union. She is has also coursed a Expert course on Town Planning in Extremadura and is working as technical ressearch support at the Research Group for Regional Development - at the Univerity of Extremadura (UEx)

Jacinto Garrido Velarde - PhD. in Graphic Expression with European mention from the University of Extremadura. Assistant Professor at the University of Extremadura. Specialist in Geographical Information Systems (GIS), Remote Sensing, Urban Planning and Territorial Planning. Research on topics related to physical and human geography, cartographic representations using GIS and 3D modeling.

Ana Vulevic, Ph.D. in Spatial Planning(University of Belgrade) and scientific researcher at Institute of Transportation CIP, Department of Architecture and Urban planning (from 1996. year) engaged in fields of work covered by the Institute include the so-called public sector - urban planning, spatial planning, transport planning, environmental planning, analyses for adapting spatial and urban plans). Thesis title: Infrastructural Corridors and their Influence on Spatial Development Example Pan European Corridor VII - Danube, in Serbia. Her research interests are spatial and transports analysis, empirical research and applications (e.g. accessibility indicators, spatial and statistical analyses) bridging the gap between theory and practice.

Łukasz Wróblewski (PhD in the field of management science), Head of the Department of Management and Production Engineering at University of Dąbrowa Górnicza, member of the Polish Academy of Sciences (Commission for Polish-Czech and Polish-Slovak Relations), Vice President of the Scientific Society of Organisation and Management, Branch in Dąbrowa Górnicza. Since 2016, doctor Łukasz Wróblewski, has been the Polish rapporteur at "Arts Management Network" in Weimar. He is a representative of University of Dąbrowa Górnicza at "The European network on cultural management and policy" in Brussels. He also acts as an expert of the American Marketing Association. Since 2017, he has been the editor-in-chief of the renowned scientific journal "Cultural Management: Science and Education" published by Logos Verlag in Berlin. He is the author of nearly 100 scientific publications (including three independent monographs) in Polish and English dealing with the subject of cultural management. He is the author of the first book entirely devoted to strategic marketing in cultural institutions published in Poland: Strategie marketingowe w instytucjach kultury (Marketing Strategies in Cultural Institutions), PWE, Warsaw 2012. Mr. Wróblewski was a scientific editor for eight.

Ahmet Hakan Yüksel is an academic at Işık University, Istanbul/Turkey, where he received his Ph.D. degree in contemporary management. He has received his M.A. degree in Organizational Behavior and B.Sc. in Economics from Istanbul University. He has worked as a corporate finance executive in Turkish capital markets for five years during when he was in charge of many initial public offering projects, debt restructuring projects, due diligence and private placement projects besides providing consultancy to foreign investors. He teaches 'Leadership', 'Principles of Management', 'Organizational Behavior' and 'Knowledge Management' at undergraduate and graduate levels. His academic areas of concentration include theories of leadership, organizational behavior, management theory and complexity thinking.

Index

www.ingramcontent.com/pod-product-compliance
Lightning Source LLC
LaVergne TN
LVHW080600300926
849162LV00005B/1007